RESEARCH ON

Wole

Soyinka

RESEARCH ON
Wole Soyinka

Edited by
James Gibbs &
Bernth Lindfors

Africa World Press, Inc.

P.O. Box 1892
Trenton, New Jersey 08607

Africa World Press

P.O. Box 1892
Trenton NJ 08607

Cover Design by Carles J. Juzang

RICLAC gratefully acknowledges
a grant from the MOREL Trust
to aid in the publication of this book.

ISBN: 0-86543-218-X   Cloth
0-86543-219-8   Paper

Comparitive Studies in African/Caribbean Literature Series

Series Editor: Stephen H. Arnold
Associate Editor: George Lang

African and Caribbean Literature Section
Research Institute for Comparative Literature
The University of Alberta
Edmonton, Alberta
CANADA T6G 2E6

Contents

SOYINKA as a POET

SOYINKA as a NOVELIST

SOYINKA as a JOURNALIST

SOYINKA as a CRITIC

SOYINKA and the CRITICS

Introduction

Most of the articles in this volume were originally published in *Research in African Literatures*, the exceptions being a few essays of our own covering topics or materials that others have not yet studied. Our intention has been to provide a reasonably broad introduction to the works of Soyinka and to the varieties of criticism they have elicited. There are many different critical methodologies represented, ranging from those concerned with verbal texture (linguistic, structural and textual approaches) to those focusing on cultural context (historical, mythological and comparative studies). One will also find plenty of metacriticism—critics quarreling with one another about fine points of interpretation or surveying a wide range of response to a particular text or issue. Soyinka's complex, nuanced art affords an inexhaustible source of stimulation to sensitive readers, so it is not surprising that there are so many different readings of his works. We do not expect that the essays collected here will bring an end to such controversies; rather, we would hope that they will prompt rigorous new research leading to fresh appraisals of the achievements of one of Africa's most abundantly gifted writers. Although more has been published on Soyinka than on any other anglophone African writer, much more needs to be written before we will be able to comprehend and measure the expansive dimensions of his creativity. This book is meant merely as an appetizer for the feast of commentary to come.

Bernth Lindfors
James Gibbs

SOYINKA
and the
ENGLISH LANGUAGE

Linguistic Function and Literary Style: An Inquiry into the Language of Wole Soyinka's *The Road*

Akpofure Oduaran

My main concern, in this paper, is with criteria of relevance. This, it seems to me, is one of the main problems in the study of style in language: to distinguish between mere linguistic regularity, which in itself is of no particular interest to literary studies, and regularity that is significant for the work under consideration. Linguistic regularity which is significant in a literary text – that is, one which helps to build the semantic system of the text – is functional. It is characterized by consistent and systematic foregrounding, which attracts attention to itself for what it is, rather than acting merely as a vehicle for information. Hence, literary language is language in context, words in relation to other words. Each detail of a literary work takes its quality from the whole work.

Thus "kill thy physician, and the fee bestow upon the foul disease" is an undistinguished sentence in isolation, but not in Shakespeare's *King Lear*. They are the right words in context. So it is in *The Road* with "may your tongue of deception be rotted in pestilence from the enigma of the Inviolate Word." This is language that is functional. The term *function* perhaps needs explanation here. The term is used in two distinct though related senses: first, it refers to grammatical (or syntactic) function; that is, to elements of linguistic structures such as subject and object. The "functions," according to Halliday, are the roles occupied by classes of words, phrases, and the like in the structures of higher units ("Language Structure"); second, it is used to refer to the "functions" of language as a whole, that is, to the notion that language plays a certain part in our lives, that it is required to serve universal types of demand.

A functional theory of language, therefore, is a theory about meanings, not about words or constructions. In other words, the language is differentiated semantically as different areas of meaning potential. This paper will be considering, as it were, the dynamics of the semantic strategies employed in the play. Represented in this way, as networks of interrelated options which define, as a whole, the resources of what Soyinka wants to say, it will then be possible to discover empirically that these options fall

3

into a small number of fairly distinct sets. Each of these distinct sets has a meaning potential that will help to determine the style of the play.

Unfortunately, an element of choice seems to be basic to all conceptions of style because the description of all the qualities of a text is an impossible task. The solution is, I think, simply to have and to state a criterion of selection, determined by relevance, while bearing in mind that a close study of the describable elements of text, however cautiously selected or correlated, only provides a less than complete story of style. But if the language of a text is carefully wrought to serve a particular need, then this should show up in some way in an investigation of the linguistic structure. The function of the language is usually built into the structure and, in fact, forms the basis of its semantic and syntactic organization. A study of style in this sense thus involves an examination of semantically motivated syntactic structures.

This paper will fall into two parts: first, an examination of certain features of the language of *The Road* and, second, a brief résumé of the question of stylistic relevance. The primary material to be examined are the various speeches of Professor, hero of *The Road*, a man dedicated to a quest for the Word. Related to this are various pieces of background information provided by other characters who stand not too great a distance from the Inviolate Word.

The language of *The Road*, it has been said, falls into two related registers: the language of religion and the idiom of the religious cult of death (Izevbaye 56-57). Be that as it may, the features that draw attention to themselves for what they are, are largely syntactic, where the syntax builds a common semantic structure that serves a vision of Professor's quest. The syntactic choices Soyinka makes enable the play to project itself as overtly metaphoric, for on the literal level it is scarcely intelligible.[1] We recognize it as a performance constructed before us by actors who speak words not their own but provided by an invisible dramatist. These syntactic choices help build the play's semantic structure which finds expression in form and through the same syntactic features.

The Road provides a remarkable illustration of how grammar can convey meaning in literature, and this relates closely to the notion of linguistic functions explained above. The particular impact of this play on readers and critics may be explained by the fact that the underlying semiotic is projected onto the grammar in the highly untypical patterns that characterize not so much individual clauses but the distribution of types of clauses in the speech of Professor as a whole. These foregrounded clause patterns are experiential ones whose meaning resides in the representation of Professor's experience; as such they express not only the content of the narrative but also the abstract structure of the reality through which that content is interpreted.

Thus the play is, in my opinion, a successful piece of imaginative dramatic writing; in the words of D. S. Izevbaye, in his penetrating critical study of language and meaning, *The Road* is "a play which satisfies our sense of dramatic rightness" (53). The *dramatis personae* of the play consist of a group of drivers and lorry-park layabouts whose lives are dominated by Professor, the central character who is involved in a quest for the Word. Now the Word which Professor seeks, according to Gerald Moore, "is surely the all-creating Word which expresses the indestructible energy of God" (53). This orthodox religion, in conjunction with the Yoruba Agemo, a religious cult of flesh dissolution, provides the background against which the syntax is foregrounded. Professor's quest in itself, it should be observed, is in several stages:[2] when the play opens we see him equate the Word with ordinary words in a language. He thus collects all printed matter he can find – journals, and even pools coupons – but he does not delude himself into accepting all such manifestations as truth and soon rejects this approach. The second stage of his quest is his realization that "the Word may be found companion not to life, but Death." At this point Professor has rejected his Christian background and has accepted the Yoruba view of flesh dissolution. His fall from ecclesiastical grace is complete. He then associates with drivers, purveyors of death on the road, and, finally he accepts ritual as the only means through which the Word may be revealed. Throughout the quest Professor's actions – his obsession with potent utterances, collection of journals and pools coupons, removal of road signs, involvement in ritual and the game of death – help build the play's semantic system, exemplified by the syntactic organization. I propose to examine an aspect of Soyinka's syntactic choices as they are used to characterize Professor's quest.

For this purpose I shall look closely at several extracts taken from different parts of the play, but representing the different stages of the quest. The extracts labeled A deal with Professor's quest after the Word in printed matter; extract B deals with his quest after the Word among the dead; and extracts C deal with the quest in ritual.

The clauses of passage A (25) are mainly clauses of action (10), process (9), or location (5); the remainder (1) is transitional. Usually the process is expressed by a finite verb in simple past tense, but there are also non-finite progressive participial forms. Almost all of the action clauses describe simple activities (provides, led, plucked, made, to find, etc.); and of these the majority are intransitive; the exceptions are "surrender the fruit of my vigil," "I plucked it" ("it" here referring to a road sign). The typical pattern is exemplified by the opening clauses of extract A: "Almost a miracle," "Almost stingy"; there is no clear indication of what the subject of the clauses might be. Some of the clauses of action and process also specify location, for example, "led to where this was hidden," "led here by spells," "it was growing from earth."

The picture is one in which Professor engages himself in some sort of activity that takes him to sundry locations, but as he concedes, "There is a mystery in everything." Even such normally transitive verbs as "grow" occur intransitively: "this word was growing." Moreover, a high proportion of the clauses lack a subject; they frequently begin with adjectives, verbs, articles, or a demonstrative. The only exceptions begin with a personal pronoun: "I am used to that"; "I shall not surrender that fruit of my vigil." This latter clause, indeed, is one of the rare instances of a transitive clause in the extract. An illusion is therefore set up, a kind of syntactic mirage between verbs that are, in the simple past tense, normally finite and dynamic, on the one hand, and on the other, the paucity of a specific subject and the almost total absence of an object to fill the transitivity gulf. It is particularly the lack of transitive clauses of action with the Professor as actor and the Word as goal (there are only two clauses in which he is indicated as subject) that creates the play's semantic system. The scenes are ones of constant movement (the Professor comes and goes; Murano disappears at dawn to appear at dusk) but the movements are ineffectual because what would normally be the object of the transitive verbs, the Word, is difficult to find at the mundane level. The quest for the Word, therefore, could not but be difficult. The syntactic tension expresses this difficulty.

Thus it is the syntax of the play to which we respond when we view Professor's quest as unsuccessful to this point. The transitivity patterns are not imposed by the subject matter; they are the reflection of the underlying theme, or rather of one of the underlying themes — the inherent difficulty a living being encounters in a quest for the Word. In terms of the events and actions in which Professor engages himself in this section of the play, there is grammatical justification for the predominance of intransitives because his quest so far is not a goal-directed activity. This syntactic foregrounding in the play, of which this extract provides a typical example, is thus relevant and has an important function: the predominance of intransitives reflects, first, Professor's limitations and, second, a dim apprehension of the possibility of finding the Word, represented by the rare intrusion of a transitive clause such as "I shall not surrender the fruit of my vigil," but the occurrence of a modal verb with it makes it uncertain, at least, for now.

Extract A is both text and sample. It is not only these particular clauses that determine our response to the play but the fact that they are part of a general syntactic and semantic scheme. That this extract is representative in its syntactic features can be seen from comparison with other extracts (186-88, 205-06). It also exemplifies certain other relevant features of the language of this part of the play. There is an abundance of adjuncts (10), which are either time or place adjuncts consisting of preposition plus noun (e.g., "those signs arrived lately," "say the Word in our time O Lord," "led here by spells," "it was growing from earth"). The place adjuncts have reference to environments where the Word may be found, and the time adjuncts express Professor's wish for finding the Word soon enough.

It is now possible to formulate a grammatical description of a typical clause of what may be called language A, the language in which the major part of the play is written and of which extract A is a sample, in terms of Professor's quest (see Appendix):

1. There is one participant, Professor, who is therefore actor.
   a. Professor in a non-goal-directed action (activity clauses are intransitive).
   b. Clauses lack subjects which are generally omitted. But where present, are
   c. unmodified, other than by a determiner which is either an anaphoric demonstrative (this, that).

2. The process of the quest is expressed in (a) normally dynamic, finite, non-modalized verbs in simple past tense; (b) lexical verbs of agricultural nature, but modalization renders the search there illusory.

3. There are often other elements that are adjuncts, treated as environments in which the quest takes place and as time in which the Word may be revealed.

Brief as this may seem, it forms the essence of the grammar of language A, the language in which most of the play is written. It tells us not merely what clauses occurred in the text but also the linguistic function of the clauses in relation to the subject of the quest. That is, the grammar of language A is functional, a deliberate stylistic choice of motivated foregrounding.

Such are some of the characteristics of language A, the language which tells the story of Professor's quest for the Word. The language which tells the story of the second stage of Professor's quest is not much different from that of language A. As a matter of fact, it occupies a point of transition between the first and the third stages of the quest. The major syntactic highlight of language B, as we may call it, is the preponderance of prepositional verbs: "seek out," "fled up," "clamber after," "crucified on," "sunk along," "sit above," "broken over." Again, these are activity verbs, and many of the intransitive clauses have potentially transitive verbs in them, but instead of a direct object there is a prepositional phrase.

In extract B, at least, we begin to observe the occurrence of potentially transitive verbs, an indication that Professor has moved one step in the direction of the Word. At this stage of the quest, the Word may be found companion not to life but death. This recognition gives some sort of direction to Professor who begins to haunt road and accident sites. Significantly, the complements of the prepositional verbs seem to indicate where the Word may be found: "disgruntled swarm of souls full of spite for their rejected bodies,' "seek out unpleasant sights," "three souls . . . fled up that tree," "all three of them crucified on rigid branches," and so on. The Word, however, remains elusive.

In the language of extract B, Professor becomes increasingly active. Subjects to clauses begin to occur much more frequently than in language A. The majority of these (6) have reference to Professor; others relate to the object of the quest or refer to other participants. There are some adjuncts of place, and there are more modifiers here. None of these features occurs for the first time, for we have had the instances in extract A. But there is a greater concentration of them in B, a linguistic phenomenon that is in harmony with Professor's increasingly active pursuit of the Word, which has been built up in much of the language of extract A. The syntax in extract B thus expresses this increased activity, and with the occurrence of transitive prepositional verbs, also provides forward-looking flashes to the outcome of the quest in ritual.

Thus the true path to the Word is never an accident, and if Professor's adversaries trouble him too much, he will counter with a resurrection. This resort to ritual marks Professor's recognition of the fact that he could no longer wait for Murano's tongue to become unglued. The spirit of a god in him (Murano) will have to be reawakened in the confrontation, events which form part of extract C. In this section of the play, Professor's fall from ecclesiastical grace and his rejection of orthodox religion is complete. Language C, the language of the last ten pages of the play, tells the story of the last stage of Professor's quest. Here we begin to observe a preponderance of action clauses: "I am a gleaner," "I make daily pilgrimage in search of leavings," "I uprooted it," "I held a god captive," "I wandered on my favourite roads," and so on. Almost all of the action clauses describe simple activities connected with the quest, and of these, the majority are intransitive. There are exceptions, however: "we formed a syndicate," "God painted the sign," "he also carved the symbol," "tapping wine from trees"; but these are unrelated to Professor's quest, being limited to providing the background of religion in which the quest occurs.

Finally, in the throes of death Professor becomes one with the Word, and this is significantly suggested by the total lack of subjects to numerous transitive clauses. The questor is about to bridge the transitional gulf to a knowledge of the Word and, perhaps, attain self-rehabilitation. The syntax thus expresses this transition in transitivity: "Be even like the road," "Flatten your bellies with the hunger," "power your hands with the knowledge of death," "wobbling reflection of two hands," "Spread a broad sheet for death," and so on. The concentration of these transitive structures in this part of the play foregrounds a linguistic function that is in harmony with Professor's knowledge of the Word in death.

We can now see the complementarity in the "languages" that describe the three stages of the quest for the Word, difficult as these have been to state. *The Road* provides a perspective for a linguistic study of a sort whose relevance and significance is hardly in doubt in view of the problem of comprehension the play poses, but difficult to assess because it is an inquiry into the language of a full-length play. The language of the play is not in any way deviant, and my analysis, therefore, is not intended to offer anything in the way of new interpretation of particular sentences in terms of their subject matter but to establish certain regular patterns that appear significant over a broad spectrum that involves much comparison.

In this study the focus of my inquiry has been on clause types and their function, the verb and its complementation; and grammar and semantics in general, on the language system and its relation to the meaning of the play as art. In the study I have observed that particular syntactic options have been selected with a greater than required frequency, a selection that is "motivated" by the exigency of the quest; and it appeared, also, that by considering their function in context, it is possible to demonstrate that they are relevant both as the language which tells the story of the quest and as an illustration of the underlying difficulty of finding the Word. In the present context, therefore, the syntactic prominence that we have observed can be said to be "motivated," and thus, it is clearly possible to speak of foregrounding here as an explanation of stylistic impact.

In *The Road* the syntax is part of the whole story, and the establishment of the syntactic norm is thus a way of expressing an important level of meaning of the work: the fact that a particular pattern constitutes a norm is the meaning. The linguistic function of the pattern is therefore of great significance. This is what I take to be "relevance" – the fact that a syntactic construction "belongs" in some way as part of the whole semantic framework of *The Road*.

APPENDIX

Extract A1

Almost a miracle... dawn provides the greatest miracles but this ... in this dawn has exceeded its promise. In the strangest of places ... God God God but there is a mystery in everything. A new discovery every hour – I am used to that, but that I should be led to where this was hidden, sprouted in secret for heaven knows how long... for there was no doubt about it, this word was growing, it was growing from earth until I plucked it.... But is this my station? I could have sworn.... If this is a trick I swear they shan't take it from me. If my eyes were deluded and my body led here by spells I shall not surrender the fruit of my vigil. No one can take it from me!   (17)

Extract A2

Economic. Almost stingy. But there are the cabalistic signs. The trouble is to find the key. Find the key and it leads to the Word ... very strange... very strange... a rash of these signs arrived lately... that woman of Tapa knows something, or else she is an unconscious medium. Oh God, Oh God, the enormity of unknown burdens, of hidden wisdoms... say the Word in our time O Lord, utter the hidden Word. But what do these mean? These signs were made by no human hands. What in the power of hell do they mean!   (203)

Extract B

My bed is among the dead, and when the road raises a victory cry to break my sleep I hurry to a disgruntled swarm of souls full of spite for their rejected bodies. It is a market of stale meat, noisy with flies and quarrelsome with old women. The place I speak of is not far from here, if you wish to come... you shall be shown this truth of my endeavors –
Samson: No thank you very much. I don't willingly seek out unpleasant sights.
You are afraid? There are dangers in the Quest I know, but the Word may be found companion not to life, but Death. Three souls you know, fled up that tree. You would think, to see it that the motor-car had tried to clamber after them. Oh there was such an angry buzz but the matter was beyond repair. They died, all three of them crucified on rigid branches. I found this word growing where their blood had spread and sunk along plough scouring of the wheel. Now tell me you who sit above it all, do you think my sleep was broken over nothing, over a meaningless event?   (159)

Extract C

See Professor's speeches in the last ten pages of the play.

NOTES

1.   Aristotle, in *Rhetoric* III, 1410b, acutely describes metaphor as "midway between the unintelligible and the commonplace."
2.   Izevbaye also identifies three stages of the quest; his third stage, however, is somewhat different from mine.

REFERENCES

Halliday, M. A. K. *Language as Social Semiotic: The Social Interpretation of Language and Meaning.* London: Edward Arnold, 1978.

---------. "Language Structure and Language Function." *New Horizons in Linguistics.* Ed. John Lyons. Harmondworth: Penguin, 1970, pp. 140-65.

Izevbaye, Dan S. "Language and Meaning in Soyinka's *The Road.*" *African Literature Today* 8 (1976), pp. 52-65.

Moore, Gerald. *Wole Soyinka.* London: Evans, 1978.

Soyinka, Wole. *Collected Plays.* Vol. 1. London: Oxford UP, 1973.

The Stylistic Function of Pidgin English in African Literature: Achebe and Soyinka

Tony Obilade

"... my life done spoil. My life done spoil finish.... a no' get eyes for my head. ...Na big lie. Na pretence 'e de pretend that wicked woman! She no go collect nutin! she no' mean to sleep for outside house. The prophet na 'im lover... ." (Chume, in Soyinka's *The Trials of Brother Jero,* p. 170) [1]

"Me? Put poison for master? Nevertheless!... why I go kill master?... Abi my head no correct? And even if to say I de craze why I no go go jump for inside lagoon instead to kill master?" (a servant, in Achebe's *A Man of the People,* p. 39) [2]

It is now generally accepted that linguistic theory provides some insights into the interpretation and evaluation of literary texts despite the fact that it is often argued that linguists rarely offer concrete guidelines that might be useful in objectivizing the literary analyst's impressions. However, although Halliday, Leech, and others have adopted the linguistic approach in their stylistic studies, the sociolinguistic aspects of literary texts have received little or no attention. It is true that literary critics often examine the social setting of literary texts, but the recent findings of sociolinguistics have not featured prominently in the current studies in linguistic stylistics. This essay examines the stylistic effect of one sociolinguistic phenomenon: Pidginization. It is assumed here that the implications of the sociolinguistic definition of Pidginization are of great relevance in the study of style in African writing in English, particularly when analyzing the stylistic use to which the English-based Pidgin spoken in West Africa is put in the writings of Chinua Achebe and Wole Soyinka.

West African Pidgin English (PE) as exemplified in the passages quoted is spoken primarily along the West African coast between Sierra Leone and Cameroon. The exact number of speakers is unknown, but there are probably at least five million speakers of PE in Nigeria, one of the major centers where the language is extensively used. The type of Pidgin found in literary works by Achebe, Ekwensi, Soyinka, and some other African writers is not the same as that often referred to as "trade jargon," "makeshift language," or "a language devoid of morphological characteristics." [3] PE plays a very important role in West Africa – especially in areas where there is no other common language. Since literature tries to represent all aspects of human experience, it is only natural to expect references to PE in the works of writers who are part of the sociolinguistic situation that gave rise to the language.

The idea of incorporating a pidgin language in a literary text written in the pidginized standard is not new. In many literatures of the world, pidgins have been recorded (though they were not introduced as a stylistic device). Taking an example from early eighteenth century English literature, we find that Daniel Defoe utilized a sizable amount of Pidgin English in *Colonel Jacque:* "Master, me speakee de true, they never give Mercièè, they always Whippee, Lashee, Knockee down, all Cruel: Negroe be muchee better Man do muchee better Work, but they tell us no Mercièè."[4] Although Defoe's Virginian pidgin is different from PE both temporally and geographically, a Nigerian speaker of PE would have little or no problem in understanding it. In Defoe's work, Pidgin English has no stylistic value; indeed, Defoe's pidgin represents a subjective characterization of its speaker as a linguistically incompetent and (possibly) a racially inferior individual: "all those Natives, as also those of Africa, when they learn English, they always add two E's at the end of Words where we use one, and make the accent upon them, as makèè, takèè, and the like."[5]

Of more relevance to the subject under discussion is Cronise and Ward's book, *Cunnie Rabbit, Mister Spider and the Other Beef,* a book of folktales collected in the nineteenth century; "All dem beef en Cunnie Rabbit bin meet up to one place. Now dey pull all dem horn, en put um'pon de groun'. Any beef pull ye yown...."[6] These examples only serve to emphasize the fact that Pidgin English has been in literary studies for a long time. However, the mere presence of PE in an African literary text does not mean that it is used as a stylistic device. It is only in the works of Achebe and Soyinka (and probably a few others) that PE rises above the level of a slot-filler or a curiosity item to that of a vehicle to express certain meanings. In other words only in Achebe and Soyinka are pidginized forms to be regarded as foregrounded elements.[7] Foregrounded elements are those that are stylistically relevant. They are made prominent so as to project deeper meanings beyond the "normal" linguistic reading. Hence, they are elements whose prominence must be motivated. In the works of Achebe and Soyinka, the pidgin forms are immediately recognized as being prominent, although this prominence is not of the statistical type that has no stylistic value. PE forms are effectively used as foregrounded elements by both of these writers, although there is a great deal of difference in the type of effect achieved through their use by each writer.

Achebe uses PE primarily as a means of presenting the human aspects of a character to the reader, who only needs to examine the frequency with which a character uses PE to fully understand that character's behavior and capabilities. Consider the "one-eyed stalwart's" language:

"Who you want?" he scowled.
"Chief Nanga."
"He give you appointment?"
"No, but…"
"Make you park for outside. I go go hasham if he want see you. Wetin be your name?" [8]

The rough stalwart appropriately speaks in PE to the hero of the novel. It may be the only language he knows (though the linguists would dispute this), but the stylistic function of PE here lies beyond mere characterization. Achebe here accurately typifies thugs and strongmen who know little or no English and rely mostly on their physical build to communicate their wishes. When Chief Nanga later says "I no follow you black white-men for drink tea and coffee in the hot afternoon" (*MP*, p. 37) he is not just putting in a touch of humor; he is using PE as an instrument of integration. He is trying to dissociate himself from the "black white-men" and at the same time he desperately wants to identify with "the people." And what better way to do this than to speak the language commonly known as "the tongue of the people"? Achebe is fully aware that PE is the language often associated with the common people, and so to qualify fully as a man of the people, Chief Nanga has to use PE. When Dogo, the one-eyed stalwart, talks to Chief Nanga, it is in PE, and Chief Nanga has to respond in the same language:

"Na this boy de halla so for master im face?"
"Don't mind the stupid idiot,… Leave am, Dogo. Make e carry im bad luck de go. Na my own mistake for bring am here. Ungrateful ingrate!" (*MP* p. 82)

Chief Nanga starts speaking in English, then, quickly realizing it was Dogo who asked a question, he switches to PE. Here we have a good example of two contrasting functions of PE within the same conversation. Dogo speaks PE because that is the language in which he can best communicate forcefully (communicative function); Chief Nanga uses PE to identify with Dogo, to show he is humble and to spite the "black white-men" (identification function). In introducing PE in such situations, Achebe gives us an insight into the character of participants in the speech situation. More importantly, he also gives an indication of the nature of the conflicts they are engaged in. Through the use of PE, the point is also being made that the characters are bilingual to some extent and they are used to discussing certain topics in PE. When Maxwell Kulmax (who is a lawyer) says to Odili, "Good gracious!... Na your eye be this?" he is not being inconsistent. He is merely emphasizing the sociolinguistic fact that sharing a common language does not diminish the use of PE. He is also using the appropriate code when in contact with a close friend. Nor are we surprised when Odili, a university graduate and the narrator in the novel, says to Max, "Na matter of can't hep,... He na my old teacher...." Achebe finds it stylistically sound to utilize PE where he would have had to engage in prolonged explanations. It would have been stylistically unwise to describe the gateman at the hospital in any detail since he plays a very negligible role in the story. However, no character is totally negligible in Achebe. Through the use of PE, Achebe makes this particular character very impressive and important, even though we come across him only once:

> "Abi you no fit read notice?"
> "Don't be silly," I said, "and don't shout at me!"
> "Be silly!" he shouted. "I don't like you. Look him motor self. When they call those wey get motor you go follow them comot? Foolish idiot... Na him make accident de kill am for road everyday. Nonsense!" (*MP*, pp. 116-17)

His speech could not have been more effective in any other medium.

PE is so much a part of *A Man of the People* that the characters often mix the language with standard English during the course of a conversation:

> "How de go de go?" I asked.
> "Bo, son of man done tire."
> "Did you find out about that girl?" I asked.
> "Why na soso girl, girl, girl, girl been full your mouth. Wetin? So person no fit talk any serious talk with you. I never see." (*MP*, p. 23)

Only these forms could adequately express the meanings Achebe is trying to communicate. "How de go de go?" would be translated as "How are you?" but the PE form *means* something more than the English translation suggests. The literal translation is "how is the going going?" and this is in fact nearer the Pidgin original.

Similarly, in "Girls at War," PE is extensively used, not only to portray character but also to probe deep into the nature of the effect of a troubled atmosphere on the behavior of the ordinary people in the street who, in most cases, are totally ignorant of the issues at stake in the war they are forced to involve themselves in. Thus, when a servant sees jet fighters and says "I see dem well well,... If no to say de ting de kill person e for sweet for eye...."[9] we are immediately reminded of the grim irony implicit in the statement.

Here, disguised in "ordinary everyday language," is the main problem
Achebe presents. The typically childlike thought evidenced in this man's
statement is arresting. In his own humble way he touches on the core problem – what to do in a situation one is not directly responsible for. His statement signifies the seriousness of the situation – a type of seriousness which
under normal circumstances is never expressed in PE. With Achebe, PE has
risen beyond the level of a humorous device; it has become a vehicle for the
portrayal of universal tragedy.

Sometimes Achebe uses PE to signify matters that are not particularly
relevant to the flow of the story. PE comes in casually – almost as an aside
whose importance could be inferred only on deep reflection. For example, in
Arrow of God, we have the following:

> "Shut up you black monkeys and get down to work!... Tell them this bloody
> work must be finished by June."
> "The white man says that unless you finish this work in time you will know
> the kind of man he is."
> "No more lateness."
> "Pardin?"
> "Pardon what? Can't you understand plain, simple English? I said there will
> be no more late-coming."
> "Oho. He says everybody must work hard and stop all this shit-eating."
> "I have one question I want the white man to answer." This was Nweke
> Ukpaka.
> Unachukwu hesitated and scratched his head. *"Dat man wan axe master
> queshon."* [10]

Unachukwu's use of PE would not have been significant but for Achebe's
remarks that he hesitated and scratched his head. Here Achebe is slowing
down action in order to focus on the single occurrence of PE in the entire
episode. Achebe deliberately uses the preceding material as background for
the foreground pidgin element. Unachukwu is not the type of man who hunts
for words to express himself – witness his unusual translations. The fact is
Nweke's demand is almost unheard of; it throws Unachukwu off balance.
He hesitates. Certainly, the white man is a common enemy; but to question
him – that takes some nerve. Instinctively (and we must mention, rather
appropriately), Unachukwu switches to the language he uses in tense situations: PE. Naturally, he could not address the white man in PE, so he speaks
half to himself: "that man wants to ask master a question" – almost as if he
couldn't believe his ears. It is also significant that he never speaks to the
laborers in PE; that would be too familiar an idiom. Thus, with the use of
this little bit of PE, Achebe has effectively communicated the basics of the
episode: the complex linguistic situation, the stratified nature of the society,

and the master/servant relationship between the white man and the workers. This use demonstrates the potential of PE as a device that not only gives deeper meanings to what is said but also leads the reader to fill in what is left unsaid.

Soyinka, too, uses PE for character portrayal as well as for humorous effect. However, unlike Achebe, Soyinka has his characters use PE principally because they can express deeper meanings in that medium. It appears that Achebe's characters often opt for PE whereas Soyinka's characters *have to use* PE. In Soyinka, there are no flashy characters like Nanga or the girls (of "Girls at War") who consistently switch from some kind of English to PE. Chume, Soyinka's expert PE speaker, can speak English equally well. A study of the development of this particular character from *The Trials of Brother Jero* through *Jero's Metamorphosis* will illustrate the stylistic effect of PE in Soyinka's writings.

In *The Trials,* Chume is a dull, unintelligent fool who slavishly follows Brother Jero, the exploiter of weak minds. In more ways than one, Chume leads a double life. At home with Amope, he is a patient but firm boss, but in the company of Brother Jero, religious fanaticism robs him of his reason. It is interesting to note that he almost never loses his temper with his wife and never speaks PE to her. When in the presence of Jero, however, the situation changes. He mixes PE and English. When he is at ease he uses English, but as the situation becomes progressively tenser and he becomes more involved, he changes to PE, and the reader cannot but feel that this, at last, is the real Chume:

Jero ...Pray with me, brother. Pray with me...

Chume: ...Help him, Lord. Help him, Lord.

Jero: Against this one weakness, this weakness, O Abraham...

Chume: ...Help him, Lord. Help him, Lord.

Jero: Against this one weakness David, David, Samuel, Samuel.

Chume: Help him. Help him. Help'am. Help'am.

Jero: Job Job, Elijah Elijah.

Chume: ...Help am God. Help am God. I say make you help am. Help am quick quick.

Jero: Tear the image from my heart. Tear this love for the daughters of Eve...

Chume: Adam, help am. Na your son, help am...[11]

This is very effective, but we must not forget that it appears that Soyinka is really experimenting with PE here. Or else why would he refer to Chume's PE as "animal jabber"? Soyinka uses PE not merely to make us laugh but mainly to show us the inner character of Chume. Through his brand of PE, we realize Chume is a very emotional man who easily gets involved in a situation and apparently loses control of himself. Here lies the explanation for his otherwise irrational behavior at the end of the play where he chases the prophet across the stage with a machete. Yet we are indirectly prepared for the eventual reconciliation of the two at a later date in the *Metamorphosis*. Jero only had to work him up to get what he wanted out of him: slavish obedience. It is not only in the religious aspect of life that Jero gets Chume worked up. He has a secret wish that Jero will not grant: he wants to beat his wife. For this emotional topic, Chume naturally turns to PE – this despite the fact that the conversation that led to the topic had been conducted in English:

Chume: ...make you let me. Just beat 'am once.

Jero: Apostate!

Chume: I n' go beat am too hard. Jus' once, small small.

Jero: Traitor!

Chume: Jus' this one time. I no' go ask again. Jus' do me this one favour, make a
      beat am today.   (*Trials*, p. 155)

We have a feeling that this kind of emotional involvement is different from that due to religious experience. Chume is not too involved. His PE is decidedly different (the punctuation marks are intended to reflect the spoken PE form as much as possible). He seems to be teasing Jero, enjoying himself in the process. Knowing fully well Jero would disapprove of wife-beating, his one concern seems to be to enjoy the sensation of beating in words; he repeats the "beat 'am" part in every sentence. It is not surprising that he is having his "asides" as Jero was praying. He isn't in the mood for prayers at this particular time. It is also interesting to note that despite Chume's annoyance at the end of the play he never speaks PE to his wife, not even after the prophet has given him permission to beat her. But when he finally figures out Jero's real reason for granting the permission, he delivers his famous soliloquy that culminates in "Adulterer! Woman-thief! Na today a go finish you!" and a threatening cutlass!

In writing a sizable portion of the play in PE, Soyinka has raised the language beyond the level of the usual embellishment function and established it as an indispensable part of the play. *The Trials* and *Metamorphosis* without PE would be like leaving out Chume in both plays. We are forced to explore the meanings expressed in PE and we become aware of the shortcomings that would have resulted had any other language been used in such situations. Chume thus soars above the flashy Nanga and the carefree Jagua Nana of Ekwensi. Nanga and others like him are recognized as being in touch with the ordinary people who engage in little everyday events. It is only Chume who is recognized as being part of that world. He speaks PE not because he wants to get in touch with the "common" people: he is already with them and it is only natural that he express himself in their (and his) language. Chume's problems and aspirations may seem trivial to the sophisticated, but they are distinct and they affect his life to such an extent that he has to express himself in the language he uses in emotionally charged situations: PE.

In *Metamorphosis,* Chume is no longer the simple idiot who slavishly follows Jero. He is a wiser, though sadder, man. Jero's betrayal and a few months in the lunatic asylum have finally restored his reason, though his gullibility still remains at a very high level, as Jero will soon prove. In short, Chume is still the same basic character, but Soyinka does not bring him back in another play only to speak PE to outsiders in emotional situations. Chume now speaks PE partly in defiance of the rapidly changing society, and partly in contempt of Standard English:

Silva (severely): Corporal Chummy, can you read music notation at all?

Chume (Angrily): I no talk so? You done come with your trouble. I say I go wait for Captain Winston you say you go fit teach me. Now you come dey bother me with music notation. Na paper man dey take trumpet play abi na music?[12]

He now speaks PE to cover his ignorance. He isn't really annoyed. And when he finds out he can push Silva around, he continues to tease him, using a language Silva cannot understand:

Enh, pepper. When you cook soup you go put small pepper. Otherwise the thing no go taste. I mean to say, 'e go taste like something. After all, even sand-sand get in own taste. But who de satisfy with sand-sand? If they give you sand-sand to chop you go chop? (*Metamorphosis*, p. 191)

Obviously, PE is no longer "animal jabber" for Soyinka. Like Achebe, he has discovered its full potential and now even those who do not understand the language are shown to be missing a lot. Chume is still enjoying himself, speaking casually in PE, when Jero enters. Naturally, Chume switches to another mood. He no longer uses PE to poke fun – he is now upset. Listening to him, one would have to say PE is his mother tongue (except that linguists claim that pidgins do not have native speakers): "commot here before I break your head" – hardly a fitting welcome for a prophet, but in the case of the Jero/Chume relationship, the best Jero could hope for. Chume is soon tamed by the prophet who knows that "the black blood of the Bar Beach brotherhood" is stronger than the clownish antics of the Salvation Army.

Contrary to popular opinion among linguists as to the incompleteness of pidgins, Soyinka demonstrates that PE can be used as a medium for serious thoughts and philosophical deliberations. Chume's words assume more weight when it is realized that they come from his "ignorant and illiterate mind." He can still reflect on his fortunes in the language he is most familiar with. His words may sound funny (and they are) but they mask a deep seriousness which underlies the play as a whole:

> If nonsense no to big insult for man of my calibre, den I no know wetin be insult again. (*Metamorphosis*, p. 191)

> If to say I get my cutlass inside your head that time this world for done become better place. They can hang me but I for become saint and martyr. I for die but de whole world go call me Saint Chume. (*Metamorphosis*, p. 193)

> *Jero*: A white man. He is not one of us. And you know yourself
> he's a hypocrite. All white men are hypocrites.
> *Chume*: Na him come save me from that lunatic asylum, not so?
> If dat na hympocrisy then thank God for hympocrites... I am
> not unfortunate inmate... The day I fust meet you, dat day na
> my unfortunate.... . (*Metamorphosis*, p. 193)

In these few funny lines reside deep themes that run throughout Soyinka's works. Simple people like Chume are often mistaken for simpletons and are usually taken advantage of. Soyinka's plays are often set in worlds where values are perverted and insults become so fashionable that they lose their sting. Despite Chume's relative insignificance he still retains enough of his independence of thought to realize that calling his traditional food nonsense is an insult. Thus, PE is being used here to show that there is virtue in being unsophisticated. Those that remain firm, unswept by the current wave of sophistication, may still be heroes in literary texts.

It was Jero who, at the beginning of the play, was speaking of "burying the hatchet in the head of one of the prophets." We have a less idiomatic version of the same thought in Chume, who regrets he did not "get my cutlass inside your head that time." Chume may sound wild but he has touched on a major enigma of life: what a society should do with undesirable characters like Jero. Chume would be doing the world a favor but he would have to risk death by hanging. He would have to die to become a saint. As far as Chume is concerned, it is not a difficult choice. He chooses to get rid of Jero. His religious fanaticism makes him opt for death with the chance of becoming a saint. Soyinka somehow suggests that it is not desirable to be a dead hero, to die for the sake of robots like Major Silva. These thoughts are especially troubling not because of their substance but because of the way they are expressed. PE gives them a certain freshness that makes them linger. Thus, a character like Chume, who on the surface appears to be a mere foil for Jero, assumes a central importance and becomes the real hero of the plays.

Chume also attacks the traditional mode of group integration based on the existence of "the others" who are not with "us." When Jero, for his own selfish interests, dismisses all white men as "hypocrites," it is Chume, a comparatively ignorant person, who rises to the occasion to say that if it is hypocritical to rescue a sane man from a lunatic asylum, then we have to thank God for hypocrites. In other words, even Chume is willing to judge people just on personal merits rather than on the basis of race or ancestry.

Much of what I have been saying here has to do with the use of PE in the works I have considered. In Achebe and Soyinka, PE is used for humor as well as for character portrayal. In Soyinka, however, it is very subtly employed to explore deeper meanings, to explain the reasons behind a character's actions, and to project and foreground certain themes that are central to the plays concerned. Needless to say, much of the stylistic potential of PE is lost due to the unavailability of conventional orthography. Nevertheless, through this brief study we see that PE can become a powerful stylistic device in the hands of a skillful artist, provided, of course, that artist is fully aware of the details of the extremely delicate semantic system of the language.

NOTES

1. All quotations from Soyinka's plays are from the following edition: Wole Soyinka, *Collected Plays*, 2 (London: Oxford Univ. Press, 1974).

2. Chinua Achebe, *A Man of the People* (London: Heinemann, 1966), p. 39.

3. For a thorough discussion of the incompleteness of pidgin languages in general, see John E. Reinecke, "Trade Jargons and Creole Dialects as Marginal Languages," in Dell Hymes (ed.), *Language in Culture and Society* (New York: Harper and Row, 1964), pp. 534-46. For additional discussion of pidgins, see Anthony Obilade, "The Nominal Phrase in West African Pidgin English (Nigeria)," Northwestern University Ph.D. dissertation, 1976; and Loreto Todd, *Pidgins and Creoles* (London: Routledge and Kegan Paul, 1974).

4. Daniel Defoe, *The History and Remarkable Life of the Truly Honourable Col. Jacque, Commonly Call'd Col. Jack* (1722; rpt. London: Oxford Univ. Press, 1965), p. 137.

5. Daniel Defoe, *Farther Adventures of Robinson Crusoe* (1796; rpt. Oxford: Blackwell, 1927), p. 76.

6. G. Cronise and H. F. Ward, *Cunnie Rabbit, Mister Spider and the Other Beef* (London: Sonnenschein, 1903).

7. For a detailed discussion of the concept of foregrounding as it applies to African literature in English, see Anthony Obilade, "Functional Linguistics and the Problem of Stylistic Relevance in African Literature in English," paper read at the University of Louisville, Ky., Interdisciplinary Conference, May 1976.

8. Chinua Achebe, *A Man of the People,* p. 36. Hereafter cited as *MP.*

9. Chinua Achebe, "Girls at War," in *Girls at War and Other Stories* (London: Heinemann, 1972), p. 108.

10. Chinua Achebe, *Arrow of God* (New York: John Day, 1967), p. 102, italics mine.

11. Wole Soyinka, *The Trials of Brother Jero,* in *Collected Plays,* 2 (London: Oxford UP, 1974), p. 154. Hereafter cited as *Trials.*

12. Wole Soyinka, *Jero's Metamorphosis,* in *Collected Plays,* 2, p. 189. Hereafter cited as *Metamorphosis.*

Wole Soyinka and the Horses of Speech

Bernth Lindfors

The Yoruba have a saying that "proverbs are the horses of speech; if communication is lost, we use proverbs to find it." [1] In actual practice, of course, the Yoruba, like any other people, command a whole stable of gnomic horses and groom them to serve a variety of rhetorical purposes. They can be employed not only to retrieve communication gone astray but also to speed it up, slow it down, convey weighty messages, deliver lighthearted jests, sharpen arguments, blunt criticism, clarify difficult ideas, and disguise simple ones beyond easy recognition. The same proverb, in fact, can be an ordinary beast of burden or a rare racing thoroughbred, depending on its use – and user. The real master of proverbs is one who is able to summon the entire cavalry at will and make them spontaneously perform precisely those tricks he has in mind. To do this, he must be in complete control of their movements at all times, harnessing their versatile energies with such skill that they cannot bolt off in directions he did not intend. He must be an expert wrangler with words.

Wole Soyinka, Nigeria's most talented playwright, is one of these. No other African writer – except possibly Chinua Achebe or D.O. Fagunwa – has displayed so much agility in manipulating traditional verbal formulae. Of course, Achebe and Fagunwa write prose fiction, a pliant kind of literature which affords them the opportunity to insert proverbs into narration as well as dialogue. Soyinka, as a dramatist, must put all his words into the mouths of his characters; he can never speak in his own voice or in the guise of an omniscient chronicler. Yet even this formal limitation does not prevent him from getting more literary mileage out of African oral art than any other writer on the continent. Indeed, the limitation may actually work to his advantage, since it forces him to employ proverbs and other forms of fixed-phrase folklore in situations where they are dramatically appropriate, situations of dynamic human interaction in which formulaic sayings are expected to have some influence on the course of subsequent events. Soyinka returns folklore to the folk, and in so doing, enriches his theatrical art immeasurably.

Take characterization, for example. The personalities of Soyinka's characters are often very clearly defined by the proverbs they use. In *A Dance of the Forests* it is not difficult to determine that Agboreko, ironically called the "Elder of Sealed Lips," is a garrulous old windbag. Everytime he opens his mouth, ponderous proverbs tumble out followed by tag lines such as "Proverb to bones and silence" or "Oracle to living and silence," which identify them as words of traditional wisdom. The trouble with Agboreko's sayings is that they contribute little or nothing to any conversation he enters because they bear only the most oblique relation to the matters under discussion. He appears to be citing proverbs merely for the sake of impressing others with his erudition, not for the sake of improving communication. To Agboreko, conventional form is obviously much more important than significant content. When advising an Old Man to be patient, he unreels a string of ancient adages, only a few of which seem relevant to the message he wishes to convey:

> The eye that looks downwards will certainly see the nose. The hand that dips to the bottom of the pot will eat the biggest snail. The sky grows no grass but if the earth called her barren, it will drink no more milk. The foot of the snake is not split in two like a man's or in hundreds like a centipede's, but if Agere could dance patiently like the snake, he would uncoil the chain that leads into the dead... (38).

This is colorful language but little else. The proverbs are not without overtones of applicable meaning, but their primary function is to display Agboreko's flair for dredging up miscellaneous tidbits of prefabricated wisdom. The situation may have called for the recitation of a few pithy proverbs, but offering them in such dense profusion seems a classic example of pseudo-intellectual overkill. Agboreko is plainly a pedantic fool.

Makuri, the old barber in *The Swamp Dwellers*, is a very different kind of person. Humble, content with his meager lot in life and obedient to his gods, he does not quote proverbs in an effort to prove himself superior to others. He quotes them only when they might serve to soothe someone in a state of emotional discomfort. In his long discussions with the blind beggar he resorts to proverbs three times: once to persuade the beggar, who has become irritated by his pointed questions, to remain with him, twice to comment sympathetically on the beggar's unhappy past experiences. The proverbs he uses ("the blind man does not hurry for fear he out-walks his guide" (14); "every god shakes a beggar by the hand" (15); "the hands of the gods are unequal" (26)) reflect his conviction that men, while dependent upon one another, are ultimately at the mercy of unpredictable gods. The proverbs also illustrate that even a deeply religious person like Makuri may find it necessary to adopt a fatalistic attitude toward human existence in order to cope with the harsh uncertainties of life in the swamps. For despite his stubborn show of faith in men and gods, Makuri is a resigned pessimist at heart.

The blind beggar, on the other hand, has great hopes for the future. Though he has been exposed to the cruelties of nature and his fellow man, he believes the world can be changed for the better. He plans to spend the rest of his life sowing seeds of renewal in fertile lands he has reclaimed from the swamps. The beggar's optimism is apparent in the proverbs he cites when trying to persuade Igwezu to return to the swamps to join in the good work:

> The swallows find their nest again when the cold is over. Even the bats desert dark holes in the trees and flap wet leaves with wings of leather. There were wings everywhere as I wiped my feet against your threshold. I heard the cricket scratch himself beneath the armpit as the old man said to me ... (41-42).

All the imagery suggests that the season has changed, that the time is now becoming ripe for the kind of revolution that the beggar envisions for human society. The proverbs define the beggar's attitude toward the new world to which he has totally committed himself.

If Soyinka's proverbs functioned only as agents of characterization or as cheap dabs of local color, they would be no more remarkable than the proverbs in plays by many of his less talented contemporaries. However, Soyinka frequently weaves them so intricately into the fabric of dramatic action that they become a vital part of the total artistic design, a part which could not be altered or eliminated without destroying the complex patterns of human interaction upon which the drama itself depends. In other words, they are not meaningless exotic decorations but elements central to the intense theatrical experience Soyinka attempts to create. An examination of their dramatic function in three comic plays will reveal the skill with which Soyinka exploits their aesthetic possibilities.

Perhaps it would be best to begin with *The Trials of Brother Jero*, a play which contains only one proverb. Why should this play be so empty of proverbs while others are so full? One answer may lie in the nature of the comedy itself, another in Soyinka's strategy of dramatic presentation. *The Trials of Brother Jero* is a farce with a religious charlatan as hero; it begins with Brother Jero revealing to the audience that he makes his living by pretending to be a prophet. He then offers to show us "one rather eventful day" in his life when his deceitful propheteering was almost brought to a catastrophic end. Thus, right from the start, we are made aware not only of Jero's duplicity but also of his ultimate survival as a rogue-hero, and this enables us to sit back without qualms of conscience and enjoy the precarious maneuvers he employs to maintain his false position. The play turns into a parade of hilarious picaresque adventures, with Jero occasionally stepping outside the action to comment on the brilliance of his strategems or the follies of his followers. Jero's schizoid role is crucial to the comedy, for as both actor and observer in the drama, he fluctuates freely between total involvement and total detachment. He is a player who wears more than one mask, and much of our delight comes from seeing him switching them so swiftly and speaking so honestly about his dishonesty. He is a human paradox.

Farce, of course, is not a subtle medium, so its capacity to exploit paradox is rather limited. Farce demands sharp outlines – nothing ambiguous, everything clear, blunt, direct. The audience must be able to follow the thread of dramatic discourse without getting tangled in hidden nuances of meaning or led astray by loose ends of tangential thought. In Soyinka's play, it is "Articulate Jero," our talkative host, who sees to it that no one loses the central thread. He may be a paradox, but he is a very transparent one who does not in any way obscure our vision of essential matters. In fact, through him we see things more clearly than we otherwise would. He magnifies rather than diminishes our insights into human nature.

Perhaps this is one reason he does not ordinarily speak in proverbs. If his thoughts were clothed in picturesque metaphors and symbols, he might be unable to communicate with such lucidity. Worse yet, he might run the risk of being misunderstood, and this would seriously undermine our confidence in him as an honest trickster. His role as master of ceremonies in the farce demands that he be completely frank and forthright, never deviously indirect.

The one proverb Jero quotes is therefore extremely significant. It appears at the beginning of his opening monologue, when he is detailing the different kinds of prophets one finds in the world. "There are eggs," he says, "and there are eggs" (45), the implication being that though they all look exactly alike on the surface, some will be good and others rotten. "Same thing with prophets," he declares, forcing us to recognize the ubiquity of apostasy and religious hypocrisy even in the saintliest of holy occupations. As he continues speaking, however, it soon becomes plain that he himself is a professional impostor, one who relishes duping the gullible by posing as a beach evangelist blessed with a divine gift of fortune-telling. His proverb serves not only to alert us to the possibility that he might be a bad egg but also to introduce the theme of duplicity which comes to dominate the entire play. It proves a very prophetic proverb.

In *The Lion and the Jewel* Soyinka makes use of a similar theme but adopts a different strategy of comic presentation. The play recounts how wily, old Baroka, through a clever ruse, succeeds in seducing young Sidi, a conceited village girl who has refused to marry him. The comic thrust is once again provided by an elaborate act of deception, but the audience is not made aware of the subtlety of Baroka's maneuvers until the very end.

Surprise is an important element in the play. Because Baroka is not a transparent trickster, we cannot predict how or even whether he will manage to win the "jewel." His climactic treachery is therefore almost as delightfully astonishing to us as it is to Sidi.

The proverbs in the play help to define the nature of the dramatic conflict as a battle of the sexes. Most of them can be found in the seduction scene where they serve both parties as ammunition, Sidi playfully firing them as taunts at Baroka for his supposed impotence, Baroka answering with a barrage of well-placed barbs by which he bullies and eventually corners his prey. It is evident that Baroka also knows how to use gentler means of persuasion, for once he has cornered Sidi, he turns on his verbal charm and overwhelms her with wise-sounding apothegms pregnant with erotic imagery. Indeed, the entire scene is a study in the art of rhetoric, for Baroka achieves his purpose primarily through the skillful selection and manipulation of accepted truths. He constructs an argument in aphorisms, clinching his points with pertinent proverbs.

One brief illustration will suffice. When Baroka shows Sidi the stamp-making machine in his bedroom and says he wants to put her image on the first stamps to be printed in Ilujinle, Sidi is struck speechless. The stage directions say she "drowns herself totally in the contemplation" of this idea. Baroka, meanwhile, talks on, first in simple, straightforward language, then in elaborate metaphors. Aware that she is only half-listening, he indulges in double-talk, occasionally pausing to ask her questions:

> Among the bridges and the murderous roads,
> Below the humming birds which
> Smoke the face of Sango, dispenser of
> The snake-tongue lightening; between this moment
> And the reckless broom that will be wielded
> In these years to come, we must leave
> Virgin plots of lives, rich decay
> And the tang of vapour rising from
> Forgotten heaps of compost, lying
> Undisturbed ... But the skin of progress
> Masks, unknown, the spotted wolf of sameness ...
> Does sameness not revolt your being,
> My daughter? (52).

By this time Sidi "is only capable of a bewildered nod," and Baroka, having seated himself beside her on the bed, resumes his mystifying patter. Soon Sidi is feebly protesting, "I can no longer see the meaning, Baroka ... words are like beetles/ Boring at my ears, and my head/ Becomes a jumping bean."

Baroka then closes in for the kill, bombarding her with old saws clearly honed to make a single voluptuous point:

> The proof of wisdom is the wish to learn
> Even from children. And the haste of youth
> Must learn its temper from the gloss
> Of ancient leather, from a strength
> Knit close along the grain ...
> The old must flow into the new, Sidi,
> Not blind itself or stand foolishly
> Apart. A girl like you must inherit
> Miracles which age alone reveals.
> Is this not so? (53-54).

Sidi, completely under his spell, replies, "Everything you say, Bale, / Seems wise to me." Baroka immediately pours out another aphrodisiac analogy:

> Yesterday's wine alone is strong and blooded, child,
> And though the Christians' holy book denies
> The truth of this, old wine thrives best
> Within a new bottle. The coarseness
> Is mellowed down, and the rugged wine
> Acquires a full and rounded body (54).

By now Sidi is "quite overcome," but Soyinka cannot resist letting Baroka conclude the scene with a singularly appropriate image of another sort:

> Those who know little of Baroka think
> His life one pleasure-living course.
> But the monkey sweats, my child,
> The monkey sweats,
> It is only the hair upon his back
> Which still deceives the world (54).

The proverbs in this scene are working brilliantly at several different levels simultaneously. They are being used to befuddle Sidi, to graphically spell out Baroka's erotic intentions, and to keep the audience amused and alert to what is going on. We understand every *double entendre* in the colorful pronouncements that Sidi, in her confusion, finds "wise," for Baroka is communicating with us in a decipherable code even while impressing Sidi by appearing to speak in unfathomable riddles. Soyinka moves easily from one level to another, juggling meaning and meaninglessness with dazzling dexterity.

But that is not all. As authentic bits of native gnomic lore, the proverbs are also functioning autonomously as independent statements about the nature of human wisdom, the deceptiveness of outward appearances, the complementary interaction of opposites – age and youth, male and female, tradition and change, etc. Yet every one of these statements is of relevance to the drama and is therefore contributing something of its own to the network of meaning in the play. They are individual resonators of important themes, electric transmitters of germinal ideas. Proverbs function in all these ways in *The Lion and the Jewel* because Soyinka knows how to take advantage of the opportunities afforded by their very nature as vehicles of indirect communication.

Kongi's Harvest is Soyinka's most proverb-riddled play, and it is probably significant that it deals with African politics. Perhaps nothing straight can be said in a world so crooked. Perhaps indirection and equivocation are essential for survival. One must either learn to speak in ambiguous conundrums or lose the privilege of speaking at all. This appears to be the only choice – unless, of course, one is at the very top of the pyramid of power. Kongi never speaks in proverbs. He simply does not find it necessary or expedient to do so, for as an enlightened modern despot, he knows that there is no one left outside prison walls for him to fear or placate. He knows too that if worse were to come to worse, he has at his command means of persuasion more powerful than mere words. So there is no reason for him to resort to circuitous speech: he can afford to be direct.

He also happens to be opposed to all things traditional, for he intends to completely modernize his state, even to the point of reforming the language of government. Early in the play one of his ghostwriters reminds another that "The period of isolated saws and wisdoms is over, superseded by a more systematic formulation of comprehensive philosophies" (24). To Kongi then, proverbs are not just unnecessary; they are downright passé and potentially destructive of the ideals of the modern nation-state. He does not want anyone to use them.

To squelch traditionalism and enshrine himself in power, Kongi plans an impressive formal inaugural ceremony. It is to take the form of a ritualized festival,[2] the highlight of which will be the moment that Oba Danlola, a traditional ruler, presents Kongi with the New Yam, an act symbolizing Danlola's spiritual submission to the new regime. Danlola, of course, is currently under preventive detention. There's the rub. How does one persuade a political enemy to participate in a phony ritual designed to rob him forever of power? Kongi's answer is to offer him a small bribe – the promise of a reprieve for a group of political prisoners awaiting execution. All this is done in the clearest clinical language.

Danlola's response to any gesture made by Kongi or his followers is to babble in proverbs. In fact, in the first scene, Danlola is revealed to be living in a state of near verbal anarchy. He is technically in a detention camp, but he and his retinue are singing, dancing, drumming, and carrying on like frenzied performers in a folk opera. When the Superintendent attempts to intervene and stop their fun, Danlola quickly puts him down with a string of proverbs. His words and subsequent threats are so intimidating that the Superintendent is soon apologizing profusely in Danlola's own idiom – proverbs:

> I am only the fowl droppings that stuck to your slippers when you strolled in the backyard. The child is nothing; it is only the glory of his forebears that the world sees and tolerates in him (6).

Danlola has forced him to change his language and sing a different tune.

Danlola has no intention of obediently participating in Kongi's festival, but his words and actions are designed to give the impression that he will do as he has been told. His task is to deceive the deceiver. This he does by pretending to get ready for the festival, pretending he will take part, and pretending he knows nothing about a revolt planned by Segi and Daodu. To conceal his true feelings yet still speak the truth, he normally hides behind equivocations couched in proverbs. A number of his sayings reflect his preoccupation with disguise:

> The ostrich also sports plumes but
> I've yet to see that wise bird
> Leave the ground (48).

> When a dog hides a bone does he not
> Throw up sand? (48).

> Only a phony drapes himself in deeper indigo
> than the son of the deceased (64).

Danlola and Kongi's other enemies eventually succeed in spoiling the festival and cursing its chief celebrant. It has been a contest between Might and Cunning, with Cunning winning because he knows how to work by indirection. It has also been a struggle between Old and New, Ornate and Plain, Tradition and Modernity. The side with the greatest maneuverability always seems to triumph.

Soyinka's proverbs are capable of carrying us to the heart of his drama. By studying how they function and what they mean in a play, we can gain not only a better understanding of his intentions but also a deeper appreciation of his art and craft as a playwright. Soyinka's plays reward this kind of study; for if proverbs are truly "horses of speech," Soyinka is undoubtedly one of Africa's greatest verbal equestrians.

NOTES

1. This proverb was collected in 1968 from Oyekan Owomoyela, a Yoruba doctoral candidate in Theater Arts at UCLA. Printed versions can be found in Leslau 5 and Delano v, ix, 109.

2. Soyinka's debt to traditional Yoruba festivals in this and other plays is discussed in Ogunba 2-18.

REFERENCES

Delano, Isaac O. 1966. *Owe L'Esin Oro: Yoruba Proverbs – Their Meaning and Usage.* Ibadan. 368.

Leslau, Charlotte and Wolf Leslau. 1962. *African Proverbs.* Mount Vernon, New York.

Ogunba, Oyin. 1970. "The Traditional Content of the Plays of Wole Soyinka." *African Literature Today* 4.2-18.

Soyinka, Wole. 1963a. *A Dance of the Forests.* London: Oxford Univ. Press.
------. 1963b. *The Lion and the Jewel.* London: Oxford Univ. Press.
------. 1967. *Kongi's Harvest.* London: Oxford Univ. Press.
------. 1969. *Three Short Plays.* London: Oxford Univ. Press.

SOYINKA
as a
BROADCASTER

"A Storyteller on the Gbohun-Gbohun": An Analysis of Wole Soyinka's Three Johnny Stories

James Gibbs

> I grew up an avid reader of fiction and biography and, one day, exasperated beyond measure by my neglect of geography, chemistry etc. for these idle pastimes, my father scathingly remarked that I would end up no better than a storyteller on the *gbohun-gbohun*. I felt there was something seriously the matter with me – as I did not consider it such a terrible fate.
>
> Wole Soyinka, "Gbohun-Gbohun,"
The Listener (London),
2 November 1972: 582

While in England as an undergraduate at the University of Leeds, Wole Soyinka devoted much of his creative energy to writing short stories. In three of these, "Johnny Just Come," "The Trials of a Bowler," and "Johnny versus the Post Office," he brought to fictional life an extraordinary character in whom he combined several existing traditions and through whom he communicated passionately held opinions. These Johnny Stories, not entirely satisfactory but always vigorous and disturbing, represent the fusion of a variety of popular and literary traditions with a maturing artistic personality. They represent a step in the emergence of Soyinka as a writer, or at least as a storyteller on the *gbohun-gbohun* (radio).

I shall begin this essay by drawing attention to some of the cultural and moral concerns which preoccupied Soyinka as a young man, then consider his view of various Nigerian and non-Nigerian traditions, and finally examine the Johnny Stories.

Soyinka's Early Concerns

During his first period in England, between September 1954 and the end of 1959, Soyinka wrote for publication in Nigeria, for the BBC, and, in a more private way, to contemporaries and friends. The available relevant work includes "Our Letter from London," "A Holiday Camp in Nieuwekerk," "A

Bar-Man's Lot," "The Immigrant Poems," "Telephone Conversation," and a letter to Professor Molly Mahood, which is on file at the University of Ibadan. In this section I shall examine these sources for indications as to the experiences and attitudes of the young Nigerian and hope to show that he expressed himself with wit and passion in autobiographical writing and verse and that he adopted certain distinctive attitudes.

"Our Letter From London" was written shortly after Soyinka's first Christmas in England and was published in *The Eagle*, a student publication at University College, Ibadan, during January 1955. It is signed "Cap'n Blood," the name Soyinka adopted as a member of the Pyrates Confraternity. In the opening paragraph, he adopts a swaggering tone, a larger-than-life persona:

> Hello Ed.,
> I'm sure you must be hoping that I'm dead – and when I say you I mean of course your readers (usually no more than six or seven) who must be glad that I no longer smear the pages of the "Eagle" with my nib. No such luck, I'm afraid. You ought to know I'm pretty hard to kill. Why, only yesterday a car bumped into me and had to be taken to the scrap iron-dealer, while I walked home with no worse damage than some engine-oil on my trousers.

He goes on to give his reaction to England ("it's a wonderful place to live in") and to describe his "quarrel" with the frequent gales:

> These gales, you'd better know, don't come once in a grey sun.... they are strong enough to blow your teeth into your throat. But I must admit to myself that it does me a world of good to watch men and women (the fatter the better) chasing their hats or shawls for a couple of thousand yards.
> Only yesterday I stood at the bus stop and one of these gales was fooling around just then. Well, a friend of mine came along and he stretched out his hand for a handshake. D'you know what happened? The wind bent his hand gradually backwards, and before he knew where he was, he was shaking hands with the person standing behind him.

After referring to the flight to London (apparently a group of students "held a jazz session in the plane, to the stark terror of one or two of the others"), Soyinka describes his experience at Windsor Great Park, where he had spent Christmas with a group of students. "The female section of that party was," he wrote, "a hundred percent what Father Christmas ordered," and one of the "belles kept stealing glances at [his] dusty [dusky] face." Her attention was so close and persistent that Soyinka/ "Cap'n Blood" thought she was going to ask if he were married. It turned out however that she "was just wondering... how many average-sized noses [could] be made out of [his]."

The persona is a "superstudent," and cars are destroyed on contact, but he is also linked to the large-nosed Nobelist. The letter is written with a robust sense of the ridiculous and an attractive, self-deflating sense of humor; it draws attention to sights and weather conditions in Leeds to which Soyinka returned when writing his short stories. Indeed, the letter hovers on the border between epistle and short story.

Among Soyinka's radio scripts lodged in the BBC's Written Archives Centre at Caversham is an account of his experience at a Dutch work camp where he spent part of his summer vacation during 1955. Clearly the experience had been a happy one, but the accident-prone Soyinka had come close to trouble on a number of occasions. He almost missed the boat to Holland because he had to get his passport "endorsed" for Holland and the Post Office only "got it back" to him just before he had to leave. Once in Holland he had difficulty in finding his way. When he reached the work camp, he began building a wall, very slowly: "at the rate of two bricks an hour... it was either that, or a wall swaying at a definitely drunken angle." He reported that his skills improved and claimed that he "seriously considered going in for a diploma in masonry." The locals were so curious about him, and in particular about the texture of his hair that "if [he'd] granted them their final request, [he] should have left Nieuwerkerk with no hair at all." An exaggeration no doubt, but then exaggeration is a feature of Soyinka's autobiographical writing – as it is in his fiction.

The following year Soyinka spent his long vacation working as a bartender in the Douglas Hotel, Isle of Man. He began his account for the BBC by saying that he had always wanted to be a waiter in a first-class restaurant: he was attracted by the clothes and the gestures required. But, lacking appropriate experience, he found himself a job behind a bar that had a Wild West theme, with "broken bits of wagons nailed to the walls, harnesses, saddles, horse-shoes, buffalo horns, Red Indian arrows, scalping axes," and bartenders in cowboy jeans and checked shirts. He clearly met "all sorts of people" and enjoyed playing tricks on some of them. He described how he sometimes served Irish whiskey to Scotsmen who had ordered scotch – and vice versa – and watched them drink the alien and scorned tots with satisfaction. "Occasionally," Soyinka admits, he "picked on one who knew his drinks, and then what he thought of [him] was not fit to print."

Soyinka found amusement not only in the ignorance and affectation of the inhabitants of the British Isles, he also turned his penetrating and mischievous eye on his fellow Nigerians. An example of his scrutiny is "Insulation," one of the "Immigrant Poems," first published in February 1959. The dramatic monologue is spoken by an African who is obsessed by clothes, by his "crisp Van Heusen collar," his "All-Wool Tootal tie," and his "three-piece suit." He adopts an arrogant, superior attitude, closes his mind to "niceties of judgment," shouts slogans, "[floats] / Upon the crest of / An alien, white society," lives in "round-the-year-entombment" surviving on "two square/ Semolina meals per day," and dreaming of home.

This poem is often linked with "Telephone Conversation," which was part of Soyinka's Evening at the Royal Court (November 1959) and which is perhaps his most frequently anthologized verse. In it an African seeking accommodation pits his wits against a hypocritical, affected, prejudiced English landlady. The African's triumph lies in stripping away the "pressurized good-breeding" until truthfulness "clanged her accent/ Hard on the mouthpiece." He reduces the oh-so-polite woman with her "long gold-rolled" voice to a vulnerable bigot about to slam down the telephone receiver.

The final text I want to draw attention to in order to suggest something of Soyinka's inner and creative life during this period is, like my first, a letter. Unlike "Our Letter from London," this was not written for publication, but I do not feel I am invading anyone's privacy by reproducing part of it here because it is in an accessible file at the University of Ibadan Library and because of the nature of its subject matter. The letter was written to Mahood at University College, Ibadan, from rue de Citeaux, 4, Paris 12 on 8 August 1959. Soyinka was visiting Paris and trying to get engagements as a singer. He had met a Lebanese student who had given him "sleeping space" in his "attic wonder" and was subsisting (just) on a diet of French rolls and jam, with milk or wine. He describes walking through a square "and noticing how closely packed the houses were, and how high, knowing full-well they had no fire-escapes." He continues:

> I began to wonder what on earth happens when there is a fire. (This incidentally was the first thing I looked for when I went to see the student's attic – which was the best way out in case of fire?) Anyway before I could control my thoughts, I began to say to myself that the fire mightn't be such a bad thing at that, because then a Red Cross group was bound to find its way there in no time, and a soup-van would draw up and the evacuees would be comforted with warm mugs of soup. (In mitigation, I must say that I was very hungry that afternoon.) And I thought if I happened to be passing, no one would notice if I slipped among the rescued and drew a similar mug of comfort, and the people would probably make room for me because I would look more burnt than any other person there and so on and so forth. Well, that same evening – have you guessed – walking along the Seine, I saw a terrific glow from that area, and after I realised it was no search-light beamed on a church, I ran there, same square, of course, but thank goodness, it was a motor car depot, so I stood and watched and ever [sic] so often, a petrol tank exploded and delighted the crowd. There was no Red Cross van with or without soup, so it made no difference.
> (Soyinka to Mahood, 8 August 1959)

This generous and delightful example of Soyinka's letter-writing ability reveals the vigor of his imagination. He entertains the preposterous (passing himself off as a victim of the fire) and the prodigious (feeling that he might have caused the fire in some supernatural way) in a manner that is both absurd and amusingly grotesque. When I first read the letter, I thought of Masterbuilder Solness in Henrik Ibsen's play about the architect who builds his career out of the ashes of a destructive fire. In the present context I would want to relate it to the same playwright's Peer Gynt, a character bred out of the Norwegian folk tradition, as Soyinka's imagination fed on the Nigerian folk tradition. In the section which follows, I want to draw attention to Soyinka's understanding of precedents and parallels during the 1950s.

Soyinka and Narrative Traditions

Soyinka's choice of the nom de plume "Cap'n Blood" has already been remarked. Peter Blood first appeared in a novel by Rafael Sabatini, but he made his most memorable impression on the twentieth-century imagination in the film starring Errol Flynn. Soyinka has taken a long and informed interest in film: his early work was particularly influenced by the silent comedies of Charlie Chaplin, that London-born, Hollywood-cultivated comedian who slipped across cultural boundaries so effectively that he inspired African mask makers and concert party performers (see Soyinka 1987b).

Soyinka's youthful literary tastes have not come down to us in any detail. He has mentioned that Dickens provided favorite boyhood reading – perhaps the sort of fiction his father inveighed against. While editor of *The Eagle* in 1953, Soyinka reproduced a list published by Columbia University Press of the world's "Ten Most Boring Books" which included works by Melville, Milton, Spenser, Boswell, Johnson, Richardson, George Eliot, Scott, Cervantes, and Goethe. He observed,

> A good choice I would say, except in Scott's "Ivanhoe" and Cervantes' "Don Quixote." How the latter in particular was included in the list beats me completely. And evidently those lucky people have never heard of Newman's "Idea of a University" – oh, maybe it isn't a classic.

Bernth Lindfors makes the appropriate comment: "It is perhaps significant that Soyinka, as a young student, was turned off by all but the prose chivalric romances on the list" (1979, 178). Soyinka and Johnny as Ivanhoes out to challenge the power of an empire with the weapons of that empire, including humor and satire expressed in the very language of "the master race," is attractive and apt. But the young writer and his creation are also akin to that Spanish remnant of an age of chivalry who set out on quests, challenged great odds, and not infrequently made an absolute idiot of himself.

During the first term of his second year at the University of Leeds (October-December 1955), Soyinka wrote six talks for the BBC's African service program *Calling Nigeria.* He appears to have written them quickly, and, as it were, off the top of his head. Indeed, the learning is so lightly worn that it is wafted away by a style that is anecdotal and conversational.

In the first talk, on "The Origin of West African Myths," Soyinka related some of the etiological myths about the origin of different races and ethnic groups and touched on the myths and superstitions surrounding eclipses. The second, entitled "Permanent Mythological Figures," opened with the story of how the tortoise put all wisdom in a gourd and tried to carry it slung in front of him to the top of a tree. Seeing him in difficulty, a fly told him to put the gourd on his back; the tortoise, Ijapa presumably, was so angry that he smashed the gourd and so scattered wisdom to all parts of the earth. Soyinka then pointed out the parallels between Ijapa and Anansi, whom he characterized as cunning, ruthless, sly, selfish, and greedy. In an aside on the trickster's marital status, he mentions Yarinbo, but says he has never heard a story about Anansi's wife.

Soyinka maintained that "the West African imagination is such that he accepts all the prodigious feats of these mythical figures" – even accepting that a tortoise can kill an elephant, or marry a princess, or change his shape. He continued: Ijapa and the spider are products of a long tradition through which West Africans "sub-consciously make a satire of their own impulses." He then compared the Yoruba monster child Ajantala with Tom Thumb, arguing that Ajantala is the more accomplished and aggressive because he could talk at birth, eat like twenty men, and fight like a hundred and twenty. He concluded by explaining the expression "Alfajona, o nbere irugbon" by relating it to the story of an ambitious "native doctor" who thought he could control the newborn Ajantala.

The talks were, inevitably, no more than introductions, but they are nonetheless surprisingly off-hand and superficial at times. At one point in the first, Soyinka ducked the issue of which came first, the myth about eclipses or the superstitions that cause people to beat tins during eclipses: he simply left the mystery to the anthropologists. In the second, he said that he had not heard a story about Anansi's wife, an admission that indicates a very limited exposure to the genre.

In a subsequent talk Soyinka spoke about the validity of English as a vehicle for African writing. He said, "More and more of our stories are being written in English," and he advocated fusion of inherited myths with "a more modern form of writing." It seems to me that this is what he managed to do in the Johnny Stories, the three narratives I want to examine now in the light of the qualities and attitudes I have identified above.

The Johnny Stories

During March 1955, Soyinka recorded "Johnny Just Come," an account of Johnny's arrival in England. He has made the journey to study in Britain, but he is not prepared to make any concessions to British ways. In Liverpool he expects to find palm wine; later he embarrasses his friend when, on stepping onto a moving staircase (escalator), he shouts "Bafi! The stairs are sinking!" His friend is glad to keep him at arm's length, finding accommodation for him at Queen's Gardens because the British Council Hostel at Hans Crescent is full. Johnny begins to fight back against the British: when shop assistants laugh at him, he "floors them" with "Have you ever seen a palmtree in all your life?" When he notices how many times a bus conductor says "Q" ("Thank you"), he suggests that the conductor play a recording of the expression or write it on a card and hang the card around his neck.

Johnny, we are told, "didn't take to the English people. They drive one slowly mad with their courtesy and politeness." He decides to get his own back: he dresses for dinner, insists that the other students serve themselves before him, and then, when dinner is over and the diners move to the door, he leaps up, holds the door open and engages in a battle of "you go first." A stalemate is quickly reached, which Johnny eventually shatters by slipping out through the door and locking it behind him.

There are qualities in this character that recall the youthful Soyinka, particularly the African in "Telephone Conversation" who uses wit to rip off a veneer of politeness. There are also moments – the comments on the bus conductor's mannerism provide one – when the humor is similar to that of British comic writing, that of Malcolm Bradbury, for example. But Johnny is to some extent an original: a monster child waging an Ajantalesque war against the British and "subconsciously satirising" Nigerian impulses.

In "The Trials of a Bowler," broadcast during August 1959, Johnny, whom details indicate is now a student at Leeds, decides to "embrace the English way of life." Naturally, he wants to do so in style: he considers wearing a kilt, but decides against it because "he had bow legs like a cowboy." He ponders the possibility of dressing like the Teddy boys, but finds he cannot get his kinky hair to fall over his forehead in the prescribed Edwardian fashion. And so, shades of the "Immigrant," he rigs himself out like a city gent with bowler and umbrella. He feels, we read, "as important as any board director." He had, however, to contend with what Soyinka described to his friends at Ibadan as the gales which are "strong enough to blow your teeth into your throat."

> He was prepared to suffer the tortures of the people's courtesy, was prepared to stuff himself day and night with mashed potatoes and boiled vegetables. He was even prepared to allow the icy winds to cut through his natty suit and freeze his bones; but he was not going to allow the wind to blow off his hat.

Johnny holds on to his hat in the street, but when his umbrella becomes stuck while getting on a bus, he has to let go of his hat for a moment and that is enough. Johnny stalks the hat, but it eludes him; he snatches at it, but it is blown beyond his grasp; he lies in wait for it, and it remains out of reach; he blocks its progress with his body, but it is blown neatly through his legs and carried into a copse. Next morning Johnny goes to lectures in a simple lounge suit. He does not see his hat again until spring, when he catches sight of it from a bus: it is caught in a tree near Otley Road. He walks back to the tree; then he phones the fire brigade. They are sympathetic when they think he is talking about a cat, but when they realize it is a hat, they refuse to turn out. Determined to "put the British Fire Brigade to shame," Johnny climbs the tree, an action which attracts a curious British crowd. When he reaches the hat, he finds it contains a bird's nest and is "bespattered with the remnants of many dinners, and the more unpleasant evidence of a maternity home." Johnny swears vigorously and falls; he is however – "have you guessed" – caught on a branch and hangs suspended by his jacket. At this point the fire brigade is called and saves him. Johnny asks his rescuers whether they can get his hat for him, but the reply is "unprintable" and, Johnny decides, "very, very unenglish. Well at any rate he hadn't yet come across it in his studies at the University."

Interwoven in this comedy are themes encountered in the account of Leeds (the wind, the hat chase), the Dutch work camp (Johnny is accident prone), of Douglas, Isle of Man (the obsession with distinctive clothes, eruption of "unprintable" language), of Paris (the arrival of the fire brigade), of "Telephone Conversation" (the testing of the English "reserve"). There is a particularly happy mix so that Johnny is both Soyinka and quite clearly a figment of Soyinka's imagination. The writer has put part of himself and some of his experiences and attitudes into his creation, but he has also distanced him. The Johnny of this story has brothers on the silver screen, but he is less Peter Blood than Charlie Chaplin – or a Mack Sennet creation. There is evidence that Soyinka is beginning to master the art of sharing his sympathies with his characters.

The third of the Johnny stories, the last that I have found, is entitled "Johnny versus the Post Office" and was broadcast near the end of 1955.

The eponymous hero – closely related to previous Johnnys – is described as "a mischief maker from Abadina." (Abadina is the name of the workers' quarters on the campus of the University at Ibadan, and Soyinka used it occasionally in *The Eagle* as a substitute for the institution.) He is staying with friends in the welcoming village of Rishton, a town just outside Blackburn, where Soyinka spent part of his holidays when a student. Johnny begins to behave as he did in Abadina. He tries to cash a postal order, but going strictly by the book, the clerk sends him to fetch his passport in order to provide proof of identity. Johnny meets a friend, Sheila, with whom he goes to dances and the cinema. One evening they quarrel and Johnny marches home "three yards to every step"; he writes a letter breaking off their friendship and posts it. As soon as he gets into bed, Johnny regrets writing and posting the letter. He determines to retrieve it from the postman when he empties the box the next morning. Johnny waits from 8:30 to 9:30 before he realizes that, since it is a Saturday, there will be no collection until 10:30. When the postman eventually arrives, he goes by the book and refuses to return Johnny's letter. Johnny complains at the post office but is told once again that his letter cannot be returned to him; however, he takes great delight in the information that the letter will be delivered at 5:30. That afternoon Johnny lies in wait at Sheila's house, meets the postman at the garden gate, and repossesses his letter. He is trimphant, rejoicing that "he alone and unaided had licked the British postal service, and flouted its red tape with the greatest ease." His joy is, however, short-lived for on returning home he finds a letter from Sheila waiting for him; it reads, "Johnny, You're the most unreasonable creature I have ever met. I'm never going to see you again." The story concludes, "Why, oh why, muttered Johnny, didn't the stuffy old Post Office win the battle?"

In this story Johnny has evolved: he is part trickster, part fall guy, part Ijapa, part Ajantala, part Quixote, part Chaplin. There is the deflation of the presumptuous male ego that was foreshadowed in the account of Christmas at Windsor Great Park, and there is the encounter with the postal system that nearly thwarted Soyinka's plans to go to Holland. But the major ingredient is the extensive examination of Johnny as trickster – not a wholly successful trickster, of course. But then even Ijapa did not always win: a fly could teach him a lesson even after he thought he had put wisdom in a gourd. The story reads well, and qualities not communicated by my summary heighten the mounting tension, Johnny's desperation, and the neat reversals that cluster at the end.

Conclusion

In the three Johnny Stories examined, Soyinka uses his central character to comment on and criticize both British society and Nigerian emigrants. Wittily and effectively, the stories show a rather gauche, unstable, quixotic, eccentric, accident-prone, mischief maker from Nigeria loose in Britain. Johnny champions some causes that are close to the heart of his creator, but he is carefully distanced, held up to ridicule as well as for guarded approval. Through him, Soyinka transforms his own experience into entertaining narratives.

Johnny stands at the beginning of a line of Soyinkan creations that stretches through Lakunle and Queen's Broken to Jero and beyond, characters who provide a disturbing and exciting mixture of attractive and repulsive qualities, energetic, full of life, and in some ways distant cousins of both Soyinka and Ijapa. In the best of these stories for *Calling Nigeria*, Soyinka managed to fuse African and non-African traditions, the fruits of his reading fiction and biography, of thinking about folk stories and going to the cinema, and of his own experience in that peculiar oral literature, the story for *gbohun-gbohun*.

NOTE

I would like to express my gratitude to the staff at the BBC's Written Archives Centre at Caversham for giving me access to the texts referred to here and to the library staff at the University of Ibadan for letting me see the Mahood-Soyinka file.

PRIMARY TEXTS

Soyinka, Wole
- 1953   "Literature." *The Eagle,* (Ibadan) 3.2 (Jan.), p. 5.
- 1955a   "Our Letter from London." *The Eagle,* (Ibadan) 4.2, p. 4.
- 1955b   "Johnny Just Come." *Calling Nigeria.* Caversham, 23 Mar.
- 1955c   "The Trials of a Bowler." *Calling Nigeria.* Caversham,
          10 August.
- 1955d   "A Holiday Camp in Nieuwekerk." *Calling Nigeria.*
          Caversham, 16 Sept.
- 1955   "Johnny versus the Post Office." *Calling Nigeria.*
          Caversham, 21 Dec.
- 1956   "A Place for West African Literature." Six talks for *Calling
          Nigeria.* Caversham.
- 1956   "A Bar-Man's Lot." *Calling Nigeria.* Caversham, 13 Dec.
- 1959a   "Insulation." *Ibadan* (Ibadan), 5 (Feb.), p. 24.
- 1959b   "Telephone Conversation." Royal Court Evening, Nov., Ts.
- 1987a   Soyinka on Bandung file. Channel 4, Feb.
- 1987b   "Soyinka in Zimbabwe." *Literary Half-Yearly* (Mysore), 28 (2), pp. 50-110.

REFERENCES

Lindfors, Bernth. "The Early Writings of Wole Soyinka." In *Critical Perspectives on Nigerian Literatures*. Ed. Bernth Lindfors. London: Heinemann, 1979.

SOYINKA
as a
DRAMATIST

The Masks Hatched Out

James Gibbs

Introduction

The title of this essay, "The Masks Hatched Out," is taken from an early poem by Wole Soyinka entitled "The Stage." I have used it to suggest the process by which the private experience of the playwright, confided to paper, becomes, in performance, the shared experience of the audience. Literature and technology are often regarded as enemies of a vigorous oral culture and of eagerly celebrated communal events. Man moves apart from man and sits with his head in a book. Man holds his transistor-radio to his ear and is deaf to invitations to join in the ceremonies being performed around him. But the playwright and his drama occupy a special place in this configuration. The child of the playwright's vision and experience is cocooned within a written text, printed and distributed by technological processes, and then, with the help of many heads and hands and of more technology, it is hatched out to delight the community which responds directly to its brief life and its butterfly colors. A somewhat similar process transforms the vision of the film-maker. The pictures and sounds which once existed only within his head are "shot," "canned" and then blazoned and blasted forth in a dozen places simultaneously at a touch on a dozen switches.

PART ONE

Production Histories of Soyinka's Plays

The Swamp Dwellers
First produced by Soyinka at the National Union of Students' Drama Festival, London 31.12.58, with the Nigerian Drama Group: Francesca Pereira (Alu); Jide Ajayi; Banjo Solaru; Soyinka (Igwezu).

See: Soyinka, Wole, "And ... *The Swamp Dwellers*," *Radio Times* (Lagos), March 1960, p. 5.

Other notable production:
Produced by Geoffrey Axworthy at the Arts Theatre, University College, Ibadan (hereafter "the Arts Theatre"), during February 1959: Christine Clinton (Alu); Dapo Adelugba (Beggar); Bernard Mafeni (Igwezu); Gabner Olusanya (Kadiye); Adisa Ajetumobi (Makuri).

See: Browne-Wilkinson, Virginia, *The Horn* (Ibadan), 2,6 (1959), p. 10.
Maclean, Una, M.M. Mahood and Phebean Ogundipe, "Three Views of *The Swamp Dwellers*," *Ibadan* (Ibadan), June 1959, pp. 27-30.

Other productions:
Nigerian Broadcasting Service (1960); Ibadan (1960); Cleveland (Karamu, 1964); Nairobi (1965); Stony Brook (New York, 1966); Ibadan (G.S., 1967); Cross River Theatre Group (1968); Ibadan (1967); Ibadan (School of Drama, 1968); Navrongo Sec. School (1969); London (BBC African Service, 1967); London (Keskidee, 1975); London (Drum, 1976); Leeds University Workshop Theatre (1978).

Film:
Directed by Dennis Duerden, produced by the Transcription Centre, London.

The Lion and the Jewel

First produced (in earlier, shorter version and with cuts) by Ken Post at the Arts Theatre, during February 1959: Abiola Irele (Lakunle); Remi Gbàdebo (Sidi); Bridget Akwada (Sadiku).

See: Akanji, Sangodare, *Black Orpheus* (Ibadan), 6 (November 1959), pp. 50-1.
Browne-Wilkinson, Virginia, *The Horn*, 2, 6 (1959), p. 10.
Maclean, et al., *Ibadan*, June 1959, pp. 27-30.

Other notable productions: Produced by Soyinka with Orisun Theatre in Lagos.

See: John MacDermott, *Sunday Times*, 21.3.65. (I have not included the place of publication of newspapers where this is obvious from the place of production of the play.)

Directed by Desmond O'Donovan at the Royal Court Theatre, London, with the Ijinle Theatre Company, 12.12.66: Jumoke Debayo (Sadiku); Hannah Bright-Taylor (Sidi); Lionel Ngakane (Baroka), Femi Euba (Lakunle), and with music by Marc Wilkinson and Sanya Dosunmo.

See: *Cultural Events in Africa*, 25 (December 1966), pp. 2-3.
         "Sheer Ingenuity of Soyinka's Plot," *The Times*, 13.12.66, p. 6.
         Young, B.A., *Financial Times*, 13.12.66.
         (This is a much abbreviated list of reviews and compilations. For fuller lists of
         reviews in this case and others see James Gibbs, *Wole Soyinka: A Selected Bib-
         liography* [1976]).
         Directed by G.A. Wilson and A.M. Opuku at the Drama Studio, Accra, in 1967 and
         revived in 1968.

See: K. E. Senanu, "Thoughts on Creating a Popular Theatre," *Legon Observer*, 29.9.67,
         pp. 25-6 and 13.10.67, pp. 22-3.
         Also in James Gibbs, ed. *Critical Perspectives on Wole Soyinka*, London: Heinemann,
         1981.
         Directed by Dapo Adelugba at Ibadan in April 1968: Val Oyelami (Lakunle); Edith
         Ekem (Sidi); Jimmy Solanke (Baroka); music by Tunji Oyelana and choreography by
         Betty Okotie-Barrett.

See: Banjo, Ayo, *Ibadan*, 26 (1968), pp. 82-3.
         Directed by Joel Adedeji with the Unibadan Masques.

Other productions include:
         Kano (1963); Eastern Nigeria (1964); London (BBC African Service, 1965); London
         (BBC Third Programme, 1966); Ibadan (1968); Mpemba (Malawi, 1971); Akure (c.
         1969); Dakar (in French and in honor of Senghor's birthday, 1976); Morgan State
         (Baltimore, 1979); Leeds University Workshop Theatre (1972).

The Invention:

First produced by Soyinka at the Royal Court, 1.11.59.

See: "African Poet and Playwright," *The Times*, 2.11.59, p. 3.
         Brien, Alan, "Where Spades are Trumps," *The Spectator*, 203 (6.11.59), pp. 629-30.

The Trials of Brother Jero

First produced in the Dining Hall at Mellanby Hall, University College, Ibadan, during April
1960: Remi Adeleye (Brother Jero); Ben Norohunfola (Chume); Kate Kehinde (Amope).

See: Banham, Martin and Abiola Irele, *The Horn* (Ibadan), 4.1 (1960), pp. 17-20.
         Maclean, Una, "Three One-Act Plays," *Ibadan*, June 1960, p. 21.

Other notable productions:
         Produced by Soyinka at the Mbari Club, Ibadan, during 1962.

See: Armstrong, R.P., *Ibadan*, 15 (1963), pp. 29-30.
         Horizon (Ibadan), 1, 2 (1962), p. 58.
         Nwankwo, N., *Nigeria Magazine*, 72 (March 1962), p. 80.
         Produced by Athol Fugard at the Hampstead Theatre Club, London, June 1966:
         Jumoke Debayo (Amope); Zakes Mokae (Jero); Femi Euba (Chume); Robert Seru-
         maga (M.P.). With additional material.

See: Bryden, Ronald, "The Voice of Africa," *Observer*, 3.6.66.
        "Harsh Comedy on Lagos Beach," *The Times*, 29.6.66.
        Jones, D.A.N., "Soyinka," *New Statesman*, 72 (8.7.66), pp. 63-4.
Presented by Farris-Belgrave Productions in association with Afolabi Ajayi at the Greenwich Mews Theatre, New York, 31.10.67: Harold Scott (Jero); Cynthia Belgrave (Amope).

See: Clurman, Harold, *The Nation*, 205 (4.12.67), p. 606.
        Bunce, Alan N., "A Brace of Double-Bills on Broadway and Off," *Christian Science Monitor* (Boston), 20.11.67.
        "Infectious Humanity," *Time*, 90 (17.11.67), p. 50.
        Sullivan, Dan, "Two Plays by Nigeria's Wole Soyinka," *New York Times*, 10.11.67.

Other productions include: Kano (1963); Ibadan (1964); Cleveland (1964); San Francisco (1965); Ibadan (Theatre Express, 1965); Ibadan (Orisun, 1965); Columbia University(1966); Limbe (Malawi, 1967); Ikole-Ekiti (1967); Cape Coast (1967); Port Moresby (P.N.G., 1968); Copenhagen (by Yulisa Maddy, 1969); Keffi (1968); Legon (Ghana, 1969); Accra (1969); Navrongo (Ghana, 1969); Kampala (1971); Mzuzu (Malawi, 1971); London (British Council, 1973); UK Tour by Dark and Light (November, 1973); Leeds University Workshop Theatre (1973); Bristol (Drama Department, 1974); Abidjan (in French, 1975); U.C.L.A. (1977).

A Dance of the Forests

First produced by Soyinka at Yaba Technical College and the Arts Theatre, 20.9.60 with 1960 Masks: Ralph Opara (Council Orator); Segun Sofowote (Murete); Femi Euba (Crier); Olga Adeniyi-Jones (Rola); Yemi Lijadu (Demoke); Patrick Ozieh (Old Man); Remi Adeleye (Eshuoro); Soyinka (Forest Head); designed by Demas Nwoko.

See: Bare, "Forests," *African Horizon*, 2 (January 1961), pp. 8-10.
        Cockshott, Una, *Ibadan*, 10 (November 1960), pp. 30-2.
        Pan, Peter, "Wole Has Overdone It This Time," *Daily Times*, 7.10.60.

Other notable productions: Extracts produced by Soyinka in Paris during mid-1972.

See: Osofisan, Femi, "Soyinka in Paris," *West Africa*, 21.8.72, p. 23.

Other productions include: Nairobi High School (September 1976); Leeds (TV version of extract, mid-1970s).

Revues (1963/64/65)

During 1963, 1964 and 1965 Soyinka worked with Yemi Lijadu, 1960 Masks and Orisun Theatre on three satirical revues:

See: *The Republican*, produced by Lijadu, November, 1963.
        Daily Express, 27.11.63, p. 3.
        The (New) Republican (as above, but with new material, some by Soyinka, March, 1964).
        Daily Express, 11.3.64, p. 3.
        Before the Blackout, produced by Soyinka, March 1965.

Barbooze, Sam, *Sunday Express*, 21.3.65, p. 5.
Daily Express, 9.3.65.
MacDermott, John, *The Sunday Times*, 21.3.65.
The company included: Olga Adeniyi-Jones; Yemi Lijadu; Wole Soyinka (he performed an "Anti-Logwu" dance); Francesca Pereira; Wale Ogunyemi; Gaius Anoka; Christopher Kolade; Jimmy Solanke; Yemi Ogunbiyi; Eddy (now Femi) Fatoba; Yomi Obileye; Tunji Oyelana; Sola Odunfa; Yewande Akiboh; Patrick Ozieh; with Aig-Imoukhuede and Kofi Pereira (Stage Management).

Childe Internationale

First produced as part of *Before the Blackout*, see above.

Other productions include: Mpemba (Malawi, 1973); Roma (Lesotho, 1974); Zomba (Malawi, 1974); Ibadan (Orisun, 1969); Benin City (1979); Ibadan (1979); Performance in Zimbabwe; Leeds University Workshop Theatre (1973).

Kongi's Harvest

First produced by Soyinka with 1960 Masks and Orisun Theatre at AMSAC's First Annual Assembly, Independence Hall, Lagos, on 12.8.65:
Gaius Anoka (Kongi); Betty Okotie (Segi); Dapo Adelugba (Daodu); Femi Johnson (Secretary); Sehinde Arigbade (Danlola); Tunji Oyelana (Ogbo Aweri); Wale Ogunyemi (Dende); Ralph Opara (4th Aweri); Sola Odunfa (Captain); Jimmy Johnson (Right Ear); Jimmy Solanke (Left Ear). Stage-manager: Bayo Oduneye.

See: "Kongi's Harvest," *Morning Post*, 8, 65. (Also in *Cultural Events in Africa*, 12 [November 1965], p. 6).

This production of *Ur-Kongi's Harvest* was taken to Ibadan following the performance at Lagos. It was rewritten and redirected during 1966, presented in Ibadan and taken to the Dakar Festival – by the Nigerian Festival Theatre Company, i.e., substantially the same cast as above.

See: Barry, Boyd. M. *Ibadan*, 23 (October 1966), pp. 53-5.
         Dathorne, O.R., *Black Orpheus*, 21 (April 1967), pp. 60-1.
         Nzekwu, Onoura, "Nigeria, Negritude and the World Festival of Negro Arts," *Nigeria Magazine*, 89 (1966), pp. 80-94.

Other notable productions:
         Soyinka's second production, begun by Dapo Adelugba, presented at Ibadan 1969 and at the Ife Festival, 1970: Adelugba, Johnson, Ogunyemi and Arigbade played the parts they took in the earlier production; Uriel Paul Worika (Kongi); Aina Lewis (Segi); Jimmy Solanke (5th Aweri).

See: Dedenuola, Jibola, *Ibadan Literary Review*, 1 (December 1969), pp. 1-3.
         Oke, Ola, "Tragedy Beautifully Rendered," *Nigeria Magazine*, No. 102 (September-November 1969), pp. 525-7.

Negro Ensemble Production at St. Mark's Theatre, April 1968.
Staged by Charles M. Schultz: Moses Gunn (Kongi); Robert Hooks (Daodu).

See: Clurman, Harold, *The Nation*, 206 (29.4.68), p. 518.
          Kerr, Walter, "Tantalizing but Blurred," *New York Times*, 21.4.68, II, 5, 3.
          Time, April 26th, 1968, p. 97.

O'Connor, Garry, "Impressive Soyinka Gallery," *Wall Street Journal*, 17.4.68.

Other productions include:
          Agbowa-Ikosi (1967); Accra (1970; "pirate" production by G. A. Wilson); Nairobi (late 1970s); Abeokuta Grammar School (1980); Zimbabwe (c. 1980).

Film:
          Ossie Davis directed a film of *Kongi's Harvest* for Omega/Calpenny Films, during 1970: Soyinka (Kongi); Adelugba (Daodu); Johnson (Secretary); Nina Baiden-Semper (Segi). (The film-script differs from both play and final film version.)

See: Ita, Bassey, *Sunday Post*, 11.4.71, p. 5.
          "Kongi on Film," *West Africa*, 15.8.70, p. 950.

The Road

First production by David Thompson for Stage Sixty at the Theatre Royal, Stratford East, during the Commonwealth Arts Festival, September, 1965, with Soyinka as an adviser: Bari Johnson (Samson); Horace James (Professor); Rudolph Walker (Kotonu); Dapo Adelugba (Murano); Alton Kumalo (Say Tokyo Kid); Pat Maddy (Chief in Town); set by Ken Calder.

Other productions include:
          Kampala (1969, produced by David Rubadiri); Kano (1978, by Derek Bullock); Port of Spain (Trinidad, by Derek Walcott); Ibadan (by Zulu Sofola).

The Strong Breed

First produced by Derek Bullock and Chris Groves at Ibadan during 1966 with pupils from Government College, Ibadan, and St. Anne's School, Ibadan.

Other notable productions:
          Produced by Betty Okotie with a University of Ibadan Company and presented at Ibadan and the World University Festival at Nancy, April 1967.

See: *Cultural Events in Africa*, 30 (May 1967), p. 2.
          Mbari News (Ibadan), 7 and 8 (1966), pp. 2-3.
          Moore, *Wole Soyinka*, p. 45.
          Presented by Farris-Belgrave Production in association with Afolabi Ajayi at the Greenwich Mews Theatre, 21.10.67.
          Harold Scott (Eman); Mary Alice (Sunma).

See: Items listed under *Brother Jero*, the other half of the double-bill at the Greenwich Mews.

Other productions include:
          Afikpo (1964); Nairobi (1967); London (Mercury Theatre, directed by Lionel Ngakane, November 1968); Zomba (Malawi, 1976); Dar es Salaam (1976).

Madmen and Specialists

First produced by Soyinka at the Eugene O'Neill Center, New Haven, Connecticut, 1.8.70, with the University of Ibadan Theatre Arts Company. Revised and slightly recast in Nigeria and presented at Ibadan and Ife in March, 1971, in the printed version: Femi Johnson (Aafaa); Femi Osofisan (Blindman); Wale Ogunyemi (Goyi); Tunji Oyelana (Cripple); Gbenga Sonuga (Priest); Dapo Adelugba (Old Man); Deola Adedoyin (Si Bero); Nguba Agolia (Iya Agba); Bopo George (Iya Mate); Nat Okora (Bero).

See: Bunce, Alan, "Soyinka's Nigerian Play," *Christian Science Monitor* (Boston), 15.8.70.
        Irele, Abiola, "Portrait of a Catching Sickness," *Sunday Times* (Lagos), 28.3.71.

Other productions include:
        London (Holland Park Link Group at Mercury Theatre, 1972); London (BBC Radio Three, Soyinka's radio version, 1973); Zaria and Ibadan (ABU Studio Theatre, 1980); Leeds University Workshop Theatre (1978).

Jero's Metamorphosis

First produced by Glynne Wickham with students of the Bristol University Drama Department, February 1974.

See: Foot, David, "Wole Soyinka," *The Guardian*, 2.3.74.

Produced at the Leeds University Workshop Theatre (1978) and at the National Theatre, Lagos, 1.6.81.

Note: The fact that these are the only productions I have listed reveals more, I suspect, about my ignorance and the inadequacy of my sources than about the production history of this play. It may also indicate that the overt anti-militarism of the play caused some potential producers to be cautious. The Nigerian production claimed to be the world premiere; this was not the case.

The Bacchae of Euripides

First produced by Roland Joffe with the British National Theatre Company at the Old Vic Theatre, August 1973: Martin Shaw (Dionysus); John Shrapnell (Pentheus); Constance Cummings (Agave); Julian Curry (Tiresias); set designed by Nadine Bayliss.

See: Darlington, W.A., "A Case of Believe it or Not," *Daily Telegraph*, 3.9.73.
        Hunt, Albert, "Amateurs in Horror," *New Society*, 9.8.73, pp. 343-8.
        (Predictably the most extensively reviewed of Wole Soyinka's productions to date. See *Selected Bibliography*, and "Press Reactions to the *Bacchae of Euripides*" by James Gibbs, "Travelling Theatre Survey" [Zomba], 20.9.73. The two reviews listed are the most revealing).

Other notable productions:
        Directed by Carroll Dawes with the National Festival Theatre at the Little Theatre, Kingston, Jamaica, 1975.

Death and the King's Horseman

First produced by Soyinka at the University of Ife, December 1976:
Jimmy Solanke (Elesin Oba).

See: Moore, Gerald, "Soyinka's New Play," *West Africa*, 10.1.77, pp. 60-1.

Other notable productions:
        Directed by Soyinka at the Goodman Theatre, Chicago, mid-October 1979,
        transferred to the John F. Kennedy Center for the Performing Arts, Washington D.C.,
        December 1979.

See: Sander, Michael J. "Soyinka's Play Captivates US Audience," *Nairobi Times*, 6.1.80.
        "A Tale of Two Cultures," *Topic* (Washington D.C.) 127, pp. 31-4.

Other productions:
        Ghana (Produced by Francis Say with Kokoroko Theatre, 1980).

Opera Wonyosi

First produced by Soyinka at the University of Ife, with staff and students of the University,
mid-December 1977: Bola Popoola (De Madam); Segun Bankole (Capt. Macheath), Gbola
Sokoya (Boky); Femi Euba (Col. Moses); Gbemi Sodipe (Anikura; Soyinka had wanted Femi
Johnson for this part). Music directed by Tunji Vidal.

See: Jeyifo, Biodun, "Drama and the New Social Order," *Positive Review* (Ife) 1978, p. 22.
        Relich, Mario, *West Africa*, 30.1.78, pp. 188-9; also in *Critical Perspectives*, ed.
        James Gibbs.
        Osikomiya, Jide, *"Opera Wonyosi* Drives Home New Message," *Sunday Times*,
        1.1.78, p. 13.

Before the Blowout

First produced by Soyinka and Chuck Mike, with the Guerrilla Theatre Unit of the University of
Ife, in and around Ife, 1978. Under this title two scripts are available: "Home to Roost" and
"Big Game Safari."

(I have not been able to locate any reviews of these productions. This may reflect censorship or
autocensorship or simply the lack of curiosity editors of Nigerian newspapers often show on
cultural matters.)
* * *

PART TWO

The Text

Question: Do you edit your plays as the need arises?
Soyinka: Oh yes, I'm good at slashing my own plays.[1]

It is necessary to establish from the beginning that to Soyinka the text is far from sacrosanct. In his view it is a means to an end, not an end in itself. While he clearly takes pains to prepare his texts for his publishers, for his readers and directors, he is by no means a typical London-published playwright. He has one foot in the English theatre/publishers tradition with its emphasis on a text as the basis for *most* productions. But the other foot is in the world of the Yoruba Festival and also of the *Alawada* Theatre,[2] where innovation within established limits is expected and where the text, if it exists at all, is more likely to have *followed* than *preceded* the production. This kind of tradition is not strange to Europe; it has flourished in the Commedia dell'Arte and in Living Newspaper plays, but it is overlooked by some academics who confuse the literary with the theatrical aspects of drama. There is an excuse for this even in considering Soyinka's work in that his texts have great literary complexity and contain detailed stage directions. Our attitude to them has to be qualified by an awareness of Soyinka's working methods and his recognition that the director stands between the text and the audience.

Soyinka's own methods were illustrated in an extreme form by his production of *Opera Wonyosi*, and were described by Yemi Ogunbiyi in the following lines:

> As directed by Soyinka himself *Wonyosi* was handled experimentally but in the typically loose way in which Soyinka works. This meant that the text of the play was never completely written as it was ever being re-written and reshaped during rehearsals. Neither was there a sanctimonious attitude towards it. Soyinka would change and discard details that did not work at rehearsals. Nothing was finally arrived at until the play closed … For him the text, even his own text, was merely a map with many possible routes.[3]

In the pages which follow some of the routes which Soyinka has taken – and the changes of routes he has made – will be indicated. *Wonyosi*, it must be remarked, is a work which falls between the stools of being a full-length play and being a series of revue sketches. The production methods adopted reflect this. With other full-length plays Soyinka pays more attention to the script, but his attitude is still "irreverent." With his revue sketches, his "shot-gun writing," he is constantly changing, adapting, updating.

As a final observation in this section, it is appropriate to point out that one of the shortcomings of Soyinka's texts as he presents them to the director is the absence of guides to pronunciation. This has sometimes led to mispronunciations which Soyinka has regretted. For instance, during the first production of *The Swamp Dwellers* at Ibadan (1959) parts of the audience hugely enjoyed the Beggar's pronunciation of the name of his home-town, "Yakarta."[4] Soyinka later explained that no humor was intended and that a Northern pronunciation, not a "Yoruba brogue," was appropriate.[5] In published versions of the play he changed the name of the town to "Bukanji" perhaps to prevent a repetition of this "mistake." Other words which have caused confusion include "Eshuoro" and "Ifada"; only when they are pronounced in the playwright's productions can the critic be sure he has heard the correct pronunciation.[6] These instances draw attention to the point I made at the start of this section: the text is the beginning, not the end; it also contains a few areas of possible confusion.

The Company

Soyinka: "... The first thing I wanted to do when I got back to Nigeria [in 1960] was to get my own company together."[7]

Like many other playwrights, Soyinka has written some of his best plays for a specific group of actors. He has written for particular talents and he has allowed particular talents to affect his work.

Prior to returning to Nigeria, Soyinka had written a number of plays. But there is no evidence, except in the case of *The Invention* which was written for a largely "white" cast, that he was affected in any way by the actors who were likely to perform his plays.[8] Within a month of his return, Soyinka had begun to gather a group of old and new friends together to form an acting company. In October 1960, as "The 1960 Masks," they were ready to put on *A Dance of the Forests*. Most of the company were experienced, but many of them had very demanding jobs which allowed them only a limited amount of time for drama. In the '60s this group encouraged the emergence of a company of younger, "professional," more or less full-time actors, "Orisun Theatre." A glance at the cast list for *A Dance of the Forests* and at a list of Orisun Theatre members indicates some of those involved in these two companies. The names in those lists, Adeleye, Adeniyi-Jones, Euba, Imerion, Kolade, Lijadu, Ogunyemi, Opara, Osisioma, Oyelana, Ozieh, appear repeatedly in the cast-lists of Soyinka's productions, particularly up to 1966. They were in one or other of the two co-operating companies which affected the texts of Soyinka's plays and sketches. Three instances will indicate the nature of their impact.

When in England for the production of *The Road* (1965), Soyinka said that the play had an all-male cast because men were more reliable at attending rehearsals than women.[9] There may have been an element of facetiousness in this comment – Soyinka had after all worked with some distinguished and enthusiastic actresses. But in Orisun Theatre there were initially few women, and it may have been this that prompted Soyinka's comment and affected the decision to have an all-male cast in *The Road*.

One of Soyinka's closest friends, in the theatre and outside, was Femi Johnson. He was not in *A Dance*, but he became associated with Soyinka in productions shortly afterwards. Johnson played Kongi's Secretary in the two stage productions of *Kongi's Harvest* during the mid-60s and in the film. From his performance in the film it is tempting to say that the part fits him like a glove and to speculate that perhaps the glove was tailored to the size of his hand. Soyinka may have had him in mind for the part when he was writing it; he may have anticipated the brisk efficiency with which he would play it. The movement of the play depends considerably on the reliability and presence of the Secretary and, in turn, of Johnson.

Insulated for a period of intensive writing, re-writing and rehearsing at the O'Neill Center (1970), Soyinka moulded *Madmen and Specialists* around the Ibadan Theatre Arts Company with which he was working. The Mendicants, played by veterans of Soyinka's productions, apparently caught the required mood well and their roles were expanded.

Since 1972, Soyinka's Nigerian productions have been mostly with actors based at the University of Ife. Some members of the company, such as Femi Euba, have long performance records in Soyinka's plays, but many were inherited from Ola Rotimi's groups: The Ori Olokun Company and the University of Ife Performing Company. Rotimi's theatre is very different from Soyinka's and this may be one of the reasons why the '70s saw new patterns in Soyinka's writing and producing. However, with *Wonyosi*, *Before the Blowout* and *The Biko Inquest* there may be signs that new working relationships have become established.[10]

The last two years have seen a new development in Soyinka's international career: he has directed his work in the United States. Producing *Horseman* (1979) was not without difficulties. Soyinka commented that Black American styles of moving and speaking were different from those of Africans; some performers clearly found the Yoruba music difficult to relate to and proved incapable of turning in the performances the director required.[11] All in all the success of the production of *Horseman*, despite these difficulties, must be seen as being due in part to the effectiveness of Soyinka's re-training program.

It is a pity that circumstances and finances have not enabled Soyinka to hold Orisun together, to realize his plans for a fully professional theatre and to travel abroad more often with "his own people." In estimating Soyinka's output, it seems that the mid-'60s were a particularly creative period and it is no coincidence that it was the period when he was working closely with 1960 Masks and Orisun. It appears that a playwright can be influenced for the better by the companies he keeps.

Cultural Barriers

In preparing *Horseman* for audiences in the United States, Soyinka made a few changes in the text. He said: "It was necessary to take out a word or two that would have been meaningless, or add a phrase or two to clarify an expression. But the heart of the play is the same, and any audience willing to be intellectually curious and able to remove the block that arises with plays from any other culture will find itself totally at home."[12]

Not everyone would agree with this assessment, certainly not if it were extended to all his plays. Some of Soyinka's countrymen have responded to his productions by saying that the work is too heavily influenced by foreign forms. Some non-Nigerians have come out of performances thinking that a Yoruba key is necessary to unlock the mysteries of the work. There are undoubtedly barriers, some of them cultural barriers, to the appreciation of Soyinka's drama: one of the most frequently mentioned is that of pace. An American critic wrote that "the opening of *Horseman* is rough on Western audiences," but such assertions do not represent a consensus.[13] The issue of the "longueurs" in *The Lion and The Jewel* provides an illuminating case study of this issue of cultural barriers – a study which reveals the impact of the director's ideas, the performers' skills and the critics' prejudices.

The first production of *The Lion and the Jewel* was by Ken Post and was of the "earlier, shorter" version. Geoffrey Axworthy, who feels that the play has "one joke" and must be played fast, says "The Hair-Plucking Scene" was cut and the play lasted an hour.[14] Despite this dispatch (or perhaps, because of it – hectic activity can become wearisome) an expatriate critic, Virginia Browne-Wilkinson, thought the play slow and thin: "One rather small joke drawn out too long."[15] At the Royal Court (1966) the play was directed by an experienced professional and acted with a cast which brought together trained and untrained performers. Since it was presented as a full evening's entertainment, it probably lasted for about two hours. Some reviewers (those on the *T.E.S.*, *Scotsman* and *Financial Times*, for example) thought the production dragged somewhat. But their opinion was balanced by that of those who found a diverting subtlety and sophistication in the structure of the play.[16] Time, it would seem, is relative; watches are soft. It can, however, be asserted that it is sometimes necessary for the director to have confidence in the text – Post may not have had enough. And, to anticipate the next paragraph, the production must be good.

It may be that the reason for the adverse critical reactions to *The Lion and the Jewel* lies in the incompetence or weakness of the productions. Browne-Wilkinson remarks that "the percussion was weak" in the Ibadan production (1959), and this may have spoilt the dance sequences. Nothing drags like a big set-piece which fails to "come off"; nothing is as tedious as the ecstatic dance which strains for effect but does not achieve it. "The Broken-Down Car" number, which several critics of the London production singled out for praise at the Royal Court, may for all I know have been inadequate in the eyes of Browne-Wilkinson in the first Ibadan production.

A more subtle cultural barrier which may have affected this issue of pace is a critical prejudice about the nature and concern of theatre. The critic who, in the manner of E.M. Forster, sighs "Oh yes. The play must tell a story" will resent all which distracts from the unfolding of the narrative. In this instance he may resent the inclusion of "the Mime of the White Surveyor" and regard it as one of Soyinka's "unnecessary scenes." Another critic, one more in tune with the conventions of Soyinka's theatre, may regard the same episode as a deft structural device, shedding light on certain relevant political and economic realities and foreshadowing Baroka's encounter with Sidi.

Given the variety of critical responses it is impossible to speak of cultural "barriers" or "blocks" in precise terms. However, to use the language of the opening quotation, some members of some audiences have shown themselves to be more "intellectually curious" than others. That Soyinka has had a major success in the United States with *Horseman* is not entirely surprising, for, as is apparent from the text, it is a play which is accessible to audiences familiar with the Aristotelian theatre. It comes from Soyinka's "Cambridge Period," a period of dialogue with the Western intellectual and artistic tradition, to which belongs *Myth, Literature and the African World*, and, by sleight of hand, the adaptation of *The Bacchae of Euripides*. In the US production Soyinka did not, incidentally, give way to all the cultural expectations of his audiences. He chose to deny them curtain calls at which they could express their appreciation. The fact that so much concern was felt by the audience about this very minor violation of customary American theatre practice reveals how well the play itself had communicated.

Filming

Soyinka said, "I first conceived [*The Road*] as a film. And I am still thinking of filming it."[17]

Before Soyinka left London at the end of 1959 he took lessons in film-making and he returned to Nigeria, thanks to the Rockefeller Fund, to a camera and some reels of film. It was anticipated that filming festivals and dances would form part of his research into African drama. In the years which have followed, Soyinka has organized film festivals, reviewed films, judged films and made films. His major film-making projects have been *Culture in Transition* (1963) and *Kongi's Harvest* (1970); the former, it seems, a rewarding experience, the latter a distressing one. Both films are helpful in the investigation of the relationship between the written word and the realization of it before an audience. At a meeting sponsored by the ILO and UNESCO to discuss the advisability of drafting new international conditions for improving the status of the performing artist, Soyinka said:

> Creative technology is one thing – no-one seriously argues whether a film-maker is an artist or not … . Ultimately, however, the problem of placing technology at the service of the artist rather than using it as an instrument of exploitation lies very much in the hands of national governments. The unarguable beneficiary of technology today is industry – the multitudes of allied conglomerates which exploit by technological explosion at the expense of the artist.[18]

The first case of film-making described below is an illustration of technology in the service of the artist, the second an instance of the exploitation of the artist by industry – at least in Soyinka's view.

The second part of *Culture in Transition* is an abbreviated version of *The Strong Breed*. This is a play which has defeated some directors and worried some critics. Is it compact or confusing? Are the "flash-backs" adequately introduced and can they be suitably "marked-off" on the stage? Opinions vary and different productions have provided different solutions – or different ways of failing. It has been observed that the "flash-backs" are a cinematic device and that the problems of the stage director would quickly vanish on the film editor's bench. It is not entirely true to say that the episodes referred to are "flash-backs" or that the technique is necessarily cinematic. Eugene O'Neill, whom Soyinka took as the subject for his MA thesis, is a likely inspiration, and the *Egungun* masquerades, through which the past erupts upon the present, provide a possible parallel. The most surprising directorial decision in making the film was to cut out all the "flash-backs" and the other episodes which run alongside the main spatial and temporal line of interest in the text of *The Strong Breed*. The film is at pains to clarify the main story-line of the play. For instance, it shows Eman bolting under the pressure of being made the Carrier – an episode, some would say the *scène à faire*, which is omitted from the text. And, as the thirsty Eman approaches the stream the camera lingers on his face, cuts to the faces of Jaguna and Oroge hiding beside the path and back to the trap which they have set. It is clear from the film, and this is once again a sequence which we do not have any detailed stage-directions for, that Eman *deliberately* places his foot in the trap. He knows it is there; he knows he will die. Pressures of time and expense may have played their parts in shaping this film version, but, taken with the film-script of *Kongi's Harvest* described below, an alternative suggestion presents itself: Soyinka may regard film as concerned with narrative rather than mood and to this end deliberately emphasizes the plot in the film versions of this play.[19]

Soyinka made extensive changes to the published text of *Kongi's Harvest* in preparing the shooting script. In the latter the assassination plot is brought closer to the surface; Segi's father is developed as a character; opportunities are provided – the most obvious change in transferring any play to the screen – for spectacular shots, in this case of motor-cycle outriders, Olumo Rock and so on; a further dimension is given to the relationship between Segi and Daodu by the visit they make to a shrine. The most striking innovations occur near the end: in the film the assassination plot succeeds in that Kongi is killed, but hopes for real changes are still-born because Segi's father assumes absolute power and is clearly set to become as repressive a ruler as Kongi. Soyinka not only prepared the film-script, he also acted Kongi, playing him so as to suggest a distinct resemblance to President Mobutu.[20] He was not satisfied with the finished film, as he made clear in a letter which provides its own context, to the Editor of *Transition*.

> Dear Sir,
>   Your note on contributors in the last issue of *Transition* (39) contains a very interesting reference to my contribution to the making of a film on the play *Kongi's Harvest*. I did take an acting role in that film (alas!) but that forms the extent of my participation. To write that I "have completed work on the film version ... etc etc" is an exaggeration in the present circumstances. Both the Director and the Producers of the film are aware of and have accepted my position in the matter.[21]

In view of the existence of the film-script it is not entirely true that the acting role was "the extent of [his] participation," but clearly he felt that his script had been distorted and he wanted to dissociate himself from the finished film. Although I have found no detailed account of the reasons for his dissatisfaction, I suspect that the following extract from his comment on the state of film production in Africa provides some clues. He criticized the film-makers in anglophone Africa

> ... because the producers attach themselves to some American principle of film producing in which the producer could lift the entire footage and say "O.K., I'm going to get a new editor," or "I don't like the way you are shooting this; I want Americans to be able to understand this film." So by the time he is finished he

has gone through about five editors. Stockholm, America, London, back again to America – you know that kind of thing. Simply because the producer and the producing company in West Africa had got themselves enthralled to the monied interests. So there have been difficulties both on the technological levels, the commercial details, the amateurishness of some of the techniques but also some genuine problems.[22]

Soyinka clearly felt that he had been exploited, that he and his work had been misused, abused. The film of *Kongi's Harvest* shows that the artist, particularly the artist who sets a very high premium on his integrity, may be compromised by the technical and bureaucratic intermediaries between his statement and the realization of it in film form. Technology should be placed at the service of the artist; it should not be used to exploit him, as Soyinka felt it had in this case.

Topicality

In the Introduction to *Before the Blackout* Soyinka wrote:

The purpose of these sketches would be defeated if performing groups feel they must be staged word for word and blow for blow. Producers should feel free to adapt them where necessary for the contemporary event and to alter entire sequences to relate the action closely to whatever is happening now. The two ballads should lose verses and be supplemented by others until eventually not one single verse is left of the original lyrics. "For Better, For Worse" must take in new acts of terror perpetrated by little Führers, and "Death Before Discourtesy" requires only a few amendments to take in every public act of cowardice.[23]

In the sketches in *Before the Blackout*, Soyinka aimed for immediacy of impact. He concerned himself with events which had occurred shortly, or fairly shortly, before the production: The Oyenuga Fiasco ("Death Before Discourtesy"); the Tiger-Fulmer World Title Fight ("Prestigious") and, rather older, the rumpus surrounding the postcard dropped by Peace Corps Volunteer Margery Michelmore ("St. Michael-More or Less"). Some of the items were amended between the time the sketches were produced and the time of going to press in order to bring them up-to-date. "Asa-gbe-fo" ("The hawk dies off") was, after the coup which overthrew Nkrumah, turned against Hastings Banda ("Babuzu, Lion of Malladi"), with little justification, incidentally, from Banda's particular brand of myth-making. Soyinka is so concerned with topicality that sometimes, in his anxiety to draw blood from a particular target, he becomes obscure to those unfamiliar with the circum- stances which provoked the sketch, but this is inevitable. On other occasions, and with the help of minor alterations to the original, he manages to cut through the specific abuse to make a general comment. In this context I will consider the following: *Childe Internationale*; Soyinka's productions of *Kongi's Harvest*; Brother Jero; *Opera Wonyosi*, and Chief Onikura.

Childe Internationale is the one sketch in *Before the Blackout* which obviously rises above the immediate context of the politics of the post-independence period and the campus crises of the early '60s. It has been produced widely and has been hugely enjoyed, because, though its origin was fairly specific, the issues raised have been duplicated elsewhere. The International (secondary) School was opened on the campus of the University of Ibadan in 1963 and stories soon began to circulate about the "outrageous" behavior of some of the students. As Soyinka's wife, 'Laide, was teaching at the School, he was well informed about the new "International" attitudes which had become current. His playlet, written according to one source in forty minutes but clearly the result of longer thought, is a minor exercise on the themes of foreign influence, attitudes to older people and courtship habits which he had explored in a more ambitious form in *The Lion and the Jewel*. Despite its general relevance to a continent in transition the sketch has its provincialisms. For example, Kotun's reference to the play "where everybody was saying 'Shit'"[24] was an allusion to Jarry's *King Ubu* which had been seen and heard on the Ibadan stage shortly before Soyinka's revue was produced. Such an allusion cries out for alteration in any context other than the original one in accordance with the advice quoted at the beginning of this section. It is a mark of lack of initiative, or of misplaced respect for the text, or of ignorance of the nature of satirical sketches, that this allusion is not always changed. In the Association of Theatre Arts Students production of the piece at Ibadan during 1979 the lines were spoken as printed and the audience was inevitably bewildered. Many suitable substitutes could have been suggested.

In his productions of *Kongi's Harvest*, Soyinka has made direct comments on developments in Nigeria and Africa within the context of a fairly tightly structured, full-length play. The play was first produced for the AMSAC gathering in Lagos during August 1965, and was subsequently taken, with minor changes, to Ibadan. The following year the script was partly rewritten and, after performances in Nigeria, it was presented in Dakar at the First World Festival of Negro Arts. During 1969, while Soyinka was in detention, Dapo Adelugba obtained permission from 'Laide Soyinka to put on the play. But while it was still in rehearsal Soyinka was released, took over the production and gave it an anti-military slant. The initial impetus for writing *Kongi* appears, however, to have been rather different, namely the drift towards dictatorships and one-party states in Africa during the '60s. When working on the script, presumably during 1964 or '65, Soyinka told David Rubadiri that he was writing a play "about

Banda."[25] Concern with developments in Malawian politics is reflected in the text by the direct quotation of Banda's "Dead or Alive Search Order" which was widely reported in the press during late November 1964. But when the play was first produced, it was the parallels between Kongi and Nkrumah which attracted most notice. Soyinka was anxious to "de-emphasize" these, and it was probably for this reason that after the first performances he cut specific references, for instance to "algebraic quantums," which had, rightly, been seen as allusions to Nkrumah. When Soyinka was released from "Gowon's Detention," he brought the second Nigerian production into the post-coup period, and gave it, as mentioned above, an anti-military slant. In answering a question about the Government of Nigeria's attitude to his work, he described the performance of this *Kongi's Harvest* to mark the twenty-first anniversary of the University of Ibadan, "one of those semi-state occasions;"

> I had reinterpreted *Kongi's Harvest* with a military image on top as a very direct reference point [presumably Yakubu Gowon], and the program itself made the message, very, very, plain. [It contained a note which began: "The play is not about Kongi but about Kongism ... It must be emphasized that Kongism has never been dethroned in Black Africa ... A current variety may be described as neo-Peronism, the cult of plaster-cast sanctity."] But there was very little that could be done. The play went forward, and in fact these people were struggling for seats for they hadn't seen the play yet. After that there was flak, but it was too late. (Interpolations mine. J.G.)[26]

Soyinka, yet to unburden himself of *The Man Died*, had clearly set out to catch the conscience of the "top brass." The "flak" was evidence of his success.

Further examples of such topicality, of using drama to provide a running commentary on the state of the nation and the continent, are provided by Brother Jero and Chief Onikura. Brother Jero may at first seem an unlikely candidate for the role of political commentator. Soyinka has described *The Trials of Brother Jero* as "a very light recital of human evils and foibles,"[27] and its production history shows how enthusiastically it has been taken up by directors in three continents and two languages. The possibility of giving the play a specific temporal and political location was demonstrated during the production at the Hampstead Theatre Club (1966). At that time of "talks about talks" between Harold Wilson and Ian Smith, a speech for the M.P was written by Soyinka or in a style similar to one he has employed (perhaps by the director, Athol Fugard). Reviewers of the production included the following intriguing snippets of it in their columns:

Gentlemen, it is an infernal triangle – Smith, Wilson, Verwoerd. No – its a diabolical quadrangle – Smith, Wilson, Verwoerd, Salazar. Wait a minute, Johnson! Gentlemen, it is a pestilential pentagon ... [and at a different point in the speech:] I name no names but certain foreign powers are trying to blacken ... or whiten ... or besmirch ... [28]

No lines are given for the M.P.'s speech in the published script of the "universal" comedy; those just quoted show how effectively the play can be used to make a point, in this case about the fatuous bumblings of politicians on a particular issue. The following year (1967), Soyinka spoke to Rex Collings about a play entitled *The Exodus of Brother Jero*.[29] But that play has never been published, perhaps it was never finished – perhaps never actually begun as a text. Instead, Brother Jero made his second appearance in post-civil war Nigeria to make a comment on military regimes in *Jero's Metamorphosis*. In this case, and in contrast with *The Trials*, the political comment is dominant and the implications are daunting.

Chief Onikura first emerged in *Opera Wonyosi* and has subsequently reappeared as the villain-hero of *Before the Blowout*, two scripts presented by the Guerrilla Theatre Unit of the Theatre Arts Department, University of Ife. Like Jero he aspires to power, but since he operates in a political context he provides a more obvious comment on political developments, a suitable figure in the late '70s and the early '80s, a period of political polarization. In *Opera Wonyosi* Soyinka took over elements from Bertolt Brecht's *Three-Penny Opera* and used them to provide a frame-work for a vigorous onslaught on a multitude of targets provided by Nigeria during the mid-'70s. The text alludes to issues associated with the Sharia Courts, the Kalakuta Republic, the Igbeti Marble finds, Secret Societies, public executions, the Cement Scandal, and the foreign exchange decree. Yemi Ogunbiyi, in the paper already quoted, has described the approach adopted in the production: "For [Soyinka] the text ... was merely a map with many possible routes."[30] There was frequent improvisation, changes were made on the opening night and topical allusions were introduced in mid-run. The results of this style included a disconcerted cast and an instantaneous response from the audience. In the scripts for *Before the Blowout*, Soyinka brought Onikura and his corrupt crew back to Nigeria and used them to expose the attitudes and activities of the political opportunists who regarded the return to civilian rule as a chance to fill their pockets and their bellies, as, in short, a "blow-out."

Many of the allusions in these works will be lost on foreign audiences, and time will dull their edge for Nigerians. It will take constant and extensive re-writing to retain the vigor and topicality of the works, and it is unlikely that many talents will emerge which are capable of the sustained wit and humor necessary for the task. The same fate probably awaits these texts as is now endured by most of the sketches in *Before the Blowout* (despite Soyinka's introduction). With rare exceptions they are not performed; instead they are occasionally given to final year University students of English as research exercises: "find out the target of this sketch."

It is sometimes objected that Soyinka attacks the individual villain rather than the species of villains or the system which produces villainy. There is some truth in this, and the estimate history has of his work will be affected by it. But his position can be defended by arguing that the stage can only be peopled by individuals, and by referring to instances when the theatre can claim to have produced beneficial change in society. In many instances change has been the result of an attack on a specific target.

Some would claim that Soyinka's approach is negative: he satirizes, he exposes to ridicule, but he does not recommend either models of behavior or appropriate political programs. To this he might reply, as he did when asked whether satire can be used for revolutionary purposes:

> ... first you have to arouse in the people a certain, well to put it crudely, a certain nausea towards a particular situation, to arouse them at all to accept a positive alternative when it is offered to them.[31]

In this strategy the tactic of contemporaneity can be very effective, whether it be a studied and consistent relevance or a quick comment, so hot that it burns the fingers. In both cases, particularly in the context of Nigeria where there are newspaper reports of violence at political meetings and of physical attacks on politicians, such contemporaneity creates an atmosphere of intense excitement. It is an excitement as old as theatre itself, but it is particularly present where there is improvisation and effective up-dating. Its presence forces us to acknowledge once again that the text is only the beginning and to recognize that characteristics of the oral performance are found in the work of this playwright-director.

Interpretation and Incompetence

In his author's note to *Death and the King's Horseman*, Soyinka wrote:

> The bane of themes of this genre is that they are no sooner employed creatively than they acquire the facile tag of "clash of cultures," a prejudicial label which, quite apart from its frequent misapplications, presupposes a potential equality *in every given situation* of the alien culture and the indigenous, on the actual soil of the latter ... I find it necessary to caution the would-be producer of this play against a sadly familiar reductionist tendency, and to direct his vision instead to the far more difficult and risky task of eliciting the play's threnodic essence. [32]

Contemporaneity is one instance of interpretation, perhaps the most obvious, but there are others. In taking on a play, director and actors have to answer certain questions and face certain issues of emphasis. In the case of Soyinka's canon these questions and issues include: what sort of a caricature is Lakunle? How is "The Mime of the White Surveyor" to be played? Is *The Swamp Dwellers* a melodrama or a poetic drama? How is the interaction of the past and the present in *A Dance* to be presented? Has Jero any redeeming qualities? Is Eman a martyr? And so on. It is an indication of the comparative wealth of literary criticism on Soyinka that these points have been taken up and widely discussed, but they have been discussed in literary rather than theatrical contexts. This is partly because the practice of writing theatre criticism is underdeveloped in many of the countries where Soyinka has been most often performed. In Britain and America productions of his plays have been extensively reviewed, but few theatre critics have shown sufficient familiarity with Soyinka's drama to recognize when a director has decisively shaped the presentation. In many of the productions of Soyinka's work, directors have found themselves faced with difficult and perhaps foreign material, they have often had to overcome their own ignorance and the incompetence or limitations of their casts and stage crews. Rarely have the directors had the luxury of interpreting to any substantial extent or with any degree of clarity.

Soyinka himself has, as noted in the case of *Kongi's Harvest*, produced his own work and offered different interpretations of it. Apart from the two productions of *Kongi's Harvest*, he has produced parts of *A Dance* twice. A notable point about the first production (1960) was that Soyinka replaced "The Dance of the Half-Child" as he had conceived it with a more modest routine. The original dance, based on "The Dance of the Child Acrobats," called for the child to be tossed from one dancer to the other. An extra element of excitement was to be provided by the fact that the dancers who caught the child were to hold knives in their hands! In Soyinka's production the Half-Child was played by a boy of nine or ten. Even supposing that suitable dancers – dancers capable of doing the dance on which the sequence was based – could be found, or that members of the 1960 Masks could learn the dance, a boy of nine or ten would probably be too big to be thrown from arm to arm. For eminently practical reasons, Soyinka substituted an alternative sequence; it was equally symbolic but considerably less spectacular. We are fortunate to have a detailed account of Soyinka's production of a sequence from the same play in Paris (1972).[33] The sequence was presented as an illustration of "The Spatial Conception of Ritual Drama" and began with the entrance of the Crier onto a darkened stage. It continued with the chanting of the invocation and the processional entrances of the protagonists carrying lighted mud-lamps. Femi Osofisan wrote:

When they are installed, in separate circles delineated by coloured lights the Crier steps into each circle and, as Master of Ceremony, makes up the faces of the protagonists who are immediately "entombed" by new chorus formations.[34]

The description continues for another revealing paragraph and it becomes clear that Soyinka had developed a physical stylization for the episode to complement the verbal stylization of the Dirgeman's chant.

The parameters of interpretation, as suggested by the playwright, have sometimes been indicated by Soyinka's comments at rehearsals of his plays. For instance, Ngugi wa Thiong'o reported that at a rehearsal of *The Lion and the Jewel* at Makerere, Soyinka said that "The Mime of the White Surveyor" should not be played as a flash-back.[35] Perhaps, we should take it as a flash sideways to a co-existent time-plane in which the past is present. But it is difficult to know exactly how to realize this on the stage, and Soyinka's comment at Makerere provides no clue. A fuller account of Soyinka as critic at a rehearsal of his play is provided by a transcription prepared by Karen L. Morell.[36] After watching a scene from *The Trials of Brother Jero* in rehearsal in Seattle, Soyinka questioned the participants in the following terms: "Do you think (Jero) is bad through and through or does he have any redeeming qualities?" The direction in which Soyinka was leading the students became clear when he said: "I have a feeling you are taking him a little too seriously," and then asked: "Does anyone have a lighter view of Jero?" He went on to describe Jero as a "warped genius" and to suggest that he might be a "likeable theatrical character." It became clear that, in the Seattle rehearsal, the negative and corrupt idea of "the articulate hero of Christ's crusade" had been overstressed and the Falstaffian vigor and roguish charm of the character had been obscured. In my experience, however, the main weaknesses of productions of Soyinka's plays are not errors of interpretation or emphasis, but the results of incompetence.

An interpretation is a coherent approach which deliberately emphasizes certain aspects of a text so as to provide a particular experience of it. Incompetence comes in various forms as a result of misunderstanding a text and its implications, or of failure to tackle the problems of staging. Thus the Blantyre production of *The Lion and the Jewel* which decked out Baroka's bedroom with an array of electronic gadgetry was incompetent – it was a fundamental misreading of the forces at work in the play, a misrepresentation of Baroka and of the reasons for Sidi's seduction. And the A.T.A.S. production of *Childe Internationale* in which Kotun was not provided with a sausage as he followed these stage directions was incompetent:

([Kotun] Quickly transfers the sausage to his plate. Picks it up again. As he lifts it to his mouth, he hesitates, tries again, stops, examines the object with his eyes almost touching it. Sniffs it. Shudders. Shuts his eyes and nibbles a bit off it ...)[37]

A potato is no substitute! And the director who allowed it on stage should have realized the fact.

Soyinka's concern that *Horseman* should not be turned into yet another drama about clash of cultures has a certain validity and deserves some respect. But given the exigencies of production – and the text itself – one wonders whether a slippery substance like "threnodic essence" is the central issue and how far it can be conveyed. For instance, did the Kokoroko Theatre in Ghana in its abbreviated, peripatetic version of the play manage to transport the "threnodic essence" from place to place? The Author's Note cannot ensure that the play will be given what the playwright considers an appropriate interpretation, nor should it. Legal protection is more likely to guarantee that the playwright's will is done. Though even that is unlikely to be fool-proof – as can be appreciated from the next section.

Legal Protection

Text of a telegram from Soyinka to George Andoh Wilson on the eve of his production of *Kongi's Harvest* (1968):

SURPRISED AND DISAPPOINTED PRODUCTION OF KONGI'S HARVEST IN PRESENT GHANA STOP NOR DID YOU ASK MY PERMISSION STOP DO NOT EXTEND PERFORMANCE BEYOND PRESENT PROGRAMME NOR SEND ROYALTIES TO ME OR MY PUBLISHERS STOP LOOK FORWARD TO JOINING YOU ON A DIFFERENT PRODUCTION [38]

Soyinka has adopted the unusual practice of acting as his own agent. Directors wishing to mount his plays, at least those plays which are protected by a statement reserving "All rights," are obliged to obtain his permission. It is pertinent to glance at directors' attitudes to this obligation, to examine Soyinka's responses to requests, and to assess the validity of his position.

The rights of authors, and musicians and *griots*, are frequently flouted with impunity. This is true in many continents and countries, and the fact that a state is a signatory of the major international copyright conventions does not, for example, guarantee the protection of the law for authors, as writers' unions have pointed out. The telegram at the head of this section refers to a "pirate production." Such buccaneering behavior as Wilson displayed is common and not all the offenders are non-Nigerians. During December 1980 the Studio Theatre of the Ahmadu Bello University presented *Madmen and Specialists* at OSFAC 80, a major arts festival in Oyo State organized by the State Council for Arts and Culture; they did not obtain the playwright's permission. These are just two instances of the failure to fulfill an obligation. It can confidently be said that Soyinka loses, or sacrifices, a considerable sum each year in unpaid performance royalties. It is notable that in the case of the Ghanaian production referred to above and presumably many others he did not threaten legal action. He was clearly more concerned, in this case, with his right to control his play rather than in any royalties which might be due to him. His integrity as a writer was more important to him than his income.

This leads to the second point: Soyinka's attitudes to requests. From the telegram it is fair to infer that if Wilson had asked to be allowed to produce *Kongi's Harvest* in Ghana in 1968, his request would have been refused. The reasons are not given but they are not hard to guess: Soyinka feared that the play would be presented as a celebration of Nkrumah's overthrow. This is in any case what happened: in Wilson's production Kongi was Nkrumah in appearance and gesture. Soyinka was probably trying to protect himself from "a ... reductionist tendency"; he was not completely successful since the text as published provides justification for Wilson's interpretation.

Soyinka has tried to prevent his plays being directed by those whom he suspects would "misdirect" them. For instance, he has prevented American moves to turn *The Lion and the Jewel* into an exotic musical, and few would blame him for this. He has also refused permission in other contexts. The issue was raised in a sensitive dimension at a symposium on Derek Bullock's production of *The Road* (1979): Bullock, an expatriate with a reputation for productions with Nigerian schools, had been given permission to produce the play. Dapo Adelugba made the point that Soyinka had refused permission to experienced Nigerian producers who wanted to direct it and wondered why Bullock had been favored. Put this way, Soyinka's position appears vulnerable, especially if it could be established that the local director had as good a record for sensitive productions as Bullock. But it may be that the issue should be seen in a different context; only then can the validity of Soyinka's position be assessed. His policy, it seems, may be summarized thus: "Let the *schools* cut their teeth on whichever of my plays they like, and let the *university groups*, those which aspire to 'professional' status, do *The Jero Plays* and do them well. I alone will be responsible for major productions of my major plays in Nigeria."[39] This would explain why Bullock, working with students at Federal Government College, Kano, was given permission, and why, for example, members of staff in the Theatre Arts Department at the University of Ibadan were not.

The reference to *The Jero Plays* introduces important exceptions to the general practices already described. In, I suspect, late 1973, Soyinka sent copies of *Jero's Metamorphosis* to friends who might be interested and asked them to produce the play since it was a statement he wanted to make. In other words, he was anxious that the play should be produced quickly, widely and frequently. That it was *not* is an indication, perhaps, of the dangerous truth it was seen to contain. It is worth noting in this regard that *Before the Blackout* was published without any statement about the reservation of "all rights." This may have been an oversight (Soyinka was in detention during an important period in the printing of the book). But it may have been part of a deliberate policy: the artist makes his most overt, immediate and unambiguous political statements as available as possible to directors and the public.

Soyinka is the victim of the printing press as well as its beneficiary. He has tried to keep tight personal control over performances of most of his work. But he has not been able to stop – or benefit from a large number of pirate performances of his plays, and in the vast majority of cases he probably would not want to do either.

Impact and Conclusion

Eldred Durosimi Jones made the following comment about African plays written in English:

> Those which are popular never get published and those which are published are never popular.[40]

This generalization does not hold good for Soyinka, some of whose published plays are extremely popular in the sense of the word which Jones is using. This point needs to be made strongly, since Soyinka is sometimes dismissed as an obscure and elitist playwright, narrow in appeal and for that reason rarely performed. The production histories of *Brother Jero* and *Childe Internationale* settle the first round of the debate: Soyinka's plays are widely produced and much enjoyed.

Having said this, the second round can be opened against the assertion that it is only the minor comedies which are produced. Once again, the production histories provide information which contradicts this statement. It is easy to be ill-informed about productions in Africa, and Gerald Moore was aware of this when he guarded his observation that *A Dance* had only been produced once with the escape clause: "so far as I can ascertain." [41] It was quite by chance that I was passing through Nairobi when a local school was advertising its production of the play. I have reason to suppose that the production histories I have prepared refer to no more than a small fraction of the actual productions. My caution extends from Africa, which is in need of documentation of its theatrical activities, to Europe and America, where one would have expected press coverage, newspaper indices, collections of theatre facts and the like to provide an accurate and full record of productions. This is not the case. It was only because I was travelling on the London Underground during 1971 that I saw fly-posted advertisements for the Holland Park Link Group's production of *Madmen and Specialists*. No information about the production was provided at any time by a normally alert press clippings agency so, presumably, nothing appeared in English newspapers or magazines about the production. It is absolutely safe to say that productions of Soyinka's major and serious plays are more widespread than is generally supposed by those vaguely familiar with the theatre in Africa and Europe (and America).

The third and final round begins with the suggestion that Soyinka has a higher reputation and has made more impact "abroad," particularly in Britain and America, than in Africa and Nigeria. Soyinka's reputation is certainly high abroad, especially among those (a tiny percentage of the populations of Britain and America, of course) who are interested in serious and Black theatre rather than those who are taken up with Shaftesbury Avenue and Broadway or uninterested in the theatre. In the London theatre Soyinka's reputation rests on four major productions: *The Road* (1965), *The Trials* (1966), *The Lion and the Jewel* (1966) and *The Bacchae of Euripides* (1973), the last being a commissioned work for the National Theatre. In all cases the productions would have benefited from casts more in tune with Soyinka's theatrical intentions, and in some cases the same could be said of the directors. Soyinka has not had a complete critical or commercial success in the UK, nor is it certain that he ever will have, given his ambitions, the London casts available, the expectations of critics and the tastes of the box-office. But his seriousness and significance are appreciated by some and, in circles concerned with Black and African theatre in London, Soyinka is, of course, recognized as a major dramatist.

In the United States the success of *Horseman* has tended to eclipse the earlier reputation made on campuses, in community theatres and Off-Broadway. After a run at the Goodman Theatre, Chicago, the play transferred to the John F. Kennedy Center for the Performing Arts in Washington, D.C. Gregory Mosher, Artistic Director of the Goodman Theatre, spoke as follows about the enthusiastic response of Chicago audiences:

> They all know they have seen something that is not just live television. It is theatre that is compelling and, even if the experience is exotic, it is absolutely understandable and contemporary. I don't think the Goodman Theatre will ever be the same after Wole.[42]

Soyinka's reputation is high among sensitive and informed theatre-loving Americans, at least in Chicago and Washington, D.C. – again a tiny fraction of the population.

In anglophone Africa Soyinka's presence has been felt, not by a small cultured, theatre-going class in certain cities as in Britain and America, but by students in schools and colleges. In those countries with nationwide schools drama festivals, Kenya, Zambia and Malawi for example, the extent to which Soyinka's plays are produced can be roughly assessed – and it is considerable. His impact on the developing theatrical traditions of these countries can be sensed from particular texts and from the orientation of those playwrights who explore the ritual basis of drama. Two examples from Malawi illustrate these influences: first, James Ng'ombe, whose play *The Echoing House* was clearly written under the influence of a production of *The Trials*; and, second, Steve Chimombo, whose *Rainmaker* employs *Nyau* rites as part of its fundamental design.[43]

In Nigeria, Soyinka is highly, and bewilderingly, contextualized. He is not seen as a "towering, foreign, dramatic genius." He is "Yoruba"; "Ijegba"; "Old Boy of Government College"; "One of the Magnificent Seven" (i.e., a Founder of the Pyrates Confraternity); "been-to"; "meddlesome journalist"; "amateur politician"; Pagan; Road Safety Marshal; Professor; "Enemy of Gowon"; "Friend of Fajuyi"; "Socialist"; "Progressive"; "Revolutionary"; "Anti-Revolutionary"; "Liberal Humanist" ... and so on. He is undoubtedly a significant force in Nigerian Theatre and society; creator of theatrical groups and of opportunities; setter of theatrical, sartorial and literary fashions; maker of powerful statements and of powerful enemies. The "flak" which flew after the presentation of *Kongi's Harvest* at a "semi-state occasion" also flew after the performance of *Opera Wonyosi*, and plans for a national tour were stymied. His plays in performance have taken elements of his intense concern for the health of society, his passion for human rights, his courage and – as the theatre is uniquely able to do – these have been welded into the experience of Nigerians. "The masks have hatched out" to haunt, to impress and to possess. I don't think Nigeria will ever be the same after the performance of Wole Soyinka's plays.

NOTES

1. Wole Soyinka, quoted in *In Person: Achebe, Awoonor and Soyinka*, edited by Karen L. Morell, Seattle, 1975, p. 103.

2. *Alawada*: "Yoruba comic theatre": àwàdà = joke; alaáàwàda=a joker, "teller of humorous stories." The term is gaining new dimensions as the comic theatre troupes develop new styles.

3. Yemi Ogunbiyi, "Soyinka Through Brecht: A Study of *Opera Wonyosi*," Seminar paper, Department of African Languages and Literatures, University of Ife, January 1979, pp. 16-17.

4. Virginia Browne-Wilkinson, *The Horn* (Ibadan), 2, 6 (1959), p. 10.

5. Wole Soyinka, "And ... *The Swamp Dwellers*," *The Radio Times* (Lagos), March 1960, p. 5.

6. Remi Adeleye, creator of the role of Eshuoro, translated the name as meaning "Eshu who lives in the Oro tree." Others have linked the trickster god of fate with orò (a cult) and oró (poison) but these suggestions are just the beginning of the debate. "Ifada" may not be a Yoruba name, but it may be and could mean "Ifa has betrayed me" or "a worthless thing."

7. Morell, 1975, p. 94.

8. The "dramatis personae" of *The Invention* include some whites and a black bishop but most of the characters were a "pasty grey" – racially indeterminate.

9. *The Road* incidentally was billed in 1965 as a forthcoming production of the 1960 Masks and so, it seems, it was not written for the London production.

10. Soyinka directed *The Biko Inquest* (by Jon Blair and Norman Fenton) in December 1978 and took it to New York in 1980.

11. "Tale of Two Cultures," *Topic* (Washington), No. 127, p. 33. Hereafter referred to as *Topic*.

12. *Topic*, p. 34.

13. *Topic*, p. 33.

14. Geoffrey Axworthy, personal communication.

15. Browne-Wilkinson, 1959.

16. "Sheer Ingenuity of Soyinka's Plot," *The Times* (London), 13.12.66, p. 6.

17. Olu Agaraogun, "Wole Soyinka," *Spear* (Lagos), May 1966, p. 18.

18. Wole Soyinka, "Technology and the Artist," *Malawi News* (Blantyre), 30.12.77, p. 20.

19. See Ann Dundun, "Soyinkan Aesthetics in *Culture in Transition*." Paper presented at the 1st Annual Literature Conference, Ibadan, 1976.

20. The Negro Ensemble production in New York had stressed the Kongi-Banda links; Soyinka suggested a new parallel by his performance.

21. Wole Soyinka, Letter, *Transition* (Kampala), 40 (December 1971), p. 8.

22. Morell, 1975, p. 125. For a critical review which may convey some of Soyinka's grounds for disapproval, see Irwin Siber, *The Guardian* (London) 26.5.71, p. 13.

23. *Before the Blackout*, Preface.

24. *Before the Blackout*, p. 58.

25. David Rubadiri, personal communication.

26. Morell, 1975, p. 106.

27. Wole Soyinka, *African Writers Talking*, edited by Dennis Duerden and Cosmo Pieterse, London, 1972, p. 174.

28. Peter Lewis, "Funny Satire," *Daily Mail* (London), 29.6.66. Sean Day-Lewis, "*Brother Jero* Full of Vitality," *Daily Telegraph* (London), 29.6.66.

29. Rex Collings, "Wole Soyinka: A Personal View." *The New Statesman* (London), 76 (20.12.68), p. 879.

30. Ogunbiyi, 1979, p. 17.

31. Morell, 1972, p. 127.

32. *Death and the King's Horseman*, "Author's Note."

33. *Collected Plays*, 1, pp. 70-2 with pp. 75-7.

34. Femi Osofisan, "Soyinka in Paris," *West Africa* (London), 21.7.72, p. 935. A video tape has been made in the Workshop Theatre, University of Leeds, which raises and resolves some of the production problems of *A Dance*.

35. Marianne Fearn, *Modern Drama of Africa: Form and Content: A Study of Four Playwrights*. Unpublished Ph.D. Thesis, Northwestern University, 1974, p. 229.

36. Morell, 1975, pp. 81-93.

37. *Before the Blackout*, p. 59.

38. Personal communication, G.A. Wilson.

39. I am very grateful to Dapo Adelugba for discussing the issue with me, and for filling in a number of gaps in the production history section.

40. Eldred Durosimi Jones, "Editorial," *African Literature Today* (London), 8 (1976), xii.

41. Gerald Moore, *Wole Soyinka*, 2nd edition, London, 1978, p. 27.

42. *Topic*, p. 34.

43. I have omitted reference to francophone Africa, although the production histories of *The Lion and the Jewel* and *Brother Jero* show that there has been a limited interest in productions of these plays in French. The impact of those productions has, I suspect, been very limited.

An earlier version of this paper was presented at the Ibadan Conference on African Literature, August 1981.

Metaphor as Basis of Form in Soyinka's Drama

'Ropo Sekoni

The discussion of form in African literature in general and in African drama in particular has been for long hydra-headed. It has, for example, featured arguments in favor of genetic connections between, on the one hand, African drama and Western dramatic forms and, on the other hand, traditional African dramaturgy and the drama written by Africans in European languages.

More specifically, Soyinka scholars have given some attention to the influence of Western and African dramatic techniques on the construction of his plays. Some of such considerations have emphasized the appropriation by Soyinka of elements of such African traditional art as ritual and other components of folk art in his plays.[1] Others have focused equally emphatically on the relation of western formal preferences, especially of Aristotle's view of organicity, to the form of Soyinka's plays.[2] One area that has not received rigorous critical investigation is the determination from intrinsic study of Soyinka's drama of the salient characteristics of the organization or structure of his plays and the aesthetic import of such features. This article will examine the nature, provenance, and aesthetic significance of the formal or structural dimension of Soyinka's drama.

Continuous research on narratological processes[3] among the Yoruba since 1975 – interviews with storytellers as well as the examination of specific stories – reveals that the Yoruba tend to show some bias for a sophisticated interplay between concealment and disclosure of cognitive elements in their verbal art as well as in such extraverbal modes as ritual. While the characterization of this conception of beauty in art by the Yoruba is still somewhat tentative, its general characteristics are (1) the multiplicity of episodes or images in complex narratives, (2) the division of such multiple episodes into two major groups – continuous and discrete episodes or episodes that of necessity advance the story from conflict to resolution and episodes that do not contribute toward such advancement – (3) the interposition of continuous and discrete episodes in the construction of stories; and (4) the implication of semantic equivalence between continuous and discrete episodes that are essentially different and unrelated at the infrastructural or material level.

A common manifestation of these characteristics in Yoruba verbal art is incremental repetition in stories and rituals. Stories and rituals are thus made of the combination of episodes that relate directly to the linear movement of action from an initial position of conflict to a terminal situation of resolution and of episodes that bear no direct relation to such a linear progression of events. Incremental repetition is basically of two types: recurrence and reiteration. Recurrence, which is a cruder form of repetition, is characterized by similar incidents happening to the same personage(s). Recurrence occurs, for example, when a character repeats *in toto* an action that he has performed earlier in time. Reiteration, on the other hand, is characterized by similar incidents happening to different personages. When it occurs, it does not necessarily contribute to the logical progression of dramatic conflicts towards any form of completion or closure. In other words, it does not share a metonymic relation with other episodes in the story. It is often the kind of plot material that Aristotle warns against as a structural defect – capable of detracting from a unified structure that is "characterized by incidents so closely connected that the transposal or withdrawal of any one of them will disjoin and dislocate the whole."[4] Incremental repetition, especially reiteration that is apparently a violation of the Aristotelian view of form, abounds in indigenous Yoruba tales and rituals as well as in some of Soyinka's plays.[5]

Since the relation between ritual and drama as performative forms is more apparent and more immediate than that between drama and the folktale, I will, in spite of the constraints of space, examine a common Yoruba ritual – "The Obatala Festival" – and some of Soyinka's plays with respect to the importance of metaphor as a basis of form.

The version of the Obatala festival being used for illustration in this study is similar in most respects to the Ede version once considered by Joel Adedeji.[6] We will in this study be referring to the Ondo version.

This festival, which usually takes place in the afternoon and lasts till dusk, started during our field work (1976) in the early part of the evening in an open space converted for the purpose and called by the priestess the Agbala, or compound, of Obatala Babarisa (Obatala: the father of the gods). At the beginning of the festival (Ajodun) the priestess led a group of singers and drummers, all clothed in white, out of a house dotted with Efun (white chalk usually used for similar sacred affairs). They were all praising Obatala as an omnipotent god who started the first human settlement at Ife and was later displaced by a strong impostor, Oduduwa. The priestess ended the song with prayers wishing all devotees and spectators a prosperous life. As soon as the priestess settled down, the other singers and drummers found places to sit around the edges of the white line delimiting a big, empty circle surrounded by devotees and spectators. Suddenly, the drummers and singers started to perform praise songs for Obatala, and, at the peak of the dance accompanying the drumming, a male character clad in white and carrying a white covered calabash emerged from the same direction from which others had previously come. The male character and others in white clothes joined in the dance. In the meantime, the male character had put down the calabash and danced ecstatically. He subsequently went out of the circle with other dancers, leaving the calabash behind. Another character then emerged amidst praises for Oduduwa from the same group of singers and drummers. This character moved back and forth in an inspectorial fashion in the circle, removed the calabash and ran out of the circle. Then, still amidst loud singing, the same character returned to the circle without the calabash and was joined in dancing by other white-clad individuals until the male character who initially brought the calabash returned and engaged him in a mock fight. The music then changed to a faster tempo and songs saying, "ojo Batala Bataasa" (the day of Obatala, father of the gods) rent the air. Shortly after, the Obatala figure (the first male character to come into the circle) was chased out of the circle by the Oduduwa figure (the character that removed the calabash). The music gradually petered out; the circle became empty and quiet. Immediately after, the two male characters returned to the circle and became locked in a mock wrestling contest amidst songs for Balufon and Oranmiyan, but the song was concerned more with Balufon than with Oranmiyan, having such praises for Balufon as the following:

> OmoSere gbogun de
> Balufon godogbo
> Omomagbo gbogun was
> Balufon joinjoin
> Ero ona parada
> OmoSere gbogun de
> Ogbogbo gbogun de
> Oyanyan gbogun was
>
> [Osere's son has brought war
> Balufon, the Stalwart
> Magbo's son has brought war
> Balufon, the unshakable
> Strangers disappear
> Osere's son has brought war
> The big-eared one has brought war
> The big-nosed one has brought war]

During the mock fight, Balufon was felled and chased out of the circle by the Oranmiyan figure. The circle once more became empty and quiet.

Amidst this quiet, Yeyerisa, the priestess who led the group out of the Orisha shrine at the beginning of the festival, emerged from the middle of the crowd with a white calabash. She was ushered into the circle with music and praises for Moremi:

Moremi, Obinrin ai be soro

Moremi, Iyalode Amulero amona dan Afewe rola l'okaramfe

[Moremi, woman volunteer for sacrifice, Moremi, the woman leader, the pillar of the house the person who makes the roads smooth, who buys honor with herbs at the hills of Oramfe]

At the peak of the song, Yeyerisa brought the two warring male characters into the circle for reconciliation. Then the song changed back to praise for Obatala and all the singers and drummers moved into the circle to dance while Yeyerisa opened the calabash from which she sprayed, with a bundle of leaves, some liquid on participants and spectators alike.

There are many ways – ranging from religious observance to ritual enactment of primordial bliss – to view this festival, but it is important, as Adedeji has said about the Ede version, to evaluate Obatala festivals within an aesthetic framework or as "a product of creative fantasy."[7] Adedeji's idea of a structure of beginning, middle, and end, correlated in the case of an Obatala festival by the re-enactment of the myth of creation, conquest, and return, says more about what happens in the reenactment than about the relation among the reenacted episodes. Our examination of the structure of the Ondo version of the Obatala ritual drama, while recognizing those that have been identified in the Ede version by Adedeji, also recognizes other structural features that we will later identify in some of Soyinka's scripts.

In the first place, the ritual consists of incremental repetitions of discrete episodes separated by time but informed by similarity of motivation and consequence of actions. Although mostly non-verbal, the songs, announcing two different male characters, suggest that there are three distinct clusters of episodes: (1) the Obatala-Oduduwa fight over the calabash, (2) the Balufon-Oranmiyan fight, and (3) the Yeyerisa's reconciliation of the two male contestants. Even though the first two episode clusters are, in historical terms, separated by many years, they are brought together in the ritual for the simple reason that they repeat the same subjective category of the struggle for power and leadership in Ife between Obatala and Oduduwa on the one hand and Balufon and Oranmiyan on the other.

Accordingly, this serial repetition of similar motifs is, in aesthetic terms, a way of intensifying the tension suggested by the first confrontation between the two characters acting the roles of Obatala and Oduduwa. Moreover, in thematic terms, it is a device for recalling and retaining essential images that pertain to the underlying concern of the performance in the minds of the audience.

A similar use of repetition is evident in Soyinka's use of different temporal dimensions in *A Dance of the Forests* for the purpose of representing and reinforcing the feeling of crisis for his audience. While Soyinka's spatialization of a category of human actions in *A Dance of the Forests* serves to establish a model of audience expectation, thereby providing a major dramatic premise for other minor actions in the script, the playwright's effort in intensifying the spatialized dramatic event is subtly objectified by his use of three different dimensions of time: ancestral, social-historical, and transitional. Essentially, these three temporal dimensions refer to three distinct points on the Yoruba cosmological space-time continuum.

The world of the ancestors, called *ancestral time* in this study, refers to a timeless frame of reference that is ahistorical in that it is not completely passé or irrecoverable; this time-unit can be recaptured through re-enactments, as in rituals.

Transitional time refers to a temporal unit set apart by the Yoruba arbitrarily as a meeting point between ancestral and social-historical time. It is generally outside verifiable human existence and is also actualizable through re-enactments by characters designated for such purposes within the Yoruba society. It is a moment of becoming or essence formation, a formless moment that is often given form only through ritualization.

Finally, social-historical time refers to the waking and sleeping period of human or anthropomorphic experience. Unlike the other two temporal categories, social time is verifiable and generally considered to be within human awareness; it is, literally, the world of the living.

Accordingly, all the episodes in *A Dance of the Forests* are arranged in three clusters around these three temporal dimensions. Episode cluster A is constituted by actions and interactions of characters from the social world: Demoke, Rola, Adenebi, and Councillor and others that are involved in organizing the celebration of "the gathering of the tribes." Moreover, it is the action within social time – the preparation for an elaborate celebration of an inter-ethnic festival – that provides the axis for the entire script and establishes the only range of expectancies possible for the audience. For instance, this episode cluster supplies the principal basis for cognitive involvement of the audience, arousing, for example, such thoughts as what is the significance of the dance, will the dance materialize or not, what forces are available for either possibility? On the other hand, Soyinka's introduction of episodes from the other two temporal categories – ancestral and transitional – into the matrix of the play is a device for manipulating audience feeling about the ramifications of the episodes already represented by Demoke, Rola, Adenebi, and Councillor.

Episode cluster B is made up of the activities of characters in the reincarnated forms of Demoke as Court Poet, Rola as Madame Tortoise, and Adenebi as Historian, in addition to the Dead Warrior, his wife, and Mata Kharibu, all of whom embody what we have hitherto called ancestral time. All these characters are, like their counterparts within the social time unit, involved in one form of persecution and exploitation or another. Kharibu sentences the warrior to death for disagreeing with his bellicose policies and Madame Tortoise flirts with the warrior in the same manner that Rola flirts with Obaneji, for instance. Court Poet is also instrumental in the death of his apprentice just as Demoke is involved in the killing of Oremole.

The third episode cluster is made up of the actions of characters drawn from the transitional temporal realm. This episode cluster details the trial instanced by Aroni, the rivalry between Ogun and Eshuoro, and the partial arbitration by Obaneji, all of whom are reminiscent of the Yoruba intermediaries between natural and supernal awareness.

The structural device of incremental repetition is also evident in a more subtle manner in *Kongi's Harvest*. There is a constant aesthetic phenomenon that holds the script together and is also capable of facilitating audience apprehension of its concern. It is the device of subtle repetitions of a single preoccupation – the love of power and public adoration – in all the three spatial categories of the play: Kongi's cell-mountain retreat, Danlola's palace, and Segi's bar. Thus, while the critics' view of Danlola and Kongi as representatives of two critical generations in African history – the waning period of monarchy and its challenge by younger products of colonial education – is insightful as an instance of referentialist criticism, an examination of both characters as well as of the Segi-Daodu unit, within an aesthetic framework, will show that, apart from the differences of style, Danlola and Kongi manifest the same obsession. They are both in love with power, obsessed with image building, and characterized by ineffective political leadership. Similarly, a dysfunctional relation with power is also suggested, as we will show later, on Daodu's part.

Soyinka's attempt to control and vary audience experience of *Kongi's Harvest* is objectified by two structural relations: multiple episodes of different objective manifestations featured in the play's matrix and the implication of inter-episode or inter-image similarities among these diverse episodes that suggest the correspondence of motivation among different characters. For instance, the notion of dysfunctional political leadership objectified by some form of excessiveness is present in each cluster of episodes. Danlola and Kongi are both in love with extremes. Oba Danlola manifests in episode cluster A – either in prison or in his palace – an excessively hedonistic disposition. He is depicted as being impervious to the existing socio-political needs of his subjects; he, for instance, hardly talks about the effect of Kongi's schemes on his subjects as a whole. Rather, he repeatedly expresses desires to savor life to its fullest as an individual. He is always fascinated by the flamboyant – heavy, colorful dresses, silver accessories, and praise songs – regardless of the immediate needs of the people over whom he reigns. Danlola's predisposition for the irrelevant in the face of the urgent is objectified by his consistent recourse to sexual imagery while important political matters are being discussed. Evidence of Danlola's lustfulness is manifested in his irrelevant response to Daodu's request for his cooperation with plans to counter Kongi's heavy-handed regime:

Daodu: It means nothing. Nothing can alter what today will bring. And your compliance is a vital part of it.

Danlola: *My vital part shall exhaust itself in my favourite's bed. Call me Wuraola.* (emphasis added)[8]

Furthermore, in spite of Kongi's curtailment of Danlola's power, both show a similar pleasure in the exercise of power for its own sake. For instance, Danlola's relationship to Dende is as demeaning as Kongi's to the members of his Aweri fraternity. One instance of Danlola's flair for drama and show of power is objectified in his attempts to curse the prison superintendent (p. 7):

Danlola [*swelling, swelling....*]:
   He paraded me to the world
   L'ogolonto I leave this abuse
   To the judgement of the...
Superintendent: Please – plead with him. Intercede for me.
Sarumi: Kabiyesi, a father employs only a small stick on his child, he doesn't call in the policemen to take him to gaol. Don't give voice to the awesome names on an Oba's tongue; when you feel kinder, they cannot easily be recalled. They must fulfill what task they were called to do.

Danlola's power, unlike Kongi's, is not to jail or shoot an opponent; it is characterized by the power to destroy the sanity of one's opponent. Danlola, like Kongi, does not hesitate to use this power until he has been copiously flattered by Sarumi, his praise singers, and his wives.

Episode cluster B concerns Kongi's life style. It details his fasting sessions on the mountain, his debates with his advisers, the reformed Aweri, and his exchanges with the organizing secretary on the latter's progress for a

successful harvest. Although there are differences between Kongi and
Danlola in terms of external manifestations of their love for power or public
acknowledgment, there is a striking similarity of preoccupation with power
between both of them. In aesthetic terms, the playwright attenuates audience
expectation of an internal mediation of the conflict between Kongi and
Danlola by evoking images that imply the love for power and position by
both characters.

Audience expectation of an internal mediation or the possibility of a
meaningful resolution of the conflict between both characters becomes
elusive with the recognition by the audience of similar images of obsession
with power in episode clusters A and B. Like Danlola, Kongi is infatuated
with flattery; his cell is populated by sycophants who are at ease in singing
Kongi's praises. For instance, Sarumi's view of Danlola

> The king is...
> He who annoints the head's pulse centre
> With the oil of sacrifice
> The king is a god. (p. 57)

– is as laudatory and flattering as the organizing secretary's suggested titles
for the photographs of Kongi: "The Loneliness of the Pure... The Uneasy
Head... A Saint at Twilight... The Giver of Live..." (p. 39) Moreover, Kongi
shows in this episode cluster a flair for displaying power similar to that
shown by Danlola in episode cluster A. Kongi, as in Danlola's attempt to
curse the prison superintendent, will only be dissuaded from killing some of
his prisoners-opponents by flattery from the organizing secretary. The fact
that Kongi and Danlola share a love of public adoration is well captured in
the secretary's and Daodu's assessment of both characters:

> Daodu: The enactment of it alone should appeal to him. Kabiyesi loves to act
> roles. Like kingship. For him, kingship is a role.
>
> Secretary: Now where did I hear that before? Seems I heard it... that's right.
> Now that's funny isn't it? One of the Aweri said exactly the same thing
> of Kongi. "A flair for gestures" he said.
>
> Daodu: Maybe that's why they hate each other's guts.
>
> Secretary: Professional jealousy eh? Ha, Ha, couldn't agree with you more....(p.
> 41)

It is against this background of a dysfunctional view of positions of
power by Kongi and Danlola that Soyinka introduces the third episode
cluster that only suggests a slight modification of relations of forms with the

two previous episode clusters. With the images of ineffective leadership objectified in cluster A on the hedonistic level by Danlola and on the pseudo-heroic plane by Kongi in episode cluster B, the playwright prepares the audience for the possibility of external mediation in which a third character, possessing more functional values and programs, may emerge to displace the two politically effete leaders. Thus, the audience is likely to be very optimistic about the Segi-Daodu episode cluster.

Episode cluster C is characterized by dancing and drinking and occasionally by the organizing secretary's visit to Daodu. Initially, audience expectation of the need for a more dynamic leadership than that of Kongi or Danlola is activated by two factors: Daodu is heir apparent to Danlola and Segi is an ex-mistress of Kongi as well as a daughter of his arch-enemy. Hope is likely to rise in the audience with Daodu's rightful claim to power and the inimical relationship existing between Kongi and Segi. Moreover, their spatial intimacy as opposed to the spatial distance between Kongi and Danlola is an icon of potential unity of forces capable of contending seriously with Danlola's and Kongi's unproductive form of political leadership.

Daodu's success on the farm contrasts him with Kongi and perhaps Danlola in terms of providing an efficient food supply to the community, but his relation to the socio-political dimension of Isma is vague and thus the audience doubts Daodu's ability to complete the Herculean task ahead of him – the displacement of his uncle and of Kongi. For instance, little is known of his background, and his political plans, if any, remain obscure. Yet audience optimism is stabilized by Daodu's acknowledged opposition to Kongi's policies. Audience sensation may even be activated with Daodu's breaking of Danlola's talking drum at the end of this episode cluster. The elevation of audience emotion and hope by Daodu's initial success – the breaking of Danlola's drum – is gradually dissipated in cluster D as soon as Daodu starts to manifest a lack of initiative and adequate self-confidence. Once again, Daodu's sphere is not without its share of the problems of achieving viable leadership in Isma. While Daodu's disposition is not characterized by Danlola's hedonism or Kongi's masochism, he is not able to assume necessary control of urgent situations when they arise. This tendency to yield the position of leadership to others for fear of mistakes is evident in his compulsive dependence on Segi for further directions after his invigorating speech:

Segi: I'll be back directly Daodu. Let everything go on as planned.

Daodu: Such as what? After what has happened, what?...

Segi: So he came back? Why didn't you tell me?

Daodu: I could do nothing to stop him... He said he had to do it and no one else.

Segi: It doesn't matter.

Daodu: We've failed again Segi.

Segi: No, not altogether.

Daodu: *What else can one do now?*

Segi: The season is Harvest, so let there be plenty of everything....

Daodu: What are you talking about? *What do I do now?* (pp.80-81, emphasis added)

With episode cluster D – the harvest and Danlola's attempted exile – the playwright subtly suggests the non-dynamic situation of Isma's political crisis. Here, in a summary fashion, Soyinka gathers all the contending characters together in the same space only to repeat their characteristic weaknesses that militate against resolving Isma's crisis.

The problem of space discourages us from detailed analysis of more of Soyinka's plays. Suffice it to say, however, that incremental repetition abounds in other plays as well. This structural device is evident in the internal reenactments in *The Lion and the Jewel*, especially where Lakunle's and Baroka's dispositions are represented in a series of tempo-causally unrelated events. For example, while the re-enactment of Baroka's bribing of the engineer bears no logical connection to his desire to marry Sidi, the fact that Baroka successfully bribed the surveyor to achieve his personal ends subtly foreshadows the possibility of his similar enticement of Sidi with the stamp machine. Similarly, the actions of Particulars Joe and Chief-in-Town in *The Road* could have been omitted without any adverse effect on the wholeness of the play, but while in it they variegate the audience's experience of the play and also serve as a modulation of Professor's exploitative disposition.

Thus, a general characteristic of Soyinka's dramaturgy is the pattern of web-like rather than tree-like internal relations of the parts of his scripts. This structural phenomenon depends more on metaphoric than metonymic imagination. It views dramatic communication as a system in which the audience learns through the recognition of similarities between apparently unrelated images with a view to emphasizing the epistemic dimension of the object with which they are confronted.

This view differs from the emphasis on tempo-causality and the emotive aspect of drama characteristic of Aristotle's organicity. Furthermore, the convoluted, rather than linear, movement or the repetitive, rather than translational, development of the Obatala Festival, and, for instance, of *A*

Dance of the Forests, Kongi's Harvest, and to some extent *The Lion and the Jewel* and *The Road*, communicate effectively through the use of metaphor. This communication is achieved, as we have demonstrated in the preceding paragraphs, through the emphasis of features of the principal or primary subjective category by using secondary or subsidiary images that imply statements about the primary vision of the writer.[9]

While the web-like, or network-like, structure described in the Obatala ritual and in some of Soyinka's drama may not produce the same emotional state achievable through organic or tree-like structures favored by Aristotle, it possesses its own aesthetic quality. It is, for instance, capable of varying audience experience with the multiplicity of images while simultaneously controlling that experience through a preponderance of inter-image similarities on the cognitive level. While its structure may not necessarily achieve the emotional satisfaction of an experience of wholeness characteristic of tempo-causal continuity or, in Aristotle's term, of unity of action, it does have its own quality; it attempts to produce in the audience the emotional satisfaction that accompanies the variation of sensations. The web-like structure, characterized by incremental repetition of diverse images capable of semantic equivalence, is indeed not devoid of emotiveness. The inter-position of continuous and discrete episodes or of plot-propelling and plot-stagnating images temporarily serves to frustrate the audience from attaining necessary knowledge of the characters' actions. The final recognition of semantic equivalence between the diversity of images in a retrospective reading or experience of such a play provides emotional satisfaction that often accompanies cognitive discovery or recognition.

Finally, this dramatic form that emphasizes connection between subsequent images of a play in metaphoric as opposed to metonymic terms, though often hard to comprehend easily, serves a metacommunicative purpose. The use of tempo-causally unrelated episodes is capable of drawing attention to the fictive process. With such attention it can effectively alienate the audience from the raw experience of primary characters and is thus capable of enhancing critical viewing of the world evoked in rituals and drama.

NOTES

1. See for example, Oyin Ogunba, *The Movement of Transition* (Ibadan: Ibadan University Press, 1975) and Joel Adedeji, "Oral Tradition and Contemporary Theatre in Nigeria," *Research in African Literatures,* 2 (1971), pp. 134-49.

2. See for instance, Gerald Moore, *Wole Soyinka* (London: Heinemann, 1971), especially Moore's view that the form of *The Lion and the Jewel* is more conventional than that of *A Dance of the Forests, The Road* and *Kongi's Harvest*; and Margaret Laurence, *Long Drums and Cannons* (London: Macmillan, 1969), especially her view of "unharnessed multiplicity of motifs" in *A Dance of the Forests.*

3.   See, for example, Ropo Sekoni, "Meaning and Mechanism in Yoruba Ijala," *Ba Shiru*, 1 (1977), pp. 31-6; and "Structure and Significance in Trickster Narratives," *Confluence*, 1 (June 1978), pp. 36-40, on the Yoruba preference for the epistemic dimension of verbal art.

4.   See Samuel H. Butcher, *Aristotle's Theory of Poetry and Fine Art with a Critical Text and Translation of the Poetics* (New York: Dover Publications, 1951), chapter 8.

5.   For examples of repetition in oral narratives, see Ropo Sekoni, "Structure and Significance in Trickster Narrative."

6.   See Joel Adedeji, "Folklore and Yoruba Drama: Obatala as a Case Study," in Richard M. Dorson, ed. *African Folklore* (Bloomington: Indiana University Press, 1972), pp. 321-29.

7.   Ibid, p. 333.

8.   *Kongi's Harvest* (London: Oxford University Press, 1967), p. 63. All quotations are from this edition.

9.   See "The Interaction View of Metaphor" in Max Black, *Model and Metaphors* (Ithaca, N. Y: Cornell University Press, 1962) and Colin Turbayne, *The Myth of Metaphor* (New Haven: Yale University Press, 1962).

Four Alternative Endings to Wole Soyinka's *A Dance of the Forests*

Robert Fraser

It has not always been noticed that there are four extant versions of the conclusion to Wole Soyinka's early play *A Dance of the Forests*. The first, and least well known, of these, which I shall christen "A," is the version contained in the original typescript, which has never been published in full. Then there is the printed version to be found in the original Oxford University Press edition of 1963 and subsequently reprinted in *Five Plays* (Oxford University Press, 1964) which I shall call "B." The version eventually included in the *Collected Plays* (Oxford University Press, 1973) differs from B towards the end and, hence, deserves separate tabulation as "C." Last but, from the point of view of the prospective director, by no means least, there is the adjusted version actually employed in the original 1960 production of the play mounted in Lagos and Ibadan and, as such, appended to all of the available published editions. In the discussion that follows, this version will be referred to as "D." A comparison between these various versions would certainly seem to be both timely and instructive, since it reveals multiple and far-reaching variants and, hence, provides us with a fascinating glimpse of the practicing dramatist at work sifting through successive drafts.

The section under consideration runs from the stage direction *"The Half-Child continues slowly towards the Mother"* on p. 70 of the collected edition to the end of the play. In constitutes the *ampe* sequence, which is part of the protagonist Demoke's trial by ordeal, followed by the tussle between the rival *orisa* Eshuoro and Ogun over his destiny, and culminating in the stated reactions to these events, first by Forest Head himself and second by the mesmerized humans. These events represent the climax of the dance sequence, and an understanding of them is hence crucial to our interpretation not only of the ritual but also of the play as a whole.

Since version A exists only in typescript it is only fair to the reader, with Soyinka's permission, to reproduce it in full from the point specified to the end of the text. It must be made clear at the outset that this version is not in any sense available for stage performance, being reproduced here simply as an archaeological curio, albeit one of surpassing literary interest. The typescript from which the extract is taken is in the possession of my colleague Martin Banham of the Workshop Theatre, University of Leeds, to whom I am indebted for its perusal. One other prefatory remark ought to be made, to avoid confusion. The character who appears in this extract as Chunebi is in fact none other than our old friend Adenebi, the Court Historian, whose more familiar name would seem to have been adopted at some stage between the penning of the play and its going to press.

A. From Soyinka's Typescript.

the child continues slowly towards the Mother, Eshuoro imperiously offering his hand, furious as each step takes the child nearer her. looks up sharply and finds Ogun on the other side of the woman, with similarly outstretched hand. snaps his finger suddenly at the interpreter, a sudden clap of drums, and the interpreter resumes his ampe *with the third triplet. The Woman's and the half-child's hand are just about to meet when this happens, and the child turns instantly.*

The ampe *gradually increases tempo and soon involves the three protagonists themselves. they are all performing at once, or nearly, and the tempo gets faster and faster. eshuoro snaps his hand again and the Interpreter turns to the child, throwing off his mask and revealing himself as Eshuoro's jester. performs all sorts of antics along with his* ampe *to maintain the child's attention. suddenly, with the half-child practically mesmerized by the jester, eshuoro picks him up and throws him towards the third triplet who makes to catch him on the point of two knives as in the dance of the child-acrobats. Role screams suddenly, the child is tossed up by the third triplet who again goes through the same motion, the other two triplets continuing the furious ampe round him and yelling at the top of their voice. Demoke, Rola and Chunebi against cluster together. The half-child is now tossed back to Eshuoro, and suddenly Demoke dashes forward to intercept. Eshuoro laughs pretends to throw the child back. the Interpreter, Eshuoro and the third triplet keep up this game for a brief period, with Demoke running between them, until Ogun appears behind the Interpreter, pulls him aside just as the child is thrown towards him, makes the catch himself passing it instantly to Demoke who has come running at the same time. All action stops again, including the first and second triplets who have never ceased to* ampe *they all look at Demoke, who stands confused, not knowing what the next step should be. Decides eventually to restore the child to the Dead Woman, and attempts to do so. Eshuoro partially blocks his way and appeals to Forest Head.*

Forest Head: *turning away* Trouble me no further; he knows the meaning of his acts. And if he does not, nothing is lost, or gained – but it is not given to you to know that. They are all thinking beings; even you Eshuoro, child that is overgrown. And Ogun, you are another. And like the humans, you all weary me. Play out the pattern since I desire it, but no interference must be demanded of me. Aroni, does Demoke know what he has done?

Aroni: Demoke, you hold a doomed thing in your hand. It is not light matter to reverse the deed that was begun many lives ago. The Forest will not let you pass.

the woman appeals, mutely to Demoke.

Forest Head: *more to himself* How slowly they drag this out, while I grow old fast and readily. The fooleries of beings whom I have fashioned closer to me weary and distress me. Yet I must persist, knowing that nothing is ever altered. My secret is my eternal burden – to pierce the encrustations of soul-deadening habit, and bare the mirror of original nakedness – knowing full well, it is all futility. Yet I must do this alone, and no more, since to intervene is to be guilty of contradiction, and yet to remain altogether unfelt is to make my long-rumoured ineffectuality complete; hoping that when I have tortured awareness from their souls, they might play out their own – futile – expiation – of their own will... ... ..

demoke appears to make up his mind; hands the child to the dead woman.

eshuoro gives a loud yell of triumph, rushes off-stage, accompanied by his jester. the triplets follow gleefully

the dead man comes forward, eagerly

Forest Head: *continuously* ... . And he? Must I tell him that from his first life-time, he played out, willingly, his self-immolation?

Dead Man: And I? Will not one take my case? Have I waited in vain and borne this shame for so long that I must find no release at the welcome?

aroni takes him gently by the hand, leads him off.

forest head follows, slowly.

A silhouette of Demoke's totem is seen, people dancing round it, also in silhouette, in silence. Eshuoro's jester leaps on stage bearing the fetish basket which he clamps onto Demoke's head; performing a wild dance in front of him.

Ogun steps between Demoke and the totem, dances to bar Demoke's path. Eshuoro enters with a heavy club, joins his jester and they manouvre Demoke past Ogun. Ogun tries to transfer his cutlass to Demoke, but each time he attempts to take it, letting go of his hold on the basket he is unbalanced, and has to restore his hold with both hands. Ogun's attempts to lop off the growth from the basket are ably defended by Eshuoro, the jester doing his best to confuse Ogun's movements. Ogun eventually attempts to trip Demoke and thus upset the pot, but Demoke is saved by Eshuoro's prompt interference. Ogun thereupon rushes off-stage.

dance of the unwilling sacrifice, in which Demoke is relentlessly headed towards the totem and the silent dancing figures. Rola and Chunebi are made to sprinkle libation around the scene.

Demoke, dancing towards his handiwork is faded away, and re-appears at the foot of the totem, the crowd parting in silence. He begins to climb, hampered further by the load on his head. there are only the drums, eshuoro and his jester have stopped dancing. slowly, but eventually, demoke disappears from view, and the crowd cheer wildly.

eshuoro rushes out in a frenzy. returns at the totem with fire-brand; sets fire to the tree. ogun, ridiculing this gesture by Eshuoro, catches demoke as he falls.

black-out behind. the front gets increasingly lighter as eshuoro returns and dances out his frenzy, lashing his jester with a branch. noise of the beaters from a distance. the dead woman looks anxiously at the sky and vanishes with the half-child. dawn is breaking. demoke re-enters, dressed like a hunter. ogun follows him, eyeing the sky anxiously. in his hand, a gun and his cutlass. the sun creeps through; ogun hurriedly hands Demoke the weapons, embraces him and flees. eshuoro is still dancing as the beaters come quite close and break on the scene and then he flees after his jester.

full morning light. agboreko and the Old Man push their way through the crowd, murete, very drunk, dragging them on.

Murete: Here. I said it was here.

Agboreko: I will not forget my promise.

Old Man: Sefe. What did you see? What did you see?

Agboreko: Let them be old man. When the grains have been winnowed, it will be time enough for the sparing of the crops. Prov … … .

Murete: *drunkenly* Proverbs to bones and silence.

Agboreko: It is time for the fulfillment of vows.

Old Man: *to demoke* We searched all night. Knowing who your companion was … . .

Agboreko: Madame Tortoise ... . the one who never dies ... . never . .

Old Man: And then I was troubled by the mystery of the fourth. The Council orator I knew. And Madame Tortoise. But the fourth ... ... *he looks round*

You are back to three. Did the other reveal himself?

Demoke: The father of ghommids. Forest Head himself.

Agboreko: At first we thought it would be Eshuoro, tricking you onwards like the echo in the woods. And then I thought, Murete cannot be silent only from fear. It must be Forest Head himself.

Old Man: Forest Head. And did you see the lame one?

demoke nods

Fools we were to pit our weakness against the cunning of Aroni, chasing souls whom he was resolved to welcome.

Agboreko: We paid dearly for this wisdom newly acquired.

Old Man: Cruelly. Look, look at me. Behind every sapling, there was the sudden hand of Aroni, and he aims well.

gingerly feels a weal across his face

Demoke: There was a path that brought us here. Could not Murete find it?

Old Man: We would have done better without him. Sometimes I suspect his drunkenness. We have tasted the night thickness of the forest like the nails of a jealous wife.

agboreko nudges the Old Man. he becomes suddenly uncomfortable, hems and coughs.

Old Man: Demoke my son. It became necessary as our search ate up the progress of the night and we fell in one bog after another without trace of you or the others ... ...

Agboreko: Is your son not a man? Out with the truth. Don't drag this out ...

Old Man: Demoke, we made sacrifice and demanded the path of expiation ...

Agboreko: The pronouncement was clear on the matter ... . It is hard ... for you. But it is meaningful, it will bear fruit ... .

Old Man: It means a new beginning my son … .

Demoke: We three who lived many lives in this one night, have we not done enough? Have we not felt enough for the memory of our remaining lives?

Old Man: What manner of a night was it? Can you tell us that?

Agboreko: It makes no change in the path he must follow. Better that you tell him that.

Old Man: Where we found you, there we must begin from the old beginnings. Your habitation – can you make it here?

Rola comes forward. She looks chastened.

Agboreko: I did not think to find her still alive, this one that outlasts them all. Madame Tortoise … .

Demoke: Not any more. It was the same lightning that seared us through the head.

Agboreko: *snorts.* Does that mean something wise, child?

Old Man: Shush. *Draws Demoke aside.* Would she stay?

Demoke: Here?

Old Man: Why not? If you went together through the same night of fires … …

Demoke: For my part, I find it easy to be a child again, playing the game of elders … … . Yes, why not … … . ?

Old Man: *eagerly* Then you are reconciled. It is a wilderness, but it was here we found the kernel of light.

Demoke: Ogun warned me. *Showing his weapons and apparel.*

He prepared me.
And I … . I find it is within my nature.

Old Man: We shall make it easier. We must not let it be another waste. Agboreko … .

Agboreko: They are here old man … … can't you see, they have begun.

the crowd is building fires. some enter with the parts of a loom. they set it up, working, rapidly.

a mortar is rolled in. cooked yams are transferred from a pot and two men start to pound

a cloth-beater's log and dumb-bells. the beaters kneel and start to beat dyed cloths. everyone is busy: the bustle affects the entire atmosphere,

wood-cutters, a small group made up of a story-teller and his young listeners, a woodchopper etc. etc. etc. all move rapidly but easily to build an instant village.

the shuttle, the beaters, the pounders, the woodcutter set up a rhythm. Demoke comes forward, Rola running after him with something he has probably forgotten, his hunting-bag which she adjusts over his shoulders.

Agboreko: *sneaking up to Demoke.* Of the future, did you learn anything?

Demoke: What are you attempting – now? The past?

Agboreko: I thought it was your … … . .

Old Man: *comes up and pulls him away* "When the grains have been winnowed … … "

Agboreko: *reproved.* Proverb to bones and silence.

Demoke: Darkness enveloped me, but piercing,
  Through I came
  Night is the choice for the fox's dance
  Child of the Moon's household am I.

Agboreko: Pumice is my choice for scrubbing
  Ever seen a crocodile that itches?
  And my veins run with the oil of palms.

Old Man: *truculently*
  The lion looked at me, and he turned blind
  the wicked lifted his arm, and it broke in two
  Ruler of the Forest depths am I.

Rola: Witches spread their net, trapped emptiness
  Does the tear in the wind's eye pause to dry?
  Palm of the storm's hand am I.

Chunebi: When the rock fell, alone I caught the boulders.
  My saddle is the torrent of the flood.
  Serpent of the ocean depths am I.

Demoke: And the lightning made his bid – in vain
  When she cooks, is the cloud ever set on fire?
  Father of the Fetish House am I.

To the rhythm of the shuttle, cloth-beaters, mortar, etc., the story-teller sings this song of the conquest of the elements, casually, as if this is the song to the story he is telling. The dance seeps in gradually, building up.

The first major source of departure between the different texts is the alternative versions presented of the *ampe* sequence itself. In all versions the *ampe* game is initiated by Eshuoro and his triplets in an attempt to distract the Half-Child from rejoining his mother. When this has been done, the child then becomes a party to the game, though, whereas in versions A, B, and C, it is the Half-Child itself who is tossed between the arms of these malevolent agents, in version D it is a wooden *ibeji* twin figure. The primary consideration in this particular alteration presumably was humane: no human mother of a human child actor is likely to remain patiently in the audience while her flesh-and-blood offspring is hurled around the stage by actors more careful of their own performance than of the child's safety. This discrepancy, however, is not the most significant one between the two versions. In A, B, and C it is Ogun who retrieves the Half-Child, which he then hands "instantly to Demoke" (*Collected*, p. 71). After some hesitation, Demoke then returns it to its mother. In D, however, it is Demoke himself who retrieves the *ibeji* figurine. He then attempts to struggle over to the Dead Woman with the Half-Child on his shoulders. Eventually, as dawn breaks, he sags, and the mother recovers the child.

What precisely is happening at this point in the play? In his substantial monograph on Soyinka, Eldred Jones, after a lengthy consideration of this episode, which he admits is crucial, ultimately has to confess himself baffled by its import.[1] This is a pity since it is he who, at the beginning of his perceptive chapter, brings in an idea from the poem sequence *Idanre* (1967) that is clearly pertinent to understanding this episode. This is the notion of the Mobius Strip, invoked in a footnote to that poem, where we learn that it corresponds in Soyinka's thinking to the "self-devouring snake" hung by the devotees of the Ogun Cult around their necks. We further learn that it is relieved at one point by a kink which, in figurative terms, comes to represent a hypothetical point of release from an apparently inexorable destiny. The release is only hypothetical, however, since, on examination, the pattern is continuous, the interruption being but an optical illusion.[2] Cannot this notion be applied to Demoke's moment of indecision? When he stands hesitating with the child in his hands has he not in effect reached the kink in the historical cycle, from which he is fleetingly entrusted with the possibility of release? In that case Ogun's handing the child to him in A, B, and C would make much sense: as his protector and guide he is giving him the creative possibility of redemption. What is confusing in A, B, and C is Eshuoro's reactions. A stage direction tells us that when Demoke first attempts to hand the child to its mother, "Eshuoro blocks his way and appeals to Forest Head." When Demoke eventually succeeds in returning the child, however, "Eshuoro gives a loud yell of triumph" (*Collected*, p. 72). Does Eshuoro want him to hand the child back or not? In D, all of this is much clearer. When Demoke grabs hold of the *ibeji* child substitute, everything stops and Eshuoro "silently appeals to Forest Head" (p. 75), presumably to stop Demoke from returning the figurine either to the child or to the mother. When, after Aroni's admonishment, Demoke returns the figurine to the child, whom he then picks up and attempts to deliver to its mother, the triplets, Eshuoro's agents, impede him at every step, while a contest with staves between Ogun and Eshuoro emphasizes that Demoke is trying to enact Ogun's wishes in the teeth of Eshuoro's resistance. The fact that it is the mother who eventually snatches the child from the fainting Demoke is also suggestive and fitting: the force of human love perhaps achieves more than the most scrupulous heroism.

The A, B, and C texts try to reinforce the point of the *ampe* sequence by a later scene, cast in silhouette on a backcloth, in which Demoke is forced to reenact the circumstances of his crime by scaling the totem from which he had plunged his apprentice Oremole to his death. Eshuoro, Oremole's protector, fires the tree in vengeance, whereupon Demoke falls to the ground, only to be saved by Ogun who rushes to catch him. The feasibility of this episode has often been cast in doubt, and the fact that it does not occur in the D version actually used in the original production presumably endorses this view. Gerald Moore for one also finds it tedious and irrelevant:

> The back-projection scene by the totem-pole. Suggested in the main printed text, is also a piece of staging whose complexity is not justified by its apparent significance; the contest between Eshuoro and Ogun has already occupied enough dramatic time and threatens to become a bore.[3]

It remains true, however, that in the A, B, and C versions, in which, as we have seen, the issues are not clarified in the first instance, this second sequence is needed to inform the audience of precisely what is going on; it enacts the process of propitiation in a way which the *ampe* sequence fails to. It furthermore elucidates the battle of principle between Ogun and Eshuoro that the earlier ritual had merely confused. The only semblance of it in the D version, where, as we have shown, it is unnecessary, is the brief duel with staves between the two rival *orisa*. It is thus not only for practical reasons that the D version is the more satisfactory text at this point.

But this is somewhat to anticipate. In all versions before the completion of the rite Forest Father is made to declare his unwillingness to intervene in a pre-ordained process. Again, in all instances, his statements are seen to be a response to Eshuoro's silent appeal for decisive action. While the tone of personal reproach is everywhere unmistakable, the speech given in the published editions is relatively short and elusive. A, on the other hand, gives Forest Head three speeches straddling Aroni's address to Demoke, which comes a lot earlier than in the available published texts. Thus, after the opening remarks "Trouble me no further," A adds these words:

> He knows the meaning of his acts. And if he does not, nothing is lost, or gained – but it is not given to you to know that. They are all thinking beings, even you Eshuoro, child that is over grown. And Ogun, you are another. And like the humans, you all weary me. Play out the pattern, since I desire it, but no interference must be demanded of me.

This speech is considerably more explicit than anything in the more familiar texts and serves to direct Forest Head's comments not only against the impulsive Eshuoro, but also towards Ogun his metaphysical rival and, beyond them, the whole envenomed messiness of the human situation. Hence a general impression is conveyed of a much bitterer Forest Head, one who has lost faith, not simply in human prudence, but also in the *orisa* and in the redemptive possibilities of the universe in general.

Moreover, immediately after Aroni's admonishment, and before he takes up the test as we know it, Forest Head is given a further additional remark: "How slowly they drag this out, while I grow old fast and readily." Then, tacked onto the end of the published speech, and immediately before Demoke actually hands the child to the dead woman, we have this: "they might play out their own – futile – expiation – of their own free will ..." Last, after the child has been returned and just before his own exit, Forest Head is heard to murmur "And he? Must I tell him that from his first life-time, he played out, willingly, his self-immolation?"

The overall effect of these remarks, taken with Forest Head's opening address, is doubly to stress the fundamental pointlessness of the act of expiation that is about to be completed. Does this rob the ritual of its impact? To the extent that it does so, this factor may have caused Soyinka to withdraw these remarks in later versions. However much sense they make philosophically, it would appear to be dramatically unwise continually to emphasize the irrelevance of what is about to happen. Nevertheless, regarding them in relation to the play's total world view, we can see that these remarks do have considerable cogency. Once again we have to refer to Soyinka's note on the Mobius pattern appended to *Idanre*. Here we are told that the snake configuration gives an "illusion of a 'kind' in the circle and a possible centrifugal escape from the eternal cycle of horrors that has become the history of man. Only an illusion but a poetic one ... . " Thus the strip itself expresses a paradox, since, viewed from the human eye, it offers a point of exit from a rigid pattern, whereas, viewed from above and, as it were, objectively, it is constrained and predictably unilinear. Much the same can be said about Demoke's action. To Forest Head it is all futile, fully conscious as he is, in accordance with text A, that "from his first life-time" Demoke has "played out, willingly, his own self-immolation." Yet for Demoke himself the moment is one of considerable indecision and hence opportunity. For the audience, following these events vicariously, Demoke's action in handing the child back to its mother makes all the difference. We are all in this position, audience, character, even the *orisa* themselves, who seem to have only partial insight; everyone, that is, except Forest Head, who thus in text A seems to make his concluding remarks almost to himself. After all, nobody else would understand them, and, if we do not pay close enough attention, that statement will also go for the critics.

Admittedly, these events are difficult to decipher. One strong contributing factor to this difficulty is a lingering uncertainty as to the status of Forest Head's personality. He is clearly, like the *orisa* themselves, supernatural; yet he seems to regard himself as in some way superior both to Ogun and Eshuoro. He is certainly gifted with more knowledge. The reference in all texts to "the fooleries of beings whom I have fashioned" would seem to identify him with Obatala, the god of creation (as opposed to creativity), himself an *orisa*. In what way, then, can Obatala lay claim to precedence? For an answer to this question we have to turn to a portion of Soyinka's explanatory criticism, to that mine of creative Yoruba concepts *The Fourth Stage*, originally published two years after *A Dance of the Forests*, now reprinted in a remarkable collection of essays.[4] Here Soyinka identifies Obatala as "the representative ... of the first disintegration experienced by godhead," and then goes on to explain:

> We are further back to the origin, not now engaged in the transitional battle of Ogun, but in the fragmentation of Orisa-Nla the primal deity, from whom the entire Yoruba pantheon was born. Myth informs us that a jealous slave rolled a stone down the back of the first and only deity and shattered him in a thousand and sixty-four fragments. From this first act of revolution was born the Yoruba pantheon. [5]

Soyinka then clinches the matter by saying, "Yoruba myth equates Obatala, god of purity, god also of creation (but not of creativity!) with the first deity Orisa-Nla."[6]

Thus, behind the character of Forest Head as we have it in the play with all its transmutations, we discern the shadow, not merely of Obatala, but, further back, of the first, now cruelly fragmented, deity. Text A makes this much more obvious by stressing his immense age – "I grow old, fast and wearily" – and the depth of his ancient despair. He does not intervene because he is restrained, not simply by reluctance, but also by metaphysical circumstance. (One must remember at this point that the imprisonment of Obatala is also a constant theme of Yoruba legend.) Thus text A, while it may be theatrically clumsy, does make the issues at stake somewhat clearer. Its cancellation must be of considerable help to the prospective director; it has the unfortunate minor effect of hindering the critic.

The last major source of divergence between the different texts is in the reactions of the human characters to the events projected. For instance, straight after Forest Head's reproof to Eshuoro, A gives the Dead Man this: "And I? Will no one take my case? Have I waited in vain and borne this shame for so long that I must find no release at the welcome?" This speech makes it evident, as no other fact does, that Demoke is acting not merely in his own behalf, but also for the scorned ancestors. The statement was presumably omitted later for the sake of conciseness and because the idea that it makes explicit is in any case largely implicit in the whole mechanism of the Mother and the Half-Child.

The greatest discrepancies, however, occur right at the end of the play during the concluding conversation between the redeemed culprits and, specifically, after the stage direction "Agboreko nudges the Old Man. He becomes suddenly uncomfortable, hems and coughs" (*Collected*, p. 73). This is beyond the point at which the D text rejoins the others, and there are thus only three texts to consider, A, B, and C-D. Here a comparison reveals a process of drastic, systematic pruning, so that what in A occupies sixty spoken lines together with a great deal of stage business, has by B been whittled down to a mere thirty-five with minimal business, and by the collected edition has dwindled further to sixteen with almost no stage directions. A prominent factor here must have been the need to cut down so as to avoid anticlimax or, worse, tedium. All versions center on the idea of Demoke having in some sense saved both himself and the community, but A has a strong tendency to belabor the point. For instance, after the Old Man's question, "What manner of a night was it? Can you tell us that?" which all versions have, A gives him and Agboreko these lines:

> Agboreko: It makes no change in the path he must follow. Better that you tell him that.

> Old Man: Where we found you, there we must begin from the old beginnings. Your habitation – can you make it here?

This at least contains a note of interrogation, but the same two characters are also given distinctly gnomic lines:

Agboreko: The pronouncement was clear on the matter ... . It is hard ... for you. but it is meaningful, it will bear fruit.

Old Man: It means a new beginning my son.

In general, in version A, Agboreko appears to be nearly as pompous as he was at the beginning of the play. Later versions relieve him of many of his heavier remarks and hence leave out much that is ponderous, not merely in him, but in the dialogue as a whole.

Text A gives us a rapid accumulation of theatrical events which looks like a build-up towards a culminating curtain call. Cooks, cloth beaters, a wood-cutter, and a storyteller and his young audience gradually gather and resume the feast. The point presumably is that, cleansed from guilt, the human community can now get on with constructing its life, a point that the suggested action makes eloquently but expensively, the surviving dialogue with a stark simplicity. The decision between these two methods of achieving a similar result is once again predominantly a practical one, but the verdict seems, here as elsewhere, to have fallen for simplicity.

Simplicity too must have dictated the last noticeable change. Both A and B conclude with a passage of lyrical identification, in which each of the main protagonists is made to declare the essential principle that rules his being. In C-D, on the other hand, these statements are missing, the text ending with Agboreko's final pronouncement (with ponderous finality), "Proverbs to bones and silence." This statement, cropping up as it does as a constant refrain throughout this work, would seem to make a fitting and recognizable conclusion, and so we are forced to ask ourselves what the earlier versions gain or lose from the additional lines.

At first these culminating testimonies seem almost impenetrably hermetic (a sufficient reason in itself, perhaps, for excluding them). Fortunately Gerald Moore provides us with a suggestion that helps to crack the code: "the last speeches made by the three mortals at the end of the play give us clues linking each of them with one of the spirits who spoke through them during the Dance of Welcome."[7] This is true enough; a simple glance back is enough to substantiate Moore's statement. Moore also, however, adds a note of complaint. The correlation is not perfect, he says, because "the Spirits of Precious Stones, of Volcanoes and of the Pachyderms, who also speak, are not accounted for." Taken as a comment on text B this is fair, but a glance at the typescript serves to establish why this is so: the appropriate statements have been edited out or altered so as to mask the equation. For instance, here Agboreko's declaration begins not with "I made a sponge of nettle ponds," as in B, but with "pumice is my choice for scrubbing," a clear reference to volcanic activity. The Old Man is given a pronouncement that seems to identify him clearly with the Pachyderms, giants of the forest.

The only item on Moore's list that is not easily detected in A is the Spirit of Precious Stones, but a last look at text B, where Demoke ends the whole play with the line, "I lodge below with the secrets of the earth" would seem to point to this final link.

Last, it is hard to escape the critical question as to the relative worth of these four versions. Has Soyinka meddled too much with the form of his original inspiration, thus muddying the design, or have the revised texts a superior thrust and clarity? We have already seen that the first major revision, that incorporated in the first published edition of 1963, does away with much that is cumbersome or duplicated elsewhere. The sacrificed portions often, however, make the process of exegesis easier and clear up a number of interpretational puzzles. On the other hand, it is doubtful whether even this version is completely stageworthy, pragmatic considerations alone driving one to prefer text D. This, as we know, was the version employed in the original production; a recent realization for the University of Leeds Television Service has again re-emphasized its immense theatrical effectiveness. In summary, then, one must settle for dramatic integrity rather than the satisfaction of scholarly curiosity in concluding that Soyinka has acted as a wise editor and the shrewdest critic of his own work. The suggested acting version is, in these terms, the finest.

NOTES

1. Eldred Jones, *The Writing of Wole Soyinka* (London: Heinemann Educational Books, 1973), see especially pp. 46-47.
2. Wole Soyinka, *Idanre and Other Poems* (London: Methuen, 1967), p. 87.
3. Gerald Moore, *Wole Soyinka* (London and Ibadan: Evans Brothers Limited, 1971), p. 40.
4. Originally in D.W. Jefferson, ed., *The Morality of Art* (London: Routledge and Kegan Paul, 1965). Also in Wole Soyinka, *Myth, Literature and the African World* (Cambridge: Cambridge University Press, 1976).
5. Jefferson, *Morality of Art*, p. 127.
6. Jefferson, *Morality of Art*, p. 128.
7. Moore, *Wole Soyinka*, p. 40.

The Last Bridge on *The Road*: Soyinka's Rage and Compassion

Robert M. Wren

In this article I propose to discuss several examples of Wole Soyinka's writing that may be seen as preliminary essays toward his play *The Road*. One has been noticed before, without elaborate comment; it is "Epitaph for Say Tokyo Kid," which appeared in the University of Ibadan poetry magazine *The Horn* early in 1962. Another, an amusing radio talk having to do with lorry drivers and police, was printed in *Radio Times* (Nigeria) a year and a half earlier; a substantial part of it has been reprinted.[1] The third has not, so far as I can learn, been noticed before: a prose article published in the (Lagos) *Daily Express* on March 28, 1962, p. 4, as a contribution to a lengthy series by prominent Nigerians titled "What Infuriates Me About Nigeria." Soyinka's piece is headlined, "Bad roads, Bad users, Bad deaths." Taken together, the poem, the radio talk, and the essay suggest the combination of outrage, satirical energy, and compassion that underlie Soyinka's most fascinating play. They also contain some details that helped develop the play's dramatic action.

Outrage dominates the *Daily Express* piece. A short time before, Soyinka says in it, he noticed that "Mile 34 from Lagos" on the Lagos-Ibadan road had "claimed yet another victim." This fact leads him to some observations, which will be returned to, regarding that point in the highway. He then notes "the death-trap at Ife" before pausing to dwell on "the last bridge on Ikorodu road," a special horror to which he devotes about one-sixth of the article. He credits a demonic road engineer with this last and discourses on the failures of civil servants and police to correct such situations. Finally, he tells of "one memorable accident" that makes "infuriate" seem a silly word. A senator declines to carry a victim with a spinal injury on to Ibadan, and his heartless behavior causes Soyinka uncharacteristic shame because two "foreigners" witnessed it.[2] Fully a third of the article is devoted to the incident.

The outrage occasioned by the senator is specific. Soyinka's rage against road engineers is, on the other hand, general and therefore appropriately expressed in satire. "As you would have gathered by now," he says, "road signing, other than the regulation eighteen by nine-inch plate, is simply anathemic [sic] to any intelligent, sober Nigerian road-builder." He goes on, "Probably it is not listed in the Local Purchase Order book. Or perhaps it is against the regulations, general orders, not to mention Native Law and Custom." With this last stroke, Soyinka ridicules the whole official order that mindlessly repeats the errors of established authority.

It is arguable that *The Road* too is a satirical attack on the official order of things, expanded theatrically, through the Professor, to the pervasive corruption of Nigerian life. A mild satire of senators at one point may reflect the offensive real senator: a messenger wins a lottery and as a result "owns half the houses in Apapa and now they have made him a Senator."[3] Soyinka's article in the *Express* was followed the next day by a Bishop's on "Bribery and Corruption"; might the announcement of that sequel, trailing on Soyinka's piece, have helped set in motion the idea of Professor as a corrupt churchman, evicted by his bishop? The question is unanswerable, of course, but it is surprising that death at a curve in a road approaching a bridge should be the motive for a play about political and religious problems and conflicts.

The Road concerns a group of lorry drivers and associated persons whose activities revolve around the palm-wine feast offered every evening by the Professor, sometime lay-reader, now proprietor of the Aksident Store where loot from wrecks is collected and sold; the store is adjacent to Professor's old church. Minor characters include Chief-in-Town, a corrupt politician; Particulars Joe, a corrupt policeman; and a gang of thugs available for political use, led by Say Tokyo Kid. Other notable characters are a former driver Kotonu, his tout Samson, a would-be driver Salubi, as well as a man-god Murano. Through Murano the church's Christianity is juxtaposed with the *agemo* mask of traditional Yoruba belief. How these elements are woven together is beyond the scope of this paper.

The *Express* article shows the critic only something of Soyinka's state of mind regarding roads sometime before composing the play. The playwright had a richer experience than most Nigerians of the terrors of the roads. Of Mile 34 on the Lagos-Ibadan road he said, "at this spot I have myself skidded – a mild initiation both times – and at least six times been with a driver who splashed his vehicle all over the road." Upon his return to Nigeria in early 1960, Soyinka had undertaken extensive travel to study manifestations of drama in Nigeria, using his post at the University of Ibadan as a base. As part of the same project he later traveled between Lagos and Ibadan almost as a commuter, rehearsing a theatrical company in the former while living in the latter.[4] As a result he came to know the major highways with painful familiarity. The rolling countryside of western Nigeria, cut by creeks and streams, some of them with deep channels, required that these highways include tortuous curves and bridges subject to damage in the heavy rains. Sometimes bends and bridges existed in close association.

In *The Road* a major accident occurs when a speeding lorry is not sustained on a "rotten" bridge (pp. 34, 55-59). Nearby apparently is a curve, marked by a sign (p. 8). That the two are associated is not clear in the play; that is, it is not said directly that the damaged bridge is concealed by a curve. Rather, the doomed kola-nut lorry, carrying passengers, arrives at, and goes off, the bridge; a following lorry makes a sudden halt in time to avoid the partially destroyed bridge. The sudden halt could – but need not – imply an associated curve.

Whether the curve and the bridge are associated or not, the "rotten" bridge is a spiritual sister of "the last bridge on Ikorodu road" mentioned earlier. The terror of that bridge was not the result of neglect (it was not rotten) but rather the result of apparently insane officiousness: "the genius of a road engineer has gone and built an island in the middle of that bend just before the bridge." Worse, "a concrete pillar guards it at either end." The pillar was the object that caught motorists coming around the bend, and what enraged Soyinka was that as often as the pillar was destroyed it was replaced as an "unmistakable warning of the narrow bridge" ahead. Soyinka asked, "has the repeated evidence of this island not persuaded the fool [engineer] that warnings are no good to dead men?"

Soyinka cares that living people should be the victims of official fools. In its capability to murder, the bend-pillar-bridge near Ikorodu is like "the road" in the play that, in diffused personification, waits like a spider for its victims (p. 34). The difference between the play and the article is that in the play the road is an aspect of the god Ogun, who demands sacrifice – if not a dog, then people (p. 59) – while in the article the road is the creation of human beings, and its dangers are the result of human folly or malevolence. The gods do not enter into it. Apparently Soyinka, like Gloucester, thought it futile to be infuriated by gods.

The spirit world, the world of the gods, dominates much of Soyinka's work. The contrasting objective, material, non-spiritual cause of death in the *Express* article is a matter of some critical importance. The article externally defines the fact that use of the *agemo*, the *egungun*, in *The Road* is metaphor. Although the Yoruba spiritual world is alive artistically, the critic must not confuse that artistic reality with any defined Soyinka world view. The Yoruba world view does not control Soyinka; Soyinka controls the Yoruba world view in so far as he can manipulate it to his aesthetic purpose. How far, to what extent, Soyinka can manipulate Yoruba religion is of course limited. He is conscious of the limits of the religion and knows that informed Yoruba readers are among his critics. After such limits are taken into account, however, it is clear that Soyinka creates the precise spiritual world in *The Road* that suits his artistic purpose.

That purpose is served in the play through characters who are believers in the Yoruba gods and believers in the world view those gods imply. The degree of belief varies as does the quality of belief. Kotonu, a kind of apostate, will not kill a dog for Ogun (p. 59), while Murano, killed by Kotonu while an *egungun*, is more than a believer. He is a god, captured by Professor in his life-death-spirit transition, or *agemo*, state.

At the same time, the religious, the spiritual, characters live in a practical world of automobile parts, licenses, political meetings, and the like. Thus when Professor first appears in the play he carries an object of practical value in the objective world of ordinary highways: *"a road-sign bearing a squiggle and the one word, 'BEND'."* This sign is a direct borrowing from Soyinka's infamous Mile 34 mentioned earlier. It seems that Mile 34 too had a sign "CORNER" – "at the most eighteen inches by nine." This is a convenient size for Professor to carry, though the design has changed. The sign at Mile 34 was, Soyinka says, completely covered by weeds for "at least a total of fifteen months" during which period this sole warning "remained totally invisible [to the driver] travelling from Ibadan." The Professor's sign too was hidden. Of it he says (p. 8),

> God God God but there is a mystery in everything. A new discovery every hour – and I am used to that, but that I should be led to where this was hidden, sprouted in secret for heaven knows how long... for there was no doubt about it, this word was growing, it was growing from earth until I plucked it.

The link to Mile 34 is fairly obvious. It is confirmed when Professor reveals that three people died in an accident at the sign – an accident, ironically, that exposed the hidden sign (pp. 11-12).

Of course the horrors of roads in Nigeria are familiar still to travelers there; Soyinka did not need to write the *Express* article to prepare himself for the play. Rather, the article serves to show that, early in 1962, the idea of those horrors was well in Soyinka's mind.

Published September 18, 1960, and presumably broadcast shortly before, Soyinka's radio broadcast satire "Oga Look Properly" shows no similar outrage. Rather, it seems a pure amusement. It is the monologue of a passenger lorry, created, it says of itself, from the impact of two lorries at a roundabout. Perhaps Soyinka had not yet been sufficiently traumatized by the horror of the highway, so in this playful piece there is no death. Although little of the monologue is relevant to the drama, a few elements show that the intellectual process that created the drama had already begun.

Rasaki, the driver who caused the accident at the roundabout, was high on marijuana when he misread a sign, "Keep Left," as "Keep Right" – with spectacular consequence. Marijuana is, of course, the delight of Say Tokyo

Kid and his fellow layabouts in *The Road*. The policeman in the play is anticipated in the satirically portrayed police inspector Ogun Epe – who is the "Oga" of the title. Ogun Epe inspects the reconstructed lorry for violations (obvious without search) while the driver, his apprentice, and, finally, even the passengers chorus "Oga look properly," leading the Inspector at last to find and collect his bribe: shillings hidden in a niche in the roof. The alertness, probity, and corruptability of Ogun Epe all delightfully anticipate the character of the drama's Particulars Joe.

Then, at about the same time the *Express* article was published, *The Horn* published what is unquestionably a preliminary sketch for a character in *The Road*, Say Tokyo Kid – a preliminary sketch, that is, for a play that Soyinka had almost certainly not yet contemplated writing.

Say Tokyo's fate in the poem would seem to preclude his appearance in the play. "The Kid," says the poem at its end,

Lay up-axled, his head ungeared, his proud
Dakar-to-Yola lungs, rudely decarbonised.

In contrast, in the last moments of the play, Say Tokyo stabs Professor fatally and then is lifted by the *egungun* (mask) and smashed on a bench. "*Say Tokyo tries to rise, rolls over onto the ground and clutches the train of the mask to him.*" The audience can hardly fail to suppose that, like Professor, the Kid is dead at the play's end.

Before proceeding to similarities between the two Say Tokyos, it would be well to dwell for a moment on his death in the play and its implications. Say Tokyo is, as Oyin Ogunba asserts, "a disreputable character," but I see no reason why Ogunba should for that reason deny the Kid's devotion to his traditional religion.[5] Say Tokyo and the Professor are two poles in relation to Murano, the palm wine tapper, killed while in the *egungun* state, the living god of the play. To Professor, former Christian lay reader, Murano is a captive god (as was noticed above) and a means, Professor believes, toward the Word he failed to find in the church. Professor believes in Murano rather as Samson believes in the spider he repeatedly examines during the course of the play; Murano is an object to Professor. On the other hand, to Say Tokyo Kid, Professor's use of the *egungun* is "sacrilege" (p. 95). Salubi, terrified, looks to the Kid to stop the mad action and gives him the knife with which he stabs Professor. Say Tokyo Kid respects the god and fears its power; Professor does not. All three, Professor, Say Tokyo, and the god, pass into what Professor calls "death's revelation" (p. 93) in the final moments of the play. It is they who by accident (Murano), by over-curiosity (Professor), or by choice (Say Tokyo) have lived throughout the drama intimately with the spirit world. Their deaths, and their deaths only, are appropriate at the end.

Say Tokyo's connection with the spirit world links most profoundly the poem and the play: in the poem as in the play it is the god, or spirits, that kill him. This point will be returned to in a moment; there are other correspondences that should be noted first.

In both forms, Say Tokyo loved and hated the same things. The poem reads,

> Timber he loved. Women – fares – abominated.
> Their children fouled the deck, their leisure
> Saw rival klaxons blare mockery....

The faults of women, their haggling over fares, their fears of speed, and their "incessant" tongues, led him to find "refuge" in the forest. "Timber was/ A male clerk passenger" who, in disdain, was silent, "And he asked no change." In the play, Say Tokyo tells of his contempt for passengers. He tells the world of passenger lorry drivers:

> You carrying rubbish. You carrying lepers. The women tell you stop because they's feeling the call of nature. If you don't stop they pee in your lorry. And whether you stop or not their chirren mess the place all over.

And in the play he not only loves timber but timber loves him (pp. 26-27): "timber don't turn against her own son see? I'm a son of timber. And I only drive timber see?"[6]

The more profound correspondence is spiritual, and it is complex. A driver on the road, the Kid has a "gift," "death," in the poem – death as "painless" as his "loves," who are not relevant here. At the start of the poem his utter indifference to the road slaughter of which he is an agent is implied by his footprints, left

> on the grease of taxi parks,
> More prints on police files, and some, in blood,
> Have caked the joints of neoned joints where
> Say Tokyo called for rest.

He is immune to "the curse of travellers" evoked "When sleep/ Betrayed him." He is in the poem thus an agent of death, himself a killer – yet as innocent in killing as in sex (or, if not innocent, indifferent). He is then an appropriate member of Professor's commune since it is organized around the quest for the Word that death conceals from the living.

His appropriateness is intensified by the reciprocal evocation of the spirits of timber in the play and poem. In the play he says, "There is a hundred spirits in every guy of timber trying to do you down cause you've trapped them in, see?" And it is the timber that kills him in the poem:

... the wild
Rebellious wood whose savaged earth unleashed
Its primal spirit, summoned
Death by the centrifuge.

In "the centrifuge" the poem connects back to the *Express* article. The force summoned by the timber spirit is the spirit of the bend in the road. The poem identifies the bend as at "Mile Forty-Six" not thirty-four, and the highway is not identified. In the realm of art, they are all one perhaps – thirty-four, forty-six, and whatever mile post it was where Professor found the word "BEND" growing. The play, the poem, and the article are all about death – absurd and senseless in an indifferent world. The play reflects the satirical rage of the *Express* article, combines with it the compassion for the predator-victim found in the poem, and is rich, too, in the comic sensibility that Soyinka showed in "Oga Look Properly."

The Road is a puzzling, exciting, and rich work of art. No small part of its beauty arises from the complex of motives suggested here. It is impossible to be indifferent to the play because it invokes paradoxical responses. The paradoxes, it may be concluded here, preceded the play, and *The Road* is an attempt to reconcile them.

NOTES

1.   Bernth Lindfors, "The Early Writings of Wole Soyinka," *Journal of African Studies,* 2, 1 (1975), 84-85, and idem, "Wole Soyinka Talking through his Hat," in *Commonwealth Literature and the Modern World,* ed. Hena Maes-Jelinek (Brussels: Didier, 1975), pp. 115-125. Lindfors generously provided me with a photocopy of the radio talk. Earlier, he had allowed me to photocopy issues of *The Horn,* including that containing Soyinka's poem.

2.   The foreigners were a doctor from the "SDA" (Seventh-Day Adventist) hospital and "a Dutch factor"; both had stopped, given aid, and were using their cars to carry victims.

3.   *The Road* (London: Oxford University Press, 1965), p. 66 (further parenthetical references are to this edition).

4.   Gerald Moore, *Wole Soyinka* (London: Evans, 1971), p. 15.

5.   *The Movement of Transition* (Ibadan: Ibadan University Press, 1975), p. 146.

6.   There is another, a verbal, correspondence when Say Tokyo greets Kotonu as "Dakar to Yola" (p. 77), Soyinka's epithet in the poem for the Kid's lungs. This correspondence seems merely coincidental hyperbole.

A Nigerian Version of a Greek Classic: Soyinka's Transformation of *The Bacchae*

Norma Bishop

There are numerous translations of Euripides's *Bacchae* into English. Why, then, would Wole Soyinka, who had previously written plays, novels, and poems primarily focused on his native Yoruba culture, want to write an adaptation (in English) of this Greek play, making it applicable to African peoples? In his introduction (1973), Soyinka explains his interest in this play in both religious and political terms. After stressing its "subversive" message and relating Dionysus to the Yoruba god Ogun, he states summarily, "I see *The Bacchae,* finally as a prodigious, barbaric banquet, an insightful manifestation of the universal need of man to match himself against Nature."[1]

Soyinka has long been recognized as a writer who probes particular situations in terms of universal human themes. Yet while recognizing this fact, Western readers may perhaps gain deeper appreciation of Soyinka's impact by understanding the contexts from which his art derives. Having had the benefit of both African and European theatrical traditions, Soyinka forges a unique brand of theatre. This essay investigates certain political and mythic elements, which, though present in much of Soyinka's writing, are highlighted in their explicit juxtaposition to Greek tradition.[2] Andre Lefevere suggests that Soyinka has achieved a consummate translation with *The Bacchae,* because of his "attempt to translate not only the linguistic circle but the cultural circle and the circle of literary procedures as well," further, by his attempt to influence "the cultural and/or the literary circle towards change."[3]

Speaking at Harvard in March of 1981, Soyinka described the roots of African guerilla theatre.[4] In situations of cultural oppression, actors and writers are forced to use "hit and run" tactics, at times performing in abandoned buildings or on the backs of trucks, and risking arrest or even death for offending government leaders. Even audiences are at risk, where such performances are known to be illegal. Soyinka's comments brought to mind the role of the Greek chorus, since like the audience of guerilla theatre, the chorus is forced to be involved, not simply to react to the play. Here the term *participant theatre* has especially real significance; it is not merely an intellectual construct.

Soyinka spent twenty-seven months in jail for his involvement in the Biafran War, so he is certainly aware of political oppression. In rewriting *The Bacchae* of Euripides, he has made Euripides's treatment of oppression and religious conflict "relevant" to a new context. He has translated Euripides's temporal setting, after the Peloponnesian Wars, to the period of the post-colonial African Wars.[5] This transformation may lead readers to look at both the original and new versions of this play with revived intensity. Soyinka demonstrates a certain political affinity with Euripides, who in 407 B.C., in his seventies, had written *The Bacchae* in a spirit of alienation from the Athenians. There are, however, other reasons for finding *The Bacchae* relevant to Yoruba and other African societies, reasons both mythic and cultural. Most important is the fact that Soyinka uses the Yoruba god Ogun as a close analog to Dionysus. In fact, both gods may have sprung from similar roots; yet, while Soyinka's Dionysus is clearly indebted to Ogun, Soyinka does call him *Dionysus*. Other cues, more obvious in performance than in reading, contribute to his African character. After describing the similarities between Ogun and Dionysus, I will suggest how these gods relate to a broader sense of cultural and literary vitality.

According to Greek myth, Dionysus is the son of Semele (a mortal who represents closeness to the earth) and Zeus, from whose thigh he sprang forth. The conflict in *The Bacchae* originates in doubts over Dionysus's divine birth, and hence his claims for homage by the people of Thebes. Pentheus, the young king, asks Dionysus, "You have some local Zeus who spawns new gods?" (Euripides, 1. 466). Pentheus is a skeptic; he feels Dionysus is a foreigner and a charlatan, rather than a true son of Zeus. As Semele's son, Dionysus cannot realistically be very old. Yet mythically he belongs to a more ancient tradition, that of the earth gods who were the original source of fertility. According to Mircea Eliade,

> The Eleusinian mysteries – like Dionysianism and Orphism in general – confront the investigator with countless problems, especially in regard to their origin, and hence, their antiquity. For in each of these cases we have to do with extremely archaic rites and beliefs. None of these initiatory cults can be regarded as a creation of the Greek mind. Their roots go deep into pre-history. Cretan, Asiatic, and Thracian traditions were taken over, enriched, and incorporated into a new religious horizon.[6]

The earth gods are generally conceived to be older than the Olympian gods. According to Herodotus, Dionysus came to Greece from Egypt, so he may well have roots in such non-Greek divinities as Kybele, an Asiatic mother-goddess.[7] This point raises further ironies, since in Euripides's *Bacchae* Dionysus, though born in Thebes, has been traveling in Asia and is considered an alien by Pentheus. Although his worshippers, the Bacchantes, are Asian, Dionysus is a mediating figure between Hellenistic and Asian cultures.

> Dionysus is not the anti-Apollo that Nietzsche considered him to be. He is in the center between the opposite poles, not the god of metamorphoses, but the god of dichotomy. He is in the middle between man and woman, between Asia and Europe, between Hellas and the barbarian world, between heaven and hell (according to Heraclitus, his other name is Hades), between death and life, between raving and peace.[8]

Underscoring the possible connections between Dionysus and the Yoruba god Ogun, a Nigerian religious historian writing in 1948 reported a popular (though subsequently undermined) tradition that the Yoruba probably migrated from Asia, via Egypt and the Sudan.[9] Compare Soyinka's description (in *Myth, Literature, and the African World*) of Ogun, the chthonic god of metals, creativity, the road, wine, and art:

> No other deity in the [Yoruba] pantheon correlates so absolutely, through his own history and nature, with the numinous temptor of the fourth area of existence which we have labelled the abyss of transition.... Ogun is also the master craftsman and artist, farmer and warrior, essence of destruction and creativity, a recluse and a gregarious imbiber, a reluctant leader of men and deities.... His was the first rite of passage through the chthonic realm [10]

Soyinka has implicitly chosen Ogun as his patron deity. Throughout his writings, it is apparent that he molds Yoruba tradition to suit his artistic purposes, which of course is a method not uncommon to any artist (T. S. Eliot or James Joyce being outstanding examples of this approach).

In Soyinka's description of the tradition, the Yoruba believe that the spiritual unrest of the gods began when a slave rebelled and hit the original being, Atunda, with a rock, shattering him into 1,001 fragments that turned into 1,001 beings. "The shard of original Oneness which contained the creative flint appears to have passed into the being of Ogun."[11] Ogun then journeyed into the human realm and was made king. All went well until the trickster god Esu gave Ogun some palm wine. After that, Ogun confused friends with foes and began slaughtering his own men. When he realized what he had done, he shrank from the human realm but did not forbid the use of palm wine, since the wine was essential to his own self-realization.[12]

From both plays and from this description of Ogun, it is evident that the god's effect on mankind is both beneficial and malevolent, gentle and terrible, as Euripides said of Dionysus (1. 861). Both gods mediate between earthly and heavenly realms, but whereas Dionysus represents dichotomies Ogun, is transitionary. The difference, according to Soyinka, lies in

European and traditional African conceptions of reality. European thought has tended to operate in Manichean terms, opposing good and evil, reason and emotion, and so forth, whereas the Yoruba have what Soyinka calls a "cohesive cultural reality."[13] Furthermore, whereas Euripides's Dionysus is soft and effeminate, Soyinka's is "a being of calm rugged strength" (p. 1), one who merges both Apollonian and Dionysian characteristics. Soyinka's conclusion to *The Bacchae*, a communion ritual, as he sub-titled the play, illustrates the continuities of Yoruba experience. The people drink wine (and, by implication, regeneration) flowing from the head of Pentheus.

The sub-title "A Communion Rite" is essential, since communion and sacrifice have an inevitable relation in Soyinka's play. He draws on the ancient Greek notion (well known to all myth and ritual critics of literature) that to ensure the fertility of the crops, a scapegoat must be sacrificed to the gods (specifically, to Dionysus). This idea of sacrifice does not occur in Euripides's play; it is brought out in Soyinka's version. At first, the chosen scapegoat is not the king, but an old slave. Of major importance to Soyinka's theme is the transference from sacrificing the slave to sacrificing the king. As the rebellious slave leader argues, "Why us? Why always us?... the rites bring us nothing. Let those to whom the profits go bear the burden of the old year dying" (p. 4). The responsibility for the ritual is thus transferred from the elite to the masses, who adopt Bacchus as their god and reject the "state religion" that demands their sacrifice. Through communal participation, they enhance their social power, as Soyinka emphasizes in his introduction to the play (p. x). By drinking the king's blood, the community as a whole partakes of his power and all are revitalized and unified.

This theme of communal participation is latent in Euripides's version, but Euripides ends with retribution, not communion or regeneration. According to William Arrowsmith (upon whose translation Soyinka depends), this play is not an "anthropological passion-play of the mystical scapegoat or Year-Daimon" (Euripides, translator's introduction, pp. 143-144). Nor is Soyinka's version, although he makes more use of this theme, which also appeared in *The Strong Breed*.[14] The idea of sacrifice and communal ritual unifies political and religious themes in both of these plays by Soyinka.

Both Euripides and Soyinka deal with the problem of stale, empty ritual traditions, as well as jingoistic attraction to the new. Cadmus and Teiresias represent the inherited wisdom of the elders. Euripides has Teiresias say,

> We are the heirs of custom and traditions hallowed by age and handed down to us by our fathers. No quibbling logic can topple them, whatever subtleties this clever age invents. (11. 201-204)

Pentheus, on the other hand, is an iconoclast who would rather trust his own wisdom (Apollo is the only god he worships) and not accept anything foreign, strange, or undignified. He tries to suppress Dionysian ritual, but this attempt only leads to its extreme expression as the god demands his due.

In *The Strong Breed* as in this play, it is a central concern that the scapegoat is no longer just symbolically flogged (as Teiresias was) or an unimportant person soon to die anyway (as the old slave is), but a vital young leader, here passionately slain by his mother. Whereas Eman's people believe in the efficacy of symbolic sacrifice, in *The Bacchae* the actual death of Pentheus is the necessary dramatic act by which Thebes can be reborn and freed from the dragon's teeth with which Cadmus sowed the land. Soyinka has Teiresias say,

> Perhaps our life-sustaining earth
> Demands... a little more... sometimes, a more
> Than token offering for her own needful renewal. (p. 96)

Soyinka's implications go beyond Greek mythology and culture. In other plays (such as *Kongi's Harvest*), he shows the insidiousness of empty rhetoric, be it traditional platitudes or modern political jargon, and the need for sincerity and human concern.

In *The Life-Giving Myth*, A. M. Hocart's discussion of ritual and emotion sheds light on the relation between enactors of ritual and those who benefit from ritual and between token ritual and sincerely felt ritual:

> Ritual is a social activity, and so requires an organization, and organization means hierarchy. Emotion breaks up the organization as it breaks up the performance. Emotional cults are at once individualistic and gregarious, individualistic in so far as all the actors do it together, and their whims are monotonously alike.... Emotional rituals are democratic.[15]

Hocart theorizes that "the greater the emotion the less the ritual," that rituals are worked out so consistently that emotions cannot be totally freed.[16] Ritual is thus a way of controlling emotion, while at the same time a way of expressing some degree of controlled emotion. Hence, in Soyinka's play Teiresias is outraged that the floggers, having forgotten that this is only a ritual, have really hurt him.

> Can't you bastards even tell the difference between ritual and reality?... Symbolic flogging, that is what I keep trying to drum into your thick heads. (p. 9)

One flogger, overcome by the emotional effect of Dionysus appearing among the slaves and vestals, responds, "It's all that incantation. It soaks in your brain and you can't feel yourself anymore" (p. 9). Similarly, Eman in *The Strong Breed,* after offering himself as victim, condemns the brutality of the actual killing, which in his village is purely symbolic (his father tells him that he has carried off their village's evil for over twenty years).[17]

The theme of ritual and emotion in *The Bacchae* eventually spills over into the sphere of political and social reality. The question is, who will be in control? Recognizing the power of strong emotion, Pentheus tries to suppress these Dionysian rites based on religious emotion. Yet it is Pentheus's own internal chaos that causes him to see corruption in others, despite Teiresias's comment, "But even in the rites of Dionysus, the chaste woman will not be corrupted" (Euripides, 1.3 18). Pentheus cannot understand how people can enjoy festive release without corruption.[18] He smells rottenness all around him. Euripides has him say, "When once you see the glint of wine shining at the feasts of women, then you may be sure the festival is rotten" (11. 260-262). Pentheus's own sense of corruption destroys him; Dionysus lets Pentheus see what he expects to see.

Soyinka also recognizes this problem of Pentheus and emphasizes it by having him say, "I shall have order! Let the city know at once, Pentheus is here to give back order and sanity" (p. 27). Yet Pentheus violates order by striking the Old Slave, which the crowd knows to be an abomination:

> We are strangers but we know the meaning of madness
> To hit an old servant
> With frost on his head
> Such a one as has stood
> At the gateway of Mysteries. (p. 37)

When even one person steps out of place, he disrupts universal order. The consequences are even greater when this disruptive element is a king. He must be sacrificed to restore harmony. Euripides's play stresses the theme of order. His chorus cries out, "O Justice, principle of order, spirit of custom, come! Be manifest; reveal yourself with a sword!" (11. 991-992).

In not recognizing Semele's worth, the women too reflect Pentheus's madness and the kingdom's disorder. As punishment, Dionysus removes them from their proper realm, their homes, saying (11. 33-35),

> I have stung them with frenzy, hounded them from home up to the mountains where they wander, crazed of mind... Every woman in Thebes – but the women only – I drove from home, mad.

As if it were not enough to remove them from their looms and their children, when Pentheus becomes more recalcitrant and stubborn, Dionysus turns the women into vicious, wild beasts, and so maddens Agave that she cannot recognize her own son, Pentheus.

Thus the principle of order is used to extact vengeance. Pentheus is pulled down from the tree-tops and torn apart like a beast. Agave mounts Pentheus's head high above the doorpost, only to bring it down later when she discovers her errors. Euripides's characters, too late, learn that Dionysus is an agent of divine justice.

Another medium for revenge is the perversion and destruction of rationality. Pentheus prides himself on his reason, as we see in his spirited stichomythic debates with Dionysus, when he condescendingly tells Dionysus, "You wrestle well – when it comes to words" (Euripides, 1. 490). Yet, Dionysus comes out the victor through his subtlety. Dionysus not only out-reasons Pentheus, he hypnotizes him and makes him drunk, until Pentheus says, "I seem to see two suns blazing in the heavens. And now two Thebes, two cities, and each with seven gates. And you – you are a bull" (11. 919-920). This, it turns out, is both a drunken vision and a true vision.

The ultimate degradation and delusion of Pentheus, however, occurs when he lets himself be dressed as a woman so he can spy on the Maenads. Soyinka develops this image more fully by having Dionysus wrap Pentheus in a chain of delusion (Ogun, remember, is a god of metal). Soyinka's Dionysus creates two visions of weddings, first a traditional but cold, formal one, among nobles, then one with the warm, loving image of Christ turning water into communion wine (pp. 68-69). Here Soyinka has temporarily underplayed Euripides's political implications and stressed the religious connotations. Sardonically, Dionysus tells Pentheus to reject illusion and seek truth on the mountain:

> You are a king. You have to administer.
> Don't take shadows too seriously. Reality
> Is your only safety. Continue to reject illusion. (p. 69)

Is Dionysus telling Pentheus indirectly that mercy is not for him or should this be read ironically? Soyinka creates a gentler Dionysus than does Euripides, one who reveals his divine poser to the audience (although Pentheus is too blind to see it) and who plays a Christ-like role.

The fragility of reason is clearly evident in Agave, Pentheus's mother, whose madness is her punishment and the medium of Pentheus's punishment. In Euripides's version, the return of her sanity only makes things worse, but in Soyinka's she sees better because of her former insanity. Cadmus cries out, "Why us?" and she replies, "Why not?" (p. 97).

Euripides's sacrificial ritual ends in merciless destruction of the royal family, Pentheus dismembered, Agave banished, and Cadmus and his wife doomed to become serpents leading a barbarian host. All have come to a horrified realization of Dionysus's divinity, but realization comes too late. "When there was time, you did not know me" (1. 1345). Cadmus seeks pity from Dionysus, but Agave recognizes that Dionysus is necessity, the hand of fate, and cannot be propitiated. Pity in Euripides's world can exist only among these doomed mortals:

> Agave: I pity you, Father.
>
> Cadmus: And I pity you, my child, and I grieve for your poor sisters. I pity them. (11. 1372-1374)

In Euripides's conclusion, the people of Thebes are sentenced by Dionysus to slavery in other lands for blaspheming him and threatening him with violence.

Soyinka's conclusion is quite different, with no sense of violent revenge. Not merely a just conclusion, but a re-ordered world, is foreshadowed by the Bacchante as Pentheus goes to his death:

> Come dawn, herald of the new order....
> the hunter's shrieks
> Forgotten. Let the new order bring peace,
> Repose, plenitude.... (p. 75)

In a lyrical passage, which Soyinka took from his own poem *Idanre,* that is sung by one slave as Pentheus goes off to his death, the slaves' new-found freedom is stressed:

> Night, night, set me free
> Sky of a million roe, highway of eyes
> Dust on mothwing, let me ride
> On ovary silences, freely
> Drawn on the reins of dreams. (p. 75)

The stage directions tell of "casting off of the long vassalage in the House of Pentheus" (p. 79) as Pentheus goes to his death. Dionysus tells him,

> Yes, you alone
> Make sacrifices for your people, you alone.
> The role belongs to a king. Like those gods, who yearly
> Must be rent to spring anew, that also
> Is the fate of heroes. (p. 78)

This is partly ironic, since Soyinka seems to believe in the involvement of the total community. Still, it is more believable than it would be coming from Euripides's Dionysus. One senses a return to equilibrium, not the angry endless revenge of Furies. "Now we shall see the balance restored/ O Justice! O Spirit of Equity, Restitution, Be manifest!" (p. 81).

Although Dionysus does not appear in Soyinka's final scene, his music, a red glow, and a wine fountain, wonderful and terrible, spurt from Pentheus's head. Thus the cycle is complete. Pentheus, the rejecter of Dionysus, has become the source of Dionysus. In this version, unlike that of Euripides, there is no need for pity because no one suffers without finding some positive resolution.

I have described the final communion rite in some detail to stress the religious syncretism latent in Euripides's play that Soyinka brings to the fore. Many readers of Euripides know little about the historical context of the play. Soyinka creates a new historical context, which in some ways violates the original Euripidean spirit.

Not only Ogun, the transitional Yoruba deity, but also Christ, the transitional, mediating Christian deity, is foregrounded. This syncretic mixing of traditions, which includes the Asian origins of Ogun-Dionysus's worshippers, is common in Africa and in Latin America, accounting for the continued strength of numerous co-existing (though often conflicting) belief systems. In *Myth, Literature, and the African World*, Soyinka again highlights the importance of his own favored deity:

> Ogun for his part becomes not merely the god of war but the god of revolution in the most contemporary context – and this is not merely in Africa, but in the Americas to where his worship has spread. As the Roman Catholic props of the Batista regime in Cuba discovered when it was too late, they should have worried less about Karl Marx than Ogun, the re-discovered deity of revolution.[19]

Within Soyinka's theoretical framework, religion and politics cannot be separated. For example, the slaves join the Asian Bacchantes in Soyinka's play because both are minorities. A reviewer for *The New York Review of Books* comments that "Soyinka's *Bacchae* is... a third-world revolutionary communion rite, in which Dionysus sometimes speaks with the voice of Frantz Fanon."[20] But in my view the political dimensions of Soyinka's play are integral to the myth and are not a grafted-on Marxist interpretation.[21] Although Soyinka's version of *The Bacchae* is verbally similar to that of Euripides, it is Yoruba, written while the African states continue to battle for independence. Therefore, we cannot read this *Bacchae* as we might a classical Greek play, if indeed we should ever have read the original in such pristine fashion. Soyinka's situation, and that of his culture, continually intrude.[22] Soyinka mediates between our European sense of literary tradition and the immanence of political events.

In his introduction to *The Bacchae*, Soyinka admitted without hesitation that his Greek, studied twenty years earlier, was "rusty" and that he therefore relied on Gilbert Murray and William Arrowsmith's translations of Euripides, at times lifting lines verbatim. But the beauty of this adaptation is precisely that, despite similarities, it transforms the work by transferring its context, as we do in reading it. The successful interpreter captures not just the words, but also an implied spirit, from a text. Soyinka's re-creation, in its suggestion that a Yoruba deity named Ogun filled a cultural role similar to that of Dionysus, enriches the implications and evocations of Euripides's play.

NOTES

1. Wole Soyinka, *The Bacchae of Euripides: A Communion Rite* (New York: W. W. Norton, 1973), p. viii, x. *The Bacchae*, trans. William Arrowsmith, *Euripides V: Three Tragedies,* ed. David Grene and Richard Lattimore (Chicago: University of Chicago Press, 1959). All further references to these two plays will be made within the text of my essay.

2. Soyinka is not at all unique in his use of classical Greek drama. Ola Rotimi and Duro Ladipo, for example, both wrote versions of *Oedipus Rex*. See, for example, Robert Plant Armstrong, "Tragedy – Greek and Yoruba: A Cross-Cultural Perspective," *Research in African Literatures,* 7 (1976), pp. 23-43.

3. Andre Lefevere, "Translation: Changing the Code. Soyinka's Ironic Aetiology," *Babel* (Spring 1981), p. 80.

4. "The Guerilla Movement in African Theatre," Theodore Spencer Loeb Memorial Lecture, March 4, 1981, at Harvard University.

5. Lefevere, "Translation," p. 80.

6. Mircea Eliade, *Rites and Symbols of Initiation* (New York: Harper Colophon Books, 1975), p. 111.

7. W. K. C. Guthrie, *The Greeks and Their Gods* (Boston: Beacon Press, 1966), pp. 153-154.

8. Siegfried Melchinger, *Euripides* (New York: Frederick Ungar, 1973), p. 189. James Folsom, of the University of Colorado, suggests that Dionysus may have come from Egypt, which would support his mediatory status, since the Greek columns were modelled on Egyptian ones made of papyrus reeds (hence their scalloped form). Furthermore, the columns of the Parthenon were originally painted in bright colors and drawings of horses were decorated with bright gold phalluses – features that violate the notion of Greek restraint and fit more with the freedom of Dionysian revels (personal communication, Boulder, Colo., November 30, 1978).

9. Olumide Lucas, *The Religion of the Yorubas* (Lagos: C. M. S. Bookshop, 1948), p. 15.

10. Wole Soyinka, *Myth, Literature, and the African World* (Cambridge: Cambridge University Press, 1976), pp. 26-27.

11. Ibid., p. 28.

12. Ibid., pp. 29-30.

13. Ibid., p. 124.

14.   Wole Soyinka, *The Strong Breed,* in *Five Plays* (London: Oxford University Press, 1964). In *The Strong Breed,* Eman is the willing victim who, according to his tradition, is essential for regeneration. Eman takes the place of Ifada, the "village idiot," who would have been unaware of his fate (ironically, Eman too is unaware of his own ultimate fate).

15.   A.M. Hocart, *The Life-Giving Myth* (London: Methuen, 1970), p. 59.

16.   Ibid., p. 54.

17.   Soyinka, *The Strong Breed,* p. 259.

18.   Like the man in *Summer's Last Will and Testament* (by Thomas Nashe), of whom Bacchus said, "wine is poison to a sick body... poison to all corruption" [quoted in C. L. Barber, *Shakespeare's Festive Comedy* (Princeton: Princeton University Press, 1972), p. 69].

19.   Soyinka, *Myth, Literature, and the African World,* p. 54n.

20.   *New York Review of Books,* anonymous review of Soyinka's *Bacchae* (February 5, 1976), p. 12.

21.   Anyone who has read Jorge Amado's Brazilian novel, *Tent of Miracles,* written in 1971, understands the complexity of traditions coexisting (not always congenially) in that culture. The majority of slaves taken to the New World were western Africans, and their traditions and religions still persist, the Yoruba, especially, in Cuba, Trinidad, Haiti, and Brazil. Like the followers of Ogun or Dionysus, they are also still threatening to political authority, precisely because of the power of strong emotion that I mentioned earlier. *Tent of Miracles* addresses the same problem as *The Bacchae,* with Ogun prevailing throughout the novel. For example, the Pentheus figure says, "we must cleanse our country's life and culture of this mud of Africa which is befouling us" [Amado, *Tent of Miracles* (New York: Avon Books, 1971), p. 177]. In the 1960s, the Brazilian government, like Pentheus's government, tried to control the African cults, by submitting the cult leaders to a standard religious examination and issuing diplomas of priesthood, to "insure the inner peace of the movement." The effect, of course, was to threaten the grassroots nature of such movements and thus their very existence [Fred G. Sturm, "Afro-Brazilian Cults," in *African Religions: A Symposium,* ed. Newell S. Booth (New York: NOK Publishers, 1977), p. 222].

22.   In one of Jorge Luis Borge's *Ficciones* [English ed. (New York: Grove Press, 1962), pp. 45-57], Pierre Menard authors a very strange translation of Cervantes's *Don Quixote.* Totally immersed in Cervantes's cultural milieu, he virtually becomes Cervantes, so that his translation, word for word, is identical with Cervantes's text, even to the point of being written in seventeenth-century Spanish. Yet because Menard's social context is radically different from that of Cervantes his is a different novel and must be read on different terms from the original. The same holds true for Soyinka's work.

Self-Sacrifice and Human Sacrifice in Soyinka's *Death and the King's Horseman*

James Booth

The published criticism of *Death and the King's Horseman* is dominated by discussion of the metaphysics of sacrifice. The play, most commentators agree, is best understood in metaphysical rather than sociological or historical terms. And some critics go on to argue that the values embodied in its central sacrificial ritual are, to a degree rare in literature, authentically African. Mark Ralph-Bowman asserts that in order to appreciate the "religious mystery" (82) which lies at the heart of the play we must forget "the whole western tradition of individual tragedy" (84). Although the protagonist has the appearance of a tragic hero, "the grandeur, dignity, and pathos of Oedipus; the questing anguish of Hamlet" (94), one must not be misled into interpreting the play in such terms. What it asserts, according to Ralph-Bowman, is not the tragic loss of an individual, but the communal Yoruba values by which Elesin is found wanting, and condemned. "Though a creation of such stature," Ralph-Bowman argues, "he has to be totally and unequivocally renounced" (94). Elesin is rejected by the world of the play because he allows himself to be diverted by selfish individualism from the sacrificial death that his Yoruba religion prescribes. In this perspective what may seem superficially to be the "romantic primitivism" of the play is more properly understood as the result of its quite un-Western theme and literary technique. In Ralph-Bowman's view Soyinka has succeeded in an astonishing and difficult feat. While effectively utilizing the conventions of "Western" tragedy in the play, he has triumphantly succeeded in refuting both the ideology and the aesthetic upon which these conventions are based.

Brian W. Last argues similarly that Olunde's climactic sacrifice can only be understood in metaphysical terms:

> The problem arises as to whether an educated intellectual at the time would behave like this, but the argument fades into the background on consideration of the world of the play: it has a metaphysical design, not a realistic one. It may be that this did not happen in fact, but it happened psychologically, subconsciously, spiritually. (41-42)

E. M. Birbalsingh traces Soyinka's developing "faith in self-sacrifice" (210) throughout his career. In *The Strong Breed, The Road,* and *Madman and Specialists,* the coherence of the playwright's thinking "is temporarily disfigured by encroaching pessimism." But by the time of *Death and the King's Horseman,* sacrifice is seen as asserting "cosmic totality." Birbalsingh approvingly concludes that in this play Soyinka at last presents "a story in which the efficacy of self-sacrifice is convincingly demonstrated" (210-11). Olunde's death by ritual suicide is interpreted as a powerful metaphor for all sacrifice of self – though the word "efficacy" strikes a strangely practical note in this metaphysical context. Eldred Durosimi Jones follows a similar line of interpretation, citing without reservation the Praise-Singer's view that Elesin's sacrifice is necessary "to maintain the integrity of a civilization at a crucial point in history" (115). His explication goes on to characterize Olunde's decision to die in his father's place as an indication of "the society's hope of regeneration and of continuity" (118).

To some extent the direction followed by this influential group of critics is dictated by Soyinka's own explicit admonitions in the Author's Note. Here the playwright warns the would-be producer against a "sadly familiar reductionist tendency" that might lead him or her to present its action as a facile "clash of cultures." He exhorts the producer to attempt "the far more difficult and risky task of eliciting the play's threnodic essence," going on to insist that "the Colonial Factor is an incident, a catalytic incident merely. The confrontation in the play is largely metaphysical, contained in the human vehicle which is Elesin and the universe of the Yoruba mind – the world of the living, the dead and the unborn" (7). There is thus not intended to be any comparative balance in treatment between the Africans and the Europeans in the play. It is essentially about the metaphysical theme of the Yoruba "abyss of transition" (7) and Elesin's failure to enter it. One should not exaggerate Soyinka's insistence on the exclusive Africanness of his theme here. It is the inner, metaphysical quality of the central conflict in Elesin's mind that Soyinka stresses, as much as the Yoruba identity of that mind. In the introduction to *Myth, Literature, and the African World* (written about the same time as the play), Soyinka carefully dissociates himself from the cruder forms of latter-day negritude:

> Nothing in these essays suggests a detailed uniqueness of the African world. Man exists, however, in a comprehensive world of myth, history and mores; in such a total context, the African world, like any other "world" is unique. It possesses, however, in common with other cultures, the virtues of complementarity. (xii)

He goes on to insist on "common humanity." What *Death and the King's Horseman* offers, then, is not reductive and chauvinistic negritude, but a uniquely African "context" of myth and mores. It is significant that history, the third element mentioned by Soyinka here, is deliberately marginalized in the play.

It is easy to sympathize with Soyinka's attack on the naive Euro-centrism of much clash-of-cultures criticism, and there is practical value in his advice that the play's dramatic or theatrical potential will be best realized through concentration on the inner drama of Elesin's mind – expressed as it often is in the most gorgeous rhetoric – rather than on the confrontation with the European colonialists, which is less poetically resonant. However, there is a florid tone to parts of this prefatory note ("threnodic essence," "an evocation of music from the abyss of transition") which may suggest a certain evasiveness. There is perhaps a note of anxiety in his insistence that the actual historical context of the action is irrelevant to the play's effect. The plot, after all, is based on a real incident, though Soyinka hastens to stress that changes have been made "in matters of detail, sequence and of course characterisation" (6). The author, and the critics who follow him, are extremely earnest that we should not vulgarly equate his abstract artistic world of metaphysics and "essence" with any representation of real, contextualized events. Jasbir Jain summarizes this widely held position when she refers to the purely "incidental significance" of the colonial issue and of the historicity of the play's central action (252).

There are, however, other views of the play, views less compliant to Soyinka's own directions. The Marxist Biodun Jeyifo, for instance, speaking for a new generation of ideologically rigorous Nigerian critics, seeks to restore the historical dimension, insisting that the Yoruba world is not, as Soyinka makes it seem, "a natural outgrowth, like trees and leaves, not an effusion of metaphysics, but an elaborated system of social relationships in a precise form of society" (34). He regrets that Soyinka should have chosen to celebrate an elitist (and he could have added sexist) patriarchy, rather than one of the more egalitarian forms of society also found in traditional Africa. Metaphysical systems, Jeyifo reminds us, inner and spiritual though they may be, are specific to particular social conditions and historical contexts. Elsewhere Jeyifo throws doubt on the essential or permanent Yoruba quality of the play's sacrificial theme by drawing attention to the popularity in Nigeria of a traveling theater version of the same story, *Abobaku* by Moses Olaiya. Here the vigorously presented Elesin figure rejects "primitive" superstition and derides the son who has sacrificed himself in his place (Jeyifo 116-17). With such considerations as these in mind, we may begin to doubt whether we ought, in this case, to trust Soyinka's explicit prescriptions as to our response. "Never trust the artist. Trust the tale," said D. H. Lawrence. Perhaps, less obediently appreciated, Soyinka's "tale" may be trusted to reveal more of the author's implicit, ulterior motives, telling thereby a different and more reliable story. What I wish to do in this essay, therefore, is to explore the dramatic techniques through which the play's metaphysical theme is realized and, at the risk of reductionism, to explore the relation between the literal, historical aspect of its action and the wider metaphorical or symbolic dimension.

I

Two complementary techniques are used in the play to convey its sacrificial theme: one direct and highly poetic, the other indirect and realistic. In the virtuoso first and third acts, the richly textured rhetoric of the Yoruba characters transports the audience into a world of apparently timeless natural rhythms. The community expresses itself in terms of praise song and threnody, enthralling in their metaphysical intensity, but affording only an impressionistic insight into customs and social structure.

> *Elesin:* The world I know is good.
> *Women:* We know you'll leave it so.
> *Elesin:* The world I know is the bounty
> Of hives after bees have swarmed.
> No goodness teems with such open hands
> Even in the dreams of deities.
> *Women:* And we know you'll leave it so.
> *Elesin:* I was born to keep it so. A hive
> Is never known to wander. An anthill
> Does not desert its roots. We cannot see
> The still great womb of the world –
> No man beholds his mother's womb –
> Yet who denies it's there? Coiled
> To the navel of the world is that
> Endless cord that links us all
> To the great origin. If I lose my way
> The trailing cord will bring me to the roots.
> *Women:* The world is in your hands.
>
> (17-18)

It is only through the contrasting prose of scenes 2 and 4 that the actual specifics of the sacrificial custom are explored, by means of dialogues between African and white characters. Despite Soyinka's insistence on the incidental quality of the Europeans, it cannot be denied that one of the main ways in which the play's Yoruba values are dramatically defined is by contrast with the attitudes of the uncomprehending whites. Theatrically, this is a most effective device, since the overwhelming majority of any audience (black or white) will be ideologically more attuned to individualistic ideology than to the communalist values represented in the central religious sacrifice of the play. They will need an imaginative bridge to take them into its world, and this is supplied by their anti-colonialism, which Soyinka skillfully evokes. As David Richards has demonstrated, one key strategy is to contrast the rich communal wisdom of the Yoruba proverbial idiom with the tinny vocabulary of skepticism and secularity employed by Pilkings and Jane. The problem with this indirect method is the (deliberate) thinness of treatment of the Europeans. On occasion the spectator may feel that the white characters are being perfunctorily manipulated by the playwright, and when this occurs, doubt may arise about the authenticity of the other, African side of the antithesis.

One of the central passages where a white character is thus used to define specific Yoruba values is the long conversation between Olunde and Jane in act 4, which constitutes Olunde's only appearance (alive) in the play. The scene is the crux of the action, since it is this apparently Westernized medical student's surprising decision to kill himself that constitutes the play's central act of faith in the efficacy of sacrifice. Elesin's failure to sacrifice himself is more easily understandable. Even a spectator quite out of sympathy with the play's religious theme can empathize with his guilt and remorse for surrendering to the temptations of the world and the flesh. Olunde's decision to take the opposite direction is far more problematic, both psychologically and dramatically. It is significant then that our view of Olunde should be determined so exclusively by what occurs during this single dialogue with Jane.

Soyinka appears in much of the scene to be drawing a deliberate contrast between the attitudes of the African character and the European toward self-sacrifice:

Jane: Mind you there is the occasional bit of excitement like that ship that was blown up in the harbour.

Olunde: Here? Do you mean through enemy action?

Jane: Oh no, the war hasn't come that close. The captain did it himself. I don't quite understand it really. Simon tried to explain. The ship had to be blown up because it had become dangerous to the other ships, even to the city itself. Hundreds of the coastal population would have died.

Olunde: Maybe it was loaded with ammunition and had caught fire. Or some of those lethal gases they've been experimenting on.

Jane: Something like that. The captain blew himself up with it. Deliberately. Simon said someone had to remain on board to light the fuse.

Olunde: It must have been a very short fuse.

Jane: *(shrugs)* I don't know much about it. Only that there was no other way to save lives. No time to devise anything else. The captain took the decision and carried it out.

Olunde: Yes... I quite believe it. I met men like that in England.

Jane: Oh just look at me! Fancy welcoming you back with such morbid news. Stale too. It was at least six months ago.

Olunde: I don't find it morbid at all. I find it rather inspiring. It is an affirmative commentary on life.

Jane: What is?

Olunde: That captain's self-sacrifice.

Jane: Nonsense. Life should never be thrown deliberately away.

Olunde: And the innocent people round the harbour?

Jane: Oh, how does one know? The whole thing was probably exaggerated anyway.
   (51)

The theatrical effect of this interchange is clear. The audience sympathizes with Olunde's sensitive approval of heroic self-sacrifice and condemns the white woman's obtuse failure to recognize its spiritual nobility. But although this scene works well enough theatrically, it is, on closer examination, oddly imprecise in effect. Olunde's skeptical question about the short fuse is left hanging unsatisfactorily, and the audience is in danger of becoming preoccupied with the thematically extrinsic mechanics of the blurred story rather than with its clear spiritual lesson. Jane, moreover, fails strangely to see the point of her own account, and this despite Olunde's assurance that she is "somewhat more understanding" than her husband (52). In this respect she seems thematically unhelpful. Indeed the audience may feel puzzled by her blundering struggle to understand (with her husband's help) an incident the implications of which are so patently obvious. She is in danger of appearing not as an imperceptive European, but as a simple half-wit – or worse, a perfunctory puppet of the playwright. And her frivolous reduction of the tragedy to the level of social diversion ("the occasional bit of excitement," "such morbid news. Stale too.") seems odd, even from an empty-headed socialite, since from the evidence we are given it seems reasonable to infer that the captain's action has saved the lives of some of her white compatriots on the coast.

   Clearly, the chief point this episode is intended to raise, with typical Soyinkan complexity, is that self-sacrifice is as characteristic of Europe as of Africa. The essential similarity between the sacrifices of Olunde and the captain carries a significant message of "common humanity" for the audience. Indeed the desire to include this sacrificial parallel seems to be one of the "minor reasons of dramaturgy" (6) behind Soyinka's moving of the play's action from 1946[1] to the period of the war. In the European tradition of Carton in *A Tale of Two Cities* and Captain Oates of the Antarctic, this captain has "played the white man," as it were, dying when required, that others may live. Significantly for the effect of the scene as a whole however, the sacrifice of the captain is entirely secular and practical. He dies to preserve the physical rather than the metaphysical safety of his community, and his action can be appreciated with no act of faith. The sacrifice of Olunde which it foreshadows is, in contrast, essentially religious.

This contrast between the sacrifices reinforces a consistent pattern in the play. The range of concepts and feelings exhibited by the whites is confined consistently within practical, secular, often reductive limits, while the African characters retain a monopoly of the spiritual and metaphysical, both in language and action. Olunde's language in describing his experience in Britain shows this clearly: "I found your people quite admirable in many ways, their conduct and courage in this war for instance" (50). The whites may have "conduct and courage," but these solid and useful qualities only make them insensitive to the different, more elusive values of others. Significantly it is Olunde's experience of this white obtuseness which has been instrumental in bringing him to a full appreciation of his own roots:

Olunde: Don't make it so simple, Mrs. Pilkings. You make it sound as if when I left, I took nothing at all with me.

Jane: Yes... and to tell the truth, only this evening, Simon and I agreed that we never really knew what you left with.

Olunde: Neither did I. But I found out over there. I am grateful to your country for that. And I will never give it up.

Jane: Olunde, please, ...promise me something. Whatever you do, don't throw away what you have started to do. You want to be a doctor. My husband and I believe you will make an excellent one, sympathetic and competent. Don't let anything make you throw away your training. (54-55)

Jane cannot see the health of Olunde's community in any terms but the medical: he must not "throw away" his training as a doctor. Similarly she speaks of "protecting" Elesin from the consequences of "a barbaric custom." Olunde, however, understands that his father's assent to sacrifice gives him "the deepest protection the mind can conceive" (52-53).

It may be objected that this kind of analysis is in danger of forcing a typicality on the characters that Soyinka does not intend. He is not opposing

"Europe" against "Africa," it may be argued, and the feeble Jane in particular is simply a "catalyst" here, not a representative of European culture. No larger thematic significance should be read into the fact that the playwright has chosen to make her a shallow chatterer, flustered by the first hint of deeper values, rather than (say) a thoughtful Christian familiar with the Western tradition of martyrdom and self-sacrifice. The choice of characterization is simply a theatrical expedient to throw Olunde's spiritual firmness into better relief. Nor should any significance be read into the absence from the play of any spiritually aware white character. Soyinka has explained in his prefatory note that the whites are not the center of his focus, and their treatment is only incidental to his essentially Yoruba theme.

Such a reading is naive and quite disregards the inevitable theatrical effect on any audience, white, black, or mixed, of a prolonged stage confrontation between a white, who happens to be materialistic and spiritually shallow, and a black, who is depicted as profoundly and organically religious. Without the intervention of some kind of positive theatrical check (a thoroughly Westernized black character or a religious white perhaps) no amount of prefatory protestation can stop the characters becoming, in effect, representatives for the versions of their cultures that are presented. Moreover the impact of this scene on stage is indeed one of gladiatorial combat between cultural antitheses. Its rhetoric consistently generates a sense that the characters do stand for wider cultural principles. Olunde continually uses such phrases as "your people," "you white races," of "the white races." "You white races know how to survive; I've seen proof of that," he exclaims bleakly to Jane (50, 53). Against Jane and her people he opposes "our people" (52). "We," unlike "you," he asserts, have not "mastered the art of calling things by names which don't remotely describe them." In "your" newsreels, he says to Jane, murderous defeats are described as victories (54). He bitterly concludes that by their war "the white races" are "wiping out their so-called civilisation for all time and reverting to a state of primitivism the like of which has so far only existed in your imagination when you thought of us" (53). The "you" here is clearly not simply Jane. The white woman responds with an insistence that her husband is genuinely concerned "for you. For your people" (52) and protests that Olunde has not seen "us at our best" (54). She admits that there are "many things we don't really grasp about your people" (56). The very pronouns "you" and "we" have by this time become heavily charged with generalized significance and seem to encompass whole cultures. If the scene is not intended to impress the audience as a confrontation between "Europe" and "Africa," such repeated antithetical and generalizing vocabulary is extremely unfortunate. In fact, of course, it is precisely the impression of a wider confrontation of cultures that compels the audience's involvement and makes this scene such vivid and gripping theater. Its brilliant effect on stage certainly does not derive from any subtle discussion of Yoruba metaphysics.

It is difficult not to feel, on reflection, that this crucial scene is more in the nature of a series of propaganda points than anything more dramatically respectable, though these points are scored with great skill and satiric accuracy. The frivolous "fancy dress" use to which Jane is putting the spirit mask, for instance, is a potent visual focus in performance, and Olunde's dry and telling reproach is guaranteed to stir any audience:

> Olunde: (mildly) And that is the good cause for which you desecrate an ancestral mask?
>
> Jane: Oh, so you are shocked after all. How disappointing.
>
> Olunde: No I am not shocked Mrs. Pilkings. You forget that I have now spent four years among your people. I discovered that you have no respect for what you do not understand. (50)

Jane of course has no adequate answer, not having been given the necessary philosophical depth or eloquence by her creator. This is very plausible and allows for a sharp and dramatically satisfying effect. Throughout the scene the audience is cajoled by a series of such pointed contrasts into a belief in the desirability, and the plausibility, of Olunde's self-sacrifice. He is called a "savage" by Jane and an "impudent nigger" by the aide-de-camp (55). Jane, as we have seen, fails to respond to the nobility of a parallel secular self-sacrifice performed by a fellow white, and Pilkings assaults Olunde's father with his "albino's hand" (60). The effect of these negative contrasts with the "Europe" that appears embodied on the stage is to lure the audience into an unexamined imaginative assent to the proposition that there is something peculiarly African about Olunde's sacrifice and also that it is spiritually and psychologically necessary. Olunde claims never to have doubted the necessity of the sacrificial custom. But, in dramatic terms, instead of the Europeans being "incidental" to his sacrifice, as this should imply, there is too much of an appearance that his decision has been precipitated *by* his interaction with Europeans. It becomes his way of "making a point," as it were.

But at this crucial thematic moment, when an articulate, Western-educated medical student is about to submit himself to ritual immolation, one might feel justified in expecting a more complex exploration of the question of understanding and respect between African and European cultures. This is particularly important here, since whatever cultural humility these confrontations elicit in the play's spectators will almost certainly have been imbibed from the traditions of Jane's Europe, going back to Montaigne's celebrated remark on the Brazilian cannibals he met in Rouen:

"I do not believe, from what I have been told about this people, that there is anything barbarous or savage about them, except that we all call barbarous anything that is contrary to our own habits" (108). The same Europe that produced the barbarism of the conquistadores and the slave trade also produced the tradition of cultural relativism to which Olunde appeals here. Without the intellectual tradition of Thomas More, Montaigne, Swift, Frobenius, Conrad, E. M. Forster, and Margaret Mead behind it, Olunde's remark would possess little force. But neither Olunde nor the playwright chooses to explore this complexity. Are we intended to infer that cultural relativism and humility are strikingly more characteristic of Olunde's Yoruba people than of Jane's Europeans? What are Olunde's deeper feelings and mental processes as he reproaches Jane for lacking the cultural eclecticism that he himself is about to discard? Is there no conflict in his mind between the scientific perspectives of his English medical education and the metaphysical perspectives of his Yoruba religion?

It will be objected here that this whole approach is too literal and takes insufficient account of the metaphorical impact of what is, after all, a poetic drama, not a historical documentary. The demand for a more detailed exploration of Olunde's psychology and a greater thematic explicitness reduces what is essentially a symbolic assertion of spiritual transcendence to a question of mere plausibility and realistic coherence. Soyinka is not writing a polemic aimed at securing the practical reintroduction of ritual suicide; he is merely using the historical incident as a particularly vivid imaginative symbol of sacrifice in general and of traditional Yoruba communalism in particular. It is this metaphorical level of the play which is stressed by most of the critics and on which Soyinka insists in his prefatory note. This argument carries a great deal of force. The religious motive of Olunde's sacrifice is not intended to command the audience's approval on a literal level. Very few will be inclined to accept that the gods or "cosmic totality" really require self-immolation of the kind prescribed by Yoruba tradition. Olunde's sacrifice is to be seen as the metaphorical vehicle for a more universal tenor. It symbolizes the determination to be true to one's roots and to assert the value of higher duty against both the internal threat of materialistic self-interest (Elesin's tragic flaw) and the external threat of an imposed alien culture. Viewed as the freely willed sacrifice of individual self on behalf of a religious principle, Olunde's decision achieves metaphorical universality and can command the respect of spectators with widely different views on religion and philosophy.

One major problem with this version remains the very specific and historically concrete context in which Olunde (in contrast to his father) is presented. The action at this point is firmly situated in a particular place and a recent time: colonial Oyo during World War II. And, as we have seen, this colonial context largely determines the dramatic presentation of Olunde's mind. Jane and Olunde argue, in the prose of common debate, about the nature of colonialism, the difference between white and black cultures, and about the horrors of war, their tone ranging from politeness to passionate offense. This is no stylized, poetic setting of metaphorical suggestiveness, such as was evoked in acts 1 and 3. It is more reminiscent of the realistic British drama of class antagonisms produced by John Osborne and Arnold Wesker in the 1950s and 1960s. In this context it is difficult for the audience to refrain from asking literal, unmetaphorical questions about the motivations and beliefs of the characters – and of the playwright.

There is moreover a second problem, generated by the dual nature of Olunde's sacrifice. As it is dramatically presented, in the context of the interference of the Pilkingses, it appears as an assertion of spiritual and cultural freedom. But in its Yoruba context it has a quite different meaning, as the inevitable sacrifice of human life required by cosmological necessity. In this aspect it is philosophically quite distinct from the more familiar sacrifice of self and is founded on a principle opposite to personal moral conviction – communal or – "cosmic" totality. Though both sacrifices involve the death of an individual for the sake of the larger good, they are otherwise so ideologically different that it is difficult to see how the one can stand as a metaphor for the other with any coherence. But in Olunde's case the two modes of sacrifice are thoroughly blended and confused in a most unusual way. He *chooses* to die because he rejects his European education and the colonial restraint of the Pilkingses, thus gaining the audience's anti-imperialist sympathy. But more fundamentally, he must die, irrespective of his own choice. He has inherited his unworthy father's role, and the unalterable cosmic law ordains that his blood must be spilled. The conflict between the levels of the metaphor seems unresolvable.

II

So far the central motif of the play has been defined as a ritual suicide which affirms a specifically Yoruba cosmology. But the apparent adequacy of this definition depends very heavily on the metaphysical abstraction of the theme. If we pay regard to the historical practice of ritual suicide in the Yoruba culture and others, it quickly becomes apparent that the apparently unrelated and free-standing status, which Soyinka's dramatic treatment gives it, is very artificial. The social institution, of which ritual suicide is one specialized manifestation, is human sacrifice. It is human sacrifice, not ritual suicide, that, properly and philosophically speaking, is at the play's center. Ritual suicide does not stand as a unique and isolated custom, and it is extremely unlikely that any society has ever existed in which the self-slaughter of a privileged and aristocratic male, such as one finds in this play, is the only form of human sacrifice to be practiced. Indeed, as the Yoruba historian, the Rev. Samuel Johnson tells us, the form of the *alafin's* funeral as it was conducted at Oyo until the later nineteenth century involved a large number of sacrifices, only some of these being such "honourable suicides" as that of the King's Horseman or Ona-Olokun-esin, whose title implied that he must die with the king. The other sacrifices were of a less psychologically complex kind:

> At certain stations on the route between the palace and the *Barà*, eleven in all, they halt and immolate a man and a ram, and also at the Bara itself, four women each at the head and at the feet, two boys on the right and on the left, were usually buried in the same grave with the dead monarch to be his attendants in the other world, and last of all the lamp-bearer in whose presence all the ceremonies are performed. (55)

Nor is such sacrifice in any way specific to Yoruba or African societies. The propitiation of the gods by the spilling of human blood is depicted in early literary works from both the Hebrew and Greek strands of "Western" civilization, in the stories of Abraham and Isaac (Gen. 22) and Agamemnon and Iphigenia (Aeschylus 48-51). The related practice of burying servants or wives in the grave of a chief or king also occurs at some stage in the development of most cultures. The earliest Chinese emperors were accompanied into the next world by real soldiers before symbol replaced reality in the form of their famous terracotta successors. The Hindu custom of suttee whereby the wife burns herself on her husband's funeral pyre was practiced in India until the present century. Judging from the archaeological evidence, the Pilkings's Celtic and Anglo-Saxon ancestors both practiced the custom.[2] And an account by a tenth-century Islamic diplomat, Ibn Fadlan, of the funeral of a Swedish Viking, which involves just such a sacrifice, is often cited by Anglo-Saxon scholars as indirect evidence for the pre-Christian practices of the Vikings' English cousins, since the burial of this chief, in a ship, so closely parallels the famous seventh-century burial at Sutton Hoo in Suffolk (Gwyn Jones 425-30).

This Viking ceremony shares striking similarities of detail with that in Soyinka's play. In each case a servant of the dead chief voluntarily follows the master into the grave. Both the Swedish servant girl and Elesin have visions of the world to which their master has already gone, which they relate to the approving mourners. The old woman named the "Angel of Death" in the Viking ceremony fulfills very much the same supportive and encouraging function as the praise singer in *Death and the King's Horseman,* and both victims enter a rapt and prolonged trance before their death. It seems then that this particular custom, asserting as it does a universal desire for continuity between the world of the living and the dead, evidences "common humanity" as much as any specific "universe of the Yoruba mind." The Yoruba version of the institution does indeed possess that distinctive intricacy and elaboration characteristic of all aspects of Yoruba social life, from the seemingly endless system of civil and military titles to the complex traditional customs for naming infants. But the fundamental religious and metaphysical beliefs that underpin the Yoruba sacrifice are much the same as those of other cultures.

The Swedish servant girl and Elesin both embrace their roles willingly, out of religious duty. Significantly, however, the instinct for self-preservation still supervenes in both cases. Elesin admits to being defeated by "a weight of longing on my earth-held limbs" (65). The servant girl in Ibn Fadlan's account spins out the last stages of the ritual in a kind of terrified religious hysteria, until hustled impatiently into the burial ship. The Yoruba historian, the Rev. Samuel Johnson, cites the case of Queen Alayoayo, wife of the late nineteenth-century Alafin Adelu, who experienced a similar reluctance to follow her husband into the grave. She "begged hard that her life should be spared" before reconciling herself to the inevitable:

> When the hour was come she bade all farewell and repaired to her chamber and the fatal cup was placed in her hands. But owing to the preventives she had fortified her system with, the effects were neutralized; this was repeated again and again, with the same result. So towards sunset the disappointed relatives in order to prevent an indelible disgrace to the family had to strangle her, and then gave her a decent funeral. (397-98)

The flagging resolve of Elesin in Soyinka's play, so effectively portrayed through his ambiguously sensuous verse, is thus a familiar psychological element in such ritual, though, as Johnson observes, other victims (particularly women and slaves) were perfectly willing, some even choosing to kill themselves when not strictly obliged to do so by tradition.

Quite frequently however the victims were wholly unwilling and were chosen arbitrarily. Johnson remarks of Adelu's rites that

> apart from those who were bound by their special office to die with the King immolation was more or less indiscriminate in order to furnish the monarch with a large retinue in the other world. Hence every one tried to hide himself or herself in every nook and corner imaginable and in the ceilings of their apartments. (397)

Naturally enough, in the vast majority of such cases, the victims were those who could least defend themselves, such as slaves, hostages, or convicted criminals. Such is the case in the sacrifice of the slave girl depicted in Buchi Emecheta's *The Joys of Motherhood* (23) and of Ikemefuna, the boy hostage in chapter 7 of Achebe's *Things Fall Apart* (though this is not a funeral sacrifice). By the time the Rev. Samuel Johnson was completing his *History of the Yorubas* in the 1890s, he could assert that the practice was dying out at Oyo: "With the exception of the women, all the men now refuse to die and they are never forced to do so" (57). In fact he underestimated the force of tradition, and the custom continued, increasingly fragmented and clandestine, at Oyo and elsewhere. Enforced sacrifice has remained the more persistent form since the faltering of the old communal consensus, it being considerably easier to persuade oneself that the gods require someone else's death than one's own. The son of the historical Elesin of 1945 was very exceptional at that time in applying the tradition to himself.

With this perspective in mind, it must seem significant that the only reference to enforced sacrifice in Soyinka's play is extremely brief and is introduced in a context designed to stress Pilkings's insensitive European ignorance:

Jane: Did I hear you say commit death?

Pilkings: Obviously he means murder.

Jane: You mean a ritual murder?

Pilkings: Must be. You think you've stamped it all out but it's always lurking under the surface somewhere. (26)

Pilkings jumps to the conclusion that he is dealing with the sacrifice of a servant or a slave, a not unnatural assumption in the circumstances. The audience, however, with its superior knowledge of Elesin's intentions, and fresh from the poetic elevation of the first act, is invited to see this mistake as evidence of Pilkings's reductive racism. Predisposed to reject racist stereotypes of African primitivism, the spectators (Western or African) readily dismiss Pilkings's distasteful allusion and turn their attention to the only sacrifice that is presented in the play – a voluntary suicide.

A skillful sleight of hand is practiced by Soyinka throughout scene 2, involving the manipulation of contradictory and inconsistent reactions in the minds of the audience. Pilkings, for instance, is made to perform a dual function. He is inevitably perceived as a spokesman for "Western" values. But in this role he is somewhat ambiguous. Although he is the satirized colonialist, he also voices sentiments which evoke, in the back of the audience's minds, such concepts as "human rights," "freedom of conscience," "liberty of the individual," thereby generating a powerful implied context of liberal, pluralist freedoms. (It is important to note that none of the African characters could perform this function in the play, except Olunde, who dramatically declines to do so.) When Pilkings learns that Elesin is to kill *himself,* for instance, he reacts in accordance with just such "Western" principles, if expressed in a crude manner. He is greatly exasperated that his position as a functionary in the colonial system compels him to interfere, where he would prefer not to do so.

> If they want to throw themselves off the top of a cliff or poison themselves for the sake of some barbaric custom what is that to me? If it were ritual murder or something like that I'd be duty-bound to do something. I can't keep an eye on all the potential suicides in this province. (31)

Live and let live. The individual has both freedom of conscience and sovereignty over his or her own body, so who is Pilkings to interfere? He would only feel morally bound to do so if Elesin were violating the sovereignty of *another's* body, since this would be murder. Pilkings here expresses a liberal, non-Christian attitude toward suicide, going back to Seneca and forward to Arthur Koestler. And clearly the success of the scene relies on the audience sharing his general liberal pluralist perspective, though not his cultural arrogance about "barbarism." Such a respect for freedom of conscience and religion is after all a prime component of anti-colonial sentiment.

But this kind of liberal pluralism is, from the "Yoruba" viewpoint (as depicted in the play), quite irrelevant to the circumstances. And it is paradoxically once again the figure of Pilkings who is used to make this clear. A quite different logic applies on this level, one deriving from a more extreme branch of the liberal humanist tradition. The audience is invited to condemn the superficiality of Pilkings's "Western" ideology in comparison with a richly organic Yoruba universe which has no place for individual rights. Soyinka's Elesin has not made a freely willed decision, from a pluralism of choices, to subscribe to a sacrificial religion. Nor has he decided, like a European stoic, that his particular individual life is not worth living. His death is to take place in a totalitarian context: cosmic totality requires it. It is determined by the religious imperatives of the community – the community which governs his individuality and apart from which his individuality has, in principle, no existence. The very name by which he is addressed throughout the play, Elesin Alafin, or King's Horseman, carries with it the implication of his sacrificial function. He must needs accompany his master into the next world, or the order of Yoruba cosmology and the cohesion of society will be destroyed. This is the burden of the praise singer's and Iyaloja's poetic eulogies of the sacrificial victim in the first act. There is not, or at least should not be, any question of individual choice or free will. Indeed, if we follow this logic through, it is clear that the society which Soyinka depicts should properly make no distinction between the voluntariness of a ritual suicide and the unacceptable compulsion of what Pilkings inaccurately calls a ritual murder. The individual will is organically subsumed in a communal totality of "the living, the dead and the unborn" (7), so when sacrifice is required, individual volition is irrelevant. In such a cosmology, what Pilkings describes as murder is a service to the community rather than a detraction from it.

On the one hand then, the spectator feels outrage at Pilkings's interference, on the pluralist, individualist ground that Elesin and the other Yoruba characters have a right to do what they like with their own lives. And on the other hand, the same spectator feels outrage at Pilkings's violation of a "Yoruba" custom, which is depicted as precious and organic precisely because of its denial of any pluralism or individual rights. A familiar ideological simplification lies behind this contradiction. What Soyinka is skillfully perpetuating here, for his willing and cooperative audience, is one of the satisfying myths of negritude. And, as Roland Barthes has remarked, "myth... could not care less about contradictions so long as it establishes a euphoric security" (70). Soyinka's partial and ahistorical Yoruba society is indeed an Africanist myth of breathtaking simplicity, capable of generating great euphoria in a cooperative audience. Apparently, the entire community, with the regrettable, but only partial, exception of Elesin, is wholeheartedly committed to the sacrificial subordination of the individual. All the central Yoruba characters – the praise singer, Iyaloja, the market women, and most crucially of all, the Westernized Olunde – accept unquestioningly the necessity for such sacrifice. Even the Christian Joseph and Moslem Amusa, who, insofar as they are characterized at all, are presented as cultural mongrels, marginalized by their association with the colonialists, cannot but respect the custom, despite themselves. No Yoruba character in the play views the practice with detachment or genuine skepticism. The people are horrified by Elesin's impious and selfish concern for his own individual survival – as he is indeed himself, once his sin has been committed.

Soyinka relies on an unexamined Manichaeism about "African" and "Western" values in his audience to secure acceptance for this totalitarian myth. And within the abstract, metaphysical terms of the play, the assertion of a pure, imaginatively rich, communal African totalitarianism, juxtaposed against a hollow European secular pluralist individualism, is dramatically effective. But, as Biodun Jeyifo justly complains, "In the process of polarising the conflict between an alien, and an indigenous world view, Soyinka has suppressed the real, objective differences between conflicting groups and classes within the indigenous system" (35). The "euphoric security" which his traditional Yoruba community engenders in the imagination of the audience is the product of ideological double-think. It is an indulgence rather than an exploration.

By the 1940s the actual inhabitants of Oyo would have reflected, consciously or unconsciously, a far wider spectrum of attitudes toward human sacrifice than Soyinka presents, depending on their religion (traditional, Christian, Islamic) and also on their sex and social status. Their perspectives would also have varied significantly according to their experience of the persistent attempts to moderate or suppress the practice. Before the colonial period the custom had not remained totally static. At one time the crown prince had been compelled to die with the *alafin* to avoid the danger of parricide, but the Alafin Atiba abolished this requirement in 1858 (Johnson 69). By the late nineteenth century it was claimed that among the Ijesa division of the Yorubas at least, human sacrifice had "fallen into disuse" (Johnson 663). Then in 1886, following the mediation of the British governor in the war between the Ibadans and the other Yoruba divisions, a series of legal enactments aimed against the practice was exacted from the local rulers.

ABOLITION OF THE CUSTOM OF HUMAN SACRIFICE BY THE COUNCIL OF IFẸ.

Whereas the practice of immolating human beings is cruel, barbarous, futile and unjust; and whereas His Excellency the Governor of Lagos, to whom the Ifẹ nation is greatly indebted for having magnanimously mediated between them and their enemies, will be pleased to hear that the Ifẹ nation has abolished the said detestable practice;... the practice of immolating human beings is and henceforth for ever shall remain abolished in the Ifẹ country. (Johnson 665)

The chiefs of the different Yoruba divisions appended their marks to this or a similar formulation, and each treaty was signed and sealed in the presence of two British "Special Commissioners." Some of the versions stipulated specifically that human sacrifice was forbidden " "at the festival of any deity or before, at, or after the funeral of any king or subject," and that "no person condemned to death for a crime... shall be utilised for the purpose of sacrifice" (Johnson 663-64). As the British extended their authority deeper inland in the years following the Conference of Berlin, they nevertheless continued to encounter the custom. The excesses of sacrificial bloodletting perpetrated in 1897 by the panic-stricken Ovonramwen, *oba* of Benin, in an attempt to turn the gods against the British advance, represent only one well-known and spectacular example (Crowder 164). Of particular relevance here is a provision in the treaty between the governor of Lagos and the *alafin* of 3 February 1893 (half a century before the action of the play).

> 6th. That I, the said ALÂFIN of Oyo, solemnly promise to prohibit the practice of offering human sacrifices, and to prohibit it throughout the country under my control. (Johnson 653)

But religious practices with deep cultural roots are not extinguished by brave enlightened rhetoric, particularly when dictated by foreign intruders scrambling for loot. The district officer on whom the fictional Pilkings is based was still faced with the problem in 1946, and in the complex cultural situation of contemporary Africa there are still people who persist in expressing the communal pieties in the traditional ways, who still believe like Birbalsingh (but more literally) in the "efficacy" of human sacrifice, rather than its "futility." It is by no means difficult to find items in the Nigerian press such as the following:

MYSTERY DEATH PUZZLES POLICE
Girl Beheaded

> Does the killing of a 12-year-old pupil, Morounmubo Thompson has [sic] anything to do with ritual murder?
> This and other questions are being asked by many people in Idanre-Ifedore Local Government area of Ondo State.
> Morounmubo, a pupil of Saint Mark's Primary School, Owena, near Akure was found beheaded by an unknown assaillant [sic] in Owena at the week-end.

A case was suspected recently at the university where Soyinka himself taught for several years.

STUDENTS PROTEST MURDER OF COLLEAGUES

> Executive members of the University of Ife Student Union yesterday protested to the Oyo State governor, Lt. Colonel Olurin over an alleged murder of a student of the institution at Ile-Ife by unknown assailants.
> The student, Mr. Tokunbo Mayowa Adeyoke, a part three student of Agric-Engineering of the institution was allegedly murdered on February 11 at Ile-Ife.
> A student of Modakeke High School whose name was not given, was also murdered on the day of the incident.
> However, the students of the university alleged that the two students were victims of ritual murder.
> A protest in Ibadan yesterday, by the president of the Union, Mr. Ajayi Owoseni gave the state Commissioner of Police, Mr. Archibong Nkana a 48-hour ultimatum within which to investigate the matter in view of the complicity of the role of the police in Ile-Ife on the matter.

With this context in mind it is clearly crucial to Soyinka's success that the theme of his play should be viewed, with whatever inconsistencies, in the narrow and partial perspective of the "voluntary" suicide of a vigorous adult male. It is most important also that he begins by establishing the victim's apparently freely willed and profound acceptance of his sacrificial rôle. Were Soyinka to confront the full implications of his religious theme and require the audience's sympathy for an Elesin (or an Olunde) engaged in sacrificing a reluctant slave, child, or woman, rather than himself, the play would be most unlikely to succeed. We cannot therefore be presented with the usual sort of victim: unwilling or half willing, unused to exerting her will in any way within the social context – a mere life required by the gods. Instead we see a virile, dominant, socially prestigious man who is actively *willing* his own sacrificial death, to the accompaniment of general applause and admiration. Indeed death is even, it seems, to be induced by an act of metaphysical will, rather than by the more usual mechanical means.

Joseph: ... He will not kill anybody and no one will kill him. He will simply die. (27)

It is strangely paradoxical that the extinction of individuality at the behest of a totalitarian communalism should be depicted by Soyinka with so extravagant an appearance of individual control and personal choice. Once again contradictions are lost in the euphoric security of myth.

In dramatic terms the function of the isolation and abstraction of Elesin's sacrifice, both from the context of actual Yoruba tradition and from the historical reality of the custom in the 1940s, is to render it acceptable to the audience as a tragedy of faltering individual will and flawed nobility. It is also essential for the maintenance of the audience's empathy that Elesin should falter in his resolve; if he did not he would be in danger of seeming more an anthropological curiosity than a fellow human being. The playwright only barely evades this danger in the case of Olunde by strenuously playing the anti-colonial card and resorting to skillful stagecraft. But the play's real *dramatic* success ultimately derives not from the myth of negritude which Olunde embodies but from its ability to induce empathy with the personal dilemma of Elesin, who, as Ralph-Bowman's heady comparisons with Oedipus and Hamlet indicate, is cast very much in the Western individualist tragic mode (Ralph-Bowman 94).[3] Indeed, despite his apparent condemnation in terms of the play's theme, there seems little doubt that it is Elesin who is imaginatively closer to Soyinka's individualist heart. The part of Elesin, a virile and glamorous figure who dominates the stage through the sheer force of his poetry, is clearly written with a view to virtuoso performance by an actor of true charismatic flair. It must indeed be an extremely rewarding role to perform. The part of Olunde, in contrast, will not be coveted by many actors. Soyinka's imagination is not really fired by the character, and ideological commitment is no substitute for genuine feeling.

Despite the arguments of Ralph-Bowman, Birbalsingh, and Last, *Death and the King's Horseman* does appear to suffer from a perverse romantic primitivism. Soyinka has always been fond of generating imaginative dynamism by pushing his metaphors to the provocative limits of literalness. The effect is frequently brilliant in theatrical terms, but ultimately it is meretricious. In this case, it is to be feared, the playwright's search for a vivid and dramatic metaphor for the "universe of the Yoruba mind" has led him to confuse an irreducibly primitive human sacrifice with an authentically African sacrifice of self.

NOTES

1. In fact, as James Gibbs has pointed out, the real events on which the play is based occurred in 1944-45, and Soyinka's reference to 1946 "is an inaccuracy which serves no purpose." "In all probability he knew only the bare bones of the episode" (118).

2. Lloyd and Jennifer Laing cite archaeological evidence of apparent English funeral sacrifices:

womens' bodies have been discovered contorted as though buried alive. The same fate may have befallen the unfortunate female whose remains were found at Sewerby, East Yorkshire – the body had been contorted and weighed down with a piece of stone for grinding grain, no doubt to prevent her from climbing out of her grave. Beneath her lay the richly furnished burial of an old woman, possibly her mistress. (111)

See also Cunliffe 298-99.

3. Izevbaye's reading of the play is very much along these lines. He sees the suicidal custom of the play simply in terms of "honour" and "the need for transcendence of material goals" and refers to the essential tragic principle of "death before dishonour" (124).

REFERENCES

Achebe, Chinua. *Things Fall Apart.* London: Heinemann, 1958.

Aeschylus. *The Oresteian Trilogy.* Trans. Philip Vellacott. Harmondsworth: Penguin, 1963.

Barthes, Roland. *Mythologies.* Selected and translated by Annette Lavers. London: Granada, 1973.

Birbalsingh, E. M. "Soyinka's *Death and the King's Horseman.*" *Présence Africaine*, 124 (1982), pp. 202-19.

Crowder, Michael. *The Story of Nigeria.* London: Faber and Faber, 1962; rev. ed. 1978.

Cunliffe, Barry. *Iron Age Communities in Britain.* London: Routledge and Kegan Paul, 1974.

Emecheta, Buchi. *The Joys of Motherhood.* London: Allison and Busby, 1979.

Gibbs, James. *Wole Soyinka.* London: Macmillan, 1986.

Izevbaye, D. S. "Mediation in Soyinka: The Case of the King's Horseman." *Critical Perspectives on Wole Soyinka.* Ed. James Gibbs. London: Heinemann, 1981, pp. 116-25.

Jain, Jasbir. "The Unfolding of a Text: Soyinka's *Death and the King's Horseman.*" *Research in African Literatures,* 17 (1986), pp. 252-60.

The Jerusalem Bible. London: Darton, Longman and Todd, 1966.

Jeyifo, Biodun. *The Truthful Lie: Essays in a Sociology of African Drama.* London: New Beacon Books, 1985.

Johnson, Rev. Samuel. *The History of the Yorubas.* London: Routledge and Kegan Paul, 1921; rpt. 1973.

Jones, Eldred D. *The Writing of Wole Soyinka.* London: Heinemann, 1973; rev. ed. 1983.

Jones, Gwyn. *A History of the Vikings.* Oxford: Oxford UP, 1968; rev. ed. 1984.

Laing, Lloyd, and Jennifer Laing. *Anglo-Saxon England.* London: Granada, 1982.

Last, Brian W. "*Death and the King's Horseman:* A Note." *World Literature Written in English,* 21.1 (1982), pp. 37-42.

Montaigne, Michel de. *Essays.* Trans. J. M. Cohen. Harmondsworth: Penguin, 1967.

"Mystery Death Puzzles Police." *Daily Times* (Nigeria), 19 Dec. 1978.

Ralph-Bowman, Mark. " 'Leaders and Left-overs': A Reading of Soyinka's *Death and the King's Horseman.*" *Research in African Literatures,* 14 (1983), pp. 81-97.

Richards, David. "Owe l'esin òrò: Proverbs Like Horses: Wole Soyinka's *Death and the King's Horseman.*" *Journal of Commonwealth Literature,* 19.1 (1984), pp. 86-97.

Soyinka, Wole. *Death and the King's Horseman.* London: Eyre Methuen, 1975.

----------. *Myth, Literature, and the African World.* Cambridge: Cambridge UP, 1976.

"Students Protest Murder of Colleagues." *Punch* (Nigeria), 28 Feb. 1986.

Begging Questions in Wole Soyinka's *Opera Wonyosi*

Bernth Lindfors

In an article published in *The American Scholar* in the summer of 1963, Wole Soyinka, a young Nigerian dramatist whose first published plays had appeared in print just a few weeks earlier, castigated an older and better-known African author, Camara Laye of Guinea, for pandering to European critical condescension by writing his second novel, *The Radiance of the King*, in a Western creative idiom. Soyinka deplored the fact that this allegedly indigenous piece of fiction was modeled so closely on Franz Kafka's *The Castle*, for he believed that:

> ... most intelligent readers like their Kafka straight, not geographically transposed. Even the character structure of Kafka's *Castle* has been most blatantly retained – Clarence for Mr. K.; Kafka's Barnabas the Messenger becomes the Beggar Intermediary; Arthur and Jeremiah, the unpredictable assistants, are turned into Nagoa and Noaga. We are not even spared the role of the landlord – or innkeeper – take your choice! It is truly amazing that foreign critics have contented themselves with merely dropping an occasional "Kafkaesque" – a feeble sop to integrity – since they cannot altogether ignore the more obvious imitativeness of Camara Laye's technique. (I think we can tell when the line of mere "influence" has been crossed.) Even within the primeval pit of collective allegory-consciousness, it is self-destructive to imagine that the Progresses of these black and white pilgrims have sprung from independent creative stresses.[1]

There are two points worth noting here. One is Soyinka's condemnation of "the obvious imitativeness of Camara Laye's technique," particularly his blatant retention of Kafka's "character structure" in his own narrative. The other is Soyinka's emphasis on relying upon "independent creative stresses." These principles, which in their baldest formulation may be reduced to the caveat: "Don't imitate! Create!", appear to have served Soyinka well in his own career as a writer, for today he is widely regarded as one of Africa's most original creative artists. He has defined his own distinctive idiom in drama, poetry, fiction and criticism, never allowing himself to fall too deeply under the sway of alien or autochthonous traditions of expression. In the marketplace of modern literature, where many convertible currencies are freely available, Soyinka owes surprisingly few traceable debts.

Yet in recent years he has published two plays that are undisguised adaptations of well-known European masterworks: *The Bacchae of Euripides*, which Soyinka "conceived as a communal feast, a tumultuous celebration of life,"[2] and *Opera Wonyosi*, an Africanization of John Gay's *The Beggar's Opera* and Bertolt Brecht's *The Threepenny Opera*.[3] Soyinka had been commissioned to prepare the Greek play for performance by the National Theatre at the Old Vic in London in the summer of 1973, and in December 1977 he had made his directorial debut as Head of the Department of Dramatic Arts at the University of Ife by staging *Opera Wonyosi* in an impressive new theatre built on campus to accommodate large-scale productions. What is interesting to observe in both of these adapted works is the degree to which Soyinka modified the original texts in order to achieve his own ends. We might well ask, how much did he blatantly retain and how much did he transform in obedience to independent creative stresses?

The Bacchae of Euripides has already been commented on by a number of drama critics and scholars, the consensus view being that Soyinka succeeded in reinvesting the play with greater dimensions and complexity by introducing African elements that harmonize with the original theme but do not radically alter the nature of the drama. In other words, though he extended its basic structure and rearranged its furnishings, he did not tamper with its original design.[4] The play was renovated, not demolished and rebuilt from the ground up according to a new architectural blueprint. One might venture to say that in form as well as content Soyinka's *Bacchae* remains more Greek than Camara Laye's *The Radiance of the King* remains German or Austrian.

The same kind of statement could be made about *Opera Wonyosi*, which follows Brecht rather slavishly in places and transforms far less of *The Threepenny Opera* than Brecht's play transformed of John Gay's eighteenth century musical drama, *The Beggar's Opera*. Soyinka seems content to pour local palm-wine into European receptacles rather than devise wholly new containers for his home-brewed spirits. *Opera Wonyosi* is a very topical Nigerian satire, but it gains much of its thrust and momentum by delivering its message in a dependable, racy vehicle of foreign manufacture. Indeed, at times Soyinka looks more like a hitchhiker than a trailblazer.

Take the "character structure" of the opera, for instance. Soyinka does not bother to change the names of a number of his *dramatis personae*, retaining the traditional Captain Macheath (i.e., Mack the Knife), Hookfinger Jake, Police Commissioner "Tiger" Brown, Jimmy, Polly, Jenny, Sukie and Lucy. Even when he does introduce a new name, the name itself does not necessarily signal a change in the role or personality of the character to whom it is given: Chief Jonathan Anikura, proprietor of a business school for beggars known as the

"Home from Home for the Homeless," clearly mirrors Jonathan Jeremiah Peachum, and his wife, "De Madam," plays essentially the same part as Mrs. Celia Peachum in the Gay and Brecht operas. The only new characters of any significance are representatives of various professions: a military man, Colonel Moses; a university academic, Professor Bamgbapo; a lawyer, Alatako; and a media man, "DeeJay," who serves as a Master of Ceremonies throughout the play, usurping and enlarging the role of the Street-singer in *The Threepenny Opera*. One comically inflated character readily identifiable as a notorious contemporary personage is Emperor Boky, a hilarious caricature of Emperor Jean-Bedel Bokassa of the Central African Republic,[5] whose imperial coronation, like that of the Queen in Brecht's rendition, serves as the occasion for Macheath's royal reprieve at the end of the melodrama, thereby providing the happy ending that Gay, Brecht and Soyinka sardonically agree light opera demands.

In addition to populating *Opera Wonyosi* with such clowns and clones, Soyinka also took over most of Brecht's plot, organizing the dramatic action into virtually the same sequence of scenes as had been used in *The Threepenny Opera*. Among Soyinka's most notable innovations was a marvelously funny scene in Part One, said to have lasted about twenty minutes on the stage,[6] in which Emperor Boky rants about revolutionary culture, denounces his friend Idi Amin for daring to wear more medals than he himself does, and vigorously drills his goon squad in murderous mayhem. One reviewer of the University of Ife production noted that the disarmingly gay and rollicking manner in which Soyinka presented human decadence and stupidity in this scene, reminding the audience all the while of their own complicity in such inane corruption, made him feel like he was "being served a mixture of poison and excrement on a platter of gold."[7] Another innovation, introduced in Part Two, was a kangaroo court scene in which Colonel Moses, Nigerian Legal and Security Adviser to Emperor Boky, is tried by Anikura's beggars and associates and is found guilty of belonging to a Secret Society, the very kind of organization that Colonel Moses has been striving to eradicate through use of military force. Ironically, the Secret Society to which Colonel Moses is accused of belonging is the Army itself, which is shown to operate according to principles identical to those of other covert organizations and blood brotherhoods officially defined as illegal. Here Soyinka is having fun with the same kind of paradox that had intrigued his predecessors: that people high and low, powerful and powerless, were equally corrupt, the only difference being that those at the bottom of society often got punished for their crimes.

The songs Soyinka used in *Opera Wonyosi* came from a variety of sources, hardly any of which were African. He grafted new words onto well-known Euro-American tunes, much as Gay had done with old English airs in

The Beggar's Opera. For instance, he borrowed Kurt Weill's famous score for the theme song, the "Moritat of Mackie the Knife," but changed Brecht's lyrics to suit his Nigerian audience; he also retained Weill's music for "Pirate Jenny" in a later scene.[8] Similarly, the English ballad "Who Killed Cock Robin?" became transformed into "Who Killed Nio-Niga?" Other melodies recognizable from Soyinka's lyrics include such popular favorites as "The Saint Louis Blues," the hippopotamus song from Michael Flanders and Donald Swann's *At the Drop of a Hat,* and at least one Nigerian "highlife" tune,[9] but there is no evidence that any traditional African songs or indigenous musical instruments were utilized. Musically *Opera Wonyosi* was an eclectic Western medley.

This is not to say that Soyinka's effort to adapt an alien art form was unsuccessful. *Opera Wonyosi* may have retained a Brechtian structure and a Gayish agility of wit, but Soyinka managed to turn the flavor of the farce into something characteristically African. Indeed, though all the action is presented as taking place in the Central African Republic, it is not difficult to identify specific Nigerian targets of his satire.[10] Even Emperor Boky is a representative figure hand-picked from an extended family of African military rulers, some of whom were in power in Nigeria when this opera was composed and performed. Military rule itself is mercilessly lampooned, and the charges brought against Colonel Moses at his trial – charges of arson, rape, assault, and murder alleged by the government to have been committed by "unknown soldiers" – have an uncomfortably close correlation with real happenings in post-war Nigeria. It is not surprising that at least one member of Soyinka's cast felt that a good deal of the military satire might have to be toned down or eliminated if the opera were to be performed outside the university campus.[11] Soyinka was tweaking some very prominent public noses, just as John Gay had done 250 years before.

To illustrate how Soyinka gave his adaptation of a foreign entertainment a local resonance, here is a portion of the scene in which a fresh recruit to Peachum's Establishment for Beggars is being introduced to the costumes that will enable him to ply his new trade most effectively.[12] Gay did not have a scene of this sort in *The Beggar's Opera,* so we'll start with Brecht's version in *The Threepenny Opera*:

(*He draws back the linen curtain in front of a showcase in which are standing five wax models.*)

FILCH: What's that?

PEACHUM: These are the five basic types of misery best adapted to touching the human heart. The sight of them induces that unnatural state of mind in which a man is actually willing to give money away.

Outfit A: Victim of the Progress of Modern Traffic. The Cheerful Cripple, always good-tempered – *(He demonstrates it.)* – always carefree, effect heightened by a mutilated arm.

Outfit B: Victim of the Art of War. The Troublesome Twitcher, annoys passers-by, his job is to arouse disgust – (*He demonstrates it.*) – modified by medals.

Outfit C: Victim of the Industrial Boom. The Pitiable Blind, or the High School of the Art of Begging. (PEACHUM *displays him, advancing unsteadily toward* FILCH. *At the moment when he bumps into* FILCH, *the latter screams with horror.* PEACHUM *stops instantly, gazes at him in amazement, and suddenly roars:)* He feels pity! You'll never make a beggar – not in a lifetime. That sort of behaviour is only fit for the passers-by! Then it's Outfit D!

Now here is Soyinka's Nigerian elaboration of the same scene:

AHMED: (*recoiling*) What's that?

ANIKURA: (*in formal lecturing voice*) These represent the five types of misery most likely to touch people's hearts. The sight of them brings about that unnatural state of mind in which people are actually willing to give money away. (*Selects one.*) That's the cheerful cripple – victim of modern road traffic. We call it the Nigerian special. The next model – War Casualty. Can't stop twitching you see. Now that first puts off the public. But the sight of the war medals he's wearing softens them. The third model – we call it the Taphy-Psychotic.* It's got a whip you see. He rushes around in a frenzy as if he's going to flog you. But that's where we put in the variation. He doesn't actually flog you. He stops with his hands raised and breaks into an idiot's grin – and you realize he's only soft in the head. You are so relieved you give him money. Number Four. Victim of Modern Industry. Collapsed chest. That sits down well with the business tycoons. Remember the Cement Bonanza? Well, to clear those ports they had the hungry sods moving the cement bags round the clock. Pay was – good to decent, and every labourer earned all the overtime he could. What no one bothered to tell them was the effect of breathing in cement dust 12 to 18 hours a day. It's called Fibrositosis. Same as in asbestos factories. Wait, I'll tell you all about it in a song. (*Looking up at Dee-jay.*) Accompaniment please.

DEE-JAY: Ladies and Gentlemen, Chief Anikura and present Company will now sing a song entitled: Big Man Chop Cement; Cement Chop Small Man.

Big Man Chop Cement; Cement Chop Small Man

A labourer's life is a healthy one
It's fresh air from dawn till the sun goes down
Clean exercise; see how those muscles bulge
Power beyond you my bookish don
And what if a man does himself indulge
At night when the bloody labour is done

Every cloud has its silver lining
Clouds of cement ensure my dining
A mound of eba washed down in palm wine
And overtime pay brings the suzies** in line.

Chorus:

I know now it's true – life is a wheeze
The proof's in my lungs when I sneeze
Well, my chest is congested
But the port's decongested
While I breathe like a dying accordion
Seven more years says the surgeon
And you end on a slab of cement
It ends on a slab of cement.

No thought for tomorrow, this Jack's all right
Grind all day long and grind all night
Udoji*** will come when things grow dull
Then watch me jump on a Saturday night
I tell you this cat's right on the ball
Like a sailor in town, high as a kite
Twelve-inches platform, dig the sky-scraping geezer
Superfly/dandy, sharper than razor
Easy come, easy go, God bless Udoji
And the season of ships and cement orgy.

From port to horizon the ships lay spent,
Cement in the holds, on the decks, cement
And I gave up my nights of leisure and fun
For overtime pay makes the worker content
Right round the clock I had a good run
The money came handy, now I repent
A man's lungs for clean air is meant
Not for breathing in clouds of cement
And overtime pay comes to mere chicken feed
When the cement tycoon has filled out his greed.

ANIKURA: Well now to the next model. (*Turning round suddenly with the costume before him. Ahmed recoils in horror.*) A Blind Man, heart-breaking very effective. (*He notices Ahmed's reaction for the first time. Bawls.*) He feels pity! My god, look at you. He actually feels pity. You feel the same way as the passers-by should feel. You're only fit to be begged from. Lead him away – give him the Bleeding-Heart outfit.

Obviously, Soyinka's scene is not wholly original, but he does supply a sufficient number of local details to Nigerianize it. His home audience would immediately grasp such topical references as Taphy, Udoji, and the Lagos cement-loading scandal, and even the jokes borrowed from Brecht about the victims of road accidents and war take on a grisly parochial relevance in Nigeria. Brecht may have furnished the basic skeleton for this scene, but Soyinka is the one who animates it in *Opera Wonyosi* by adding familiar flesh and blood, then clothing the whole conception in national dress.

In the scenes in which Soyinka departs entirely from Brecht's text, he gives free rein to his antic imagination and achieves some extraordinary theatrical effects. Emperor Boky's foaming tirade, one of the comic high points in the opera, would test the versatility of any professional actor. Here is a portion of the conclusion to it – the goon squad drill:

BOKY: (*Examines his watch*) Time for culture. I know I should sing for you, but you can't do much with the voice in the way of Social Reality. With boots on the other hand, with or without hob-nails ... Ready!

Rhythm Section! Ready ... Two – Go! One-two-three-a' four! One-two-three-a' four! Come on! One-two-three-a' four! One-two-three-a' four! One-two-three-dig! In! One-Two-Three-Heels In! I said Stomp! Stomp! See their eyes – Dig In! Skulls! Imperial Stomp! Stomp! Stomp! Studs In! Studs In! Toe-caps! Grind! Grind! Crotch movement! Crotch! Dig In! Dig In! Spinal Column! Aim for the pelvic junction! Pelvic junction! Grind! Grind you bastards, I said Grind! ... Come on Inspector Brown – give us that Lagosian lynch-mob rallying rhythm.

BROWN: (*Snaps into action from a confused state*) Yes your Imperial Majesty. One-two-three –
O nse mi ki-ki-ki
O nse mi ki-ki-ki
O nse mi mon-ron-yi
O nse mi mon-ron-yi
O nse mi ki-ki-ki

BOKY: (*Alternating between himself stopping and exhorting the squad to greater action.*) Those are ingrates at your feet. Juvenile delinquents. Future criminals. Little ingrates! Putative parricides! Pulp me their little brains! Wastrels! Prodigal sons! Future beggars! Suspects! Vagabonds! Rascals. Unemployed. Subversives, Bohemians. Liberals. Daily paid labour. Social menaces. Habeas Corpusites. Democrats. Emotional parasites. Human Rightist Vagabonds. Society is well rid of them. They disgrace Imperial dignity. Louts. Layabouts. Now their heads are under your feet. Your chance to clean up the nation once for all. Protect property. Protect decency. Protect dignity. Scum.

Parasites. What do you do with parasites? What do you do with fleas! Bugs!
Leeches! Even a dog is useful. But leeches on a dog? Ticks? Lice! Lice! Lice!
Crab-louse! Stomp! Imperial Stomp! Studs in. Grind! Pre-frontal lebotomy [sic]
– the Imperial way! Give your Emperor a clean empire. Sanitate. Fumigate,
Renovate. (*He clubs the squad right and left to give them encouragement,
decimating them until the very last one keels over. Finally realizes he's alone.*)
Hey, what's this? A mutiny?[13]

This matches in manic intensity some of the looniest harangues in
Soyinka's canon – everything from Brother Chume's prayers in *The Trials
of Brother Jero* to the Professor's philosophizing in *The Road* to the Old
Man's curse in *Madmen and Specialists*. It is vintage Soyinka, not leftover
Brecht or mock Gay. By taking such liberties with the text and making it say
something entirely new, Soyinka stamps his own individuality on the vehicle
he has borrowed. Thus, *Opera Wonyosi*, though a lineal descendant of
European light opera, has enough native strains in it to stand on its own as a
separate but equal work of pop art. Like Brecht's reworking of Gay, it is a
hardy hybrid achievement, a bastard with admirable integrity.

Soyinka's purpose in writing this opera was to satirize Nigeria in the
mid-1970's, a period marked by military rule and an economic boom fueled
by oil. In a prefatory note to the original playscript Soyinka stated that:

Opera Wonyosi has been written at a high period of Nigeria's social decadence
the like of which will probably never again be experienced. The post Civil-war
years, after an initial period of uncertainty – two or three years at the most – has
witnessed Nigeria's self-engorgement at the banquet of highway robberies,
public executions, public floggings and other institutionalized sadisms, arsons,
individual and mass megalomania, racketeering, hoarding epidemic, road abuse
and reckless slaughter exhibitionism – state and individual, callous and
contemptuous ostentation, casual cruelties, wanton destruction, slummification,
Nairamania and its attendant atavism (ritual murder for wealth), an orgy of
physical filth, champagne, usury, gadgetry, blood ... the near-total collapse of
human communication. There are sounds however of slithering brakes at the
very edge of the precipice ... .[14]

Opera Wonyosi apparently was meant to restore human communication, to
put more pressure on the slithering brakes. Soyinka attempted to do this by
holding up to ridicule and scorn many of the social atrocities committed in
the morally confused post-war era. The story of Mack the Knife was a convenient peg on which to hang his charges against his countrymen, for the
underworld ambience of such a traditional villain-hero was sufficiently
distanced in time and place to provide a large-scale perspective on the
subject of human depravity, thereby imbuing the dramatic action with a

semblance of "universality," yet at the same time that ambience resembled so closely the cut-throat, dog-eat-dog atmosphere of the "high period of Nigeria's social decadence" that Mackie could be easily assimilated as a local folk-hero/villain. Nigerian audiences would not be likely to question the stylized squalor of the beggar's world portrayed in this opera, for that would be tantamount to denying the surreal dimensions of their own corrupted world. Soyinka had chosen an excellent warped mirror to reflect the absurdities of an unbalanced age. As he said rather playfully in the playbill to the original production at the University of Ife:

> We proudly affirm that the genius of race portrayed in this opera is entirely, indisputably and vibrantly Nigerian. We therefore insist, in view of all the above, that the characters in this opera are either strangers or fictitious, for Nigeria is stranger than fiction, and that any resemblance to any Nigerian living or dead, is purely accidental, unintentional and instructive.[15]

It may be no mere coincidence that both Brecht and Soyinka reworked the story of Mack the Knife in a postwar era, for both must have felt that their countrymen had learned nothing from the horrors of the holocaust. Man's unreluctant return to depravity after such catastrophe must have struck them as dangerously idiotic. To show up this dark, benighted side of human nature, both turned to light opera, sugar-coating the bitter message they wished to convey to a complacent populace. By making people laugh at something absurdly close to home, they sought to make them think.

Brecht, however, fashioned his opera as a comment on the evil inherent in all mankind and reinforced by man-made institutions. As Peachum sings in the finale to Act One:

> There is of course no more to add.
> The world is poor and men are bad.
> We would be good, instead of base
> But this old world is not that kind of place.[16]

Soyinka, on the other hand, spoke primarily of the evils visible in Nigeria. Like Gay, he was striking out at specific targets in his own society, so his was a more topical satire than Brecht's.[17] But whereas Gay was content to expose social evils without denouncing them or inquiring into their origins, Soyinka was interested in provoking his audience to raise questions about what their world was coming to and why. At the end of *Opera Wonyosi* Anikura sings:

> What we must look for is the real beneficiary
> Who does it profit? That question soon
> Overtakes all your slogans – who gains?

> Who really accumulates and exercises
> Power over others?[18]

Soyinka thus stands in a middle ground between Gay and Brecht. He has more social commitment than Gay but less pessimism than Brecht. He appears to believe that reform is possible so long as one can recognize and speak out against the evils that man brings upon man. *Opera Wonyosi* is his attempt to contribute to the reform of contemporary Nigeria through song, dance, and satirical laughter.

NOTES

*TAPHY: A by-word now for the authorized flogging of Nigerian citizens by soldiers for alleged traffic infractions, etc. Neither women nor the elderly were spared this experience of public humiliation.
**SUZIES: Local for dashing young women.
***UDOJI: Named for the 1975 wages review commission which created Nigeria's record inflation.

1. Wole Soyinka, "From a Common Back Cloth: A Reassessment of the African Literary Image," *American Scholar*, 32 (1963), 387-88.

2. Wole Soyinka, "Production Note," *The Bacchae of Euripides: A Communion Rite* (New York: Norton, 1973), n.p.

3. *Opera Wonyosi* (Bloomington: Indiana University Press, 1981). The play was initially called "The Wonyosopera," and the explanatory note on the title page of the original playscript which read, "Also known as *The Beggar's Opera, The Threepenny Opera*. In the manner of Bertold [sic] Brecht from a theme by John Gay," suggests that Soyinka was more in debt to Brecht than to Gay. I am grateful to Deirdre La Pin and Yemi Ogunbiyi for providing me with copies of this playscript.

4. See, e.g., E.J. Asgill, "African Adaptations of Greek Tragedies," *African Literature Today*, 11 (1980), 175-89; K.E. Senanu, "The Exigencies of Adaptation: The Case of Soyinka's *Bacchae*," in *Critical Perspectives on Wole Soyinka*, ed. James Gibbs (Washington, D.C.: Three Continents Press, 1980), pp. 108-12; and Albert Hunt, "Amateurs in Horror," *New Society*, 9 August 1975, pp. 342-43, and reprinted in Gibbs, *Critical Perspectives*, pp. 113-15.

5. In the "Acknowledgements and Disclaimers" printed on page 2 of the playbill for the University of Ife production of the play, Soyinka stated: "The author both on his own behalf and that of his collaborators, the late John Gay and Bertolt Brecht, acknowledges his indebtedness to His Imperial Dimunitive [sic] Emperor Bokassa I of Central Africa, who solved the geographical dilemma of this opera by taking a timely stride backwards into pre-history." I am grateful to Deirdre La Pin for providing me with a copy of this playbill.

6. Biodun Jeyifo, "Wole Soyinka, 'Opera Wonyosi,'" *Positive Review* (Ile-Ife), 1 (1978), 22.

7. *Ibid.*

8. Mario Relich, "Soyinka's *Beggar's Opera*," *West Africa*, 30 January 1978, pp. 188-89, and reprinted in Gibbs, *Critical Perspectives*, p. 128.

9. Kole Omotoso [interviewed by Alex Tetteh-Lartey], "Arts and Africa," *BBC African Service*, No. 228 (n.d.), p. 4.

10. Soyinka states in the "Acknowledgements and Disclaimers" page of the playbill for the original University of Ife production that aside from Emperor Bokassa, "the genius of race portrayed in this opera is entirely, indisputably and vibrantly Nigerian." See quotation, above, p. 151.

11. Omotoso, p. 6.

12. Bertolt Brecht, *The Threepenny Opera* (New York: Grove Press, 1964), pp. 8-9; Wole Soyinka, *Opera Wonyosi*, pp. 7-9.

13. *Opera Wonyosi*, pp. 26-29.

14. Preface to unpublished playscript of *Opera Wonyosi*. Not included in published play.

15. "Acknowledgements and Disclaimers," playbill for University of Ife production of *Opera Wonyosi*, p. 2.

16. *The Threepenny Opera*, p. 41.

17. For comparisons of Brecht with Gay operas, see Judith Johnson Sherwin, "The World is Mean and Man Uncouth," *Virginia Quarterly Review*, 35 (1959), 258-70, and Ulrich Weisstein, "Brecht's Victorian Version of Gay: Imitation and Originality in the *Dreigroschenoper*," *Comparative Literature Studies*, 7 (1970), 314-35.

18. *Opera Wonyosi*, p. 83. The question is similar to that asked in Ayi Kwei Armah's novel *Why Are We so Blest?* (London: Heinemann, 1974), by the one-legged veteran in the hospital who is seeking to understand the results of the French Revolution: "Who gained? That is all I want to know. Who Won?" (p. 24). It is probably safe to assume that Soyinka would have been familiar with Armah's novel.

SOYINKA
as a
POET

The Voice and Viewpoint of the Poet in Wole Soyinka's "Four Archetypes"

Tanure Ojaide

Wole Soyinka's international reputation as a playwright tends to obscure his stature as an accomplished poet. Cosmopolitan in outlook, he shuns cultural restrictiveness and freely absorbs the alien into his receptive personality. As a result of this inclusiveness, he successfully blends traditional African culture with Judeo-Christian and Western literary traditions. He belongs to a tradition that, though African, is an extension of modernism. He thus occupies a unique position in African poetry.

In "Four Archetypes," Soyinka displays his poetic gift as he expresses strong views about himself, his country, and human existence at a critical period in Nigerian history. To give universal validity to the events in Nigeria during the civil war, he uses Joseph, Hamlet, Gulliver, and Ulysses as masks to express his predicament at the time. His voice and viewpoint deserve to be heard.

"Four Archetypes" is the second section of *A Shuttle in the Crypt,* a collection of Soyinka's poems about the Nigerian crisis between 1966 and early 1971 and his own detention by the federal authorities for allegedly sympathizing with the secessionists. The four archetypal figures are analogues of the poet. Though unique in some ways, these four personae have certain similar qualities, and the poet sees their experiences as reflecting his own during the Nigerian crisis.

All four are strangers in the situations in which they find themselves; they are lonely, and hanker after truth and ideals. Joseph and Gulliver are imprisoned, Ulysses is detained by Circe, and Hamlet is exiled from Denmark to England. Through these personae, the poet identifies the values he seeks and cherishes. He thus uses the archetypes to universalize his condition. His loneliness is not unique because he is one of many wanderers. His problems of isolation, alienation, persecution, and pain are human and natural. In the course of dramatizing his condition, the poet indicts the military establishment, which was responsible for his arrest and detention.

Two kinds of voice are heard in these poems: the self-dramatizing and the critical. The voice is self-dramatizing when the poet defends himself against false accusations and when he explains his idealistic motivations.

The voice is critical when he denounces the federal establishment as hypocritical, tyrannical, and mean. In both voices, there is passion because of the personal involvement of the poet. It will be clear that the two voices heard in these poems belong to one personality with a unified sensibility because pursuit of ideals inevitably results in rejection of negative values. In these poems, especially "Joseph" and "Gulliver," the poet seems to write with a motive, as he does in his prison record *The Man Died,* aimed not simply at socio-political criticism but at history – a determination, as a witness, to get down a record of the abuses of the violators of his person and society. The poet's self-dramatization should not be seen as the antics of a deluded soul or a narcissist; rather it is a strategy through which he uses his particular experiences to expose the evil nature of his persecutors.

The poem "Joseph" is indebted to the story of Joseph and Potiphar's wife in Genesis. Joseph, the eleventh and favorite son of Jacob, is known for two major qualities: discipline in resisting the temptation of his master's wife and insight in interpreting dreams. "Joseph" is a dramatic monologue, and its speaker is pungent in his denunciation of the hypocrisy of "Mrs Potiphar." He denies the charge of sexual harassment Potiphar's wife levels against him. By presenting herself as the victim, and hiding the fact that she is a victimizer, she lays claim to a virtue she does not possess. The speaker shifts from accusing Potiphar's wife of hypocrisy to rejecting the quality of sainthood associated with Joseph. Since saints are agents of divine fulfillment, they are passive and patient, but the speaker sees times of evil as demanding a "renunciation of the saintly vision" for "instant hands of truth to tear/ All painted masks"[1]; in other words, there should be no passivity in evil times because action is needed. Since he curses and wants quick solutions, he is unlike those holy men who are pious, passive, and patient. He accepts martyrdom, dying for a cause, which is not necessarily a saintly act; he is interested in moral responsibility, not holiness. The Joseph-"Mrs Potiphar" case represents a universal problem because "Time's slaves" continue to be "eunuchs of will," attending the "Mrs Potiphars" of the world. Those who are like the poet, "whose dreams of fire resolve in light," emulate Joseph, "the old ancestor," in the "pursuit of truths" and the "interpretation of dreams." The poet accepts Joseph, not as a saint, but as a worthy ancestor.

The poet employs many poetic devices to achieve vindication of himself and castigation of the establishment. In the Biblical story, Potiphar's wife is left holding the clothes she has herself torn in order to fabricate evidence for the rape. In the poem, irony and metaphor are particularly effective in exposing the hollowness of the woman's chastity. Her "trophy" is "Tattered pieces of your masquerade/ of virtue." A trophy is something won and prized, but not rags. Besides, her virtue is a masquerade, a counterfeit. She hides her guilt in "scarlet pottage," trying to cover up her moral deficiency. The result is negative because the "grim manure" raises "weeds of sick ambition." She rests on a "Whitened couch of bones," another underscoring by the poet to expose her hypocrisy. Irony, metaphor, possessives, and negative epithets puncture Potiphar's wife's claim to virtue and expose her for what she really is: a liar and a hypocrite.

"Joseph" is both self-dramatizing and anti-establishment, a mixture of self-defense and satire. It is an analogue of Soyinka's situation during the Nigerian Civil War: the federal military government is like "Mrs Potiphar" lying against the dutiful, honest, and foresighted poet; and Joseph's imprisonment is akin to his solitary confinement because he was neither tried nor given an opportunity to defend himself. The poet succeeds in defending and universalizing his predicament in a self-dramatizing and critical voice by means of such effective poetic devices as irony and metaphor.

"Hamlet" is related to Shakespeare's tragedy of the Prince of Denmark. The relevant scene is that in which Hamlet falls victim to his uncle's conspiracy with Laertes to kill him in a duel. Realizing the treachery, Hamlet quickly stabs the king using the poisoned sword with which he has been mortally wounded. He thus takes his revenge before he dies.

Written in the third person singular, "Hamlet" does not attempt to achieve the dramatic voice of "Joseph." Instead, it presents a controlled, introspective, and impassive voice analyzing what spurs Hamlet into action in the very last moments of his life. Before Hamlet makes up his mind, doubts halt and lame his "resolution on the rack"; his desire to avenge treachery and villainy is dampened by caution. Even after the ghost of his father appears to him, he is still doubtful about proceeding. Then he decides to use a play to test his uncle. He is "passionless" as he does not betray his motives – he is controlled, disciplined, and deliberate. "Passion" is repeated to draw attention to the contrast between Hamlet's self-control and the king's lack of emotional restraint. Furthermore, it is ironic, and yet appropriate, that he uses passionless behavior to expose the guilt of passion.

Too much intellectualizing made Hamlet vacillate, but this state of inaction stopped when he discovered treachery against him by his uncle. After learning that the wound from Laertes' sword is fatal, he acts promptly:

It took the salt in the wound, the 'point
Envenom'd too' to steel the prince of doubts.[2]

The latter part of the last line, "steel the prince of doubts," echoes the first, thereby unifying the poem. There is a pun on "steel," and it not only contrasts with "still" but evokes "steal." To Soyinka, the discovery of further treachery spurs one to decisive action.

Soyinka uses certain techniques to shape voice and viewpoint. The poet is distant to avoid sentimentality. While it is apparent that Hamlet is a metaphor for the poet, the analogy is drawn in a rather cold way. The poetic distance and use of rhyme and stanzas reflect Hamlet's self-control, a fusion of poetic art and theme. There are many possessives and epithets, which give weight to statements. The repetitions of "passion" and "doubts" and the pun on "still" and "steel" help to draw attention to Hamlet's vacillation and sudden action.

Though it is the poet who speaks about Hamlet, unlike Joseph who speaks for himself, "Hamlet" and "Joseph" both concern treachery against innocent individuals. Hamlet is a metaphor for the poet: the discovery of treachery against him makes the poet bold to say what he would not otherwise say. Hamlet would not have acted decisively after resolving his uncle's guilt if he did not have final evidence of treachery. Somehow, he is an agent of divine justice.

"Hamlet" is a mask through which Soyinka expresses his position during a Nigerian crisis. Soyinka believes that the January 1966 coup formed a good basis for positive changes in Nigeria. He says, "with its lapses, self-betrayals, incompletion, and ultimate desecration, was January 15th acceptable or not as a basis for national struggle?...There were no qualifications to my affirmative answer."[3] The poet thus sees the July 1966 counter-coup as a form of political betrayal. Soyinka liked Adekunle Fajuyi, who was the military governor of the Western Region during the Aguiyi-Ironsi administration. The poet's sense of betrayal was intensified since he had supported the unitary government which the July counter-coup terminated. It is possible the poet sees the counter-coup as a form of murder of his father and the usurping of his mother, Nigeria, by the Gowon administration – hence the Hamlet analogy.

"Gulliver" has as its background Gulliver among the Lilliputians in Swift's classic. After being washed ashore in Lilliput, Gulliver is secured by Lilliputians and is later freed on certain conditions. He gets himself into trouble when he extinguishes the fire consuming the apartment of the empress by urinating on the flames. His action is useful but against the law, which forbids urinating in the palace grounds. Later, four articles of impeachment are brought against Gulliver: urinating in the palace precincts, refusing to join the killing of the innocent people of Blefuscu for conscience's sake, having good relations with ambassadors of Blefuscu, an enemy state, and trying to leave Blefuscu with only oral assurance, not with a legitimate permit.

Gulliver's plight is analogous to the Nigerian situation that gave rise to Soyinka's detention and to this poem. Lilliput seems to be Nigeria and Blefuscu, Biafra. Soyinka would not support the federal side, and he went to Biafra without permission from the Lagos authorities. He also fraternized with such people as Victor Banjo and Christopher Okigbo, who could be metaphorically described as ambassadors of Biafra. With this double background of *Gulliver's Travels* and the Nigerian crisis in mind, the maudlin, complaining, and denouncing voice of the poet who is victimized for being farsighted can be better understood.

From the first line of the poem, one gets the impression of a satire, especially with the symbolic "ship-(of state)-wreck."[4] This wrenched cliché has political overtones in its apparent reference to the Nigerian state wrecked by crises. The word *necropolis*, the allusion to Lethe, the Latinate *obtruding* and *famished*, and the many compounded words in the first verse paragraph create a sophisticated and learned voice. The poet uses antithesis to convey the contrast between Gulliver-himself and the Lilliputian-Nigerian rulers. Gulliver is an "alien hunk" in the "thumb assemblage." In *Gulliver's Travels* and this poem, physical stature is an exteriorization of moral standing.

The speaker describes the opposing side in negative terms. He calls the participants in Lilliput's council meetings "Peacock vain, mannikin cruel, sycophant(s)." It was not surprising that he should "sagely err" in the midst of such people. His urinating to extinguish the flame is paradoxical (p. 24):

> In plainsight I decried an earthly burn
> And squelched the puny flames in fountains
> Of urine.

This "indecent act" produces positive results. This ironical theme of means and ends is also dealt with in *Ogun Abibiman,* where the poet approves of violence as a legitimate means of gaining freedom from oppressors if peaceful means fail. In both poems, the poet sees the end result as paramount. The means, indecent behavior and violence, are geared towards highly positive results.

As the poem progresses, the self-vindicating voice becomes more articulate. Gulliver's "act was rain/ Upon long stunted passions,/ Customs, taboos, parched sensibilities." Not long after he was pardoned, war broke out between Lilliput and Blefuscu. The speaker mocks the Lilliputians, who were the aggressors (p. 25):

> From Us the Lillywhite King Lillypuss
> To you obfuscating Blefuscoons
> From Us the Herrenyolk of Egg
> To you Albinos of the Albumen...

The Lilliputians' false claim to superiority is subtly presented. They talk of "Us," starting with a capital U, a sign of egotism; and the "you" of the "Blefuscoons" starts with a small y. In addition the Lilliputians claim to be "Lillywhite" and the yolk, and their enemy "obfuscating," albino-like, and the albumen, qualities the egotists consider inferior to theirs. "Blefuscoons," with its "coons," a pejorative term for black people, shows the Lilliputian contempt for the enemy. "Herrenyolk" is a variation of *Herrenvolk,* the German Nazis, who felt superior to other races in Hitler's time. The Lilliputians are racists and facists. Soyinka seems to be throwing jibes at the current rulers of Nigeria, whom he sees as arrogant.

During the war, Gulliver "pressed a reasoned course/ Of temperate victory," but the Lilliputians (like the federalists of Nigeria) would not accept a "temperate victory" as enough. He turned to arbitration, but the belligerent Lilliputians were bent on wiping out the enemy. This is a kind of self-justification and self-absolvement from the crimes associated with the war. This section of the poem recalls Soyinka's trips to the northern part of Nigeria and to Biafra. After his arbitration efforts were spurned, old accusations were brought up as an excuse to get rid of a peacemaker. The speaker is accused of being a blasphemer and an arsonist. The antithetical views of the speaker and the Lilliputians are emphasized in the speaker's being too big intellectually to abet their petty ideas.

The speaker is condemned to "capital doom" because his elimination would save those to whom he had been a threat, but the Court Hygienist voices a "dread"; that the speaker could even in death infect others with his disease. Since the poet's death could incite anti-government activities, there is need for a compromise. At this stage, the poem has gone beyond its Gulliver-in-Lilliput base to a Soyinka-in-Nigeria poem. The mask has become more transparent. The symbolic language helps to make this section highly effective. The Court Hygienist is a political-internal security adviser, perhaps an inspector general of police or director of prisons, who weighs the pros and cons of government action against a dissident.

The final verse paragraph is ironic. The speaker is condemned, and his "fault is not ill-will but in seeing ill." "Seeing" and sight-related words are repeated to emphasize the "offense" of the so-called culprit. The good qualities of foresight and insight are considered dangerous in this state. The sentence is not based on justice or law, but on the whims and caprices of the tyrannical state.

In "Gulliver," the poetic voice is self-dramatizing, self-vindicating, and critical of the establishment. Gulliver's sojourn in Lilliput is Soyinka's analogue of the Nigerian crisis as it affected him. The poet succeeds in portraying himself as misunderstood, and his reasonable efforts spurned by the military rulers, who were too mean to see clearly the advantage of his insight. He was victimized for not supporting the petty designs of the ruling clique.

Gulliver is like Joseph and Hamlet in the pursuit of truth. All are reasonable, disciplined, and victimized in their different ways. Soyinka uses the techniques of antithesis, irony, and wit to demonstrate the fate of the intellectual in his society, his alienation in a time of crisis.

"Ulysses" is related to a long literary tradition. Ulysses is the Greek Odysseus, who helps to take Troy and is known for his travels, resourcefulness, endurance, and experience. He is also an agent of salvation; Circe transforms his men into swine, but with the help of Hermes he avoids personal dehumanization and brings his men back to their human shape. In James Joyce's *Ulysses*, as Leopold Bloom, he is no longer an aggressive figure but a peaceful man, acting as a kind of stepfather to Stephen. He is a man of average feeling and intellect, neither as earthy as his wife Molly nor as imaginative as Stephen. In Joyce's novel, he is a kind of Everyman. In Soyinka's poem, the references to sea, wind, rocks, straits, and Circe are Odyssean.

The speaker of "Ulysses" is involved in an internal quest, and his voice is introspective. The use of possessives and epithets holds back the rhythm and gives the voice a languorous and elegiac tone. The enjambements help to create slow movement. The image of a storm, compared to a bird with cold wings that beat "an interchange in time to death and birth," shifts to that of a woman in labor delivering a "newcomer-wanderer."[5] The speaker/ Ulysses is searching for profound values:

I, sleep-walker through
The weary cycle of the season's womb
Labouring to give birth to her deathless self,
One more reveller at the rites, I watch
The years re-lay their yeasting dregs
Beneath the froth, hard soles travel pressed
In poultice of new loam. (p. 27)

These lines suggest a ritual in which the participant drinks and dances to lighten the burden of life. The poet allegorizes the human condition, which is full of cyclic attempts to create immortal values out of painful experiences.

The speaker reveals that he had been toying with "concepts." His theoretical "concepts" in the classroom were a "crystal cover on the world," and everything was held in suspension until the storm of experience came with its thunder and broke things into fragments. (After all, the poem is subtitled "Notes from here to my Joyce class.") He implies that previously he was living in a world of concepts, but that now he is going through the reality of those ideas. There is some connection between the classroom and his prison, between the concept and reality; but the harsh reality of experience is more telling to the poet.

The latter part of the poem concerns the speaker's quest. He is a lone wanderer, and the quest takes him to and through various difficult experiences. Here, Circe's imprisonment of Ulysses, her turning his companions into swine, and the figures of Scylla and Charybdis are evoked. Soyinka's "Swine-scented" and "wine-centred waves" are variations of Homer's description of the "wine-dark" sea. These anecdotes are relevant to Soyinka's position during the Nigerian crisis. He was detained like Ulysses and like him survived dehumanization, while others turned to human swine. The poet's mental activity, a kind of Odyssean resourcefulness, saved him from the fate of others. The choice between Scylla and Charybdis is that between facing trouble in criticizing the military rulers and drowning in the corruption of the government. After all, "the man dies in all who keep silent in the face of tyranny."[6] Despite the dangers and pain of the quest, it results in a new awareness, "our lighted beings."

Like "Gulliver," "Ulysses" ends with images of light and darkness. To the poet, a lonely quest leads to knowledge, and pain brings wholesome effects. The meaning of life comes from experiences gained in action or involvement, not the theoretical talk in the classroom. "Ulysses" is mentally taxing in its rather abstract reasoning. Stuart Gilbert sees Joyce as using the technique of dialectic in the Scylla and Charybdis episode of *Ulysses* related to this poem,[7] and Soyinka might be matching his literary sources to his recreation. His word play and use of compound and nonce words, such as "rain-becoming," "manger-haven," "Swine-scented," and "wine-centred," are Joycean. The language is as difficult as the quest itself.

The experiences of the four archetypes are analogous to Soyinka's during the Nigerian crisis. The working out of the kinship between the poet and the four figures reveals Soyinka's poetic imagination, learning, and genius. Each persona is an objective correlation of the poet's state. The intellectualization elevates the voice from that of a common victim to that of the victimized hero. Joseph, Hamlet, Gulliver, and Ulysses are all heroes; and the poet implies that he too is heroic, having gone through the same kind of experience.

The two kinds of voice – the self-dramatizing and the critical – are interrelated, since expressing one's personal predicament in a political context involves criticism of one's persecutors. By assuming the mantle of the questing hero who has been arbitrarily imprisoned and betrayed, the poet denigrates the establishment that persecuted him. There is therefore, especially in "Joseph" and "Gulliver," a strong satirical edge in the self-dramatization as the speakers in the poems hammer at hypocrites, traitors, and perverters of justice. There are some shades to the self-dramatizing, such as the passivity in "Hamlet" and the dialectic in "Ulysses," but in each case the poet defends his position. In "Four Archetypes," the voice of the poet is passionate and firm and relays the views he wants to be heard.

NOTES

1. Wole Soyinka, *A Shuttle in the Crypt* (London: Rex Collings/ Eyre Methuen, 1972), p. 21. All other quotes from this poem are from this page.
2. Ibid., p. 22. All other quotes from this poem are from this page.
3. Wole Soyinka, *The Man Died* (New York: Harper and Row, 1972), p. 161.
4. *A Shuttle in the Crypt*, pp. 23-26. All quotes from this poem are from this text.
5. Ibid., pp. 27-29. All other quotes from this poem are from this text.
6. *The Man Died*, p. 13.
7. Stuart Gilbert, *James Joyce's Ulysses: A Study* (New York: Knopf, 1952), p. 208.

Myth, Metaphor, and Syntax in Soyinka's Poetry

James Booth

Soyinka's poetry is a great divider of the critics. The spectrum of their verdicts is very wide. At one extreme it is grudgingly admitted that *some* of his verse just manages to escape the gaudy incoherence which is its normal element, while at the other it is claimed that his poetry is a uniquely coherent embodiment of Yoruba myth. Some critics irascibly tug at the intricacies of Soyinka's individual phrases, while others, winged with quotations from *Myth, Literature, and the African World*,[1] soar into realms of metaphysical abstraction, leaving the words on the page far below them. Then there are others who compromise, conceding that there is an element of stylistic mystification in Soyinka's poetry, but finding it either an unfortunate blemish or, alternatively, a source of poetic interest in itself. That the critics of Soyinka's poetry are so deeply and sometimes so passionately divided seems to me the inevitable consequence of the particular qualities of his rhetoric. It is the poet's attitude towards his medium of language which brings out the profound ideological and aesthetic differences in his readers. I propose therefore in this essay to examine the responses of the various critics as a means of focusing more clearly on Soyinka's qualities as a poet. "Dawn," the first poem in the *Idanre* volume, has been given the most extensive critical attention among his poems to date and will provide a convenient focus for comparisons.

It will be useful to distinguish two main strands in the criticism of Soyinka's poetry, although they are not always clearly separable from each other. One strand is represented in a particularly forcible form by Roderick Wilson's essay "Complexity and Confusion in Soyinka's Shorter Poems."[2] With a rigor reminiscent of F. R. Leavis, Wilson distinguishes the fifteen poems in the *Idanre* volume which he considers "almost wholly successful"[3] (note the "almost"). The rest, in his view, exhibit, in varying degrees, "inadequate working out of images and metaphors, slightness of theme, and insufficiently full presentation of the theme or experience involved."[4] He offers incisive verdicts on the expressiveness and coherence of Soyinka's use of words, employing a critical vocabulary which seems exact and judicious. One poem is "annoyingly bardic," another shows "a parade of verbal fireworks," another a preference for "sound at the expense of sense."[5] Many readers, punch-drunk and reeling from Soyinka's verbal assaults, must have felt that Wilson's authoritative, unintimidated judgments have given them courage to fight back against the poet's rhetoric. A less acerbic version of this first critical strand, which we may call "traditional practical criticism" is provided by Ken Goodwin in his book *Understanding African Poetry*. Goodwin is more patient and forbearing than Wilson in his attempts to riddle out Soyinka's metaphors and syntax, and he devotes much attention to a discussion of the literary sources of, and parallels for, Soyinka's methods. But like Wilson he continually returns to a very basic dissatisfaction with Soyinka's obscurity and ambiguity. He finds particular poems "overloaded with possibilities and deficient in clear statement." Sometimes, he says, Soyinka's syntax "seems to float in moody description rather than come to an indicative statement."[6]

No critic, it appears, is prepared actually to deny that Soyinka is on occasion a willfully obscure and confusing poet. Even Stanley Macebuh, whose "Poetics and the Mythic Imagination"[7] represents an approach virtually opposite to that of Wilson, concedes that "Soyinka is, without doubt, a difficult, sometimes infuriating writer."[8] He differs markedly from Wilson and Goodwin, however, in the critical weight which he attaches to this infuriating quality. Much of his essay is devoted to a demonstration that any detailed analytical concern over Soyinka's stylistic and syntactical incoherences is a sure sign of the critic's failure to respond to his mythic dimension. What Macebuh terms the "harsh inscrutableness" of Soyinka's language is, in his view, the inevitable result of the attempt, common to many African writers, to penetrate the psychological barriers erected by colonialism "and to reach towards the primal sources of their being."[9] Obscurity and difficulty are thus an essential part of the poetic effect. Mere verbal coherence is not to be expected on so profound and primal a mythic level. More specifically than this, Macebuh attributes the qualities of Soyinka's mythic language to his role as "translator."[10] His English is, in fact, essentially a "translation" from Yoruba, Macebuh argues.

> The roots of Soyinka's English are uncompromisingly Anglo-Saxon rather than Hellenic or Latinate because they represent for him the closest proximation to the primal roots of Yoruba cultic diction. But the virtue of "originality" lies not merely in its freshness or quaintness but indeed in its vitality, in its ability to evoke in the mind a memory of the dynamism of the original Yoruba.[11]

Macebuh's essay is a powerful and thought-provoking piece, but some of his contentions invite close scrutiny. His judgments about the uncompromisingly Anglo-Saxon basis of Soyinka's language and the uncompromisingly African derivation of his imagery,[12] for instance, are simply wrong. Both these elements in Soyinka's poetry are continually compromised. And Macebuh's argument that the vitality of Soyinka's poetry derives from its "ability to evoke... *a memory*... of the original Yoruba" seems dangerously close to a kind of mandarin exclusivity whereby the only readership deemed qualified to appreciate Soyinka's poetry in English will be that tiny minority who know the Yoruba language and are thoroughly steeped in Yoruba culture.

Macebuh represents, in unusually explicit theoretical form, the second strand in Soyinka criticism, which we may term "mythography." It is perhaps the dominant vein in recent criticism. Inevitably all critics give some attention to Soyinka's mythic concerns and his Yoruba roots. But what distinguishes this particular approach is the conviction that his mythic qualities provide a triumphant justification of, or at least an effective excuse for, the obscurity and confusion which preoccupies critics like Wilson. Indeed some mythographic critics simply ignore the difficulties of the poetry in favor of broad myth explanation. Such explanation may throw light on Soyinka's themes and allusions, but it is important to realize that it is not in itself a guide to poetic effectiveness. Afam Ebeogu's "From *Idanre* to *Ogun Abibiman*: An Exploration of Soyinka's Use of Ogun Images,"[13] for instance, offers a detailed and illuminating account of the particular legends of the Yoruba gods referred to in the two poems. In particular Ebeogu focuses on Ogun's slaughtering of his own people in a moment of rage and his subsequent suicide and deification. Particular passages in the poems are carefully related to this myth and also to the story of Atooda's smashing of the original unitary godhead into fragments. Ebeogu traces an underlying pattern of death and rebirth in these mythic references. All this is valuable explication. But, unlike other critics, Ebeogu offers no analysis of Soyinka's actual poetry, beyond the assertion that the two poems with which he has chosen to deal are "two great works of Soyinka" and that "*Idanre*" is "a most edifying artistic creation."[14] The difficulties of syntax and imagery which preoccupy Wilson and Goodwin are not acknowledged, and no treatment of Soyinka's poetic artistry is attempted, except insofar as the broad account of themes can be considered as such.

A third mythographic critic, D. I. Nwoga, attempts a certain combination of practical criticism with the mythographic approach. He admits to the presence of "problems both of language and imagery"[15] in "Dawn," and shows some analytical incisiveness in condemning the poem's obscurity. "Within the poem an occasional appositional image is difficult to fit into the poem," he says, and complains of the lack of "context" for particular images.[16] Nevertheless, Nwoga remains committed to the mythographic camp, going on to justify Soyinka's poetic oeuvre as a whole on the grounds of its uniquely cogent perception of cosmic realities. Soyinka's characteristic mode, according to Nwoga (quoting C. M. Bowra), is a "primitive symbolism" going deeper than the mere self-expression of other poets. "Images transcend the status of means of expression to become the means of vision."[17] One recognizes here a version of the argument frequently invoked in relation to writers such as William Blake, Emily Brontë, and D. H. Lawrence, whose works are considered to generate a particularly resonant and "organic" union between metaphor and reality. Like Macebuh, Nwoga locates the roots of this quality in Soyinka's Yoruba cosmology. He goes even further than Macebuh, however, in contending that Soyinka's difficulties in retracing his roots are ultimately resolved in a harmonious and "optimistic" expression of traditional Yoruba wisdom.

> The "wisdom" which he finds, and what I think emerges from his poems and gives significance to them, is recognition of the cyclic nature of death and resurrection, of destruction and new creation. If then the situation is catastrophic and largely sad, the informed vision holds on to the promise of renewal. [18]

As in Ebeogu's account we arrive at the universal cycle of death and birth and at the striving of humanity towards harmony with Nature and the gods. This is a metaphorical pattern familiar not only in Africa, of course, but also in much European writing. Nwoga's reading may be felt to understate Soyinka's skepticism. Some may even feel that it has something sentimental about it, untrue to the poet's tortured inability ever to rest in an unambiguous commitment. Undoubtedly the most serious problem with the mythographic strand of criticism, whatever individual differences are shown by its exponents, is its unwillingness to confront the slipperiness of Soyinka's poetic language, which is in practice a primary and persistent difficulty for all readers. Ebeogu ignores it in favor of thematic commentary. Nwoga does acknowledge it, but then leaves it on one side and moves on to wider issues. Macebuh is more consistently combative, vigorously dismissing any dissatisfaction with it as irrelevant. His remarks on Soyinka's language thus deserve further examination. Soyinka, Macebuh says, "has not been preoccupied with language merely as the index of style, but rather with language as a vehicle of mythic meaning."[19] The antithesis here between "style" and "meaning" is surely problematic. In what sense can these elements of literature ever truly be said to be alternatives? It is true that some poetry seems to be "all style and no content," but this is merely a form of words. Even if the language is used as a "vehicle of mythic meaning," that meaning can only be conveyed through the way in which the language is ordered, that is, through its "style." It is indeed precisely Soyinka's knotty, elusive style which Macebuh so admires, that conveys to his readers that his meaning is a mythic one. The idea that language can convey meaning independently of the rhetorical strategies which govern it is mere naïveté. A more extreme version of this argument is given by Robin Graham in his essay "Wole Soyinka: Obscurity, Romanticism, and Dylan Thomas."[20] Of the problematic elements in "Dawn," Graham remarks:

> These "obscurities" belong to the processes of mythology rather than to the arbitrary potentialities of language. Myth is a faculty which flourishes on sudden and unexpected analogies and recurrences. This in itself makes the products of the Mythic Imagination impenetrable to the anatomizing, analytical mind. [21]

Once again the role of mere language in the creation of the poetic effect is denied. And this denial may seem the more strange in that the characteristics which Graham assigns to myth are, as readers of seventeenth-century poetry or of T. S. Eliot will be aware, precisely those usually assigned to poetic language ("sudden and unexpected analogies and recurrences"). The question arises as to how Graham conceives that the Mythic Imagination can convey these analogies and recurrences to the reader of a poem if the potentialities of its medium of expression, language, are deemed merely "arbitrary."

But Graham's comment about the impenetrability of myth to "the anatomizing, analytical mind" introduces a second, perhaps even more crucial weakness in mythographic criticism: namely, the simplistic conception of myth on which it bases itself. Macebuh, Graham, and others have a tendency to make the mere adumbration of myth or Yoruba theology in a work by Soyinka the end and goal of their critical effort. The poem is then to be admired with religious respectfulness. The concept of myth which justifies this approach is a universalist or essentialist one. Myth is placed beyond, or beneath, the reach of that analytical discourse which places artistic or cultural productions in particular contexts of society, where they can be compared and criticized. Nwoga, as we have seen, is not afraid to use the word "primitive" of the symbolism which conveys myth. For Macebuh, Soyinka's preoccupation with his roots is the restoration of a primal Yoruba essence which has been deformed by the historical distortion of colonialism. This is too simple. Myth does not exist in a realm of primal purity, transcending history, innocent of politics, immune to manipulation by particular groups and individuals. Roland Barthes, for instance, has ridiculed the notion that myth transcends history as an ideological deception. However ancient and permanent a myth may appear, its roots lie not in primal essence, but in particular social conditions, in politics:

one can conceive of very ancient myths, but there are no eternal ones; for it is human history which converts reality into speech, and it alone rules the life and the death of mythical language. Ancient or not, mythology can only have an historical foundation, for myth is a type of speech chosen by history: it cannot possibly evolve from the "nature" of things.[22]

Myth is the historically determined self-assertion of a particular society, or rather of its ruling group. It is, in fact, ideology which in the form of myth, masquerades as universal nature in order to protect and preserve the status quo. It is this relativity of myth which Lewis Nkosi asserts in his irritated attack on Soyinka's theology: "After all, if it comes to that, there is really neither Ogun nor Jesus! There are only mystified forms of our consciousness."[23] Thus, for example, the ancient myth of Ogun slaughtering his own people and then becoming their deified protector is, like the very similar Celtic myth of Cuchulain, the product (even the propaganda) of a warrior society dominated by patriarchal aristocrats for whom such a savage, unpredictable being will seem the worthy focus of an ideology of awe and submission. Such a myth will be bound to be re-evaluated, recast, or even rejected as the society which produced it develops new physical and social conditions through history. Ideologies and myths are as historically determined as techniques of building of methods of travel.[24] It is absurd to imagine that the postcolonial Soyinka can evade history and regain access to the primal myths of his ancestors, pure and without ironies. It is a sentimentalism to desire to "correct" the colonial "distortion" by such atavism. The clock will not turn back. Indeed, as we shall see later, properly understood, Soyinka is to be seen not as "returning" to primal myth in his poetry, but as rewriting and transforming myth for his new historical context.

I

With these wider theoretical distinctions in mind, I would like now to turn to the particular analyses offered by the critics of Soyinka's "Dawn." Not only should our examination provide specific tests of the different critical approaches but a clearer view of the real nature of Soyinka's obscurity may perhaps emerge.

Breaking earth upon
A spring-haired elbow, lone
A palm beyond head-grains, spikes
A guard of prim fronds, piercing
High hairs of the wind

As one who bore the pollen highest

Blood-drops in the air, above
The even belt of tassels, above
Coarse leaf teasing at the waist, steals
The lone intruder...[25]

Roderick Wilson cites this poem as an example of Soyinka's "inadequate working out of images and metaphors." Its "pervasive sexuality," he argues, confuses the reader as the tree seems to change from male to female in the course of the poem, "the lone intruder," the sun, taking over its initial masculine role. More specifically, Wilson remarks, "The pun in 'spring-haired elbow' conveys both new growth and a coiled energy. There is a tense expectancy, but the 'elbow' is not after all attached to anything and the image remains disembodied."[26] Wilson states carefully what can safely be said to be conveyed by the imagery and syntax of the first lines. His reading seems accurate and incisive. But some readers may feel his approach is imaginatively parsimonious in its response to the challenge of the poem's unconventional imagery and syntax. Ken Goodwin, in contrast, takes up the challenge, and confidently attaches the elbow to the palm.

The palm is seen as if just stirring, resting on its buttressed trunk as if on an elbow. "Springhaired," a notorious difficulty, I take to mean covered in the hairy filaments produced in the spring or growing season, with "spring" hinting also at the springing of an arch, such as the buttressing root provides. The filaments will obviously pick up and reflect the first rays of light.[27]

Despite his reference to one particular "notorious difficulty," Goodwin's is a remarkably unhesitant explication. It seems, indeed, too sure of itself by half. I can find no "buttressing root" in Soyinka's poem, and the explanation of "spring-haired" as referring to "hairy filaments produced in the spring or growing season," which "will *obviously*... reflect the first rays of light," though persuasive, is not inevitable. Hesitation may also be felt about both Wilson's and Goodwin's perception of a Eurocentric reference to the season of spring in relation to this tropical palm (although Soyinka frequently *does* use "unAfrican" images based on temperate zone seasons). Goodwin reveals his own uneasiness about this in the phrase "spring or growing season." Nor do either Wilson or Goodwin mention what must surely be the most natural interpretation of "spring-haired": that it is the hairs *on* the metaphorical arm which are "springy," and then only secondarily, by transferred association, the trunk/root(?)/ elbow itself. Thus, while Wilson refuses to probe into the ambiguities which irritate him, Goodwin seems to be imposing too detailed and literal an interpretation on them.

D. I. Nwoga does for the syntax of the poem what Goodwin does for the imagery. He is unique among the critics in following through the syntax of the poem as tenaciously as he follows the metaphors. This leads him to solve Wilson's problem of the disembodied elbow by attaching it, not to the palm, but to the sun, "the lone intruder." A little reflection will confirm that if the syntax of the poem is to be disentangled at all (and it may be, as we shall see, that we are not meant to disentangle it), then Nwoga is most probably right. "The lone intruder" is the subject of the single sentence which constitutes the poem, and the participial phrase in the first two lines is properly read as modifying it. Nwoga does not explain why other critics should attach the elbow to the palm, but the reasons are evident. First, there is the strongly appositional style. "A palm beyond head-grains" does *look* very much like the subject of the sentence at first, and we only begin to suspect that it is not as the subsequent phrases continue to multiply without yielding a main verb. And then, when the verb ("steals") finally appears it is unmistakably governed by "The lone intruder." There is also the grammatical ambiguity of "spikes" at the end of the third line, which the reader may first take to be a verb governed by the subject "A palm," only later realizing that it is more probably to be read as a noun in loose apposition to "A palm." But by this time the short circuit between elbow and palm has been established. Nwoga, having made his "correct" syntactical attachment of elbow to sun, is not afraid to admit the problems to which it gives rise, placing his heavily conjectural explanation in parentheses. "(Perhaps this may refer to the myth of the sun being an earth being from whom the light emerges when he wakes in the morning, lifts himself on an elbow, and opens his armpit?)"[28] The opening armpit here is surely a touch which few readers would have discovered in the lines without Nwoga's help. And in view of the large claims he and others make on behalf of Soyinka's mythic Yoruba dimension, one would like to know if this "earth being" personification of the recumbent sun is specifically Yoruba. But Nwoga does not tell us what source for this myth he has in mind.

M. R. Salt offers an altogether more flexible reading than any we have encountered so far. He simply refuses to resolve the ambiguities of imagery and syntax which Soyinka has written into the language of the poem. Salt attacks Wilson's dismissal of the lines for ignoring the way "that figurative language radiates meaning through epithets, images, and symbols. Wilson, on the other hand, tends to identify an image with *one* particular meaning: the "lone intruder, with the sun."[29] Responding to the ambiguities of the poem instead of resolving them as Goodwin and Nwoga do, Salt sees both palm and sun as included in the phrase "The lone intruder." Both are "emblems for creative energy," intruding upon the sky and breaking earth. In this reading the elbow image must be given a looser, more evocative explanation:

the image is sensuous, and imaginative: it suggests the movement of the palm-fronds; the ascending curve of the tree-tops, with the lone palm at the apex; and the rather mystical union of the fronds with the "High hairs of the wind."[30]

Salt's is a sensitive response, attempting to register all the poem's complexities without simplifying or reducing them. However, it is, I think, significant that, in spite of his efforts to keep the elbow suggestively detached, he cannot help but, in effect, attach it to the palm. Where Goodwin has a buttressing root (which does have the virtue of looking very much like an elbow), Salt merely hints, without actually stating, that "the movement of the palm-fronds; the ascending curve of the tree-tops" may somewhat resemble an elbow. This is perhaps persuasive enough and certainly less forced than Goodwin's analysis. But as Nwoga has shown, the elbow is syntactically just as (if not more) connected to the later part of the poem, where the image of the sun has been superimposed upon that of the palm. Salt himself does not wish to disentangle the two images. But he makes no real attempt to associate the "radiating" meaning of the elbow with the sun, contenting himself with a "rather mystical union of the fronds with the 'High hairs of the wind'."

Although Salt then attempts to grapple with all the complexities of the poem in a way which the others do not, it must be admitted that his interpretation of the first lines is ultimately little more satisfying – and it is certainly less precise – than theirs. There are two insoluble problems about the elbow image. Firstly and crudely, we do not normally think of the sun as possessing an elbow, and the hinted personification in "The lone intruder" is too unfocused and too physically distant in the poem from the elbow to give the image coherence. Secondly and more importantly, an elbow – and a spring-haired elbow at that – presents a very visual and concrete image. Of itself it has little of the mystically suggestive or symbolically resonant. It is neither ambiguous enough nor abstract enough to hover meaningfully, detached from a clear syntactical or metaphorical context. It strikes clearly and vividly on the reader's visual imagination, which is then not supplied with any means of linking it convincingly to the other images, concrete and abstract. The result is that no larger, more resonant, and evocative meaning can emerge from it. Soyinka's rhetorical strategy presents the reader with a mixture of levels, concrete and abstract, literal and metaphorical, from which it is difficult to construct any definite, or coherently indefinite, response. The desire to connect the elbow meaningfully with the other images of the poem, evident in all the critics including Salt, is not then the unimaginative, analytical obtuseness which the approach of Macebuh and Graham might suggest it to be. It is a desire to make *metaphorical* sense of the words. Unattached, the elbow is a source, not of complex, unanalyzable, mythic meaning, but of verbal and visual confusion. It remains what, when all is said and done, most readers in the first instance find it (though they may be persuaded otherwise later) – a stubborn irritant, nagging the imagination without making imaginative sense. It is important to recognize that what one is seeking here is not "merely stylistic" or "analytical," or (as Graham terms it elsewhere) "commonplace" coherence,[31] but imaginative, metaphorical coherence. And it is lacking. The problem is not that these lines are grammatically or merely linguistically unconventional; it is that they are metaphorically messy.

It is in the latter part of the poem that the theological and mythical implications emerge most explicitly.

>   above
> Coarse leaf teasing on the waist, steals
> The lone intruder, tearing wide
>
>
> The chaste hide of the sky
>
>
> O celebration of the rites of dawn
> Night-spread in tatters and a god
> Received, aflame with kernels.[32]

Once again there are minor and major contradictions between the readings of the critics. Eldred Jones sees the sun coming "like Tarquin" to rape the palm. He continues:

> The last stanza [sic] delicately suggests the worship with which dawn is greeted. Not only do the words "celebration" and "rites" suggest this, but the blood-red kernels of the palm become an apt sacrificial offering to a god who is himself "aflame." In the end we have something like the character of the dawn (rather than a photographic picture of it) through images which suggest not only how the dawn comes, but what it means.[33]

No one would wish to argue against the assertion that there is some rite of religious worship in these lines, but the other aspects of Jones's reading seem questionable. It is difficult to see why he should be so certain that "Tarquin's rape of Lucrece is strongly suggested," and he offers no explanation. Also there is little inevitability about his interpretation of "a god/ Received, aflame with kernels" as referring to a metaphorical burning of the blood-red kernels in sacrifice to "a god who is himself 'aflame'" (i.e., the sun). It is a *possible* construction of the words if one reads the punctuation and the preposition somewhat freely. But it is one that is unlikely to suggest itself to many readers without Jones's help. Altogether Jones's account leaves one in real doubt as to the nature of the nonphotographic "something like the dawn" that Soyinka has conveyed and what its "meaning" is. It involves a "delicately" suggested religious rite addressed to a sun god who recalls the brutal rapist Tarquin. If this is the meaning, it surely demands some further clarification, which Jones does not give. Goodwin follows the broad outline of Jones's interpretation, though with significant differences of detail. He sees the lines as

> a theophany in which the sun rapes a lone palm-tree, "tearing wide the chaste hide of the sky" that has previously enfolded it like a "night-spread" (that is, the bed-spread of the night). It "steals" up on its (more or less willing) victim, first faintly illuminating various parts of the palm before rapidly overwhelming it in the glory of a god.[34]

There is convincing coherence here in the way that the picking out by the sun of the parts of the palm and the flooding of the tree with light are interpreted as the tenor of the sexual metaphor of teasing and rape implied by the imagery. And Goodwin's elucidation of "night-spread" is incisive and exact. In Goodwin's version, as in Jones's, the sun rapes the palm with its "leaf teasing at the waist"; but Goodwin's palm is no Lucrece, who was certainly not at all "willing." Moreover, Goodwin's reading, unlike Jones's, seeks no other implication of the rites beyond the "sacrificial" rape. The sacrificial burning of kernels remains indeed unique to Jones's version.

Salt differs from both Jones and Goodwin in interpreting these lines. This time, however, he does not preserve Soyinka's ambiguities as he did in the earlier part of the poem, but simply resolves them in a startlingly different way from the others. For him the palm tree is not a rape victim but

> a phallus, "piercing/ High hairs of the wind," bearing "the pollen highest" and "tearing wide/ The chaste hide of the sky." The tree obviously radiates one source of creative energy standing erect and "aflame with kernels." These kernels, and the shafts of early morning sunlight, combine to suggest the presence of the "Blood-drops in the air." But, why a phallus? Part of the answer might well be that Ọlọ́run, the Yoruba God, handed a palm-tree to Orìṣà-nlá when he sent this divinity to "equip and embellish the earth."[35]

Some readers may well feel that Salt's version has more to recommend it than those of Jones and Goodwin. The tree *is* a pollen bearer, and pollen is a natural metaphor for fertilizing sperm, borne "highest" by the tree. In this reading the kernels remain where they literally belong, being only metaphorically inflamed with the god's passion rather than in sacrificial flames. Clearly also the kernels on the erect stem of the tree are associated with testicles, there being a concealed Soyinkan pun on "nuts" which Salt is too delicate to mention. Moreover, Salt's reference to Yoruba mythology seems very illuminating, though it is impossible to be certain (as his "it might well be" concedes) that the poet actually intended any specific reference to Ọlọ́run and Orìṣà-nlá. The objections to Salt's reading are as evident as its strengths, however. The palm does after all have "a guard of prim fronds" and a "Coarse leaf teasing on the waist," which seem conclusively to justify a female interpretation. The "lone intruder" comes "above" the belt of tassels and "above" the leaf on the waist which would suggest a sky-inhabiting deity dominating the primly fronded tree – or is it coarsely teasing? It seems that we have arrived back at Wilson's exasperated perception of the pervasive and confusing sexuality of the poem. The palm appears in some phrases as erect phallus with kernels "aflame," in others as "prim" rape-victim, and in yet others as "teasing" seducer. Could this conflicting imagery perhaps be intended as an ingenious reflection of the botanical fact that the coco palm is monoecious, the same plant bearing male and female flowers?

None of the critics mentions the further complication of the strange and unexpected clash of register in the words "chaste hide of the sky." This phrase has a true Soyinkan ring of bold inventiveness about it and is clearly calculated (like "Coarse", two lines earlier) to create an effect of brutally ironic contradiction. But to what effect? It could be argued that this is simply a felicitous visual image, the smooth expanse of the dawn sky looking very much like an immaculate "nightspread" of pale animal-leather. But the powerful figurative associations of the words inevitably suggest contradictory metaphorical significances. Women (or men for that matter) may be "chaste," but they have "skin" not "hide"; cattle have "hides," but are not usually dignified with attributions of chastity. Here, however, we are presented with "the chaste hide" of the sky, which the sun (or the palm, or both) "tears wide" in its rape. The association of tearing hides with the rites of dawn must surely be meant to suggest to the reader the actual sacrifice of cattle in a religious ceremony such as that of the fourteen white bulls in *Season of Anomy*. However, "Coarse leaf teasing at the waist," "chaste," and "a god / Received," seem indeed to imply, as Jones and Goodwin perceive, a rape; not of course a mere human rape like that of Lucrece by Tarquin, but the awesome rape of an earthly virgin by a god, such as occurs in several Greek myths. Soyinka then weaves Greek and Yoruba figurative elements together in these lines, one phrase hinting at a rape by Zeus, another at an animal sacrifice, both being merged into a syncretic "celebration of the rites of dawn." The rape is to be seen, like that of Leda in Yeats's poem, as brutal but pregnant with creative potential; and the Yoruba sacrifice also hinted at is a similar sacrificial communion between humanity and the gods.

II

So far in our discussion the sincerity of the "celebration" of dawn enacted in the poem has not been in question. It is possible, however, to view the disruptions of style and syntax which we have been discussing as signs of a complexity and uneasiness in the poet's attitude toward his mythic theme. Such a view involves quite a different critical perspective from those that we have so far considered, one which locates the source of Soyinka's obscurity not in incompetence, nor in mythic profundity – or at least not wholly so – but rather in his continual struggle to create coherence out of an experience which denies it: to assert conviction in a world of doubt. Most critics have recourse to this line of argument at some time or other, though it is usually only a secondary critical strand in the commentators with whom we have been concerned until now. Roderick Wilson, for example, locates much of the power of "Death in the Dawn," the poem which immediately follows "Dawn" in the *Idanre* volume, in its uneasy juxtaposition of traditional African and modern European elements. "Each item in this synthesis of traditional and western questions the other," he remarks. He considers this poem "one of the best in the opening section of the book" while still criticizing its "undisciplined imagery."[36] In a similar way Stanley Macebuh contends that

> our impression of the harsh inscrutableness of Soyinka's language may be seen as an exact equivalent in words of that unease of the mind that is the lot of all those who have suffered a modification of vision through colonialism.[37]

The difficulty of Soyinka's language is seen as arising not only from his mythic depth but also in part from his struggle to overcome the alienation of colonialism.

It is Thomas R. Knipp in an impressive essay, "Irony, Tragedy, and Myth: The Poetry of Wole Soyinka,"[38] who makes this mode of interpretation the basis of his entire critical approach. Like Macebuh and Nwoga, Knipp sees the value of Soyinka's poetry as residing primarily in its mythic quality. Unlike them, however, Knipp does not locate this mythic element solely in a "primal" Yoruba aspect of Soyinka's poetry. In his version of Soyinka's attitude toward traditional Yoruba myth is a dynamic, even at times a highly skeptical one. Soyinka does not merely express, or struggle to recover, "unmodified" Yoruba myth. He is a mythopoeic writer in a more organic sense, creating new mythic patterns out of the contradiction between tradition and modernity. He is a "tragic ironist" who constantly attacks the easier forms of myth (e.g., that of the "golden age" of the traditional past, debunked in *A Dance of the Forests*). Whatever the mythic patterns he sets up in his poetry, he remains the modern skeptic. "As a result of westernization, he analyses [myth] from outside, but as an African he feels it from within.... In all of the poems [in the *Idanre* volume], however, the informing vision is that of the modern poet."[39] Soyinka's individual sensibility thus becomes the arena in which larger historical and cultural conflicts are acted out. It is perhaps not quite so clearly as Knipp's wording here makes it seem, a matter of ancient African tradition versus modern Western skepticism. To be modern is surely not to be un-African; nor is there anything particularly un-Western about myth, as Soyinka's constant preoccupation with ancient Greek myth ought to remind us. Knipp himself is quite aware that the myths with which Soyinka concerns himself (the golden age, the racist mythology of colonialism, negritude) are very often neither exclusively African nor ancient, but expressions of *modern* ideologies. Ken Goodwin, indeed, parallels *A Shuttle in the Crypt* with two of the most celebrated modern European mythopoeic poems, *The Waste Land* and the *Cantos*. Soyinka's collection, in Goodwin's view, represents "like the work of Eliot and Pound, an exploration of the poet's own being as it comes close to madness and dissolution,"[40] Soyinka is here placed, quite convincingly, in the context of the post-romantic myth of the isolated individual in an alien world.

In his treatment of the specific details of "Dawn," Knipp does not differ greatly from some of the critics we have already examined. He remarks that the lines

> above
> Coarse leaf teasing on the waist, steals
> The lone intruder, tearing wide
>
> The chaste hide of the sky

present a "lovely image," without referring to the jarring of register in "Coarse" and "chaste hide." And like Salt he gives a phallic interpretation to the tree. What is significant about Knipp's analysis is the extent to which he places "Dawn" in the wider, ironic context of the other poems in the "For the Road" section of the volume. This poem, he argues, is not to be read in isolation, as an unambiguous traditional "celebration" of the coming of day. As the following poem, "Death in the Dawn," shows, the gods do not seem to be necessarily propitiated by the sacrificial rite. The narrator sees the death of the white cock on his windscreen as a sacrifice to Ogun, warding off harm. The next thing he encounters on the road is an accident, with a man dead. Clearly the attitude towards the god in this poem is a complex one. Is Ogun punishing humankind, as Goodwin suggests, for an "insatiable desire for technological progress,"[41] a form of hubris against the god of iron? Or is he simply capricious? Knipp detects in this poem, and throughout the "For the Road" section, a radical skepticism about the nature, or even the existence, of the gods, a pervading sense of the inefficacy of traditional mythic explanations of experience. Throughout the *Idanre* collection, we find an "organizing principle of ironic juxtaposition" such as is seen at work in these first two poems.

> The first section ends with the irony and mystery of death and its possible meaninglessness more overtly confronted in the person of Ogun as the poet grieves for his dead friend Segun Awolowo, "for him who was." And note that there is no hint of African ancestors or Christian afterlife; there is only the very modern, very final past tense.[42]

The dynamism of Soyinka's mythopoeia is thus seen, in stark contrast to the views of Nwoga or Macebuh, as deriving precisely from his uneasiness with myth, which the mythographic critics would see as a lamentable distortion of his Africanness.

Although Knipp places Soyinka convincingly in an overall context of mythopoeic struggle and doubt, he is, nevertheless, unwilling to admit that this struggle causes real confusion in the poet's rhetoric, which he finds powerful and effective. C. Tighe's *"In Detentio Preventione in Aeternum:* Soyinka's *A Shuttle in the Crypt"*[43] presents an interesting contrast with Knipp's essay in this respect. His critical approach is in broad essentials the same as that of Knipp, focusing on conflicts within Soyinka's sensibility. Unlike Knipp, however, Tighe does not find the poetic expression of the tensions between African and Western, traditional and modern, in Soyinka's work wholly effective. He focuses particularly on the flippant puns and mixed metaphors in *A Shuttle in the Crypt*, which he attributes to Soyinka's "unsuccessful attempts to come to terms with the indigestible experiences of war and imprisonment." Soyinka is using the poetry – which was conceived and drafted while he was actually in prison – as a kind of escape therapy, a means of evading his frustration and powerlessness. Unable to find relief in purposive action, the shuttle of his mind weaves and weaves in the crypt of the prison. Of the characteristic puns, Tighe remarks:

> Usually the puns are a method of side-stepping the real questions that the poetry raises, a sheepish, grinning, half apology for what is being said. It is as if he finds his subject too painful to discuss seriously and dismisses it with a pun, avoiding any attempt to articulate fully what he feels.[44]

Tighe's searching analysis places what value these poems possess in their irremediable confusion of effect. Unsatisfactory though he cannot but find it, Tighe, nevertheless, prefers this vivid, unresolved turmoil to the later reworking of Soyinka's prison experience found in *The Man Died*. "This awkwardness and confusion are rare in *The Man Died* since most of that book has been put through a kind of post-imprisonment ego-blender which disguises the real moments of doubt and fear."[45] Tighe's attribution of the problematic features of the style of *A Shuttle in the Crypt* to Soyinka's specific dilemmas at the time of his imprisonment is highly convincing. However, it must be said that explicable though they are in this way, such poetic mannerisms were evident in Soyinka's writing long before the period of the civil war. Bernth Lindfors, exploring some of Soyinka's very earliest published work in undergraduate magazines, was prompted to coin the phrase "the wild and Wole idiom"[46] to describe an early manifestation of just this liking for mixed metaphor and gaudy rhetoric. And as we have seen, the *Idanre* volume shows these features also. Intensified though they may have been by the trauma of the civil war and imprisonment, these poetic characteristics seem basic to Soyinka's writing right from the beginning.

Knipp remains unconvinced by Tighe's strictures on Soyinka's stylistic excesses. Tighe's criticism of one passage, he says, misses its mark "because the language here is strong and effective. The strained quality that Tighe complains of is actually a poetic strength."[47] The argument here is one concerning degree. At what point does the expressive (or expressionist) force of metaphorical or grammatical disruption slide into self-indulgence or incoherence? In the final event this argument can be resolved only by the judgment of individual readers. To take the case of Soyinka's puns and wordplay: some may be persuaded by Knipp that "Orphans of the world/ Ignite" is effective. "The pun keeps the personal experience and the political issue at a manageable emotional and aesthetic distance."[48] Such readers may parallel the uneasy, "bad-taste" wordplay here with apparently similar examples in other prominent twentieth-century poets: "Fearful, original sinuosities!" for example, in Derek Walcott's "The Swamp,"[49] or Dylan Thomas's "I shall not murder / The mankind of her going with a grave truth"[50] in "A Refusal to Mourn the Death, by Fire, of a Child in London." But to others Soyinka's pun will seem crude and flashy, lacking either the profundity of Walcott's or the strange dignity of Thomas's. It will appear too metaphorically arbitrary, a demonstration of the author's brilliance rather than real poetry. The judgment of such readers will not be greatly altered by thematic or ideological explanations of Soyinka's rhetoric. His distinctive style may be attributed to his mythic Yoruba depths, or alternatively to his divided post-colonial sensibility. But such explanations in themselves cannot transform meretricious incoherence into subtle complexity, though they may impart a certain interest to the incoherence. It is surely difficult not to doubt the poetic worth of a work like "Dawn," which can elicit from intelligent and perceptive critics such a welter of conflicting readings. Brilliant and assured in tone as Soyinka's poetry undoubtedly is, it is also, as we have seen, metaphorically irresponsible and syntactically messy. And these are poetic sins of no small order.

NOTES

1. Wole Soyinka, *Myth, Literature, and the African World* (Cambridge: Cambridge UP, 1976).

2. Roderick Wilson, "Complexity and Confusion in Soyinka's Shorter Poems," *Critical Perspectives on Wole Soyinka*, ed. James Gibbs (London: Heinemann, 1981) pp. 158-69.

3. Ibid., p. 163.

4. Ibid., p. 158.

5. Ibid., pp. 161, 159.

6. Ken Goodwin, *Understanding African Poetry: A Study of Ten Poets* (London: Heinemann, 1982), p. 114.

7. Stanley Macebuh, "Poetics and Mythic Imagination," *Critical Perspectives*, pp. 200-12.

8. Ibid., p. 201.

9. Ibid., p. 203.

10. Ibid., p. 208.

11. Ibid.

12. Ibid., p. 212.

13. Afam Ebeogu, "From *Idanre* to *Ogun Abibiman:* An Exploration of Soyinka's Use of Ogun Images," *Journal of Commonwealth Literature*, 15 (1980): 84-96.

14. Ibid., pp. 84, 86.

15. D. I. Nwoga, "Poetry as Revelation: Wole Soyinka," in *Critical Perspectives*, pp. 173-85; quotation on p. 175.

16. Ibid.

17. Ibid., p. 178.

18. Ibid., p. 183.

19. Ibid., p. 207.

20. Robin Graham, "Wole Soyinka: Obscurity, Romanticism, and Dylan Thomas," *Critical Perspectives*, pp. 213-18.

21. Ibid., p. 217.

22. Roland Barthes, *Mythologies,* selected and trans. Annette Lavers (London: Granada, 1973), p. 110.

23. Lewis Nkosi, *Home and Exile and Other Selections* (London: Longman, 1983), x.

24. The two opposed perspectives on myth are strikingly illustrated in two recent books on African literature. Isidore Okpewho's *Myth in Africa: A Study of Its Aesthetic and Cultural Relevance* (Cambridge: Cambridge UP, 1983) takes an extreme essentialist position, seeing myth as "a creative resource from which the larger cultural values are derivative" (ix). Kinfe Abraham's *From Race to Class: Links and Parallels in African and Black American Protest Expression* (London: Grassroots, 1982), on the other hand, refers to a "whole series of myths" being "created" in nineteenth-century Europe, to justify the exploitation of blacks (22).

25. Wole Soyinka, *Idanre and Other Poems* (London: Eyre Methuen, 1976), p. 9.

26. Wilson, p. 158.

27. Goodwin, p. 112.

28. Nwoga, p. 175.

29. M. R. Salt, "Mr. Wilson's Interpretation of a Soyinka Poem," *Critical Perspectives*, pp. 170-02, quotation on p. 171.

30. Ibid.

31. Graham, p. 215.

32. Soyinka, *Idanre and Other Poems*, p. 9.

33. Eldred Jones, *The Writing of Wole Soyinka*, rev. ed. (London: Heinemann, 1983), p. 126.

34. Goodwin, pp. 111-12.

35. Salt, p. 170.

36. Wilson, p. 165.

37. Macebuh, p. 203.

38. Thomas R. Knipp, "Irony, Tragedy, and Myth: The Poetry of Wole Soyinka," *World Literature Written in English*, 21 (1982): 5-26.

39. Ibid., pp.7, 10.

40. Goodwin, p. 130.

41. Ibid., p. 112.

42. Knipp, p. 12.

43. C. Tighe, "*In Detentio Preventione in Aeternum*: Soyinka's *A Shuttle in the Crypt*," *Critical Perspectives*, pp. 186-97.

44. Ibid., p. 192.

45. Ibid., p. 189.

46. Bernth Lindfors, "The Early Writings of Wole Soyinka," *Critical Perspectives*, pp. 19-44; quotation on p. 30.

47. Knipp, p. 19.

48. Ibid., p. 20.

49. Derek Walcott, *Selected Poetry* (London: Heinemann, 1981), p. 17.

50. Dylan Thomas, *Collected Poems, 1934-1951* (London: J. M. Dent, 1952), p. 101.

Equivalent Structures in Soyinka's Poetry: Toward a Linguistic Methodology in African Poetry Criticism

Sunday O. Anozie

Introduction: Poetic Language and Generative Grammar

The advent of the generative theory in linguistics, formulated most clearly in the works of Noam Chomsky (1956, 1964, 1965, 1968), was a welcome sign, especially for those critics and linguists interested not only in finding new methods of approach to the study of literature but also in dealing with the problems of the structure and meaning of poetic language (cf. e.g., Saporta, 1960; Halliday, 1962; Levin, 1962, 1967; Jones, 1967; Levenston, 1974; Lord, 1975; etc.). The generative approach views grammar as a theory or model which ideally generates all and only the grammatical sequences of a particular natural language. A generative phonology of English, for instance, would describe all and only the phonologically acceptable sequences, the adequacy of the description being determined in part by the accuracy with which it can predict the acceptability of unobserved sequences of sound. The generative theory, therefore, approaches the study of language from the native speaker's perspective. But it does so not from a narrow, restrictive, empiricist standpoint, nor do the universals it postulates, relating to competence and performance, derive from any ethnocentric bias, but from an objective and scientific point of view.

Let us consider the following brief episode. An Italian tourist loses his bearings at a London substation. At the entrance to the station, he accosts a passerby and in halting English asks for directions to Trafalgar Square. The woman obliges. But impatient with the details, the tourist turns to the woman and says, "Excuse me, but I must ask someone else who can speak English." Offended and angry, the woman replies, "I'm English. I speak English." And with that, they part company.

A diehard empiricist, especially from the Sapir-Whorfian school of linguistics, would, when confronted with this communicative impasse, jump to the defense of the insulted English woman by recognizing her context-sensitive claim to competence. He would argue implicitly that under the sharply defined variables of the context of the situation – a foreigner, not fluent in English, lost in London, in need of help, versus a native speaker of English, familiar with London, willing to help – all basic referential semantics as well as the cognitive registers of the language point in favor of the woman's being right. (Both Whorf and Sapir in their works, especially about the Hopi Indians of North America, have formulated linguistic hypotheses based upon differential world views which can serve as models for our imaginary episode.) Generative linguists, on the other hand, would, confronted with the same situation, also recognize the woman's claim to competence, maintaining that as a native speaker of English, she is born with an innate cognitive mechanism for recognizing the grammaticalness of sentence structures of the language, but they would proceed very differently and rationally from her performance in establishing that competence: they would construct objective rules and criteria for making the competence explicit. Those explicit conventions are what is termed generative grammar.

Poetic language is only one form of language use of performance, a creative use of language. As such it is an inclusive part of the notion of competence. The symbolic system that operates within a given creative use of language, for instance, in poetry, is always context-sensitive in the largest sense of the term, but it is dependent also upon the rules of grammar of the natural language. Investigation of the context-sensitivity of poetic language leads to a semantic interpretation of poetry and the postulation of underlying universals of the experience it conveys. On the other hand, an investigation aimed at establishing the grammatical rules of a poem has as its primary purpose the making explicit of its internal mode of signification, that is, the deep structure of a poem. In the following pages we will propose a reading of Wole Soyinka's poetry which aims at doing exactly that. In other words, the analysis will demonstrate the presence of an extensional logic, that is to say, grammatical conventions which render possible the production of meaning in these poems. Thus by focusing on the actual performance of the poet, rather than on interpretational strategies, one hopes ultimately that the reconstruction of a Soyinka poetics, or the generative grammar of Soyinka's poetry, will be made possible.

Equivalent Structures in Soyinka's Poetry

Consider the following poetic proposition: "Peppers green and red – Child – your tongue arch / To scorpion tail, spit straight return to danger's threat/ Yet coo with the brown pigeon, tendril I dew between your lips" (Soyinka, "Dedication", 1975, pp. 161-62). Leaving aside the independent phonic and morphophonemic (such as stress, intonation, and juncture) infrastructure of the poem (note, however, that these external features are indispensable in any semantic interpretation of the dirge) and concentrating instead on the position of each word or group of words along the syntagmatic chain, we find that the poem breaks down easily into noun phrases (NP), verb phrases (VP), conjunctions (C), and prepositions:

NP_1 ($\downarrow$ peppers green and red) + NP_2 (Child) +
VP_1 (your tongue arch) + to + NP_3 (scorpion tail) +
VP_2 (spit straight return) + to + NP_4 (danger's threats) + C (yet) + VP_3 (coo)
with NP_5 (the brown pigeon) NP_6 ($\downarrow$ tendril dew between your lips)

Syntagmatically, the following positional equivalences are defined in the poem: $NP_1 - NP_6$; $NP_2 - NP_5$; $NP_3 - NP_4$; $VP_1 - VP_2$; only VP_3 stands unpaired. Following Levin (1962, p. 23 ff.), we define the term *positions* as "those places in the linguistic chain where alternation is possible"; and the term *alternation* as "the replacement of one form in a syntagm by other forms such that the syntagm remains grammatical under all these replacements and the replacing forms are all morphemic." On the basis of this definition, NP_3 and NP_4 are considered as having equivalent positions because each is preceded by the preposition *to*; likewise VP_1, VP_2 are equivalent by reason of being followed each by an NP; thus: "arch your tongue," "spit straight return" are equivalent.

Paradigmatically, other equivalences also exist such as between NP_1, NP_6; and between NP_2, NP_5. Although these equivalences occur within the syntagm and so are part of the external linguistic environment of the poem, they are nevertheless supra-segmental; that is, we can only explain their occurrence by appealing to extralinguistic factors, such as meaning. Hence, if we expand its semantic context, NP_1 may read as follows: "[with] pepper green and red [in your mouth]...," and NP_6 should read as "[with] tendril dew on your lips." We have indicated these zero positions, or zero promorphemes as they are sometimes called, with inverted arrows ($\downarrow$). The modifications made, though not essential, are made only in the interest of clarity of analysis. The justification for them may well be, as Levin (1962, p. 54) correctly suggested, that "we bring to bear a number of things in the reading of a poem, one of these things being a knowledge of that part of the language code which the poet and we have in common." In the case of this poem, a good part of that public knowledge has to do with generative grammar and also with meaning. For example, we know from common sense that a child does not arch his tongue in pain and coo unless he has hot pepper in his mouth. Another interesting feature of the semantic paradigm or equivalence is revealed by the poet's supplying at an unusual position within the poem's syntagm the missing promorpheme "with": "Yet coo with the brown pigeon." The position is "unusual" if we render the last line of the poem instead in the following modified form: "Yet coo – brown pigeon – with tendril dew between your lips."

Now the question arises, did the poet deliberately create "empty" slots in the poem – the so-called zero positions, or zero promorphemes (cf. Harris, 1963, p. 301 ff.) – in order for the reader to fill in the right linguistic forms? In this we embrace a technical and manipulative use of the English language peculiar to poetry, and I have not hesitated to qualify this as a sign of competence-in-performance. *A propos*, Levin (1962, p. 39) has observed that in poetry

> constructions are not merely dummies, to be filled in by just any linguistic forms as long as they are grammatical and communication is effected; in poetry the constructions are filled by words having... special kinds of equivalence.

Moreover, according to Levin, these special kinds of equivalence are of two types: positional equivalence if it depends ostensibly upon linguistic alternation, and *natural* equivalence if it depends upon extralinguistic consideration.

The extension into poetry analysis of the conventions of generative transformational grammar, such as I am attempting to do here, has of course its own inherent limitations. One of these limitations concerns the status of poetic propositions, as opposed to what linguists call the "sentence." Linguistic forms in poetry do not behave as the grammarian's "sentences" or "phrases," but rather like propositions or, more properly speaking, like illocutionary acts. They constitute, as shown in the analysis above, semantic as well as syntactic paradigms. This is so because unlike the linguist whose primary, though not exclusive, focus is upon the ordinary utterances of a natural language, the poet is inventing new "languages" and creating private grammars in which meaning is no longer dissociable from the form, nor sound from the meaning of what is being said. Given this blurring of linguistic boundaries through the superimposition of new structures – semantic, syntactic, phonological, and so forth – in poetry and given also the reference which the poet makes to extralinguistic phenomena, it becomes difficult to assert categorically that the term "sentence" has the same connotation in a casual utterance of language as it does in a poem. This inbuilt limitation of sentence-based generative grammars is beginning to be felt by critics interested not only in the relationship of linguistics to literature but also more fundamentally in finding ways to account for the production of meaning in literary texts and in units larger than the sentence. A variant of this argument has been developed in relation to pragmatics by Van Dijk (1972, 1976, 1977) and in special relation to African literature where it is linked with the idea of *pretext* by this writer (cf. Anozie, 1981, chaps. 10, 11).

The foregoing may serve as background to the second example which we wish to present here regarding the construction of Soyinka's poems. In his poetry, Soyinka presents thoughts and images (including metaphors and similes) in a pragmatic series or continuum, not as sentences or "lines." Unlike the grammarian's "sentence" (so-called "complete thought"), sentences in Soyinka's poetry form instead structures similar to Hjemslev's "thought-mass," while the *démarche* of his poetic propositions is similar to Milton's "sense variously drawn out from one verse into another" (cited in Lord, 1975, p. 6). I am unable otherwise to account for the frequent use which Soyinka in his poetry makes of this phenomenon except by saying that it acts somewhat like an attempt to erect a bridge between the poet's competence in his native Yoruba language, via his performance in the literary language of English, *and* the native speaker's intuition of English, that is, generative grammar (cf. above). Soyinka's "Gulliver" (1972, p. 23) abounds in such propositions, often arranged in a semantically equivalent order:

(1) Fearful I was
   Lest, rising, I dislodge a crossbeam
   Of their skies.

(2) I
   Proved obedient to their laws: alien minds
   Must learn recumbent postures.

(3) I took their meaning, pressed my hands
   To earth.

(4) I schooled me
   In their ways, picked a wary course
   Through egg-shell structures.

The equivalencies – all of them occur within the first two stanzas of the poem – are not structurally redundant, but purposeful. Each of the above quotations contains a set of two propositions, with the first proposition acting as a *condition*, and the second as a *conclusion*. (Later we shall see how this phenomenon is expanded by Soyinka into a global *if-then, protasis-apodosis* structure for the poem "Hamlet.") Note that the conditional parts of the four sets have positional equivalence. They may or may not also have identical deep structures, if we apply to each the following phrase structure rules for sentences in English.

The phrase structure rules (cf. also Chomsky, 1957), which apply in constituent analysis, will be employed in our demonstration in this paragraph:

$$S \rightarrow NP + VP$$
$$VP \rightarrow V + NP$$
$$NP \rightarrow Det + N$$
$$Det \rightarrow the, a$$
$$Aux \rightarrow can, may, will, must, etc.$$
$$V \rightarrow read, hit, took$$
$$N \rightarrow boy, obedience, etc.$$

Thus (1 and 2):

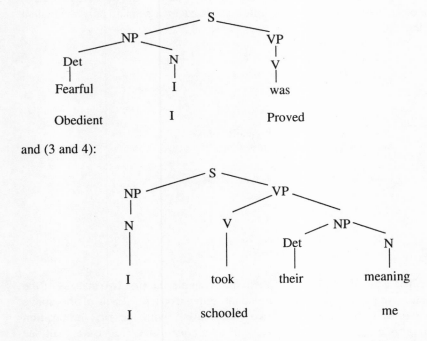

and (3 and 4):

Clearly, then, semantic equivalence in poetry does not register necessarily as identity in either surface or deep structures between equivalent propositions, and we have no reason to think otherwise because the fourth verse, which is opposed to the third by its reflexive deep structure ("I schooled me," etc.), is nonetheless semantically equivalent to it in a paradigmatic, that is, extralinguistic sense. A similar mode of analysis can be employed to show that the *conclusive* parts of the same sets of propositions, with the exception of proposition 2, have positional equivalence, although they do not constitute a paradigm: "[Lest] I dislodge a crossbeam," etc. "I pressed my hands...," "I picked a wary course." All of these are positional, not natural equivalences: no particular extralinguistic appeal is necessary in order to show that in their various contexts in the poem these linguistic forms have identical reference and meaning. The poet's art here consists in substitution, not in repetition of analogous phrases; for this reason, too, there is no structural redundancy. On the other hand, consider the conclusion in the second verse: the proposition "Alien minds must learn recumbent postures" is an independent proposition. Therefore, the semantic equivalence which it may have with the rest of its counterparts is due *not* to the linguistic environment, as defined by its position within the syntagm (although this too should be taken into account), but instead to our knowledge of its meaning, its extralinguistic connotation, as a proverbial proposition. This knowledge, I maintain, should be considered as part and parcel of competence in the poet's native language and its literary traditions – a knowledge which the poet brings surreptitiously to bear upon his relationship with the English language. I do not think that this competence is demonstrable otherwise except in actual performance. For the third example, I shall take a string of propositions occurring as a single "sentence" in Soyinka's "Ulysses":

> Lodged in barrenness of ante-rooms
> To manger-haven, I, sleep-walker through
> The weary cycle of the season's womb
> Labouring to give birth to her deathless self,
> One more reveller at the rites, *I watch*
> *The years re-lay their yeasting dregs*
> *Beneath the froth*, hard soles travel pressed
> In poultice of new loam. (1972, p. 27)

Traditional grammar would recognize in this passage certain constituent forms – such as, adjectival phrases, "lodged in barrenness"; prepositional phrases, "to manger-haven," "beneath the froth," "in poultice of new loam"; nouns in apposition, "sleep-walker through," "one more reveller at"; participal phrases, "labouring to give birth"; and, of course, the principal clause: "I watch/ The years re-lay their yeasting dregs/ Beneath the froth" – but not others, for example, the embedded deep structural substring: "the dregs are yeasting." Thus, the passage provides a good example not only of the systematic exploitation of both syntactically and semantically equivalent structures at the deep and surface structural levels but also, by logical deduction, of the infinite generative capacity of the system which the poet is using. This statement can be illustrated through a constituent analysis, using a tree-diagram, of even the main proposition: *"I watch/ The years re-lay their yeasting dregs / Beneath the froth."* This diagram makes perfectly explicit the relative positions of each constituent member of the basic proposition we are concerned with. Besides, its interpretation is transparent. It would be interesting, for instance, to account for *why* S_1, S_2, and S_3, despite the fact that they are syntactically equivalent, have different deep structures and, for precisely that reason, perhaps also different meanings. Or, inversely, *what* semantic, extralinguistic consideration is responsible for the particular transformation and reading assigned to S_3. Or, finally, *how* the prepositional phrase contracts the special relationship which it has under VP_3, and so forth. Generative grammar claims to have discovered, at the level of the human mind and intuition, the logic responsible for these *why's*, *how's*, and *what's*; in other words, the logic that would render satisfactory account for the linguistic phenomena described above. That logic is called *competence*. It is simply postulated here, for our part, that a good poet, like the generative linguist or grammarian (cf. also Anozie, 1970, pp. 54-65), has his "private" way, too, of making explicit in the poem that intuitive logic: he *performs* it.

It may be necessary, however, to remind ourselves also that, besides the type of equivalence which may subsist between forms sharing a linguistic environment (i.e., syntactical or positional equivalence) and semantic equivalence or one which may depend upon purely extralinguistic factors, there is yet another kind of equivalence. Although merely broached above with reference to metrical stress, this third type of equivalence relationship nevertheless plays a significant part in poetry by mapping syntactical structures to semantic representation. I refer to phonic (or morphophonemic) equivalence. A rather interesting example of this is contained in this passage taken from Soyinka's "Gulliver":

> From Us the Lillywhite King Lillypuss
> To you obfuscating Blefuscoons
> From Us the Herrenyolk of Egg
> To you Albinos of the Albumen... We Declare!
>   (1972, p.25)

In this text the initial parallel constructions, "From Us" and "To you," alternate. They are also semantically equivalent. Interpretationally, therefore, the pairing (the term *coupling* is sometimes also used: cf. Levin, 1962, p. 30 ff.) of semantically equivalent forms may indicate one meaning of the quoted passage as a form of exchange of diplomatic notes or

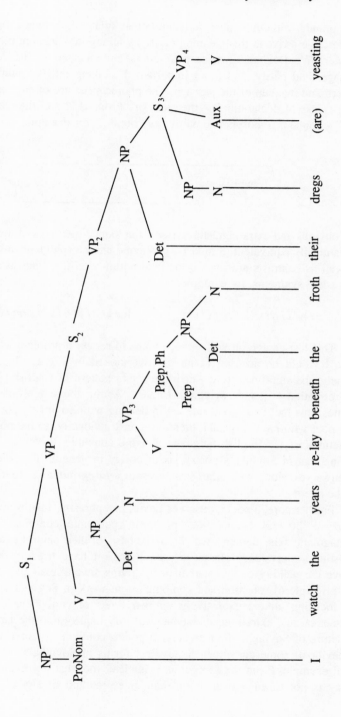

memoranda, although more unilateral than bilateral, between two hostile parties. We arrive at this meaning partly by taking into account the principal clause, "We Declare," whose position is unduplicated in the rest of the passage; and partly, and more important, by taking into account the tonal pattern and makeup of the passage. The phonic structure of each member of each "class of declaration" – the class of "From Us," and the class of "To you" – contains a morphemic pairing or coupling, for example:

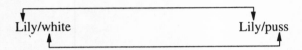

Lily/white   Lily/puss

For obvious and extralinguistic reasons, the looped members of this class are semantically equivalent. Similarly, phonemic and morphophonemic parallels as well as contrasts are linearly defined within alternate lines as within the individual syntagms, for example:

$$ɔ/b/f/\delta/s/k/ey/t/i/\eta \qquad b,/l/\delta/f/\delta/s/k/\tilde{oo}/n/s$$

This last paragraph will serve, I hope, to rectify a problem which otherwise I would be accused of having overlooked or slighted in this essay, namely, the significant role which the sound pattern of English plays in the interpretation of poetry written in English. As the above analysis briefly indicates, this fact is of great interest in dealing with Soyinka's poetry, for he is a poet who pays a special attention, constructionally, to the phonological structures of the English language. Let me conclude, therefore, simply by stating that in Soyinka's poetry, as in poetry in general, the sound pattern often serves, along with other structures, as a *foregrounding*[1] to the meaning of the poems.

Furthermore, a poem, observes Levin, paraphrasing Jakobson (cf. Levin, 1962, p. 30; Jakobson, 1960, p. 358), "puts into combination, on the syntagmatic axis, elements which, on the basis of their natural equivalencies, constitute equivalence classes or paradigms." I have tried to demonstrate above the validity of this statement by giving several examples that reveal the principle of selection and combination at work in Soyinka's poetry and by focusing almost exclusively on two types of equivalence: linguistic-syntactical and extralinguistic-semantical. My inquiry into the language and structure of Soyinka's four archetypal poems continues by investigating the behavior of some constituent equivalent forms in Soyinka's "Hamlet," the final example. From the foregoing, it is clear, too, that my intention in this essay is not to engage in a full-scale interpretation of any of the poems discussed. Nor, for that matter, is it to display in a matricial form all the equivalencies identified within the four archetypal poems. Instead, my aim has been to point out the types of paradigms present and the positions at which they may either intersect or converge with one another and with the process of meaning and interpretation. In the case of this final example, this instantiation will take the form of showing how the various linguistic phenomena discussed above appear to come to a certain head in the sonnet, "Hamlet."

This poem, it should also be noted, illustrates the use of a double archetype, one superimposed upon the other. These archetypes are (a) the story of Shakespeare's play *Hamlet* (the remaining three archetypal poems are based upon Jonathan Swift's *Gulliver's Travels*, James Joyce's *Ulysses*, and the biblical story of Joseph); and (b) by inference only, the Shakespearean sonnet form. Thus the poetic function of Soyinka's "Hamlet" is to project the principle of equivalence in a dual direction: linguistically, from the axis of selection into the axis of combination within the poem itself; and extralinguistically, that is, paradigmatically, from the axis of the experientially particular into the axis of the experientially universal. The first projection relates to the construction of the sonnet, its internal organization; the second, to its meaning and interpretation. In this analysis, as already stated, I favor the first rather than the second. This is so not because I consider interpretation of meaning in poetry as necessarily secondary to analysis and description, *but* because I consider description and analysis as a necessary adjunct to the very meaning of poetry interpretation. In the case of Soyinka's "Hamlet," a significant part of that meaning lies in the freedom from constraints, syntactic or semantic, which the poet has exercised with respect to his original Shakespearean paradigms. This freedom from accountability is, of course, the poet's prerogative. It should not deter us, however, from wishing to find out if some structural conventions governing the Elizabethan sonnet also apply in Soyinka's poem. One such convention which may be of interest is the legalistic, conditional, argumentative structure, sometimes called the *if-then* (or, latinately, *protasis-apodosis*) division of the sonnet form (cf., e.g., Shakespeare's Sonnets 12, 29, and 30).

I. [S_1: ✓ He stilled his doubts], [S_2: ✓ they rose to halt and lame
A resolution on the rack]. [S_3: ✓ (Passion's flame)
Was doused in fear of error], [S_4 ✓ (his mind's unease)
Bred indulgence to (the state's disease)]

II. [S_5: ✓ Ghosts embowelled his earth[; [S_6: ✓ he clung to rails
In (a gallery of abstractions), dissecting (tales

As "told by an idiot")]. [S_7: ✓ Passionless he set (a stage
Of passion) for the guilt he would engage].

III.   [S_8: ✓ Justice despaired]. [S_9: ✓ The (turn and turn abouts
Of reason) danced default to (duty's counterpoint)
Till treachery scratched (the slate of primal clay)]
[S_{10}: Then Metaphysics waived (a thought's delay)] –
[S_{11}: ✓ It took the salt in the wound, the "point
Envenom'd too" to steel (the prince of doubts)].

In this poem, where constructional parallelisms abound, the quatrains act as the *condition*, while the sestet acts as the *conclusion*. Also within the conditional part, the first quatrain may act as the *subcondition*, and the second as the *subconclusion*. This structure, which provisionally defines the global symmetry and unity of the octave, is registered even down to the individual "lines" and "sentences," for example, S_1 acts as the *sub-subcondition*, and S_2 as the *sub-subconclusion*. Consider the equivalent initial propositions S_1 and S_5 separating the two members of the octave:

$$S_1 \rightarrow N + V + Pron + N$$
$$S_5 \rightarrow N + V + Pron + N$$

The verbs of the propositions, "stilled" and "embowelled," appear, however, to be opposed to each other for purely semantic reasons. We might then conclude that S_1 and S_5 enjoy a relationship known as *coupling*. This term has been defined by Levin (1962, pp. 34 – 35), as "the structure wherein naturally equivalent forms ... occur in equivalent positions." This is the case with S_1 and S_5, despite the opposition between their main verbs. Since propositions which are semantically equivalent also constitute paradigms, S_1 and S_5, which are equal in positional hierarchy (cf. also the first and second quotations from "Gulliver"), also constitute a semantic paradigm by virtue of the opposition between "stilled" and "embowelled." Now consider the two terminal propositions," S_2 and S_6, which occupy identical subordinate positions vis-à-vis S_1 and S_5 respectively:

$$S_2 \rightarrow N + V + Prep + V, \text{ etc.}$$
$$S_6 \rightarrow N + V + Prep + N, \text{ etc.}$$

These two propositions, for the same reasons explained earlier, constitute a paradigm of another sort: it complements the first. At still deeper levels of embedding, in the same propositions, the poet can be seen as distributing and balancing semantically equivalent forms. This is the case with the two prepositional phrases: "on the rack" and "in a gallery of abstractions," respectively contained in S_2 and S_6, despite the fact, however, that the first prepositional phrase in S_2, "to halt and lame a resolution," appears to have a positional, though not semantic, equivalence with the adverbial phrase, "to rails," in S_6. This observation only serves to reinforce the conclusion that S_2 and S_6 constitute a paradigm whose function is to complement S_1 and S_5.

Let us turn now to S_1, S_5, and S_8, which have identical positional hierarchies with respect to the quatrains and the sestet. Whereas the quatrains have constituents exhibiting the structure described above, those of S_8 in the sestet show an opposing pattern: $S_8 \rightarrow N + V + \text{Reflexive} + N$. This pattern is similar to the one noted earlier in the expression "I schooled me": it merely indicates that when expanded, proposition S_8 will generate or yield the deep structure – "Justice despaired justice," the second "justice" being "embedded." The notion of embedding of words or meaning, especially at the deep rather than the surface structural level of propositions, corresponds with the idea of zero positions and zero promorphemes already mentioned. Since zero positions play a significant role in understanding the construction of Soyinka's "Hamlet," I have indicated, using inverted arrows, the positions in the text of the poem where they may occur. Meanwhile, because of its reflexive transformational component, S_8 cannot be said to be semantically equivalent either with S_1 or with S_5. Instead, the relationship it contracts with these two is based upon complementarity, similar to that which exists between, for example, S_1 and S_2. In other terms, S_2 and S_8 can be considered as semantically equivalent or coupled and, therefore, as constituting a paradigm. For exactly the opposite reasons, propositions S_9, S_{10}, and S_{11} (indeed, all the members of the octave) are coupled and semantically equivalent.

We, therefore, arrive at a situation where the adjusted relationships between the first (S_1, S_2) and second (S_5, S_6) quatrains and the sestet (S_8, S_9) can be stated, account taken also of the zero positions, more explicitly as follows:

I: *when* S_1... (Protasis), *then* S_2... (Apodosis)
II: *if* S_5... (Protasis), *then* S_6... (Apodosis)
III: *given* I and II (Protasis), *then* S_8... *then* S_9, etc. (Apodosis)

The reasons for these changes are consistent with those already stated. On this basis, the whole of the sestet may be changed to read:

Then Justice despaired. *Then* the turn and turn abouts
Of reason danced default to duty's counterpoint
Till treachery scratched the slate of primal clay –

Then Metaphysics waived a thought's delay
Then Metaphysics (It) took the salt in the wound...

The use of the zero promorpheme "then" and the expansion of the pronominal "it" into a zero position plus a noun thus help to bring out more clearly the unity of sestet whose function, as already mentioned, is to serve as a *conclusion.*

I am aware of the statement made earlier to the effect that, within the octave portion of the sonnet, the second quatrain may act as a subconclusion, and the first as a subcondition. If this statement were entirely correct, then the zero promorpheme in S_5 would read "then," instead of "if." However, any argument made in favor of replacing "if" with "then" in the indicated zero positions would have dubious validity if based solely on the poet's use of punctuation; even then, the semicolon (;) in S_5 might be just as misleading as the zero punctuation at the end of S_4 may be revealing. In any event, the "then"-promorpheme subordinates, whereas the "if"-promorpheme elevates the syntagmatic hierarchy of S_5 to the position of equivalency with S_1.

Furthermore, to show how the principle of selection and combination works on the syntagmatic and paradigmatic levels in Soyinka's poetry, consider the distribution within the sonnet of one category of equivalence classes: the partitive genitive or possessive constructions. In the text I have isolated these repeated parallel forms by means of brackets. Notice that in the first quatrain, they occur in terminal positions: "passion's flame," "mind's unease," "state's disease," and are all identical. In the second quatrain they assume much more expanded forms (e.g., "an idiot's tales" is expanded into the passive form, "tales as told by an idiot"), appear either in the middle of the line or as run-ons. In the sestet, finally, they revert to the original terminal position, this time with a mixture of the short and the expanded forms. Again, notice that in the octave, the possessives are almost evenly distributed among propositions with "if"-promorphemes and those with "then"-promorphemes, whereas in the sestet they all have "then"-promorphemes.

Finally, mention should be made also of the selection and distribution of rhymes within Soyinka's sonnet. Here, too, we are presented with a structure diametrically opposed to either the Elizabethan or the Shakespearean tradition: *aabb ccdd efggfe* as opposed to *abab cdcd efef gg.* The rhyming words are generally either linked to possessive nouns (e.g., "mind's unease," "state's disease") or within their vicinity (e.g., "rails" and "tales," or "stage" and "engage"), thereby indicating either positional equivalence as in the first quatrain, or opposition as in the second. Moreover, rhymes which are linked to possessive nouns and also enjoy positional equivalence (e.g., "unease" and "disease") occur in propositions containing a *then*-promorpheme; their counterparts (i. e., rhymes occurring within the vicinity of possessive nouns and enjoying equivalence only by being placed in positions of antagonism with one another: e.g., "stage" and "engage," "rails" and "tales") have a tendency to pull the propositions in which they occur toward the opposite direction. Here then, we have a possible answer to the problem as to whether the second quatrain indeed constitutes a *protasis* or an *apodosis* in the Soyinka sonnet. On the basis of the rhyme scheme and what is said above, the answer favors *protasis;* given other considerations, however, such as the syntactic division of the sonnet into three distinct parts, the choice is *apodosis.*

Conclusion

To conclude the analysis, and this essay, let us say then that the difficulty which the second quatrain presents is not a difficulty of language or of organizational structure of the quatrain, but rather a difficulty which, taking the sonnet as a whole, will normally occur when one takes a paradigm or a model of something – in this case, Shakespeare's dramatic account of the Hamlet experience and syndrome and the Shakespearean sonnet form – and then recasts and deconstructs that model or experience or form into something totally new and different from the original. As with the other poems of the "Four Archetypes," so it is with "Hamlet"; Soyinka is not in any way structurally constrained or limited by his models nor by the traditions that govern them. Vis-à-vis these models and their traditions, the poet asserts his individual freedom, as the analysis above amply shows. Earlier I described this attitude as freedom from accountability. This is so because the poet is not held responsible, at least in this analysis, for his original models and paradigms, only for what he does with and to them.

NOTES

This is an extract with a new introduction, from a more extended essay, "Linguistic Competence and Poetic Structure: An Inquiry into Soyinka's Writing," which will appear in a collection of critical essays devoted to Wole Soyinka. See *In the House of Osugbo*, ed. Henry Louis Gates, Jr. (London: Oxford University Press, forthcoming).

  1. For the original meaning and use of this word, in the Prague School of Linguistics, see, e.g., Jan Mukařosvský's article, "Standard Language and Poetic Language," trans. Paul L. Garvin, in *Linguistics and Literary Style*, ed. D. C. Freeman (New York: Holt, Rinehart and Winston, 1970), pp. 40-56.

REFERENCES

Anozie, S. O. 1970. "Poetry and Empirical Logic: A Correspondence Theory of Truth in Okigbo's *Laments." The Conch*, 2, no. 1.

──────. 1972a. "Structuralism in Poetry and Mythology." *The Conch*, 4, no. 1 (Structurology I).

──────. 1972b. "Structurology II: A Generative Transformational Approach to African Poetics." In *Language Systems in Africa*, ed. Sunday O. Anozie (Studies in African Semiotics Series) New York: Conch Magazine.

──────. 1977. "Negritude and Structuralism." In *Neo-African Literature & Culture: Essays in Memory of Janheinz Jahn*, ed. Bernth Lindfors and Ulla Schild. Wiesbaden: B. Heymann Verlag.

──────. 1981. *Structural Models and African Poetics*. London: Routledge & Kegan Paul.

Bierwisch, Manfred. 1971. *Modern Linguistics* (Series Minor, 110). The Hague: Mouton.

Chomsky, Noam. 1956. *The Logical Structure of Linguistic Theory*. Mimeographed. Cambridge, Mass.

──────. 1964. *Current Issues in Linguistic Theory*. The Hague: Mouton.

──────. 1965. *Aspects of the Theory of Syntax*. Cambridge, Mass.: M.I.T. Press.

──────. 1968. *Language and Mind*. New York: Harcourt Brace Jovanovich.

Dijk, Teun A. Van. 1972. *Some Aspects of Text Grammars*. The Hague: Mouton.

──────. 1976. *Text and Context*. London: Longman.

──────. 1978. (ed.). *Pragmatics of Language and Literature*. Amsterdam: North Holland Publishing.

Halliday, Michael A. K. 1962. "The Linguistic Study of Literary Texts." In *Proceedings of the Ninth International Congress of Linguists*, ed. Horace G. Lunt (Series Maior XII), Cambridge, Mass.: rpt. The Hague: Mouton, 1964.

Harris, Zellig S. 1963. *Discourse Analysis Reprints*. The Hague: Mouton.

Jakobson, Roman. 1960. "Closing Statement: Linguistics and Poetics." In *Style in Language*, ed. Thomas A. Sebeok.

────── and Lawrence G. Jones. 1970. *Shakespeare's Verbal Art in th' Expence of Spirit*. The Hague: Mouton.

────── and Claude Lévi-Strauss. 1962. "*Les Chats* de Baudelaire." *L'Homme*, 2, no. 1.

Jones, Lawrence G. 1967. "Grammatical Patterns in English and Russian Verse." In *To Honor Roman Jakobson. Essays on the Occasion of His Seventieth Birthday*, vol. 2. The Hague: Mouton.

Levenston, E. A. 1974. "A Scheme for the Inter-Relation of Linguistic Analysis and Poetry Criticism." *Linguistics*, no. 129.

Levin, Samuel K. 1962. *Linguistic Structures in Poetry*. The Hague: Mouton.

──────. 1967 "Poetry and Grammaticalness." Rpt. in *Essays on the Language of Literature*, ed. Seymour Chatman and Samuel R. Levin. Boston: Houghton Mifflin.

Lord, John S., Sr. 1975. "Syntax and Phonology in Poetic Style." *Style,* 9, no. 1.

Saporta, Sol. 1960. "The Application of Linguistics to the Study of Poetic Language." In *Style in Language,* ed. Thomas A. Sebeok.

Soyinka, Wole. 1972. *A Shuttle in the Crypt.* London: Rex Collings.

---------. 1975. (ed.). *Poems of Black Africa.* New York: Hill and Wang.

SOYINKA
as a
NOVELIST

"To Dare Transition": Ogun as Touchstone in Wole Soyinka's *The Interpreters*

Kathleen Morrison

One of the most illuminating of the many intricately related symbols in Wole Soyinka's novel *The Interpreters* is the god Ogun, a key figure in the pantheon of Yoruba gods that Kola is painting and for which his friends act as models. By implication, Ogun is a touchstone by which the lives of the protagonists may be evaluated, for each represents one or more facets of this god of multiple meaning.[1]

The protagonists are five young Nigerians, all of whom have studied abroad and who have returned to elitist positions in their newly independent country. Bandele and Kola are university lecturers; Egbo and Sekoni are officials in government ministries; Sagoe is a newspaper features reporter. None of them preens himself on his attainments. Rather, they scorn the pretensions and status seeking of others in similar positions. Yet although their society is riddled with corruption and in dire need of leadership, Sagoe, Egbo, and Kola are living futile lives. Only Sekoni and Bandele offer any positive contribution to the world around them. The association of these young men with Ogun highlights both their faults and their potential strengths, for the Yoruba gods, unlike those of many religions, are a mixture of strengths and weaknesses and thus are very human. By seeing how the responses of the protagonists to the difficulties of their lives resemble and differ from the conduct of Ogun, the reader can more fully comprehend the challenge that Soyinka's novel presents to his compatriots.

In his *Myth, Literature, and the African World,* Soyinka discusses at length the nature of Yoruba myth and, in particular, the symbolic import of Ogun, who, for Soyinka, is the most significant of the Yoruba gods. As depicted in Kola's canvas (224), the multiple godhead of Yoruba belief emerged from the fragmentation of the one primal deity, Orìsà-nlá, each god incorporating some of the qualities of the whole. As Soyinka explains, "The shard of original Oneness which contained the creative flint appears to have passed into the being of Ogun...With creativity, however, went its complementary aspect, and Ogun came to symbolise the creative-destructive principle" (28). Thus, Ogun, "by incorporating within himself so many seemingly contradictory attributes, represents the closest conception to the original oneness of Orìsà-nlá" (31).

In Hellenic values Ogun can be "best understood...as a totality of the Dionysian, Apollonian and Promethean virtues" (*Myth* 141): Dionysian in his ecstatic energy, in his association with wine, and through his disintegration and "spiritual re-assemblage" within the abyss of transition (142); Apollonian as the "first artist" and "the essence of creativity" (141); and Promethean as the "instinct of rebellion" (146) and the bringer of the secrets of the universe to man in the beginnings of technology (29). Among the protagonists of *The Interpreters,* Soyinka gives us the Dionysian Sagoe, the irrepressible and often drunk reveler; the Apollonian Kola, who understands "the nature of art" (227); and the Promethean Sekoni, who dares the retributive wrath of officialdom in his effort to bring power and light to a village.

The key incident in the Ogun myth is Ogun's traversing of "the transitional gulf" (*Myth* 143). When "long isolation from the world of men had created an impassable barrier which they [the gods] tried, but failed, to demolish" (28), Ogun was "the only deity who 'sought the way,' and harnessed the resources of science to hack a passage through primordial chaos for the gods' reunion with man" (27). Having "Plunged through the abyss," Ogun "called on the others to follow" (29).

As intellectuals and artists, the young protagonists of *The Interpreters* should harness the resources of their knowledge to seek the way through "the transitional gulf" for the floundering members of their chaotic society to follow. Sagoe, Egbo, and Kola are not able to do so because they are divided selves, out of touch with the deepest resources of their beings. The following passage from *Myth* is quoted at length because of its pertinence to the situation of these three young men:

> The weightiest burden of severance is that of each from self, not of godhead from mankind, and the most perilous aspect of the god's journey is that in which the deity must truly undergo the experience of transition. It is a look into the very heart of the phenomena. To fashion a bridge across it was not only Ogun's task but his very nature, and he had first to experience, to surrender his individuation once again (the first time, as a part of the original Orìsà-nlá Oneness) to the fragmenting process; to be reabsorbed within universal Oneness, the Unconscious, the deep black whirlpool of mythopoeic forces, to immerse himself thoroughly within it, understand its nature and yet by the combative value of the will to rescue and to re-assemble himself and emerge wiser, powerful from the draught of cosmic secrets, organising the mystic and the technical forces of earth and cosmos to forge a bridge for his companions to follow. (153-54)

In each of Sagoe, Kola, and Egbo, we see, in the words of the just-quoted passage, the "severance...from self," along with an unwillingness "to surrender his individuation," a lack of "the combative value of the will," and therefore an inability "to forge a bridge for his companions to follow."

The three lead fragmented lives. In their contempt for others' behavior, they express different values from those around them. They scorn people like Professor Oguazor, Dr. Lumoye, and Ayo Faseyi for whom status is so all-important that they invest much of their time and energy in trying to advance it and impress it on others. Unlike this latter group, the young friends are not concerned with upward mobility. And yet, in their bi-monthly night-club rendezvous, with unnecessary brawls initiated by Egbo (*Inter-preters*, 19), Kola's bawdy satirical sketches (22-25), and Sagoe's progressive drunkenness (19), these "superior" young men are not so different from the frequenters of the university social affairs as they like to believe. Society will not be revitalized by the self-indulgent lives of this trio.

Sagoe relies on his girlfriend Dehinwa for support in the illnesses brought on by his excesses and pesters her for sexual gratification, but he long refrains from offering her the commitment of marriage. In the fanciful exuberance of drunkenness, he plays practical jokes on people whom he sees as his intellectual inferiors. He leads an Honourable Member into making a fool of himself in parliament through a ludicrous suggestion for trading night-soil from the south for donkeys from the north; then he ridicules his dupe in his column for having done so (*Interpreters* 238-39). He spends much time in expounding his "Philosophy of Voidancy" in what he calls his "Book of Enlightenment" and reading it at great length to captive listeners. This opus is a hilarious commentary on society's coalescence of grandiose utterances and moral filth, but Sagoe's ingenious wit leaves that society uncleansed, and he continues to while away time at a newspaper in which any story revealing the truth about society will remain unpublished.

Kola also evades commitment both in his personal life and in his art. When he finds himself attracted to Monica, he fears "the leavening presence of some tenderness to weaken the laws of his own creation" (*Interpreters* 50). After beginning to express his complex feelings about the albino child Usaye, he breaks off abruptly, apologizing, "Sometimes I suffer from fluffy emotions" (49). For fifteen months he immerses himself in the creation of the enormous pantheon, knowing that it lacks "even the beginnings" of that power of true art present in Sekoni's *Wrestler* (100-01). Kola admits to himself that he has experienced "the knowledge of power within his hands, of the will to transform," but that "he dared not, truly, be fulfilled. At his elbow was the invisible brake which drew him back from final transportation in the act" (218). Therefore, Kola's Pantheon cannot empower its viewers with the strength of the gods it depicts nor reunite society with its traditional values.

Sagoe, Kola, and Egbo try to escape from personal memories and obligations of the past. Sagoe, on his return from America, does not at first let his family know that he is back, planning "a brief courtesy visit and then finish. Every man to his own business" (*Interpreters* 90). Both Kola and Egbo express the wish to be free of the past. Near the end of the novel, Kola thinks, "If only... we felt nothing of the enslaving cords, to drop from impersonal holes in the void and owe neither dead nor living nothing of ourselves" (244-45). Egbo cries, "Is it so impossible to seal off the past and let it alone? Let it stay in its harmless anachronistic unit so we can dip into it at will and leave it without commitment, without impositions!" (121). But in Yoruba belief, "life, present life, contains within it manifestations of the ancestral, the living and the unborn" (*Myth* 144). Therefore, an alienation of oneself from the past is self-destructive, a form of that "refusal to be" that Egbo sees in Noah but fails to recognize in himself (*Interpreters* 231).[2]

It is Egbo whom Kola has chosen to represent Ogun in the pantheon, but ironically Egbo is the one in greatest need of developing Ogun's "combative value of the will." Egbo's unwillingness to engage in self-sacrifice is apparent from the very beginning of the novel. The Osa Descendants Union plead with him to assume his grandfather's chieftaincy in the hope of gaining an "enlightened ruler" (*Interpreters* 12). In this request they are asking him to relive the feat of Ogun, to traverse the dangerous abyss between the old traditional ways of his grandfather and the new modern society of Ibadan and Lagos. But Egbo, unlike Ogun, shirks the task. On the canoe journey to his grandfather's creek-town domain, he tells his friends, "Over there is a blind old man and a people, waiting on some mythical omniscience of my generation" (12). That he does not have such "mythical omniscience" is his rationalization for failing their expectations, but a truer explanation lies in his subsequent selfish protest: "But what on earth can such an existence hold out for me?" (12). He could better ask this question about his work in the Foreign Office. Very little of its nature is revealed directly, but by implication his desk job is much like the one Sekoni refuses to tolerate: letters to sign, leave applications to process, bicycle advances, job applications to sort. Egbo is not "one of the keen ones" like Sekoni (27), however, and he continues to stagnate.

Later, Egbo admits another reason for his recoiling from his inherited responsibility: "My rejection of power was thoughtless.... If you seek to transform, you must not be afraid of power" (*Interpreters* 182). It is Egbo's lack of the Ogun will, rather than callous indifference, as Bandele sees it (228), that keeps Egbo from trying "to forge a bridge" between his grandfather's people and the modern world, between the past and the present. He concedes, "Oh I've dreamt of me and...the future prospects for the country's traditions. By example to convert the world" (14). Here he is joking about polygamy, but the implications are much wider, and dreams that are not energized by will are futile.

At the moment in the creek journey when Egbo must enter his grandfather's town or return to the city, Egbo tries to evade the responsibility for his own retreat by instructing the paddlers to go "with the tide" (*Interpreters* 14). To drift with the tide is Egbo's way of life. Whereas, in the passage quoted earlier, Ogun had immersed himself in the "black whirlpool of mythopoeic forces" in order to "understand its nature" and then "to rescue and to re-assemble himself," Egbo defies one such whirlpool and shrinks from another.

In the first instance, Egbo is sleeping on the rocks under the railway bridge over the river Ogun, after his sexual awakening by the courtesan Simi has upset "some balance in his life" (*Interpreters* 125). In the night he wakes to see the rushing waters "turned black, black as the deep-sunk cauldrons of women dyers and the indigo streams from *adire* hung up to dry, dripping like blood in the *oriki* of Ogun, *to to to to to*" (126).[3] At first, "alone among the rocks, and the closing forest, naked in the... dark" (126), he is filled with a metaphysical fear, as if "in the dark dwellings of an avenging God" (127), but then he grows "bold with fear, and angry, truly angry.... And his anger mounted, seeing only the blackmail of fear." Believing that his weakening has come from a sense of sin, he defies the numinous presence: "If this be sin – so – let come the wages, Death!" (127). Having survived these "terrors of the night," he feels free of sin: "it seemed to him that he was born again" (127). But as Mark Kinkead-Weekes points out, Egbo's feeling of rebirth comes from his daring of the gods rather than from communion with them (227). Making this spot "his preserve, a place of pilgrimage" (127), Egbo has many times "relived his passage of darkness" (133). But he has not let himself be "reabsorbed within universal Oneness," and never has he emerged "wiser, powerful," able "to forge a bridge for his companions to follow." Rather than reassembling himself through his mystical experiences, Egbo anesthetizes himself as he does in sexual oblivion with Simi.

Egbo's awareness of his lack of purpose is shown in his words to the girl student whom he takes to his shrine and seduces:

> I seem to go only from one event to the other. As if life was nothing but experience. When I come here I discover, it is enough. I come here...to be vindicated again, and again and again. Some day I may find that once has been sufficient. (133)

His endlessly recurring need for vindication suggests an uneasy sense that his way of life is an indefensible one.

At the end of the novel, when Egbo must choose between Simi and the pregnant girl (and analogously between continuing his drifting life and fulfilling his obligations to the past, present, and future), he experiences a second black whirlpool. In the hypnotic darkness of the concert hall where Joe Golder is singing, Egbo feels himself being sucked into the whirling blackness of dye pits with their angry bubbles calling to him: "Egbo-lo, e-pulu-pulu, E-gbo-lo" (*Interpreters* 246). This near-hallucination recalls his reaction to the pleadings of the Osa Descendants Union: "a slow anger built in him, *panic* and retraction from the elaborate pit" (12; emphasis added). Terror-stricken, Egbo hovers on the brink of the transitional gulf between irresponsible immaturity and responsible manhood, "for the abyss is the transition between the various stages of existence" (*Myth* 154). Egbo has imagined that he wants to be freed from the "creek-surface" of life where you are "controlled by ferments beyond you" (13), but now he is close to panic when faced with assuming the direction and control of his own life.

In *Myth*, Soyinka describes such a moment as Egbo experiences as a re-enactment of Ogun's ordeal:

> On the arena of the living, when man is stripped of excrescences, when disasters and conflicts...have crushed and robbed him of self-consciousness and pretensions, he stands in present reality at the spiritual edge of this gulf [the metaphysical abyss], he has nothing left in physical existence which successfully impresses upon his spiritual or psychic perception. It is at such moments that transitional memory takes over and intimations rack him of that intense parallel of his progress through the gulf of transition, of the dissolution of his self and his struggle and triumph over subsumation through the agency of will. (*Myth* 149)

Whether Egbo will summon the will to triumph is the question left unanswered at the end of The *Interpreters*. Like the other protagonists, he has within him the godlike power to transform. But in Kola's words, the act of transforming is "the process of living" and requires of each the will to overcome "the intense fear of fulfillment" (218). Without the Ogun will, Egbo, Kola, and Sagoe can only drift through life uncommitted both to some worthwhile purpose and to other people.

Such drifting not only prevents constructiveness, it occasions destructiveness. Although Noah's fear of the homosexual Joe Golder is the immediate cause of the young boy's death, the self-centered irresponsibility of Sagoe, Kola, and Egbo is the underlying cause. Sagoe's desire for an exploitative news story takes the group to Lazarus's church, where they meet Noah. Kola, struck with the purity of Noah's appearance, seeks him out and takes him to Ibadan to sit for the pantheon, but afterward ignores him, leaving him to wander where he will. Egbo, in "a sudden moment of curiosity" (*Interpreters* 231), takes Noah to Kola's studio, wanting to be present at the first meeting between Lazarus and Noah after Noah's flight from the trial by fire through which Lazarus has sought a needed miracle. But in an eruption of egotistic anger at his Ogun image, Egbo flings out of the studio, not caring what has become of Noah. Thus, Noah is abandoned to Joe Golder and to death.

Of the many myths surrounding Ogun, Kola has chosen for his pantheon "one single myth, Ogun at his drunkennest, losing his sense of recognition and slaughtering his own men in battle; and he has frozen him at the height of carnage" (*Interpreters* 233). Ogun, like Egbo, had refused to become a king, fearing the misuse of his own power, but later assumed kingship with the tragic result shown on Kola's canvas. When Egbo sees this representation of himself, he is affronted not only personally but on behalf of Ogun: "Look at that thing he has made of me... a damned bloodthirsty maniac from some maximum security zoo. Is that supposed to be me? Or even Ogun, which I presume it represents?" (233). Egbo, in rejecting this repugnant vision of himself, quarrels with Kola's selectiveness:

> Even the moment of Ogun's belated awareness would have been... at least that does contain poetic possibilities.... And then there is Ogun of the forge, Ogun as the primal artisan... but he leaves all that to record me as this bestial gore-blinded thug! (233)

We realize that, although the more positive attributes of Ogun are potentially present in Egbo, Kola has painted actuality: Egbo as destroyer, one who, during a night of drinking, erupts into "sudden violence" (219). And Egbo has not yet reached the stage of "belated awareness" of how he is living, nor has he yet benefited his society in any way.

What is lacking in the three protagonists so far discussed is the essential quality of Ogun, which Soyinka describes in *Myth* as follows:

> Ogun is the embodiment of challenge, the Promethean instinct in man, constantly at the service of society for its full self-realisation. Hence his role of explorer through primordial chaos, which he conquered, then bridged, with the aid of the artifacts of his science.... Only Ogun experienced the process of being literally torn asunder in cosmic winds, of rescuing himself from the precarious edge of total dissolution by harnessing the untouched part of himself, the will. This is the unique essentiality of Ogun in Yoruba metaphysics: as embodiment of the social, communal will invested in a protagonist of its choice. (30)

Because Sagoe, Kola, and Egbo are unable or unwilling to harness the will, they are in danger of "total dissolution" as useful participants in society and cannot explore and bridge the chaos of that society to lead others safely through it.

It is the engineer Sekoni who takes on the Ogun "role of explorer." Sekoni "with the aid of the artifacts of his science" creates an experimental village power-station, and when it is condemned by corrupt officials, he exerts his will against them in his effort to get the station opened for "the service of society." As a result, he suffers confinement in a mental hospital, but he rescues himself "from the precarious edge of total dissolution by harnessing the untouched part of himself, the will" and redirecting his creative energy into sculpting his masterpiece *The Wrestler,* "all elasticity and strain" (*Interpreters* 99). The sculpture physically resembles Bandele in face and form, but it also images the life and soul of its sculptor.

The explanation of Sekoni's superiority to Kola as an artist resides in the symbolism of Ogun "both as essence of anguish and as combative will within the cosmic embrace of the transitional gulf" (*Myth* 150).

> Ogun is embodiment of Will, and the Will is the paradoxical truth of destructiveness and creativeness in acting man. Only one who has himself undergone the experience of disintegration, whose spirit has been tested and whose psychic resources laid under stress by the forces most inimical to individual assertion, only he can understand and be the force of fusion between the two contradictions. The resulting sensibility is also the sensibility of the artist, and he is a profound artist only to the degree to which he comprehends and expresses this principle of destruction and re-creation. (150)

Sekoni, in defying the forces of authority, has subjected his spirit to be tested by daring and suffering, but Kola "dared not, truly, be fulfilled" (218). Therefore it is Sekoni, not Kola, who develops "the sensibility of the artist."

In Sekoni is reflected also what Egbo might become with the exertion of the Ogun will. Ogun permitted himself "to be resorbed within universal Oneness" and reunited the gods with men. Sekoni, a visionary and a mystic, sees the unity of life under the illusory plurality of its manifestations (*Interpreters* 122) and symbolizes this unity in his image of the dome of continuity (9). Emmanuel Obiechina explains this dome as "the dome of life, where we find religious ideas about gods and ancestral beliefs underlying the lives of men and women of modern culture and sensibility, whose present occupations and concerns anticipate a revolutionary future" (152). For Egbo, who seeks to separate himself from the past, a belief in continuity is "an optimist's delusion" (233). When he expresses a desire to forget the dead, it is Sekoni who reminds him, "b-b-bridges d-d-don't j-j-just g-g-go from h-h-here to th-there; a bridge also faces backwards" (9).

Sekoni can never fully transmit his vision of continuity in words, as perhaps his characteristic stammer is intended to signify. But his "wonder-filled, miracle-seeking hands," weighing "heavily with hope and with history," absorb power during his pilgrimage to Old Jerusalem, where "wholly awed" he stands "pitiless on his heritage before disturbing intimations, suddenly meaningful affinities" (*Interpreters* 99). "Wonder-filled" like Sekoni, Egbo makes his pilgrimage to his god-haunted shrine on the Ogun River. But because the miracle that Egbo desires is the self-seeking one of personal vindication, he draws no life-giving power from his experience. Egbo's mysticism is inward turning and lethargizing. When a woman in Lazarus's church is "taken by the spirit" (175) and becomes physically frenzied, Egbo leaves before the others: "he had seen too much like her and could never like it.... At such times Egbo longed for the other possession, the triumph of serene joys and sublimated passions" (176). What Egbo desires in spiritual experience is to be solaced, not regenerated as Sekoni and Ogun are.

If Sekoni, who takes life's necessary risks, rather than Egbo, who refuses them, had represented Ogun in Kola's pantheon, the creative and harmonizing side of Ogun rather than the destructive and disruptive one would have emerged. It is noteworthy that the final scene of the novel focuses attention simultaneously on the indecision of Kola and Egbo and the achievement of Sekoni's *Wrestler*.

Throughout the novel, as has been seen, Kola, Sagoe, and Egbo withdraw from life: Kola into his painting, Sagoe into drunkenness and his Philosophy of Voidancy, and Egbo into his isolated river sanctum. In their grief at the death of Sekoni in a road accident, they self-centeredly seek these retreats as usual. Only Bandele reaches out to the one more agonized than they, Sekoni's father. Bandele, like Sekoni, fulfills the Ogun role of acting in "the service of society." In doing so, he also embodies the mercy and justice of Ogun's multiple personality.

Traditional poetry records Ogun as "protector of orphans," "roof over the homeless," "terrible guardian of the sacred oath" (*Myth* 141). Such is Bandele, who is sought by those in need because he is always ready to help. Thus, the girl student sends messages to Egbo through Bandele, and he tries to protect her and her unborn child. Joe Golder comes to him for help after inadvertently causing Noah's death and is given succor. With sympathetic regard for the feelings of others, Bandele respects human dignity. He tries to protect people such as Faseyi from their own follies, rather than to lead them on into making greater fools of themselves, as Kola and Sagoe do. He sees the worth in others, telling the skeptical Kola that Faseyi "is supposed to be the best X-ray analyst available in the continent" (*Interpreters* 45). Unfailingly courteous to Lazarus, he chides his friends for their mockery of this preacher who has rescued others from lives of crime:

this man did go through some critical experience. If he has chosen to interpret it in a way that would bring some kind of meaning into people's lives, who are you to scoff at it, to rip it up in your dirty pages with cheap cynicism. (179)

Thinking of the possible damage that might be caused by a sensational newspaper account of Lazarus's belief that he has been resurrected, Bandele warns Sagoe against carelessly promoting another's myth (178) and issues the quiet but stern condemnation: "None of you minds much what suffering you cause" (179).

The justice for which Ogun stands and which Bandele personifies is "transcendental, humane but rigidly restorative" (*Myth* 141). Bandele can forgive his friends' weaknesses. What he cannot forgive is their inability or unwillingness to admit and repent their transgressions. Men, like the gods, must acknowledge and repent their failings to regenerate their community and restore harmony. As Robert W. July tells us, the Yoruba gods

> are held accountable for their transgressions, and obliged to make amends through ritual. Thus, as with their human counterparts, their fallibility produces discord, and requires remedial action that will contribute to the constant regeneration of the universe and the restitution of harmony. (490)

On the day after Noah's death, Bandele finds unbearable the seemingly light-hearted banter of the others, for whom Noah has become "a subject to be pushed from thought, to be wholly effaced from conscious recognition" (*Interpreters* 238). Nor can he accept Egbo's inhumanity in his refusal to assist the hysterical Joe Golder because of Joe's homosexuality, telling Egbo: "I can't forget that I came to you this morning for help and you failed me" (241). To Kola, Bandele looks as if he is "killing himself inside" (243), but Bandele asserts, "I expect Joe Golder has put years on me. But I will not snap" (244). He suffers the Ogun anguish but, like Sekoni, transcends his suffering.

In the final pages of the novel, Bandele becomes Ogun as the "terrible guardian of the sacred oath." He sits "apart from the others" (*Interpreters* 244), he stands "forbidding" (247).

> He was looking at them with pity, only his pity was more terrible than his hardness, inexorable. Bandele, old and immutable as the royal mothers of Benin throne, old and cruel as the *ogboni* [elders] in conclave pronouncing the Word. (250-51)

The Word he pronounces is intended for his friends as well as for the hypocrites who have been pompously delivering moral judgments on the pregnant student: "I hope you all live to bury your daughters" (251). It is a warning of the retribution for inhumanity – an impotent and sterile future.

In these many parallels of the protagonists with Ogun, much of the meaning of *The Interpreters* resides. "To dare transition is the ultimate test of the human spirit, and Ogun is the first protagonist of the abyss" (*Myth* 158). In the disordered upheaval of Nigerian society, passing through the perilous "transitional gulf" from colonization to independence, from a rural to an urban culture, from tradition to modernity, leaders are needed with the strength of will to link the past with the future, the material with the spiritual, the human with the divine. During the period of their lives depicted in the novel, Sagoe, Kola, and Egbo, as assessed by the criterion of Ogun, have failed to find and show the way, but the way of continuity sustained by the will in the service of society has been disclosed by Sekoni and Bandele.

NOTES

1.   Emmanuel Obiechina, basing much of his interpretation on Soyinka's article "The Fourth Stage" (now an appendix in *Myth, Literature, and the African World* on which the present study is based), asserts that "in *The Interpreters*, it is obvious that the Ogun and Obatala principles are very heavily drawn upon...in the structuring of the inner qualities and psychological details of character-portrayal" (112) and that Sagoe and Kola "share the Ogun principle with Egbo" (114). However, he does not elaborate on the relationship of the former two characters to Ogun, and he perceives Sekoni and Bandele as sharing the Obatala principle (112-14). Although Bandele and Sekoni can be seen to resemble Obatala as "suffering spirit" (112), Ogun also suffers. Moreover, Soyinka explains that "Yoruba myth syncretises Obatala, god of purity, god also of creation (but not of creativity!) with the first deity Orìsà-nlá" (*Myth* 152). It is creativity, Ogun's trait, that men and gods possess in common. It should be noted, too, that Orìsà-nlá (or Obatala) is referred to in *The Interpreters* only in the poetic description of Kola's almost-completed canvas (224), and then not by name or nature but only in the story of his being fragmented. Furthermore, there is no reference to any character's sitting for the portrait of Obatala as Egbo does for Ogun. For these reasons, Ogun seems to be the god most relevant to an understanding of all five protagonists of *The Interpreters*.

2.   Noah is an alter ego of both Egbo and Kola, just as Joe Golder is of Egbo and Peter of Sagoe.

3.   *Adire* means dyed cloth. The *oriki* of Ogun is the chant of praise names, comprised of family names, titles, antecedents, and so on.

REFERENCES

July, Robert W. "The Artist's Credo: The Political Philosophy of Wole Soyinka." *Journal of Modern African Studies*, 19 (1981), pp. 477-98.

Kinkead-Weekes, Mark. *"The Interpreters* – a Form of Criticism." *Critical Perspectives on Wole Soyinka.* Ed. James Gibbs. Washington, DC: Three Continents, 1980, pp. 219-38.

Obiechina, Emmanuel. *Culture, Tradition, and Society in the West African Novel.* London: Cambridge UP, 1975.

Soyinka, Wole. *The Interpreters.* Introd. Eldred Jones. London: Heinemann, 1981.

----------. *Myth, Literature, and the African World.* London: Cambridge UP, 1976.

SOYINKA
as a
JOURNALIST

Tear the Painted Masks. Join the Poison Stains: A Preliminary Study of Wole Soyinka's Writings for the Nigerian Press

James Gibbs

In 1967 Wole Soyinka was detained because of an article he published in the *Daily Sketch.* It was not the first time he had written for the Nigerian press, nor, despite the punishment it brought upon him, was it the last. With the help of friends and colleagues and of the facilities of the National Archives at Ibadan, I have been able to locate thiry-two pieces by Soyinka that have been published in the Nigerian newspapers.[1] They include a wide variety of different kinds of writing: there are open letters and texts of talks, letters to editors and commissioned articles, contributions to controversies, a book review, a telegram, a song, and a poem. One or two of the items show Soyinka tackling complex issues, but he avoids the erudite and obscure for writing that is clear and direct. In this body of work Soyinka is generally entertaining, concerned, hard-hitting, determined to communicate, anxious to carry his readers along with him.

This paper is a preliminary study. It is likely that Soyinka will appear in the press between the time of writing and the time of publication. It is inevitable that more material from the past will be located. There are obvious ways in which this work could be extended, for instance as a study of Soyinka's public role in Nigeria or as an analysis of the Nigerian press. I have done no more than scatter a few comments through the paper on some of the issues that are raised in order to suggest the wider context in which the writing published in the newspapers should be seen.

Soyinka has chosen the newspapers as the setting for a number of important statements, particularly on the arts, road safety, and politics, both national and international. Politics has accounted for most of the "column inches" he has produced and accordingly I have given a fair amount of space here to charting his political development as revealed in his articles for the newspapers. Some lines from "Joseph," a poem that appeared in *Shuttle in the Crypt* and that was probably written while he was in detention, provide a convenient summary of his attitude:

> ... A time of evils cries
> Renunciation of the saintly vision
> Summons instant hands of truth to tear
> All painted masks, that poison stains thereon
> May join and trace the hidden undertows
> In sewers of intrigue.

It was the tearing of "painted masks" that landed Soyinka in Kaduna Prison, and it is an activity he has frequently indulged in. There is no doubt that he regards the Second Republic over which Shehu Shagari presides as "a time of [great] evils" and there is every likelihood that his responses to the evils will lead him into danger once again.

Almost all of the material considered in this paper will be unfamiliar and unavailable to readers and so I have included résumés and quotations. I have divided my treatment into two complementary parts. In the first I provide a brief précis of each of those items published only in the press. In the second I consider these works in terms of five phases, each with characteristic attitudes and concerns. The phases should not be taken as entirely separate compartments, but as a way of organizing the material produced by one man, a man of convictions and integrity, responding to changing circumstances.

I

"The Very Last, Sir!," *Daily Express,* 31 January 1962.
Soyinka entered a controversy about the quality of the First Festival arranged by the American Society for African Culture (AMSAC). He took issue particularly with Ulli Beier for his "spurious dissection of art and entertainment," and with "Backdrop" for his cultural intolerance and insularity. Soyinka argued that the degree of success achieved by the festival had been underestimated.

"Bad Roads, Bad Users, Bad Deaths," *Daily Express,* 28 March 1962.
Soyinka castigated those responsible for road maintenance, road signs, and road engineering because of the hazards that he encountered on Nigerian roads. He accused the Ministry of Works and Transport of failing to fulfill their responsibilities. He was incensed by the hypocrisy of those politicians who delivered self-righteous speeches on international issues but who failed to help the victims of road accidents – he cited a specific instance.

"Writers for Individual Liberty," *West African Pilot,* 4 June 1962.
This, the first press release issued by Soyinka in his capacity as Secretary of

the Committee of Writers for Individual Liberty (CWIL), was published shortly after a State of Emergency had been declared in the Western Region. It argued that there was no good reason for the declaration and that far from reducing tension the government's action had increased it.

"Five Minutes of our Dances in a Theatre will Chloroform You," *Daily Times,* 7 July 1962.
Soyinka challenged the "cheap emotionalism" of Peter Enahoro's attitude to American choreographer Pearl Primus and his rejection of any contribution that she might make to adapting African dances for the stage. He argued that "authentic" dances had to go through a "necessary transition" before they could be used in the "conscious art form" of the theatre.

"Only His Friends Are Brilliant," *Daily Express,* 12 November 1962.
A review of *My Life* by Ahmadu Bello. Soyinka described the autobiography as "remarkably modest" and suggested that there were few indications of the author's own feelings. Clearly he felt that the life story left important things unsaid.

"On That Review," *Daily Express,* 17 November 1962.
Soyinka complained that his review had been edited and his strictures on *My Life* removed. He described the review as published as "a negative kind of waffle," drew attention to some of the points that had been edited, such as his complaint about Bello's picture of the Kali Courts, his "effusive attitude" to the British Royal Family, and his indelicacies. Soyinka concluded that the treatment of his review raised basic questions about the relationships between newspapers, contributors, and readers.

"Dangers of a False Sense of Security," *Daily Express,* 30 July 1963.
As Secretary of CWIL, Soyinka wrote an article that quoted a statement signed by the Committee and, of course, by Soyinka himself. The article warned against a "false sense of security following the decision to defer the Preventive Detention Act." It suggested that the threats to liberty were still great.

"Flogging Women Offenders," *Daily Express,* 4 November 1963.
In a protracted exercise in Swiftian irony, Soyinka commented on the sentencing of five women to one year in prison and to eighty strokes of the lash for "insulting behavior" towards political opponents. He sarcastically described the punishment as "an edifying aspect of Northern culture" and recommended that a film be made of the execution of the sentence.

"For Segun Awolowo," *Sunday Express,* 25 July 1965.
This well-known poem (published in *Idanre and Other Poems*) appeared a little more than two years after the accident in which Segun Awolowo died.

"An Open Letter to the Western Obas," *Daily Times,* 10 November 1966.
A delegation of Obas from the Western Region was about to set out on a tour of regional capitals. Soyinka addressed them through the press, objecting that they had nothing of value to say and pointing out that they had not backed up their expressions of concern about events in their own areas with any meaningful actions. He also attacked the Yoruba community in Zaria for the manner in which they thanked the authorities for protecting them and their property.

"Let's Think of the Aftermath of this War," *Daily Sketch,* 4 August 1967.
This strongly worded article called on the Federal Government to declare a truce in the struggle with Biafra. Soyinka argued that Odumegwu Ojukwu must have realized his secession was "at least, a miscalculation" and that the Federal response to secession was a clumsy operation, conducted with "blunt and unsterile scalpels." He asked for "a sense of the future," an attempt to answer the question "What happens after?" His suggestion was that the war was "inevitable," that there "[could] be no victory for anyone in the... conflict only a repetition of human material wastage and a superficial control that must one day blow up in our faces and blow the country finally to pieces." He was particularly indignant at the "velvet cushion commandos, cheer-leaders of national disaster" and their "warped version of the national mood."

"Dead-line for Dialogue," *Daily Times,* 31 January 1971.
Soyinka commented on a "dirge of self pity" by A. J. Isong of the University of Ibadan, which had appeared three weeks previously, in a restrained manner. He proposed a social system in which the right to a decent wage was guaranteed, there was equality of educational opportunity, and there was none of the "mutual degradation" caused by wide divisions between rich and poor. Soyinka was not surprised by the violence of the poor against the "outward symbols of all privilege" – which Isong reported – and he concluded, with a twist, that Isong's article gave cause for hope: it would encourage people to take action!

"Halt Idi Amin," *Sunday Times,* 27 July 1975.
Soyinka attacked and exposed Idi Amin (the "murderous buffoon," the "over-large child"), those who had fallen for his "diction of revolution," and those who had been taken in by his manipulation of "the Dennis Hills

Affair." Soyinka advocated the shifting of the forthcoming Organization of African Unity (OAU) summit from Kampala to Mozambique in recognition of the achievements of Samora Machel, leader of the people of Mozambique. He condemned Nigeria's position and those who employed double standards in responding to events in Africa. He concluded that 1975 "should mark the beginning of Amin's total isolation and [be] a warning to his blood brothers on the continent."

"Fresh Light on Black Arts Festival: We Must Avoid Emotional Terms," *Sunday Sketch,* 21 March 1976.
In a restrained and reasoned article (and in the context of suggestions and threats that Senegal might boycott the Second World Black and African Festival of Art and Culture, FESTAC, if North African delegates took part in the Colloquium on Black Civilization and Education) Soyinka spelled out his position regarding the categories of countries that should be allowed to participate in the colloquium. His argument, as the title partly suggests, drew attention to the danger of making political and emotional statements and claimed the right of the organizing committee to decide whom to invite.

"Soyinka's Airport Ordeal," *Daily Times,* 10 May 1976.
Another open letter, this time to the Inspector General of Police and protesting against an "aggravating search" at Ikeja Airport. Soyinka maintained that he was travelling "for the benefit of the Nigerian people" – he was a consultant to the organizers of FESTAC – and that he was working "side by side with the people, under a leadership which [did] not contradict [his] political conscience." He hoped the police would call off their meaningless harassment.

"The Scholar in African Society," *Nigerian Herald,* Part 1, 31 February 1977; Part 2, 2 March 1977.
This paper has been published in Volume 1 of the proceedings of the Colloquium on Black Civilization and Education (Lagos: Federal Military Government of Nigeria), pp. 44-54.

"The Inquisition in Uganda," *Sunday Times,* 10 April 1977.
Writing in a straightforward style and from personal experience Soyinka gave an account of his growing awareness of the nature of Idi Amin's regime. He first described meeting a Ugandan colleague in 1971 and listening to a defence of Amin; he then described meeting the same man in 1973 and hearing the truth about Amin's vicious reign of terror. Soyinka used the descriptions to draw attention to the need to be honest about violence and to speak out against brutal governments. He mentioned recent

acts of violence in Nigeria: the death of Gogo Nzeribe, secretary-general of a powerful trade union, and of Dr. Ademola, chief medical adviser to the Federal Government, and the razing of the Kalakuta Republic. He condemned the complacency and lethargy of journalists, trade unionists, teachers and students in the face of such events.

"It Owes Its Birth to *Save Journey,*" *Sunday Times,* 26 June 1977.
Soyinka entered a dissenting opinion as to the origin and antecedents of Segun Olusola's popular television serial, *Village Headmaster,* then the topic of a series of newspaper articles. Olusola had suggested that it grew out of a feature program on a headmaster; Soyinka placed it in the tradition of radio comedy pioneered in Nigeria by Ralph Opara and others. He also claimed that *Village Headmaster* owed something to a radio situation comedy series, *Broke-Time Bar,* which he had worked on with Olusola.

"National Road Slaughter: We Must Show We Mean Business," *Sunday Times,* 31 July 1977.
In an article that formed a contribution to a continuing debate, Soyinka called for the mobilization of the people against the appalling driving standards in Nigeria. He called for "enforcement saturation" on the Ife to Ibadan road to deter drivers from irresponsible actions, for intense education of passengers, and for the complete abandonment of the "current" campaigns for road safety with their jingles and pious exhortations. He recommended the imposition of crippling fines on guilty drivers.

"The Police Force: Example of Indifference," *Daily Times,* 22 September 1977.
Soyinka, who had just returned from South America, set his experience of racial discrimination in Peru against the experience of a Ghanaian journalist whose cousin's eldest son had been murdered in Ajegunle. Quoting the journalist at length and commenting on the letter, Soyinka directed the attention of the Inspector General of Police to a situation in which the police force showed no inclination to investigate a murder and in which it was necessary to pay bribes in order to recover the body of a relative for burial. He suggested that the Bar Association should be concerned but observed that they were only interested in such matters when "certain classes of society [were] involved."

"Varieties of Wasting," *Daily Times,* 23 September 1978.
In the silence and stillness that followed the Pedro Martins Committee, set up to investigate the effects of a national "purge" of administrators, Soyinka considered the fate of those who had been unjustly fired by their employers

– particularly by the government. He scrutinized two of the organizations with which he was familiar, the "thieving manipulators of the Festac administration" and the university, where he drew attention to the devious activities of lobbyists with grudges and of those who, out of jealousy and insecurity, frustrated talent. He concluded by calling for "a complete overhaul of the current militarist automatism of waste."

"Song of the Ruling Passion," *Nigerian Herald,* 14 October 1978.
This song appears on pp. 57 and 58 of the published edition of *Opera Wonyosi,* a play that was first produced at Ife during December 1977. There is no reason to suppose that Soyinka promoted its publication in the *Herald.*

"An Open Letter to Arap Moi," *Daily Times,* 7 November 1978.
In his capacity as Secretary General of the Union of Writers of the African Peoples (UWAP), Soyinka addressed the Kenyan president through the *Daily Times.* He expressed his condolences on the death of Jomo Kenyatta and "approached" Moi on the question of Ngugi wa Thiong'o's release from detention. He expressed disbelief that Ngugi could be a threat to the state and drew attention to the callous treatment to which Ngugi and his family had been subjected.

"The Censorship of Sembene Ousmane," *Daily Times,* 9 December 1978.
A correspondent to the *Daily Times* had raised the issue of the censorship of Ousmane Sembene's work in Senegal and of UWAP's action on the matter. Soyinka, writing as Secretary General of UWAP, assured the correspondent that protests had been made and he quoted a telegram sent to Senghor concerning Ousmane's film *Ceddo.*

"1979: Year of the Road," *Daily Sketch,* 1 January 1979.
Soyinka, by-lined "Special Marshal, Oyo State Road Safety Corps" (OSRSC or RSC), put the case for a more serious approach to road safety. He drew attention to the lack of funds for the corps, the bureaucratic muddles in the state administration, and the lack of concern among civil servants that a case for improvement of the roads could be made in a "positive, detailed and committed manner." After taking up a former vehicle inspection officer for some of his remarks about the Corps, Soyinka provided the "positive, detailed" document that the civil servants had failed to produce. He claimed that the RSC was potentially effective, that entrenched bad habits had to be removed, that the Vehicle Inspection Office and the system of distributing driving licenses had to be overhauled, and that maximum speed limits and a computer data bank had to be introduced. He argued that if these measures were taken, there would be a major reduction in the number of road

accidents over the next six months. He referred to the Okuwa case (see below) and the damage done by it.

"Commissioner for Partial Justice," *Daily Times,* 21 January 1979.
This was a communiqué from the Special Marshals' Unit of the OSRSC, University of Ife Branch, but it bears the marks of Soyinka's hand so clearly that I am taking it as his work. At K. G. Okuwa's trial for dangerous driving the Oyo State Commissioner for Justice, Mr. B. A. Aiku, said that the case had not been correctly brought and that there was no case to answer. In the communiqué Soyinka exposed Aiku and his "specious nonsense" and set down the terms on which the special marshals would resume their operations.

"Happy Riddance," *Nigerian Herald,* 25 May 1979.
The text of a talk given to the Ugandan community in Nigeria by Soyinka on behalf of UWAP. Soyinka opened this, his most densely textured piece to appear in the Nigerian press, with a gale of sarcasm at the expense of Amin, those who regarded Tanzania as an "imperialist's stooge," and those who excused Amin's behavior on the grounds of historical circumstances. Soyinka then gave a résumé of UWAP's concern with Uganda and the union's efforts to discover and publish the facts about Amin's rule. Soyinka referred with approval to Olusegun Obasanjo's speech at the Khartoum summit and used its radicalism to establish common cause between Nigeria and the post-Amin rulers in Kampala. He argued in favor of Tanzania's role in toppling Amin and exposed the weakness of the OAU, the maneuverings of Libya, and the "mischief making" of journalists. He claimed that there had been a "conspiracy of silence" and that African leaders and the African intelligentsia had been bemused by Amin's buffoonery and closed their eyes both to the viciousness of his reign and to the vacuity of his "economic policy." He concluded with a narrative built on Amin's confession of "love" for Julius Nyerere of Tanzania, which turned into a questioning of why "distant neighbors" mourned while the streets of Kampala were full of revelers.

"Sick Humour," *Sunday Sketch,* 24 June 1979.
In a letter to the editor, Soyinka drew attention to two tasteless cartoons that had appeared in the paper and had made light of domestic tragedies. He deplored the approval implied for such "sick humor."

"Display of Shagari's Portrait," *Sunday Sketch,* 27 January 1980.
In Soyinka's view certain elements of the press were making an issue out of whether or not the head of state's portrait was on display in government offices in certain states. Soyinka was anxious to prevent the creation of a

new test for loyalty and pointed out that in the offices of *The New Nigerian*, the paper most vigorously promoting the cause, the photographs of the current head of state had not always been on display. He accused the paper of operating "double standards."

"Telegram to Governors Balarabe Musa of Kaduna and Abubakar Rimi of Kano," *Nigerian Herald*, 5 August 1980.
The telegram read "Your so-called expulsion from PRP is a sad shock for us, former admirers of Alhaji Aminu Kano. However a commitment to the masses as opposed to narrow privileged interests far out-weighs considera-tion for individuals however much they have contributed to the unending struggle. Count me in if you plan to form a party which will vigorously pursue those ideals which your government has striven to materialize. Sincere fraternal greetings, Signed Wole Soyinka, University of Ife."

"In Defence of Aboyade," *Sunday Sketch*, 16 November 1980.
Writing as "Chief Aparologists for the Aparo Mafia (Extinct Species)," Soyinka defended the reputation and record of Tunji Aboyade, ex-vice-chancellor of the University of Ife. Specific charges had been levelled against Aboyade concerning the delayed rebuilding of a students' hostel that had collapsed, the withholding of promotion papers, and the use of the vice-chancellor's lodge as a "disco palace." Soyinka defended Aboyade, vouched for his energetic attempts to get the hostel rebuilt and alleged that the rumors about the "disco palace" were unreliable and had been "fed" to the press. He admitted that he was a member of an informal consultative body that had supported Aboyade and worked hard in the interests of the university and its students. He denied that the group had ever had anything to do with academic promotions or that it was involved in attempts to embarrass the new vice-chancellor. He called for a panel of investigators "preferably with a couple of psychiatrists in attendance" to consider the case of the "intel-lectual midget" who claimed that his professorship had been delayed.

"Police Are Brutal and Commit Atrocities," *Sunday Sketch*, 27 July 1981.
In this second open letter to the Inspector General of Police, Soyinka asserted that recent manifestations of police brutality were consistent with the government's plan to turn the force into the "strong-arm section" of an "aggressive and totally unscrupulous fascist regime." As evidence he cited the deaths at the hands of the police of an athlete, a recent graduate, and sev-eral University of Ife students; the deportation of opposition leader Shuguba Abdulrahman Darman, leader of the Great Nigeria People's Party in Borno State; the "invasion of the Nigerian legislature by the Riot Squad"; the assault on the Governor of Ogun state; the rampage in Kano, and the

"outrages" in Oyo (Ife/Modakeke), Borno (Bembem), and Sokoto (Bako-lori). He accused the Inspector General of *folie de grandeur* and of having ambitions to run the country. The final paragraphs breathed defiance: Soyinka expressed his confidence in the will of the people to resist.

"The Bogus Revolution of our Time," *Sunday Sketch,* 3 January 1982.
The text of Soyinka's address at the launching of *Aké,* his account of his childhood, in Abeokuta. Soyinka said that the launching was an act that united the forces of liberation against the forces of death. He took issue with *The Punch* that had reported that he had said that revolution was inevitable and maintained that Shagari's government was involved in promoting a "revolution" of its own. Soyinka mockingly listed the achievements of the "revolution": Shugaba's deportation; the despoilation of the country's wealth; the Bakolori Massacre, where farmers were killed by the forces of the state; the subversion of the Kano state government by a "cooperative mob"; the destruction of *The Triumph* newspaper offices; the butchering of Bala Mohammed, political adviser to the governor of Kano state; the deaths of students, athletes, and Youth Corpers, and the storming of an elected legislature. Soyinka argued that the government responsible for these "acts of public violence" was inviting a "cataclysm." He accused certain supporters of the government of conspiring against him with the assistance of "local agents of the National Security Organization." He spoke of the importance of Wale Ademoyega's book *Why We Struck* and maintained that the significance of *Aké* was to be found in the continued suffering of the masses, "the contempt and feudal arrogance" of the very rich, and in the example, recorded in *Aké,* of the uprising of the Egba women, shortly after the war, against the Alake, the "traditional ruler' who had been favored by the British in Abeokuta. He suggested that this uprising had led to a temporary liberation.

II

This material covers roughly twenty years and I have divided it into the following five phases of various lengths: Phase 1, The Western Region Emergency and After (1962-1965); Phase 2, The Drift into Civil War (1966-1967); Phase 3, Detention, Ibadan and Exile (September 1967 - December 1975); Phase 4, Military Rule under Murtula Mohammed and Olusegun Obasanjo (December 1975 - October 1979); Phase 5, The Second Republic (October 1979-).

PHASE 1, The Western Region Emergency and After (1962-1965)

Soyinka returned to Nigeria after five years in England with a fine sense of timing: he arrived in Lagos on the first of January 1960. His reputation as a poet and playwright had preceded him to Ibadan and he soon became well known in the Western Region as a writer and broadcaster, an actor, and a singer. He began writing to and for the press in, I think, 1962, and during the three years that followed expressed his opinions on the arts, the roads, and politics. It was a period of violent political confrontation in the Western Region, and Soyinka experienced censorship and circumvented it before being drawn to the center of the political conflict in a most dramatic way.

In December 1961 he took part in the first Nigerian festival organized by the American Society for African Culture (AMSAC), and his contribution to the controversy among critics and performers that followed the festival was, as far as I can ascertain, his first appearance in the Nigerian press as a contributor.[2] He took issue with the established cultural pundits, with their restrictive concepts of the function of the arts, and with their prescriptions for the arts in Nigeria. He came out strongly against cultural insularity and chauvinism, arguing for a rapprochement with relevant and virile foreign traditions.

He returned to the cultural controversy in his lengthily titled rejoinder to "Peter Pan": "Five Minutes of our Dances in the Theatre will Chloroform You." "Peter Pan," the pen-name of the established and respected journalist Peter Enahoro, was taken to task for the terms in which he had criticized Pearl Primus, the Afro-American dancer and choreographer.[3] Soyinka accused "Peter Pan" of "cheap emotionalism" and lack of logic in responding aggressively to Pearl Primus's project "to teach Nigerians how African dances can be adapted to the modern stage." The title of his article summarized Soyinka's position on the matter: he recognized that adaptation of material was essential. Indeed adaptation – a process which involves alteration of existing material for performance "in a theatre" – is a principal tenet of Soyinka's aesthetic. Put another way, he draws on his Yoruba cultural matrix but shapes the material before it is performed in the theatre.

These two articles announced the arrival in the columns of the Nigerian newspapers of a lively, mature, combative mind, anxious to take on the established cultural authorities. Since he wrote those articles, there is little evidence in the newspaper pieces that Soyinka's ideas have changed significantly. Indeed, looking forward fourteen years to the article on the origin of the idea for *Village Headmaster* (26 June 1977) we see him emphasizing the dependence of the individual on a tradition of creativity, an extension of the concept of adaptation presented in 1962.

By March 1963 Soyinka was considered important enough to be invited to contribute, along with such respected men as Bishop S. C. Phillips, to a series under the heading "What Infuriates Me About Nigeria." He was also prominent enough to be asked to review a book, but he was not respected or prominent enough to have his copy printed unedited. Soyinka was, it appears from his article, "infuriated" by the hazards encountered on the Nigerian roads. His article, "Bad Roads, Bad Users, Bad Deaths," indicates how long he has been passionately concerned with road safety. A distinctive feature of his attitude to road hazards in 1963, one that has since changed dramatically, was that he professed to be unconcerned about the identity of those responsible for creating or permitting the hazards. At one point in the 1963 article he wrote:

> Now, I do not know whose responsibility road-signing is, and quite frankly I am indifferent. In fact, such is my faith in the inevitability of poetic justice that I keep hoping that before some humane person comes into the road-signs department the criminal gang of mass murderers who were responsible for this and for other farcical warnings will meet their just deserts at the respective bends.

The same article is of interest to those concerned with Soyinka's writing for the theatre because it described in prose the road hazards which constitute the "obstacles" in the sardonic revue sketch "Obstacle Race."[4]

Apart from providing an opportunity for men to show their inhumanity, for office holders to show their irresponsibility, for the grim reaper to gather to him those sentenced to death by poetic justice, the road also provided a testing place for politicians. The final paragraphs of Soyinka's article pillory a senator, well-known for being quick to shed crocodile tears over Patrice Lumumba (the assassinated Congolese leader), who would not go out of his way, even in his government-owned car, to take a Nigerian road accident victim to hospital. Hypocrisy and double standards of this kind are repeatedly attacked by Soyinka in his newspaper articles, especially when, as in this case, they can be seen in those who aspire to be leaders.

The book Soyinka was asked to review for *The Daily Express* in November of 1962 was the autobiography of a major political figure, *My Life* by Ahmadu Bello. The values that Soyinka brought to his reading of the book are encountered elsewhere in his writing: a concern with individuality (*Aké* is an intensely personal book), a healthy antimonarchism (as in some of the poems read at the Royal Court evening), and a sense of delicacy and taste (see the letter on "Sick Humour," 24 June 1979). But it is the fate of the review, rather than the review itself, that is revealing. The editor of the *Express* cut out some of the most telling of Soyinka's criticism, and Soyinka complained strongly. He began his letter to the editor thus: "It has always been, I know, a frustrating experience to write honestly and intelligently for any of our newspapers." His penultimate paragraph read: "I hope you understand that actions like [the editing of the review] make it impossible for any trust to exist between contributor and editor."

It is not entirely clear what, apart from the treatment of the review, lay behind this weary tone ("It has always been..."), but it would seem that following the riots in the Western House of Assembly and the appointment of Dr. Moses Majekodunmi as federal administrator at the end of May there had been a certain amount of press censorship. That this affected editors as well as contributors is indicated by the fact that Majekodunmi restricted the movements of two editors, Lateef Jakande and Bisi Onabanjo. It is probable that Soyinka's writing for the press had already been affected by this "blackout' and the censorship may have nudged him towards the political stage revue as a form of protest.

Anxiety about the State of Emergency and about the direction the country was moving in – it was a "time of evils" – may well have prompted the formation of the Committee of Writers for Individual Liberty (CWIL). The members of that committee were among the brightest and most concerned Nigerian academics of Soyinka's generation. They included Mrs. B. Awe, Miss O. O. Idowu (later Mrs. Soyinka), Demas Nwoko, S. R. B. Okoro, Dr. S. A. Aluko, Dr. J. O. Ezeilo, Dr. Oyenuga, Dr. D. F. Ojo, Dr. J. Ajayi, Dr. Akin Mabogunje, B. J. Dudley, and Dr. J. C. Ene. None of these was, in the strict sense, a "writer," and it is possible that the committee chose its title with the deliberate intention of evoking the special status accorded to the creative writer or artist in order to attract attention and ensure space in the newspapers. Soyinka, who was secretary and, of course, a writer, must also have anticipated that editors would take more notice of him if he presented himself as a representative of an organization than if he simply went to them in a personal capacity. In this manipulation of the press the fact that CWIL was a small group of academics with no popular base was unimportant and Soyinka managed to get two statements on current events into the newspapers, the first on June 4, 1962, shortly after the declaration of the State of Emergency, the second just over a year later.

The title "Writers for Individual Liberty" was given to the first press release by Wole Soyinka. There is no suggestion that it was an official communiqué; rather the opposite is suggested since it was written with the wordplay, the comic exaggeration, and the use of specific instances that are features of Soyinka's own polemic writing. For instance, he described a soldier encountered on the Ikorodu road thus:

[His revolver] was not even in the holster: HE HAD IT IN HIS HAND! If someone had said Boo to this tenderfoot, there is no doubt that he would have put a bullet through his toes or dropped dead of fright.

The press release carried a creative insight into the ways in which man seeks and then hoardes power, but "the Committee's" central concern was with the rights of individuals. This concern was summarized thus, "What concerns us specifically is the destruction of an individual sense of security." "Individual" liberty was, and is, a concern of Soyinka's, but, once again, his emphasis has changed. This article reflected a conviction that has been replaced by an increased sense of communal responsibility and by calls to action.

A year later Soyinka again sounded a warning note. He regarded the government's maneuvers, such as their promise to shelve the Preventive Detention Act and the public excitement encouraged about Dick Tiger's boxing title fights, as ploys in a bid for even greater power than they already held.[5] Speaking for the Committee he described the opponent's strategy:

> What we are saying here is that it should be obvious now to everyone that these seemingly isolated outbreaks of power rash are in reality typical patterns of power experimentation.

Having indicated the conspiracy – "the poison stains" – Soyinka issued a summons to confrontation, encouraging his supporters with rhetoric:

> We have a simple choice of dying as a nation or of fighting governmental arrogance whenever it shows itself. Let us face it, we are now confronted with the final desperate twitches of a corrupt generation who have failed us, who are suspicious of any independence of mind and who would rather intrigue, blackmail and buy support than deserve it constructively and by demonstrations of idealism.

Soyinka would, I suspect, admit that the lines about the "final desperate twitches" were written out of misguided optimism rather than out of rigorous analysis of available evidence. His assessment of the spectrum of possibilities as a simple choice is one that runs through his writing both for the press and for the stage. There is a Manichean element in his apprehension of events that polarizes the forces of good and evil, life and death. He usually preaches confrontation – as here – but on some occasions he recognizes that short-term cooperation with reactionary institutions is necessary to ensure long-term victory.

In his concluding paragraphs, Soyinka, the creative writer, betrays his awareness of the English literary heritage while briskly and forcefully summing up principles. In writing "For those who believe that an elected government exists to measure out their liberty in teaspoons," he charged T. S. Eliot's world-weary image with scorn. He went on to emphasize:

1. that national security cannot be separated from the security of the individual and from a national absence of fear;

2. that the people should not permit themselves to be manoeuvred into a position where they must beg their freedom;

3. that the Judiciary is the last hope of the common man, and that any clique which intrigues to immunise itself against the law becomes, ipso facto, an outlaw clique.

This constituted a clear statement of his democratic socialism.

In September 1963, after a well-publicized tussle in which he used the pressure of publicity to hasten the issuing of a new passport, Soyinka left Nigeria to attend the International Festival at Edinburgh. It seems that Dr. S. A. Aluko, an economist who often wrote to and for the press, took over as Secretary of CWIL. Although Aluko had been an active member of the Committee, it does not seem to have survived the change of office holders, or perhaps it fell victim to the pressures its press releases had warned against. In any case the next time Soyinka's work appeared in the press it showed that he had adopted tactics quite different from those he had used as secretary of CWIL. "Flogging Women Offenders" appeared in November 1963 and took issue with the vicious punishment inflicted on five women found guilty of "insulting behavior" towards their political opponents. The satiric mode that Soyinka adopted is one that came easily to him, as his plays reveal. It has the advantages of confusing the censor and of taking the reader unawares. It is also virtually unanswerable and can express passionate anger with an intensity that mere outrage rarely matches. The characteristic tone of the piece is caught by the following paragraph:

> My only sorrow is that we in the South are deprived of participation in this edifying aspect of Northern Culture. It might be a good idea, therefore, if the Film Unit of the Northern Government would make a record of the proceedings.

"Laying it on" even more thickly, if that is possible, he wrote, "We need to conserve and display these simple touches of rural elegance in our eternal search and propagation of a national personality." The style of this writing owes something to Jonathan Swift and has much in common with that of some of the revue sketches that Soyinka wrote about this time for *The (New) Republican* (1963) and *Before the Blackout* (1964), and with some parts of *Kongi's Harvest* (1965). It would seem that the blackout was approaching and the first phase of Soyinka's writing was coming to an end. "Flogging Women Offenders" marked a change of approach in the battle to communicate with the public and looked forward to a period during which the stage and direct action provided means of getting ideas across. They became particularly necessary after the passing of the Press Bill in September 1964.

A final insight into the nature of this transitional period is provided by the reaction to the publication of "For Segun Awolowo" in the national press. The episode shows how the expression of personal grief at the death of a national figure in a tense and polarized political atmosphere can provide a focus for popular feeling. Segun Awolowo, eldest son of the imprisoned Action Group leader Obafemi Awolowo, died in a motor accident on the Ibadan-Shagamu road during July 1963, just eleven months after graduating in law from Cambridge. A memorial service was held for him a year after his death, and Soyinka's poem appeared a year later. The accident, the youthful promise of the victim, the lonely grief of the father, and the recollection of these circumstances moved many Nigerians, particularly Yorubas, deeply. Soyinka's poem was apparently much appreciated. In the course of an assessment of Soyinka's position in his society, Dennis Duerden provided the following account of its reception:

> When the nightclubs were being closed in Ibadan during the disturbances in the summer of 1965, Soyinka's praises were being sung by every band. They were sung the louder after he published a poem lamenting the death in a motor accident of the son of Awolowo, the jailed opposition leader.[6]

This popular acclaim, and the unscrupulous criminality which surrounded the elections a few months later, provided the background to Soyinka's most desperate attempt to use the mass media to communicate with the people. He decided to hold up the radio-station at Ibadan and broadcast a tape he had made which began "this is the voice of Free Nigeria" and went on "to advise Chief Akintola and his crew of renegades to quit the country." After he had put the tape on, Soyinka left the radio-station and, in his own words, "went into hibernation." He was eventually brought to trial and acquitted – on the grounds that there was conflicting evidence. He was carried shoulder high from the court surrounded by enthusiastic well-wishers.[7]

PHASE 2, The Drift into Civil War (1966-1967)

In *The Man Died* Soyinka wrote that his arrest in 1967 was prompted by his denunciation of the war in the Nigerian press, his visit to the East, his creation of a pressure group of intellectuals, and his formation of a third force.[8] In this section we are concerned with Soyinka's writing in the press about the events leading up to the war and about the war itself: two pieces appeared, "An Open Letter to the Western Obas" and "Let's Think of the Aftermath of this War." It is essential to see them in the context of events in Nigeria in 1966 and 1967, for, like almost all Soyinka's writing for the press, they are responses to a series of particular statements and events.

The military coup in January 1966 brought the First Republic to an abrupt and bloody end. Many, including Soyinka, welcomed the promise of changes that came in with Aguiyi Ironsi. In May of the same year, however, there were disorders in the North, in July a counter-coup placed Yakubu Gowon in power, and in September and October there were attacks on Igbos in the North and West. Soyinka's first foray into the press on the multitude of issues raised by these events was an open letter to a group of obas, traditional rulers, from the Western Region who, in November 1966, were about to set out on a nationwide tour. Soyinka regarded the undertaking, which was presented in terms of a peace mission, as a purposeless charade, a confusionist tactic that would try to cover with words the wounds that only actions could heal. He coupled his criticism of the obas with an attack on the Yoruba community in Zaria for the contemptible and "un-Yoruba" manner in which they had expressed their thanks for being protected during the disturbances. This was, I think, the first time Soyinka had employed an open letter as a means of communicating his position, focusing public opinion, and fomenting a debate. In this case it seems that the western obas read the letter openly addressed to them – or at least knew of its existence – but it did not dissuade them from their mission. From the correspondence that followed the publication of the open letter, Soyinka had rather more opponents than supporters among his readers.[9]

His second article during this phase was written in a far more acerbic style and was published at a far tenser time. It led to an extensive correspondence and to Soyinka's arrest. By August 4, when the article appeared, there had been significant developments in the national situation: on May 30 Biafra seceded from the Federation, in early July there were "Igbos Must Go" demonstrations in Lagos and reports that Igbos were trying to blow up the city, on July 10 *The Daily Sketch* reported that federal troops were advancing on Enugu, and on July 16 *The Sunday Sketch* reported the capture of Nsukka. The tide of fighting was presented as flowing strongly in favor of the federal forces. In fact, however, Biafra was poised to make her most decisive thrust of the war, the drive into the Midwest that took Biafran forces to Benin City. Soyinka's appeal for a truce and his attack on the "velvet cushion commandos" who were "exploiting" the chaos was thus published on the eve of a major federal setback. The appeal enraged federal supporters and prompted them to present Soyinka as the cause of their humiliation.

"Let's Think Again" was not only an appeal for a truce, it was also an appeal for plain and honest speaking. Soyinka objected to the description of the conflict as "a police action," he preferred "to give it its proper name – a civil war and a most disastrous, inglorious war." Soyinka, and it is one of the several perspectives he shares with George Orwell, is concerned about language and aware of the ways in which governments, and others, employ language to confuse and mislead. As can be seen from the line just quoted, Soyinka was not satisfied with "proper names"; he added hard-hitting condemnation to plain speaking. This tactic has often proved unproductive; no one likes to have his "painted mask" pulled off and insults hurled into his face.

Soyinka offered no coherent analysis of the causes sucking the country into Civil War. He wrote:

> Let me concede right away that this present war did become at some point or other simply inevitable. The blood cloud which hung so recognisably over the country had finally to burst.

There is no evidence in "Let's Think Again" that Soyinka had recognized what he later described in *The Man Died* as "the genocidal policies of the government of Gowon."[10] His instinct, or perhaps his "intuition," prompted him to point out and vilify those who were exploiting the confusion and chaos into which the country had been swept. These were the very men whom he would later accuse of *creating* the confusion and chaos. He described them in July 1967 as

> the now familiar brigade of professional congratulators, opportunists, patriots and other sordid racketeers who are riding high into positions of influence on the wave of hysteria and tribal hatred.

He continued in this vein of choice insult for two paragraphs and he must have realized that its effect would be like pouring paraffin on smouldering embers. Inevitably the strong words with which the article closed distracted attention from the plea that the title of the article summarized and the proposal with which he began. Tempers flared.

The idea of a truce was, in fact, taken up in a *Daily Sketch* leader, but the correspondence pages were quickly filling up with rejoinders. For instance, on August 15 *The Daily Sketch* carried two pieces which combined rejection of Soyinka's proposals with a smear campaign and a call for reprisals against him. The articles were revealingly entitled "Slow Action can only Aid the Rebels" and "We Needn't Spare Nation Wreckers." When Soyinka was subsequently asked by his Special Branch interrogator, whom he refers to as "D", what he thought about the replies to his articles, he said:

They seem to have come from a very frantic propaganda machine.... Most of the names attached to those letters are false. Seventy-five per cent of the letters were written by the same group of hacks.[11]

But by the time he said that, he was already in custody and, although he smuggled letters out of prison to combat the campaign in the press against him, he did not have anything published in the Nigerian newspapers for more than three years.

PHASE 3, Detention, Ibadan and Exile (September 1967-December 1975)

"To keep Nigeria one – Justice must be done" said Soyinka when he flew in to Ibadan after his release from twenty-seven months in detention. The newspapers reported his release and quoted his eminently quotable quote. As the months passed, however, Soyinka, who had evidently been deeply hurt by the way the press had been used against him while he was in detention, showed little enthusiasm for writing to or for the newspapers. As in 1964-1965 he preferred to use the stage to make his political comments: for instance through his anti-military production of *Kongi's Harvest,* through *Madmen and Specialists,* and through *Jero's Metamorphosis,* which all date from this period.

In January 1971, however, he was provoked into print by an article written by Dr. A. J. Isong of the University of Ibadan. Isong "paged" the "serious minded readers" of *The Sunday Times* with an "argument" entitled "In this country the top man is openly persecuted." "Persecuted," Isong maintained, by being heavily taxed to support development projects that benefit all, by being abused by young people who resent him for riding in a car, by having his car damaged by envious pedestrians, by being charged higher prices than market traders demand of their poorer customers, by being queried by the Inland Revenue who ask about earnings over and above the university salary. In a different mood Soyinka, one feels, might well have answered this "dirge of self-pity" with a "poor little rich boy" parody, but his reply to the blinkered and reactionary colleague was measured and detached rather than sarcastic. It was also radical, sounding notes that suggested that Soyinka's months in detention had encouraged him to analyze society in terms of class conflicts and to perceive a violent uprising as a means of resolving those conflicts. He wrote:

What I would have expected of an academician was the advocation of a social system whereby the right to a decent [living] was guaranteed and the benevolent patronage of the privileged groups was eradicated for all time.

> Dr Isong's cry if any should be directed against a social system which binds
> both him and his dependants in a vice of mutual degradation and limits his
> freedom of action and development by denying him equality in his association
> with all the potential inherent in every class of society.

He went on to criticize the universities for creating "little rivieras ... without
equivalent facilities for their junior staff" and to argue that "for the modern
university idea to thrive, the system must die." He indicated that he understood the pressures that drove the downtrodden to take violent action against
the symbols of the wealthy. The final paragraph added an element that indicated further Soyinka's ideological shift:

> In a way, finally, Dr Isong's article gives one hopes. A few more essays in that
> vein and no one will need to preach any ideology to the people. Events would
> simply overtake dialogue.

Soyinka is at pains not to repeat the clichés of Marxist ideologues – he is far
too sensitive to language to do that. But there has been a major shift to the
left in his thinking and this can be clearly seen by comparing the
perspectives and implications of this rejoinder with his articles of the early
1960s.

Soyinka did not, I think, publish in the Nigerian press again for four and
half years – years he spent in Britain and Ghana, and years during which his
interest in writing for the press was largely satisfied by his editorial
responsibilities for *Transition/Ch'Indaba*. These were also years during
which his more revolutionary brand of socialism may well have been
encouraged by the new vigor that informed European politics and writing in
the wake of the events of May 1968, and the new confidence expressed in
such books as *How Europe Underdeveloped Africa* by Walter Rodney.[12]

Soyinka's move towards revolutionary socialism was consolidated
during a period when the slogans of revolution were being grossly abused
by Idi Amin. Following the coup in which he toppled Milton Obote, Amin
was welcomed by some in the English press, by many African intellectuals,
and by such journalists as Deji Fasuan who wrote as follows in *The Sunday
Times* (25 February 1973) under the heading "Idi Amin and his Built-in
Sense of Humour," "We can only hope and pray that fortune and his fellow
countrymen will spare [Amin] long to enliven this dull continent."

In mid-1975 Amin was "enlivening the continent" with the Dennis Hills
Affair, posing as a revolutionary leader, and looking forward to becoming
chairman of the OAU. In July Soyinka sent an article, "Halt Idi Amin," to
The Sunday Times. From the article it was clear that Soyinka regarded
Amin's "diction of revolution" as a trick to distract attention from his brutal

regime; he saw the maneuvering with Dennis Hills as a transparent attempt to rally support and unite Africans behind a bogus banner. Soyinka shuddered to think of Amin as chairman of the OAU, for Amin not only violated all his convictions about human rights, he was also an insult to deeply felt ambitions for the African continent. In this and other writings Soyinka reveals an emotional commitment to the continent that is so strong that he claims the right to override the jealously guarded sovereign independence of nations in the interests of good government.

The campaign against Amin was one that Soyinka might have been drawn into because of his position as editor of *Transition,* a journal which had moved from Kampala to Accra, but it was in all probability part of a wider campaign against the violation of human rights and the exercise of tyranny in Africa. In the article just mentioned Soyinka condemned not only Amin but also the "calculated genocide in Burundi" and the brutality of Marcias Nguema in Equatorial Guinea. Soyinka was one of the few "leaders of thought" in Africa to make his revulsion about corrupt African regimes widely known, and this instance of his integrity and consistency in action made him many enemies. While Fasuan and a host of others were praying for long life for Amin, Soyinka was condemning him as a "murderous buffoon." The campaign Soyinka waged revealed how radical and international he had become during his detention and "exile."

PHASE 4, Military Rule Under Murtala Mohammed and Olusegun Obasanjo (December 1975-October 1979)

In December 1975, some five months after the coup that overthrew his old enemy, Yakubu Gowon, Soyinka returned to Nigeria. He returned, as he put it, to work "side by side with the people, under a leadership which [did] not contradict [his] personal conscience." The leadership was provided first by Murtala Mohammed and then, after his assassination in February 1976, by Olusegun Obasanjo, and the work partly involved preparations for the Second World Black and African Festival of Arts and Culture (FESTAC).

Soyinka's position during this phase is revealed by an incident that occurred at Ikeja Airport in April 1976 and that prompted Soyinka to write an open letter to the Inspector General of Police. Briefly, Soyinka, who was outward bound on FESTAC business, almost missed his plane because the police insisted on searching him and his luggage so thoroughly. This fourth phase was a period when Soyinka was working within the power structure in some respects (for instance, in the case of FESTAC), was shaping policy in others (in the campaign for new road safety regulations), and was combating the authorities in yet others (his "Airport Ordeal" had been at the hands of the police and he repeatedly found fault with the force and its methods during this whole period). The fact that the ordeal was at the airport and that Soyinka wrote in his open letter "my professional geography does not embrace only Nigeria but the African continent and beyond" conveniently draws attention to Soyinka's international commitments – some of which he pursued through the Nigerian press. Notable among these international activities was the continuation of his campaign against Amin and his work as Secretary General of the Union of Writers of African Peoples (UWAP) to try to prevent the repression of writers and the censorship of their works. Incidentally, Soyinka was also drawn into print on matters of artistic originality and taste ("It Owes its Birth" and "Sick Humour") and was pushed into print by editors who published material that had appeared elsewhere long before ("Song of the Ruling Passion") or that was clearly written for a specific occasion with little or no thought of publication in the newspapers ("The Scholar in African Society"). Taken together these articles show the extent to which he was involved in national life and the extent to which he was regarded as a national figure. The last four items I have mentioned, however, are peripheral to the main concerns of this period, which may be classified as FESTAC, road safety, the police, Amin, and UWAP.

Soyinka was both attracted to the idea of FESTAC and dubious about it; he was both active in the organization of the festival and critical of it. He wanted the festival to succeed and became involved with it in a variety of capacities even though, as he must have known, his involvement would entail thankless tasks, frustration, and disappointment. Almost the first issue that occupied his attention was one which threatened to wreck the festival: which countries should send representatives to deliver papers at the FESTAC Colloquium? Soyinka's article on the topic appeared in March 1976 and is a pedestrian and lifeless statement; it reads as if it were written more out of a sense of obligation than out of a sense of urgency. Not that Soyinka compromised himself and argued, or rather belabored, a case he did not believe in, but the desire to make a decisive impact, which is a feature of Soyinka's prose pieces for the press, is absent.

The tensions between Soyinka and some of the others involved in the organization of FESTAC were apparent in the paper on "The Scholar in African Society" that Soyinka presented to the colloquium when the festival eventually took place in January and February 1977. This paper was subsequently published in the *Nigerian Herald* and so it moved into the area examined here. In the course of it Soyinka paid tribute to both the Nigerian government and Leopold Senghor and so found himself in the uncharacteristic position of appearing as a supporter of the establishment. In order to make his independent and uncompromised position clear, the permanent rebel included a final paragraph that read in part:

Nothing of what I have just said shall be interpreted as presuming an ideal state of intellectual freedom in the internal policies of either [Nigeria or Senegal] ....

His dissatisfaction with elements connected with the festival is revealed by a reference in the paper to

a handful of philistines who had been successfully infiltrated into the [FESTAC] organisation for no other purpose than to serve interests decidedly inimical to those of the Black World.

And by the subsequent mention of the "thieving manipulators of the FESTAC administration." From this it would seem that the festival provided profound causes for concern, as well as some satisfaction. It, of course, also provided Soyinka, in the colloquium, with a forum in which he could make his case for the black scholar as "a historicized machine for chewing up the carcase of knowledge to regurgitate mortar for social reconstruction" and propose that Swahili be adopted as a *lingua franca* for Africa.

During this fourth phase Soyinka added his voice and his ideas to the campaign for road safety. The campaign was already under way and made use of road safety weeks, admonitory jingles on the radio, and demands in the press that improvements be made. In "National Road Slaughter" Soyinka picked up some of the points that had recently emerged in the newspapers, argued for the "reactivation of the completely comatose agencies for enforcing law, and supported the flooding [of] the highways with Road Marshals." He observed, however, that this latter measure could not succeed unless "it [was] complemented by the thorough mobilization of the general public in their own cause." Soyinka's emphasis on involving the masses ran through the whole article; for instance, he wrote, "one critical injection into the process of restoring sanity is the MOBILISATION of the people themselves." It is necessary to underline this populist dimension to Soyinka's planning. Too often his thinking, and even his road safety work, is seen solely in terms of an individualistic or elitist approach. Soyinka, as the very existence of all this writing for the daily press testifies, has taken pains to enlist the support of public opinion. He may have had more conspicuous success in his work with special marshals (Knights of the Long Road) than with mobilizing public opinion, but he has recognized the importance of the latter.

Soyinka became a special marshal in the Oyo State Road Safety Corps and exercised the powers designated to that group of handpicked, voluntary office holders. The special marshals were resented by some and criticized – Soyinka might prefer "maligned" – by others, and on New Year's Day 1979 Soyinka rebutted some of the criticisms that had appeared in the press in the closing weeks of 1978. He claimed modest success for the organization of which he was part, and, obviously more used to attacking than defending, he swept into battle:

> The point we are making here is that it is pure rhetoric to expect that decades of irrational, black-market licensed, egotistical, ignorant and fatalistic driving habits will be wiped out after a mere year of operation by a scratch team thinly stretched, starved of resources, stymied by bureaucratic obtuseness and constantly snapped at by the mangy watchdogs of petty legalisms.

Some of Soyinka's own letters of criticism might well, it is worth observing, have been dismissed by some as "pure rhetoric." It is particularly surprising, and disconcerting, to hear the eloquent upholder of human rights and the man who had written "the Judiciary is the last defence of the common man" dismissing "petty legalisms" so lightly. Soyinka's principles appear to have changed, and it is tempting to suggest that the concern for sanity on Nigerian roads or the taste of power had created an appetite for power that disregarded some of the rights of others.

Only part of "1979: The Year of the Road" was concerned with defending the record of the special marshals; most of the article consisted of plans for road safety measures that would, Soyinka claimed, halve the number of accidents in six months. The measures he proposed were far-reaching and expensive and cut across many interest groups. They showed that Soyinka could plan and prepare a proposal. He had lived long enough in the world of senate meetings and general orders to have learned that one way to bring about changes is to sit on committees and commissions, to channel passion into paperwork. In 1962 Soyinka had written: "I do not know whose responsibility roadsigning is and quite frankly I am indifferent." On New Year's Day 1979 he was proposing that a computer databank store and make available information about those who commit offences on the roads. These two positions provide an accurate indication of the distance he had travelled in seventeen years.

"1979: Year of the Road" is characteristic of the work of this period in that it shows Soyinka operating from inside an institution – in this case a young institution and one which he had shaped – and yet full of plans for improvements. Even though the national leadership did "not violate [his] conscience" there were groups and institutions that operated under that leadership that caused him great concern, notably the police and the judiciary. Inevitably his work on, and his writing about, road safety prompted him to comment on both. In "National Road Slaughter" he condemned the police as "completely comatose." In 1977 he wrote "The Police Force: Example of Indifference," in effect, a second open letter to the

Inspector General of Police, and it was far more serious in import than the first. Soyinka was, and is, a kind of unofficial ombudsman in Nigeria; his name, as he subsequently put it, suggests "instant redress," and he is constantly petitioned by those who regard themselves as the victims of the establishment. In this instance Soyinka took up the case of a Ghanaian journalist whose relative had been murdered and dumped in a swamp near Ajegunle; the journalist had had to give bribes in order to retrieve the body for burial. The Nigerian police appeared to have regarded the murder as providing an opportunity to collect a bribe and had shown no interest in investigating the circumstances surrounding the death: "an example," as Soyinka termed it, "of indifference." This "act of omission" was to be followed by disturbing "acts of commission" by the police.

Soyinka concluded the open letter with the following paragraph:

> The Bar Association of Nigeria should, I believe, be asking the questions which are embedded in the extract from this letter, but, of course, the vocal elements in this Association appear to be concerned only when certain classes of society are involved.

This jibe at a professional association for showing class allegiance rather than concern with national responsibility demonstrates Soyinka's analysis of his society in class terms. It also leads into a brief examination of Soyinka's attitude to the case of K. G. Okuwa. Okuwa, a deputy legal adviser to the Ministry of Justice in Ondo state, drove recklessly and was involved in a serious motor accident. He did not stop at the scene of the accident but drove on to Abeokuta. He was, however, tracked down by a special marshal and called for trial in Oyo state.[13] At the trial the Deputy Public Prosecutor entered a plea of *nolle prosequi* and the State Commissioner for Public Justice, Mr. B. A. Aiku, agreed that the case had been incorrectly brought. Soyinka and the other special marshals were furious at what appeared to them to be the legal fraternity closing ranks in order to protect a colleague and, in so doing, making a mockery of all efforts to make the roads safer. In a society in which "big men" have often been able to subvert the course of justice, a public humiliation such as that inflicted by Aiku's action came close to destroying the morale and credibility of the special marshals. A communiqué from the University of Ife Road Marshals, undoubtedly written by Soyinka, was published on the "Grapevine" page of the *Daily Times* under the ironic title "Commissioner for Partial Justice." In it Soyinka exposed the weaknesses in Aiku's position, emphasizing that Aiku himself had "presided over the preliminary committee which [had] worked out the structure of the Road Safety Corps and its mobile units" and claiming that Aiku had shown partiality in his treatment of a fellow lawyer. As Soyinka warmed to the task of vilification, Aiku found himself described as "partisan, totally corrupt," a "disillusioning sample." Soyinka warned (the emendation is mine):

> This level of egotism is [not] unusual in this country, but it is one which, we had hoped, had disappeared in such arrogant and impertinent forms since 1975. The pointer is ominous.

Soyinka feared that if Aiku were not checked his action would "constitute a spill-over model into conduct of the public departments of the forthcoming civilian regime." The special marshals demanded Aiku's resignation or the restoration of "fugitive from justice Okuwa" to their "judicial embrace." The communiqué may have had the desired effect since Okuwa was subsequently tried, found guilty, and sentenced.

Soyinka seems to have used the press to ensure that in this case justice was done and was seen to be done, but there is a less positive footnote to the episode: the "Grapevine" page was discontinued. I am not suggesting that the decision to stop the page was in any way related to the Okuwa Affair; it was in all probability part of an increasing caution on the part of the editor. But it had the effect of removing from the national paper an irreplaceable and unrivalled forum for muckraking, truth-telling, scurrilous attacks, hard-luck stories, petitions, and complaints. In a country in which ordinary people find it hard to make themselves heard and in which the arrogant abuse of power is often apparent, "Grapevine" had provided a service and the Nigerian press was poorer for its loss.

"Varieties of Wasting," published at about the same time as "Example of Indifference," provided a further illustration of Soyinka's position. In it he wrote once again as an "unofficial ombudsman" taking up a problem in the press in order to bring pressure to bear on the system. The article is notable for the attacks it contains on two institutions with which he had worked – the FESTAC organization and the university – and for the extent of the attack on the military rulers and their "automatism of waste." Perhaps Soyinka's concern was increased by accounts of brutality that continued to come out of Uganda at this time and the writer's fear that Nigeria might "go the way of" Uganda.

Soyinka continued his campaign against Amin and summoned the spectre of Amin to haunt Nigeria. In "Inquisition in Uganda" he called for close scrutiny of developments in Uganda and complained that Nigerian journalists neglected investigation and research. He presented Amin as an arrogant, brutal monster, but one whom Nigerian leaders might imitate. The very structure of the piece – it is written around two encounters with a Ugandan colleague – demonstrates the process of discovery and underlines the importance of honesty and of finding out what is happening. A few sentences from near the beginning of the article indicate the kind of sensitivity which Soyinka brought to his analysis of the evidence:

> My objections to Amin at that time [1971] were purely ideological. I refused to be fooled by his populist antics and was deeply suspicious of his very motive in disposing of Obote. The fact that the British and American governments, through their Press, had begun to ridicule and assail Milton Obote's efforts to bring Uganda closer to the progressive direction of Zambia and Tanzania, becoming shrill in their alarm as they woke up to the fact that Obote was matching pronouncements with action which bit deep into their pockets – these were pointers to international intrigue-hatching which could not be separated from the sudden appearance of an "unknown factor" in the seat of power.

Soyinka sniffed out a neo-colonialist conspiracy, but his use of "their Press" in such a way as to suggest that all newspapers are official or unofficial mouthpieces of Western governments is inaccurate and an overstatement that weakens his case.

Soyinka then launched an attack on African leaders, journalists, and radicals. He drew attention to the extent to which foreign influences dominate African leaders: "A good half of our national leaders are little more or less than tools of the super-powers." He deplored the lack of "investigative journalism" on Uganda and attacked the "smug, comfortable, secure, chauvinistic, self-persuaded radicals" for their belief in "abstractions." It was in this context that he stated his creed, a conviction that had already found expression in plays:

> There are no abstractions. There are only upholders of the living ideal and those who trample the human embodiments of such ideals underfoot.

He moved on to suggest that a sense of communal responsibility is a protection against the predatory state. He took the Nigerian trade unions to task for permitting silence to follow the disappearance of a leading activist, Gogo Nzeribe, and he upbraided the Nigerian Medical Association for not demanding a thorough investigation into the murder of Dr. Ademola. Soyinka used the state of chaos that existed in Uganda to argue for constant vigilance, communal responsibility, and a readiness to speak out loudly and clearly about crimes committed – even if, or particularly if, committed by the men at the very top. There is much in this article to call to mind Soyinka's prison notes and the conviction expressed there that "the man dies in all who keep silent in the face of tyranny."

Soyinka's next piece on Amin was published nearly two years later and is in a very different style, though he takes the opportunity to attack some of the same targets. "Happy Riddance" is the text of a talk given by Soyinka as a representative of UWAP at a meeting with the Ugandan community in Nigeria after the expulsion of Amin from Uganda. It celebrates, in a mood near to euphoria, the triumph of the "Upholders of the Living," the overthrow of the tyrant, and the discomfiture of the "radicals" who had supported Amin. The tone of the piece varies; the opening paragraphs are a parody, reminiscent of "Flogging Women Offenders":

> We who thought up this modest occasion know only too painfully that we are the brain-washed victims of Western propaganda who have no feeling for or interest in the welfare of the Ugandan masses.

He had the "elevated world of black intelligentsia," the OAU and the guardians of "radical socio-economic postulates" on the run and he exulted in their rout. Shortly afterwards he turned on the journalists, a group he had already castigated in "Inquisition," he called them "the mercenary moulders of public opinion" and condemned their "mischievous and hysterical commentaries," their attempts to stir up ill-feeling between Nigeria and the new rulers in Uganda. The relationship between Nigeria and Uganda was, of course, extremely sensitive since the involvement of Tanzanian troops raised the question of the sovereign independence of each state. Soyinka, who saw the issue in terms of right and wrong, life and death, poetic justice and the shared destiny of Africa, approved of Tanzania's action. Some lawyers, diplomats and journalists had their priorities elsewhere and were concerned that a disturbing precedent had been set. Soyinka felt he could distinguish between Tanzania's invasion, which was "right," and, say, Libyan involvement in Uganda and Chad, which was "wrong." There is no doubt that this distinction could not be codified. It was characteristic of Soyinka that he supported his case with an argument from a familiar image and "poetic justice": Amin, he suggested, had "bitten off more than he could chew" in attacking Tanzania in the first place and it was only fitting that he should choke to death! The final paragraphs of the piece are worth quoting in full because they show how Soyinka resolved, or rather evaded, the dilemma of justifying the Tanzanian action:

> Come to think of it, did not Idi Amin once say how much he loved Nyerere?
> "But for the white hairs on your head," joked our irrepressible humourist, "I would have liked to marry you."
> Well, the bride obviously took "her" time considering the proposal.
> When she finally accepted, she got into her bridal dress, carried her dowry and proceeded to the bridegroom's home.
> The bridegroom squealed at the approaching procession, assured relations far and wide that he was no longer thinking of marriage.

When he appealed in desperation to the Pope, the bride only pressed on faster, thinking that the Pontiff in person was coming to solemnise the nuptials.
Alas, on arrival, the bridegroom had fled.
Well, the household trooped out in their finery and welcomed the bride.
There was wild revellery in the streets of Kampala.
Why, one may ask, is there such lamentation from far-distant neighbours of the groom?

This final line turned once again on an idiom, in this case a saying made familiar by Oba Danlola's lines: "Only a phoney drapes himself in deeper indigo/ Than the son of the deceased."[14] This conclusion was elegant and witty, but it did not tackle the issue in all its complexity. Here, as on other occasions, Soyinka used his prose pieces as he used his plays: to provoke rather than to argue a case through. We may be sympathetic to his case and find his presentation satisfying on several levels, but if we are of a different persuasion or if we are wrestling with the full complexities of an issue we are unlikely to find Soyinka's treatment intellectually convincing.

The last two contributions to the press during this phase that I want to consider were written by Soyinka in his capacity as Secretary General of the Union of Writers of African Peoples (UWAP). I have already had occasion to mention this organization – most recently in connection with the function at which "Happy Riddance" was delivered. Briefly, the organization was inaugurated in Accra during February 1975 as an alliance of writers working "for the creation of a humanity that is not separated by class or race... working fraternally [with associations with similar ideals] for the attainment of humane and universal ideals for the peoples of the world."[15] Soyinka, always prominent among the organizers, was made Secretary General and in that capacity carried forward the work of the Union. He wrote two letters that appeared in the Nigerian press – one about the detention of Ngugi and the other about the censorship of Sembene Ousmane's film *Ceddo*. These letters demonstrate that, in spite of what its critics might say, the union was active and taking up matters at the highest levels. Soyinka no doubt derived a certain satisfaction from the fact that the writers of Africa were showing fraternal concern for one another in the face of opposition from prime ministers and presidents. They were demonstrating a solidarity that the trade unionists and the medical doctors had failed to show with Nzeribe and Ademola.

PHASE 5, The Second Republic (October 1979 –)

There is no reason to suppose that Soyinka ever had any particular respect for Shehu Shagari, who became the first president of the Second Republic, but his writing for the press since October 1979 has shown increasing hostility. In Soyinka's view the president came to power illegally and has maintained his position by being brutal and "fascistic"; he has created a situation in which revolution is inevitable. With this reading of political developments it is not surprising that national politics should have dominated Soyinka's recent writing for the press. In fact there is only one article from this period which is not on that issue; the exception is "In Defence of Aboyade" and I will consider it first, simply because it is a transitional work. It belongs more to the power-sharing politics of Phase Four than to the confrontation politics of Phase Five.

Tunji Aboyade, the out-going vice-chancellor of the University of Ife, had been criticized in the press for being "lackadaisical" over a students' hostel that had collapsed and for turning the vice-chancellor's lodge into a "disco palace." Soyinka came to Aboyade's defence using an assumed title, "Chief Aparologists for the Aparo Mafia (Extinct Species)," a thin disguise and one in which he was recognized by many. From the article it appears, I maintain, that Soyinka was one of a trusted group of advisors (the Aparo Mafia) whom Aboyade used to tackle some of the problems confronting the university, such problems as accommodation and water supply. Soyinka, with the benefit of inside information, argued that there was nothing lackadaisical about Aboyade's action over the hall that collapsed; he reported that they had gone together to talk to Obasanjo about the rebuilding of the hall and he had been able to see that action was being taken by the head of state. From other clues, it is possible to deduce that Aboyade and Soyinka went shooting bush fowl ("Aparo") together and that they enjoyed one another's company. Soyinka denied that the "close consultative group" ever had any influence over promotions – as had been alleged.

Soyinka has often been sharply critical of Nigerian academics – or "academicians" as he sometimes calls them – and of Nigerian universities, but on this occasion he defended the head of one of the Nigerian universities against "careless and uncharitable accusations." Characteristically he defended by attacking, and the charges concerning holding up promotions and dancing at the vice-chancellor's lodge prompted the following barrage:

> We are faced with a situation where your newsroom has been turned into bedrooms by certain dons who provide columnists with the most salacious half-truths and fabrications of what is supposed to be going on in the University.

And later on, on the same issue:

> Your newsboys were fed with the lies as a deliberate campaign of denigration by a singularly contemptible professor on this campus and his cohorts.

Soyinka is asking for a clean fight, but the very methods he has employed – such as the use of an assumed title and of name calling – are "dirty." On occasions he puts himself above the laws he lays down for others, and this leaves him open to the charge he so often convicts others on: the operation of double standards.

The Aboyade article, interesting as it is, is essentially a digression, a hangover from the kind of writing that characterized Phase Four. Soyinka's major preoccupations during the period since October 1979 have been elsewhere. For instance, he has been particularly active on the roads of Oyo state since his friend Bola Ige, who became governor of the state in October 1979, made him director of the Road Safety Corps. Soyinka now has a body of paid, uniformed, mobile men obedient to him and a group of unpaid, civvy-suited, special marshals supporting him in his efforts to improve the level of safety on the roads. He has authority and he has the attention of the media. For these reasons he has not needed to write to the press on road safety matters during this period. Instead he has issued instructions, called press conferences, and enjoyed sympathetic coverage from the UPN papers in the state – that is to say, from the Sketch group and the *Nigerian Herald*. On issues of national politics, however, he has had no such natural outlets and he has written to the newspapers or sent them copies of his telegrams and speeches. It is not surprising that he has sent his material to the *Sketch* and the *Herald* since he has good contacts with those papers and they have offices quite near to his base at the University of Ife.

Soyinka's first article to appear after the elections concerned what might at first seem a very trivial issue: the display of the president's photograph. The background to the article was to be found partly in resentment that Shagari had become president – and some would have said that he only became "president by mathematics," that is to say, as the result of a disputed interpretation of the percentage of national support that the president required. It was to be found partly in the determination of the *New Nigerian,* a paper backed by Shagari's party, the National Party of Nigeria, to make a national issue out of whether the president's photograph was appropriately displayed in government offices throughout the federation.[16] Soyinka argued that the paper was stirring up trouble, simply inventing a test for loyalty in order to embarrass opponents. He pointed out that there had not previously been any consistency regarding the display of the portrait of the head of state and that those working in the offices of the *New Nigerian* had previously shown no interest in complying with the principle they were now attempting to impose upon the country: in the past they had not displayed the photograph of the current head of state in their own offices.

Soyinka's comments on the president in this article were veiled, and it is only with the help of subsequent descriptions that their implications are apparent. His concluding paragraph read:

> If the Constitution demands it, many will gladly wear a locket of Alhaji Shehu Shagari's picture next to their hearts, if only as an example of a man more sinned against than sinning. But this is not to say that his photograph in a public office will obliterate the social anomalies of this nation which alone have given birth to quite a historical presidential prodigy.

"Social anomalies" and "presidential prodigy" are words which can be variously interpreted. An "anomaly" may be simply an "irregularity," and a "prodigy" may be "a marvellous thing." Soyinka, not usually a man to conceal his meaning in his journalistic writings and, in fact, a sharp critic of those who use language to blur their meaning, was unwilling to make his position crystal clear.

His attitude did not remain in doubt for long. I have not referred in this paper to interviews with Soyinka, but of course they provide a source from which it is possible to trace his changing position. At this point, however, an interview provides part of the essential background to the next item under consideration. In April 1980 Soyinka was interviewed on Radio Ogun in a weekend series called "Meet the Press"; his replies provided front page stories for several of the papers on Monday, April 21. In answer to one question, he said that if he were to join any political party it would be the People's Redemption Party (PRP). During July there was a deep split in the PRP between those who associated the party with its leader, Alhaji Aminu Kano, and those whose loyalty was to the party and its principles rather than to any individual in it. At the beginning of August, Soyinka sent a telegram to governors Balarabe Musa and Abubakar Rimi, the leaders of the anti-Kano faction, pledging them his support if they ever formed a party. This was a major step by Soyinka. He had long held aloof from joining political parties; he had enjoyed a maverick independence, even refusing to join a popular party with which he had much in common, the Action Group, preferring to work with small cliques, such as CWIL. In 1965 he had held up a radio-station; in 1966 he had written "Let's Think"; in 1980 he was willing to join a party, or part of a party, and one whose leaders actually held power in some states. This was a significant shift in Soyinka's approach to politics. The individualist, the lonely hero crying "a plague on all your houses," had almost become a member of a mass movement. Answers to the question: "Why did he take that step at that time?" are provided by two newspaper articles. In them Soyinka catalogued the disturbing developments that had taken place during Shagari's presidency. The articles were entitled: "Police Are Brutal and Commit Atrocities" and "The Bogus Revolution of our Time."

The disturbing developments were characterized by subversion of the rule of law and by the use of violence to silence opposition and push forward plans. Soyinka's lists included "the violation of the ballot box and the seizing of power in 1979," Shugaba's deportation, the massacre of two thousand peasants in Bakolori, the "Modakeke Riots" in Ife, the outrage at Bembem in Borno state, the assault on the governor of Ogun state, the invasion of the legislature by the police, the deaths of student demonstrators at Ife, the flamboyant display of riches by M. K. O. Abiola, the subversion of the Kano state legislature, the despoilation of the country's wealth, the destruction of the *Triumph* newspaper's offices, the attempts of "Chief O" to get Soyinka's students to plant incriminating articles in his office, the shooting – Soyinka prefers "the extermination" – of Dele Udo, and the "butchering" of Bala Mohammed. There is no doubt that most if not all of these events took place; some provided headlines in the newspapers, others were hushed up. The question is: "What is the significance of them?" Soyinka obviously perceived a pattern – he "traced the undertow" – and laid the blame for the climate of violence, the rampant exploitation, and the political maneuvering at the door of the presidential palace. It is not always easy to see the links – to "join the poison stains." Sometimes the trail leads directly to Shagari, who, for instance, must have known about the plans to bundle his opponent Shuguba out of Nigeria and deny that he was a Nigerian. Such a case as that of Dele Udo, however, is by no means so obviously traced to the president. Udo, a fine athlete, had returned to Nigeria from the American college where he was studying and training to take part in an athletics competition. He was shot dead at a checkpoint following an argument with the police manning it. There is no suggestion that Udo was of any political significance. The episode showed, however, the extent to which the police, often poorly trained and uncertain about their responsibilities, had come to regard themselves as a law unto themselves. Soyinka's use of the word *extermination* suggests a degree of premeditation and of coldbloodedness that is inappropriate. The allegation of extermination can only be understood when it is appreciated that Soyinka regarded the episode as part of the "long manifested intent to turn [Nigeria] into a police state." Soyinka has not made his case convincingly.

The second of the articles comes close to defining Soyinka's position on a fundamental political issue: Does he believe revolution is inevitable in Nigeria? The article comes close, but it does not state his position clearly and unambiguously. "The Bogus Revolution of our Time" is the text of a speech given at Abeokuta on the occasion of the launching of Soyinka's autobiographical work, *Aké: The Years of Childhood*. The launch came a few weeks after the publication of another book, *Why We Struck* by Wale Ademoyega, at which time Soyinka had spoken, according to the *Punch* (11 December 1981) of "an inevitable revolution."

In "Bogus Revolution" he wrote that the *Punch* reporter had "laid a wide track of distraction by suggesting that Wole Soyinka was calling for a violent revolution." He admitted, however, to expressing a "faith in an inevitable revolution." These two positions were easily confused, especially when the media would like them to be and when Soyinka, as he did at Abeokuta, spoke so approvingly of violence as a way of bringing change. It is indeed hard to distinguish between the statement that something is going to happen and the approval of its happening. Prophecies have a way of being self-fulfilling; alarmist talk leads to crises. Soyinka was at pains to make it clear that while revolution was inevitable, its inevitability was not to be blamed on him. It was, he said, the actions of the Shagari government that were making revolution inevitable. In the course of arguing this point he, "inevitably," reminded his readers of the outrages they had witnessed, the scandals which had been uncovered, and the provocative actions that they had heard or read about. He did not add that Shagari was an "honorable man," but if he had, then the description would have served to remind his countrymen of his dishonorable actions. Soyinka knew very well that defending himself against a charge was the best way of making his case. He was too subtle to give a yes or no answer to the question: "Do you believe in violent revolution?" especially in the tense Nigeria of 1982. Instead he seemed to say: "look out of the window, the violent revolution is in full swing!" And, "remember what happened yesterday, the Egba women rose up and put their enemies to flight."

The launching of *Aké* takes us deeper into the roots of Soyinka's political awareness than is shown by his feinting and jousting with the press. He described his view of the nature of the occasion in the following terms:

> To launch a book which deals with one's childhood, on the very soil of one's birth, is a simple act of willed rebirth, that is an act of rededication. For me it is a continuous process which takes many forms.
>
> And I want this message to be understood by those who, in our society, have allied themselves with the counter-values of death, destruction, sterility, stagnation and paralysis of the social will. It is a symbolic act of rededication which engages simultaneously, the will and the progressive aspirations of the millions of countrymen and women, the youths and the children, ranged against the conscienceless existence of a grasping, greedy and over-sated minority, those agents of death and sterility that we have already remarked.

This is a familiar Soyinka, Soyinka of the divided cosmos, for whom there is no middle ground. After cataloguing the actions of the agents of "death and sterility," he returned at the end of the article to his recollection of the Egba women's uprising against the Alake. He wrote:

> Note that this same city, roused to anger by similar acts of contempt and feudal arrogance, once rose and drove her king from his secure palace walls, routed the forces of colonial support and liberated itself, however temporarily, from the shackles of feudal exploitation and repression.

If the implications of this were not apparent enough, he continued a paragraph later in the same warning and inflammatory tone:

> So let those who by their acts deride and insult the poverty of the majority, titilate the palates of an unthinking minority of parasites and hopefuls and, finally, encourage the predatory violence of armed robbery which they are always the first to condemn – let them remember that theirs is the hand that set the violence of society in motion.

It is in the understated parallels of these rousing concluding passages that Soyinka's position on the issue of revolution can be most clearly appreciated. He has established a line of continuity between contemporary events and the Egba women's uprising against the Alake and he writes favorably of the uprising. We are left to make the obvious inference.

Aké relates how his mother, Eniola, and his "aunt," Funmilayo Ransome-Kuti, organized an adult literacy class for the socially mobile who imitated European fashions, the "gown-wearers." This became, under the provocation of taxation, a political movement that united both "gown-wearers" and those who retained strong links with indigenous customs, the "wrapper-wearers," behind Funmilayo Ransome-Kuti in demanding specific social changes. A later march on the Alake's palace and agitation – in short the "uprising" – led directly to the Alake being sent into exile. Soyinka himself has followed a course somewhat similar to that of his remarkable relation: from his position as secretary to the "gown-wearing" Committee of Writers for Individual Liberty, he has become, it seems, a supporter of a movement that brings together both "gown" and "wrapper" wearers, the People's Redemption Party. He may emerge as a spokesman and leader in the party's campaign to drive the "king" from his "secure palace walls." He will, I am sure, do this with full awareness that the best he can hope for is a "temporary liberation." Alakes have a way of returning from exile or of being replaced, thanks to the manipulation of colonial or neo-colonial, or indigenous influences by amenable successors. But he still believes actions should be embarked upon.

It is very suitable that this survey should finish with the consideration of a talk delivered at Aké for it is clear that Soyinka's upbringing deeply affected his attitude to public life as revealed in his newspaper articles. There was not only the example of the Ransome-Kutis with their determination to influence the course of events, there was also his father, Ayodele, always arguing with his friends and often filling the role of "devil's advocate," and there was the sense of the past, the "rich mustiness of age," which he responded to so sensitively at Isara. Isara, moreover, was where the remarkable Odemo held court; rooted in tradition yet a great nationalist and alert to each new development, the Odemo was anxious to hear about events in Abeokuta and, as events showed, determined to stand by his principles. Soyinka's satire and his protest writing draw strength from being related to a world view which he had acquired in childhood from such women and men as these. The shifts of emphasis and changes which have been apparent have taken place within this world view.

Conclusion

I have had to omit many enlightening and enlivening moments in Wole Soyinka's writing for the press. I have had to leave out his opinions on tens of subjects and dozens of individuals. I have had to resist the temptation to quote hundreds of telling phrases, burnished praises, revived images, subtle twists of language and eloquent insults – especially eloquent insults! This examination, though long, is by no means complete or comprehensive. It is a preliminary study. But even though it is incomplete, it shows that, partly through the press, Soyinka has established himself as a significant presence in the Nigerian political arena. His opponents cross him with trepidation; those who cooperate with him know that he will not compromise his principles; those who have his support can be confident that he is a mighty champion. Inevitably setting himself up as the scourge of vice and the foe of villainy has imposed a heavy moral responsibility on Soyinka. He has had to be above suspicion, but on occasions his judgement has been questioned and his actions have been criticized.

The newspaper articles reveal Soyinka as a versatile writer, a conscientious office holder, and a maturing thinker who draws on the world view of his childhood in responding to contemporary events. To the non-Nigerian, who knows Soyinka through the work he has published in London and New York, the articles reveal the extent to which he has been and is involved in Nigerian public life and provide valuable background to the appreciation of some of his poems and plays. It is my contention that the work for the press is, in fact, important in its own right. Despite the distortions of the editor's pencil and a sprinkling of printers' devils, these articles show Soyinka engaged in an invigorating debate with his own countrymen. As much of his genius has gone into this work as into any other.

NOTES

1. I am indebted to many colleagues and friends for such progress as I have made in locating Soyinka's contributions to the Nigerian press. It is a continuing process and I would like to thank the following for having helped me to get this far: Dapo Adelugba, Willfried Feuser, Ime Ikiddeh, D. S. Izevbaye, D. A. N. Jones, Chikwenye Okonjo Ogunyemi, Femi Osofisan, Niyi Osundare, and the archivists working in the National Archives at Ibadan.

2. For contributions to the controversy see the *Daily Times* of 22 December 1961 and 30 December 1961, and the *Daily Express* of 26 December 1961, 11 January 1962, and 24 January 1962.

3. Peter Pan, "Shame Shame," *Daily Times,* 23 June 1962.

4. "Obstacle Race" is in *Before the Blackout* (Ibadan: Orisun Acting Editions, n.d.), pp. 32-38. See also Robert M. Wren, "The Last Bridge on *The Road:* Soyinka's Rage and Compassion," *Research in African Literatures,* 13 (1982), pp. 60-67.

5. For background and comparison see Peter Pan's columns in the *Daily Times,* 27 August 1963 and 29 August 1963. Despite protests the Press Bill was passed into law (*Daily Times,* 29 September 1964).

6. Dennis Duerden, "African Sharpshooter," *New Society* (London), 8 December 1966, p. 879.

7. See the *Daily Times* of November and December 1965 for coverage of the trial. The report on the judge's summing up and the scenes that followed the acquittal are in the *Daily Times* for 21 December 1965.

8. Wole Soyinka, *The Man Died* (London: Rex Collings, 1972), p. 18.

9. In his "Open Letter" Soyinka referred to the *Daily Times* of 7 November 1966 that carried the headline "Here is a Way Out of the Fix." The obas' comments on the letter appeared on 14 November, the correspondence appeared on November 18 and 19.

10. *The Man Died,* p. 18.

11. Ibid., p. 31.

12. Rodney's book was first published by Bogle-L'Ouverture Publications, London, and Tanzania Publishing House, Dar es Salaam, 1972.

13. "Partial Justice," *Daily Times,* 27 November 1978.

14. "Kongi's Harvest," *Collected Plays II* (London: Oxford University Press, 1974), p. 115.

15. Wole Soyinka, "African Writers – A Union," *Africa Currents* (London), 2 (Summer 1975), p. 22.

16. See, for instance, "UPN States Yet to Display Shagari's Portrait," *New Nigerian,* 21 January 1980.

SOYINKA
as a
CRITIC

Soyinka as a Literary Critic

Obiajuru Maduakor

The substance of Soyinka's achievement as a literary critic is revealed in *Myth, Literature, and the African World* (1976), which contains his most important literary essays. The title itself is suggestive of Soyinka's major critical preoccupation: he is fascinated by myth as a phenomenon that exercises an unlimited appeal for the human imagination, manifesting itself in the literature, culture, folklore, and world view of a people. Because he is also a manipulator of myth in his role as a creative writer, his critical statements on works in the mythic mode are bound to throw some light on his own writings.

What is myth? An answer to this question is not directly provided in Soyinka's critical utterances on myth and literature, but we can infer it from his writing as connoting a people's world view and the moral system that sustains that world view as it is reflected in their stories of the origin of the world, of gods and of man. Among his own people, the Yoruba, this view of myth is reinforced by the Coleridgean sense of the one-life theory which binds man to the gods and to nature in the interest of the psychic well-being of the universe. But there is a more pertinent definition from Clarence Hugh Holman *et al.*, who distinguish between the traditional definition of myth and the modernist extension of this definition. In the traditional sense of the word, myths are

> anonymous stories having their roots in the primitive folk beliefs of races or nations and presenting supernatural episodes as a means of interpreting natural events in an effort to make concrete and particular a special perception of man or a cosmic view.[1]

In the modernist re-definition of the word, myth is seen as containing

> vestiges of primordial ritual and ceremony, or the repository of racial memories, or a structure of unconsciously held value systems, or an expression of the general beliefs of a race, social class or nation or a unique embodiment of a cosmic view.[2]

The two definitions are relevant to Soyinka's use of the term *myth* both in his creative works and in his literary essays. His literary essays touch naturally upon other areas of general interest in literary criticism; for example, the question of authenticity in character conception and presentation, and of probability in the execution of plot in the criticism of fiction. But he is by natural disposition a myth critic. His later excursions into a sociological analysis of works of literature is the direct outcome of the ideological controversy between him and his Marxist critics.

For convenience, I shall consider Soyinka's literary essays under four subheadings: Incidental Essays (1960-66), Ritual Essays (1976), Essays on Ideology and Social Vision (1976), and Controversies (1975-80). The early essays referred to as Incidental Essays are not reproduced in their original format in *Myth, Literature, and the African World*, but the substance of their arguments is worked into the extended framework of the essay on literature and the social vision with little or no modification of Soyinka's original impressions on the works concerned. But I discuss them here separately in recognition of their merits as literary essays and also to cover other issues of critical interest that might have been left out in Soyinka's summary of their contents in the third and fourth chapters of *Myth, Literature, and the African World*.

Soyinka's literary essays are, to some extent, one essay. His critical prejudices were formed quite early in his career as a writer and a critic. Both the early and later essays are criss-crossed by related threads of thought. The war on Negritude rages on still, even though the first shots were fired in the 1960s. Apart from his objection to Negritude on the basis of its addiction to self-glorifying narcissism, I detect in Soyinka's opposition to that movement the beginnings of his later aversion to literary ideology in general. It is a mark of Soyinka's maturity as a critic that he maintains a consistency of opinion in his evaluation of works of literature. That implies that his views are considered carefully before they are offered to the public.

Incidental Essays

Three essays that will be discussed in this section are "The Future of West African Writing" (1960), "From a Common Back Cloth" (1963), and "And After the Narcissist?" (1966). The first essay, possibly written during Soyinka's student days at Leeds, was published in the University of Ibadan poetry magazine, *The Horn*, founded by J. P. Clark and Martin Banham. Since this essay is not easily accessible, I reproduce Bernth Lindfors's summary of Soyinka's main argument. According to Lindfors, Soyinka argues that

> the real mark of authenticity in African writing was indifferent self-acceptance rather than energetic racial self-assertion. Early African writing... was dishonest

because it either imitated literary fashions in Europe or pandered to European demands and expectations for the exotic and primitive. The first West African writer to produce truly African Literature was not Leopold Senghor but Chinua Achebe.[3]

Here is part of the essay as it appears in Lindfors's study and in an article written by Martin Banham, who indeed may have been the first critic to notice Soyinka's early attempt at literary criticism:

> The significance of Chinua Achebe is the evolvement, in West African writing, of the seemingly indifferent acceptance. And this, I believe, is the turning point in our literary development. It is also a fortunate accident of timing, because of the inherently invalid doctrine of "Negritude." Leopold Senghor, to name a blatant example. And if we would speak of "Negritude" in a more acceptable broader sense, Chinua Achebe is a more "African" writer than Senghor. The duiker will not paint "duiker" on his beautiful back to proclaim his duikeritude; you'll know him by his elegant leap. The less self-conscious the African is, and the more innately his individual qualities appear in his writing, the more seriously he will be taken as an artist of exciting dignity.... Senghor seems to be so artistically expatriate... [and he and poets like him] are a definite retrogressive pseudo-romantic influence on a healthy development of West African writing.[4]

Soyinka is rather hard on Senghor and Negritude in this essay; his own writings are equally guilty of some of the charges he levels at Senghor. His novel *The Interpreters* appears to have been influenced by James Joyce, and his poetry reflects the "toughness" of such neo-metaphysical poets as Eliot and Pound. But Soyinka is no less an African poet because of his response to these Western influences. The quip on *duiker* and *duikeritude* graduated into the celebrated adage about *tiger* and *tigritude* at the African Writers' Conference at Kampala (Uganda) in 1962. On the whole, Soyinka is object-ive in his assessment of works by African writers. The same Achebe who is praised for his "Africanness" in "The Future of African Writing" is gently reprimanded in "From a Common Back Cloth" for succumbing to a slight touch of improbability in the resolution of the plot in his first novel, *Things Fall Apart* (1958). The accidental explosion of Okonkwo's gun, contributing as it does to the novel's ultimate tragic denouement, is, in Soyinka's view, a narrative expedience rather than an organically integrated episode. On the other hand, Achebe is praised for anticipating in the novel some aspects of the traditional African philosophy which Soyinka will regard later as vital elements of the African world view. This Achebe did in his allusion to the mysterious relationship between a man and his *chi*, to the mysteries of initiation, to guilt and purification whose ethics, says Soyinka, "are not those of a court of law but of the forces of Nature cycle, of the living and the dead." The logic of this phenomenon is the "philosophy of acceptance. Not blind, slavish acceptance but a positive faith, an acceptance of forces that begin where the physical leaves off."[5]

"From a Common Back Cloth" is an assessment of the African literary image in the novels of the 1950s and of the treatment in those novels of a common theme that preoccupies them; that is, the encounter between tradition and change. Soyinka labels both of these considerations the "common back cloth." In the hands of lesser writers such as Onuora Nzekwu, the "back cloth" breeds sociological novels. With such writers as Alan Paton, Peter Abrahams, and William Conton, the "back cloth" gives birth to dumb and wooden, servile character-types masquerading as human beings. African characters in the works of these writers lack human attributes because they were not conceived from within, that is, from the "dignity and authority of self-acceptance."[6] Their portraiture is dictated largely by Western stereotypical prejudices originating from what Soyinka calls "an outrageously imposed Christian forgiveness."[7] It is only in the works of such writers as Chinua Achebe, Mongo Beti, and the South African novelist, Alex La Guma, that the African characters appear as fully individuated human beings. Mongo Beti achieved this rounded portraiture in his presentation of his Africans by seeing them in the first place as individuals composed like every other human being of cunning and compassion. His is not the negritudinist, one-dimensional mode of characterization, but a rounded view of both the African and his traditional society. "Hospitality is not, as we are constantly romantically informed that it is, nearly so spontaneous. There is a mercenary edge, and this, alas, is not always traceable to that alien corrupt civilization!"[8] Paton, Abrahams, Conton, and Negritude will appear later in the essay on ideology and the social vision where they will serve to buttress Soyinka's arguments against literary ideology.

An important writer mentioned in the present essay is Amos Tutuola, whose "back cloth" is a shade different from those of his contemporaries in the writing trade. Soyinka finds Tutuola to be more original than his fellow African writer-intellectuals because his imagination is constantly amalgamating new experiences and fusing them into new syntheses. The atom bomb and the magical egg of plenty find a place in his world. The difference between him and his modern manipulators of the "back cloth" is such as can exist between a natural imagination and an intellectual imagination. Tutuola is a "storyteller in the best Yoruba tradition, pushing the bounds of credibility higher and higher and sustaining it by sheer adroitness, by a juxtaposition of analogous experience from the familiar."[9] He is best understood as "the contemporary imagination in a story-telling tradition."[10]

In the third essay ("And After the Narcissist?"), Soyinka insists that the supreme narcissist in African writing is Leopold Senghor. Narcissism is synonymous with the literature of self-worship or of self-hypnosis, one in which the self is "most clamant in its own adulation."[11] Too much concentration of emphasis on the self breeds stasis or absence of action. Thus, stasis becomes an extension of the meaning of narcissism. And this is where writers such as Achebe of *Arrow of God* (1964) and Gabriel Okara of *The Voice* (1964) qualify as narcissists. In these works there is movement which is not translated into action. Ezeulu neither dares nor ventures forth, just like Okolo, the hero of Okara's novel. There is no communication in the latter "of the psychic drive which sets a man on a course of single-minded enquiry into the heart of matter or existence."[12] Okolo's passivity contrasts with the questioning and the daring insistence of Soyinka's own quest-hero Ofeyi, equally engaged, like Okolo, in an inquiry into the heart of matter or existence. The psychic unease that impels Ofeyi is frequently the subject of Ofeyi's reflection. Ofeyi is often caught up in throes of introspective reminiscences and self-doubt.

Soyinka distinguishes between narcissism and self-exploration. Self-exploration is the burden of the tragic/ subjective artist, the soul's descent into its own world of interior which, as Hegel says in a different context, has been urged upon the artist by "a severance of mind from world, soul from circumstance, and human inwardness from external conditions,"[13] whereas narcissism is self-manipulation. Soyinka's metaphor for it is the fascination for the womb, where no distraction exists and where no opportunity tempts to action. But the true poet is one who ventures forth, who confronts experience, who realizes that

> hot sterilizing pads sealed the cord at birth but that such discouraging facts need not condemn the poet to exile. And so exploration begins from the acceptance; the poet rejects the navel's fascination, seeks his path through experience, through liberation, through self-surrender.[14]

The work that best illustrates Senghor's narcissistic indulgence, insofar as narcissism is synonymous with inaction, is Senghor's dramatic poem, *Chaka*. Chaka, the legendary man of action, is rendered effete and effeminate in the poem; and this, says Soyinka, is due to Senghor's misapprehension of the proper functions of poetry. The sentimental reduction of Chaka's will for action into a narcissistic passivity implies that, for Senghor, "poetry is not in itself a force for violence or an occasional instrument of terror";[15] whereas, for Soyinka, "every creative act breeds and destroys fear, contains within itself both the salvation and the damnation."[16] We are approaching here the delicate grounds of aesthetics, the Soyinkan aesthetic which sees the artist as the destroyer and the preserver. It was the Irish dramatist, John Millington Synge, who articulated the cardinal ideology of this aesthetic as the mingling of beauty with brutality. Synge is reported to have warned Yeats that before poetry could be human (beautiful) it must learn to be brutal. The combination of beauty with ugliness in Yeats's later verse which is so different from the ideal fantasy world of his early verse is a new development credited to Yeats's encounter with Synge. Perhaps Senghor needed to have heeded Synge's advice to Yeats to render Chaka more masculine and energetic in his poem. What we have in Senghor's poem is sentimental affirmations and the negativity of escapism rather than a vigorous tragic resolution of conflicts through the will for action.

Soyinka returns to this same theme of passive acceptance rather than of tragic engagement which is inherent in Negritude in the essay "The Fourth Stage." "The principle of creativity," writes Soyinka, "when limited to pastoral idyllism, as Negritude has attempted to limit it, shuts us off from the deeper, fundamental resolutions of experience and cognition."[17] For a more authentic approach to Chaka, Soyinka offers Senghor the example of his god, Ogun, who embodies the right attitude towards the creative principle:

> In explication of the real problem of Senghor in the interpretation of *Chaka*, which cannot be solved by the poetic self-identification, the essence of Ogun, the Yoruba god of war and the creative principle, probably offers the best assistance. ... Primogenitor of the artist as the creative human, Ogun is the antithesis of cowardice and Philistinism, yet within him is contained also the complement of the creative essence, a bloodthirsty destructiveness. Mixed up with the gestative inhibition of his nature [is] the destructive explosion of an incalculable energy.[18]

As a corrective measure to Senghor's dull rendition of the Chaka legend, Soyinka has himself embodied the myths of Ogun and Chaka in two epic poems distinguished by their conscious cultivation of the aesthetics of action.

Ritual Essays

The core of the ritual essays is Soyinka's attempt in "The Fourth Stage" to define the origin and meaning of the tragic myth in the context of the Yoruba world view. This essay was written in honor of Professor G. Wilson Knight, who was Soyinka's teacher at Leeds.[19] Knight, an eminent Shakespearean scholar and a critic in the ritual mode, influenced Soyinka significantly in his understanding of myth and ritual. "The Fourth Stage" is Soyinka's first pronouncement on what he later calls "morality and aesthetics in the ritual archetypes" and on the role of drama in the African world view. The other two essays whose titles correspond with the foregoing expressions ("Morality and Aesthetics in the Ritual Archetype" and "Drama and the African World View") merely enlarge upon the issues that have been raised in "The Fourth Stage." "The Fourth Stage" helped to establish Soyinka's reputation as a myth critic, a drama theorist, and a master of language. The citation conferring upon Soyinka the honorary degree of Doctor of Letters from Yale University acknowledges these attributes: "Poet and playwright in a language metaphorical and lyrical, you have redefined modern tragedy through a synthesis of Yoruba and Western tragic forms."[20] Like Nietzsche's *The Birth of Tragedy* which inspired it, "The Fourth Stage" was written in a youthful spirit. Its language is explosive, lyrical, and emotional. What approximates to the essay in verbal intensity is charged moments in Soyinka's prison memoirs, *The Man Died* (chap. 12). In his later literary essays Soyinka's language has grown more sober, more controlled, and less mythopoeic.

"The Fourth Stage" seeks to inquire into the origin of Yoruba tragedy. In Soyinka's account, tragedy, in the Yoruba world view, originated from the gods' consciousness of their own incompleteness or what Soyinka has called "the anguish of severance" (145). The idea of severance takes us back to what Soyinka refers to elsewhere as the principle of "complementarity" (19), that is, the need for the gods to continually experience the human in themselves and a parallel urge in man to reassume his divine essence. The interaction of the divine and the human both in god and man leads to the achievement of a full personality, a unity of being, which fosters what Soyinka terms in a larger context "cosmic totality" (3). In physical terms, the gods once lived here on earth with humans, and their partnership was marked by camaraderie and mutual regard for each other. However, either through sin or default, an estrangement occurred between man and god, and the gods withdrew into the upper regions of ether for their habitation. The estrangement is symbolized in metaphysical or religious terms as the thick undergrowth of matter and non-matter which Soyinka, borrowing a phrase from Nietzsche, calls "the chthonic realm" (2). It was the destiny of Soyinka's god, Ogun, to do battle with the forces of the chthonic realm, to bridge the gap between man and god and thus to re-establish the principle of complementarity. "Into this universal womb plunged and emerged Ogun, the first actor, disintegrating within the abyss" (121). Ogun's pathway through the abyss of being and non-being is what Soyinka has called "the gulf of transition" (149). And Ogun was able to confront the dark forces of the abyss and to hack his way through it because he was the embodiment of the will, for only the will can dare the abyss and emerge therefrom unscathed. The first actor, in the Yoruba drama, was Ogun, the first darer and conqueror of transition, and the first art was the tragic art (123).

Tragic consciousness in Yoruba drama is the protagonist's awareness of his parallel progress through the abyss of transition, for, as Soyinka has noted, "Yoruba tragic drama is the re-enactment of the cosmic conflict" (150). Tragic destiny in general is man's re-enactment of Ogun's rite of passage. Individual misfortune and tribulations are viewed as personal reflections of the god's agony:

> On the arena of the living, when man is stripped of excrescences, when disasters and conflicts (the material of drama) have crushed and robbed him of selfconsciousness and pretensions, he stands in present reality at the spiritual edge of this gulf, he has nothing left in physical existence which successfully impresses upon his spiritual or psychic perception. It is at such moments that transitional memory takes over and intimations rack him of that intense parallel of his progress through the gulf of transition. (149)

In prison Soyinka experienced an agony parallel to his god's and was able to overcome the dark forces within the "abyss of transition" through the agency of his own will. On the other hand, Elesin Oba in *Death and the King's Horseman* skirted the abyss but lacked the courage (will) to make the perilous plunge.

The will, in Soyinka's thinking, is the tragic hero's greatest asset in the abyss of transition; and music, in at least one Western philosophy, is the expression of the will. Soyinka marries the two together (will and music) in his own theory, taking his cue from Schopenhauer, who had asserted that music is the "direct copy of the will itself":[21]

> If we agree that, in the European sense, music is the "direct copy or the direct expression of the will," it is only because nothing rescues man (ancestral, living or unborn) from loss of self within this abyss but a titanic resolution of the will whose ritual summons, response, and expression is the strange alien sound to which we give the name of music. (149)

Soyinka goes beyond the Western definition of music as the manifestation of the will by relating music properly to ritual and drama. In his view music is the tragic hero's sole companion at the charged moment of his self-individuation:

> This masonic union of sign and melody, the true tragic music, unearths cosmic uncertainties which pervade human existence, reveals the magnitude and power of creation but above all creates a harrowing sense of omni-directional vastness where the creative intelligence resides and prompts the soul to futile exploration. The senses do not at such moments interpret myth in their particular concretions; we are left only with the emotional and spiritual values, the essential experience of cosmic reality. The forms of music are not

correspondences at such moments to the physical world, not at this nor at any other moment. The singer is a mouthpiece of the chthonic forces of the matrix and his somnabulist "improvisations" ... are not representations of the ancestor, recognitions of the living or unborn, but of the no man's land of transition between and around these temporal definitions of experience. (148)

However, Soyinka's explanation of the function of music in ritual drama is not so different from Nietzsche's view of it as he claims. The insight into the magnitude of creation which dawns on the tragic hero through music is the counterpart of the retreat into the maternal womb of being or Original Oneness that, Nietzsche claims, is brought upon the Dionysian artist by the magnetic spells of music.[22]

Ogun's pathway, the gulf of transition, is the fourth stage. The word "stage" underscores its connotation as a scene of action, but the fourth stage implies much more than an arena of action. Soyinka's imagination waxes philosophical in the course of the essay. The "anguish of severance," for instance, is translated in philosophical terms as the "fragmentation of essence from self, of essence from itself" (145). Religion is man's symbolic efforts to halt the separation. We must view the fourth area of experience as a physical, metaphysical, and symbolic reality. As a physical definition of space, the fourth stage is a synthesis of Miltonian hell and the Yoruba conception of the original abode of cosmic forces. Soyinka calls it "the seething cauldron of the dark world will and psyche" (142). Still, he resorts to Jungian psychology in an effort to clarify further his definition of the fourth space. One might view it as a symbolic representation of the Jungian "collective unconscious," for it is also defined as "the vortex of archetypes and kiln of primal images" (36). Soyinka is at pains to define the exact nature and topography of the fourth area of experience. Below is a conglomeration of denotations:

(1) the womb of origin or of universal Oneness (30, 153)

(2) the territory of essence ideal (1)

(3) the unconscious (153)

(4) the matrix of cosmic creativity or of essence (153)

(5) the creative cauldron of cosmic powers (145)

(6) the deep black whirlpool of mythopoeic forces (153)

(7) the source of creative and destructive energies (154)

(8) the transitional yet inchoate matrix of death and becoming (142)

(9) the seething cauldron of dark world will and psyche (142)

What immediately emerges is the identification of the fourth area of experience with the source of poetic intuition, which is hardly surprising, since Ogun is himself the god of creativity. Thus, the numinous area of transition is the home of the tragic muse. "Tragic music," says Soyinka, "is an echo from that void," and he goes on:

> The source of the possessed lyricist, chanting hitherto unknown mythopoeic strains whose antiphonal refrain is, however, instantly caught and thrust with all its terror and awesomeness into the night by swaying votaries, this source is residual in the numinous area of transition, (148-49)

Still there is a metaphysical edge to the meaning of the fourth stage. It is a connecting link (a passage) between the three areas of existence defined by Yoruba ontology as the world of the ancestor, the living, and the unborn. A diagrammatical representation of this ontological universe is shown in figures 1 and 2.

The gulf of transition is a symbol of continuity: it permits free traffic between the three areas of existence, and the transitional passage, being Ogun's pathway, establishes Ogun's primacy as the god of the "road."

Soyinka's essay endorses a view of artistic creativity that is tragic. This view holds, as Yeats would say, that all the great poems of the world have their foundations fixed in agony. Both Yeats and the Nigerian poet Chritopher Okigbo uphold the notion of a tragic creativity whose metaphoric summation is contained in Yeats's observation that "the poet has made his home in the serpent's mouth."[23] Both Soyinka and his god, Ogun, are tragic artists. Ogun immersed himself in the seething cauldron of the dark-world will to forge a bridge for both men and gods. For his courage he was rewarded with the appellations: "primogenitor of the artist as creative human" and "forerunner and ancestor of palaeotechnic man" (150). When we transfer Ogun's action to its artistic complement, we have the following statement:

> To act, the Promethean instinct of rebellion, channels anguish into a creative purpose which releases man from a totally destructive despair, releasing from within him the most energetic, deeply combative inventions which, without usurping the territory of the infernal gulf, bridges it with visionary hopes. Only the battle of the will is thus primally creative; from its spiritual stress springs the soul's despairing cry which proves its own solace, which alone reverberating within the cosmic vaults usurps... the powers of the abyss. (146)

The soul's despairing cry which proves its own solace and which alone usurps the powers of the abyss is poetry.

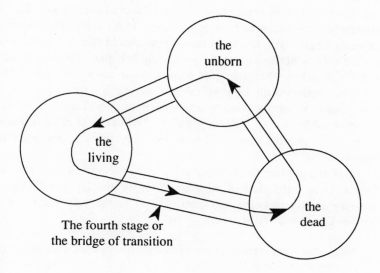

Fig. 1. Soyinka's Cosmology

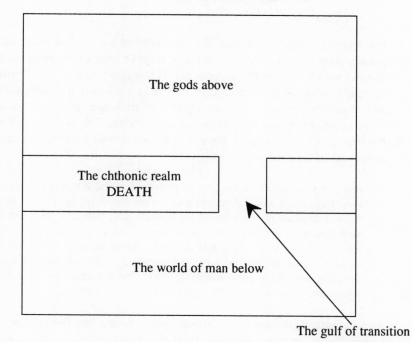

Fig. 2. Soyinka's Cosmology

Soyinka's essay is insightful on the subject of hubris. Soyinka's master, Nietzsche, sees hubris as a tragic necessity. In his view hubris is at the root of every tragic myth, for, as he says, "how should man force nature to yield up her secrets but by successfully resisting her, that is to say, by unnatural acts?"[24] Wisdom, Nietzsche goes on, is a crime committed against the gods, for it has equipped the sage with divine secrets. But the acquisition of such rare wisdom is accompanied by an attendant penalty. This, says Nietzsche, is the inexorable logic of the law of karma: "Whoever, in pride of knowledge, hurls nature into the abyss of destruction, must himself experience nature's disintegration."[25]

Soyinka applied the insights derived from Nietzsche to Ogun's act of hubris. Ogun's defiance of the cosmic forces that lay guardian to the yet inchoate matrix of being and non-being is in the very nature of Ogun's destiny and of tragedy in general.

> Tragic fate is the repetitive cycle of the taboo in nature, the karmic act of hubris witting or unwitting, into which the demonic will within man constantly compels him. Powerful tragic drama follows upon the act of hubris, and myth exacts this attendant penalty from the hero where he has actually emerged victor of a conflict. (156)

But Soyinka stretches the idea of hubris beyond the need to exact personal penalty from the hero. He weaves the concept of hubris into the fabric of the Yoruba world view. In this context hubris is a factor in the cyclic resolution of man's metaphysical situation. It triggers a chain reaction which "hurts" and "benefits" nature. The whirlpool of transition requires occasional hubristic invasions for its continuous regeneration. The role of hubris as a mechanism for guaranteeing the continuity of cosmic balance and harmony is stressed in the passage that follows:

> offences even against nature may be part of the exaction by deeper nature from humanity of acts which alone can open up the deeper springs of man and bring about a constant rejuvenation of the human spirit. Nature in turn benefits by such broken taboos, just as the cosmos does by demands made upon its will by man's cosmic affronts. Such acts of hubris compel the cosmos to delve deeper into its essence to meet the human challenge. Penance and retribution are not therefore aspects of punishment for crime but the first acts of a resumed awareness, an invocation of the principle of cosmic adjustment. (156)

And because restitution in the natural order is possible through the act of hubris, hubris becomes itself an essential element in the Yoruba concept of morality, for morality for the Yoruba, we are told, is that which creates harmony in the cosmos.

The issue of morality is taken up more fully in the second ritual essay, "Morality and Aesthetics in the Ritual Archetype." First, the problem of definition. The operative words in the title of this essay are contained in the term "ritual archetype." The term is to be understood in its specific meaning for Soyinka and in its original Jungian sense. "Ritual archetype" is used in the main body of the essay as an expression synonymous with "the drama of the gods." This drama is essentially a ritual (and a rite of passage), and the gods themselves are the first actors in the drama. It is therefore primal or primordial, that is, archetypal. Human enactments of the drama of the gods are imitations of the archetypal original. Soyinka uses the words ritual and drama interchangeably in the essay. In his view there can be no legitimate dividing line between ritual and drama. Ritual is drama and drama is ritual. Experts in dramatic literature and criticism would of course contest this view, but they do agree (especially Anthony Graham-White) that "the distinction between ritual and dramatic performances is not often made in traditional African societies."[26] And when Soyinka equates ritual with drama, he has traditional African drama in mind. From pages 34-35 the word ritual archetype reverts to its original Jungian meaning as the primordial inhabitants of the "collective unconscious," or, in Soyinka's typical parlance, "the hinterland of transition." But Soyinka quarrels with Jung for including dream images and psychotic exhalations and deliriums in the category of archetypes. These, says Soyinka, are not archetypes but mere emanations from the ephemeral and transient portions of the human psyche, whereas archetypes *proceed* from the congealed substrata of the psyche which are constantly enriched by the moral and historic experience of man. In spite of Soyinka's criticism of Jung, his understanding of myth has been enriched by the achievement of Jungian psychology.

Soyinka proceeds to illustrate the issue of morality and aesthetics in the drama of the gods by using examples from the dramatic literature based on the myth and history of his favorite deities: Sango, Obatala, and Ogun. His basic argument is that the gods are conceived among the Yoruba within the context of human fallibility. They are prone to an act of error which disrupts nature, in expiation of which the gods are condemned to penance. Their consequent penance restores order in the world of man and in the cosmos. Morality in Yoruba world view is bound up with the mandatory compensations that nature demands. It is predicated on the dialectics of challenge and response, on action and counteraction, on the hubristic infractions on nature which, in turn, compel upon nature countering contingency measures for the reassertion of its totality. The drama that develops from the history of these gods is a rite of passage distinguished by the three-part structure that is basic to all rites of passage, that is, ordeal and ritual death followed by rebirth.

This ritual dialectic has wider implications; it is linked with the cyclical dynamics of nature, that is, with the alternating cycles of death and life, dearth and plenty, drought and rain. The ordeal of the gods is nature's own mechanism for its own renewal. These gods are vegetation deities to a certain extent, for they possess affinities with such nature deities as Osiris, Ishtar, and Thammuz.

Sango's destiny at the positive end of the dialectical axis is apotheosis, aptly defined by Soyinka as "the joining of energies in cosmic continuity" (11). As the god of thunder and lightning, Sango is the "cosmic instrument of swift retributive justice"(8). Sango's history is the history of an anthropomorphic deity. A one-time tyrant of the ancient kingdom of Oyo, Sango himself became the victim of his own cunning. He had conspired with some of his henchmen to eliminate two of the most powerful war-lords in his kingdom, Gbonka and Timi. The first strategy, which failed, was to expose them to the risk of death in a war with an external aggressor. The second, which succeeded, was to set them against one another in single combat. The stronger of the two war-lords, Gbonka, defeated his rival and emerged from the combat wiser. He confronted Sango with his machinations and demanded his throne. Sango considered the challenge an affront to his royal dignity. In a fit of rage he set upon his own people and slaughtered his subjects, thereby committing a sacrilege upon nature that he had to atone for by exile and suicide. But after his death by hanging, his very subjects who had abandoned their king at his moment of trial admired the dead king for his courage to dare the abyss of transition through ritual suicide and proclaimed him a god. Sango's slaughter of his own people was the consequence of his hubristic neglect of the virtues of self-control.

Obatala's own error resulted from his addiction to palm wine. He was drunk as he was engaged with the divine duties of molding human shapes with clay, for he was the god of creation. His craftsman's fingers faltered from his excessive intake of alcohol, and he molded albinos, hunchbacks, and cripples. Obatala became guilty of criminal deviations from the aesthetics of creation. Nemesis caught up with Obatala when he visited his old friend Sango at Oyo. Suspected of an intent to steal Sango's horse, Obatala was clamped into prison, and creation came to a standstill because the god who turns blood into children was languishing in jail. The imprisonment of Obatala disrupted harmony in the cosmos and in the world of man, which was restored after the god's release. We have here an anomalous situation in which the crimes of the gods are visited upon mankind. This cannot be otherwise, says Soyinka, because "the relationship between man and god (embodiment of nature and cosmic principles) cannot be seen in any other terms but [in] those of naturalness" (15).

In Ogun's case we are already familiar with his hubristic invasion of the whirlpools of transition. The cosmic forces that guard the pool postponed Ogun's penalty till the fateful moment at the battle of Ire when, under the influence of alcohol, he massacred his own men. For that unwitting act Ogun is compelled to visit earth annually in atonement for his day of error. His visit to earth means harvest, and his withdrawal implies drought and scarcity. The alternating cycles of harvest and scarcity are rationalized in the Yoruba psyche in the myth of the god's descent to earth and his subsequent withdrawal. This myth is the subject of the long poem *Idanre:*

> He comes, who scrapes no earth dung from his feet
> He comes again in Harvest, the first of reapers
> Night is our tryst when sounds are clear
> And silences ring pure tones as the pause
> Of iron bells.[27]

The African gods retain the importance ascribed to them by the African world view in their home grounds, but those of them that survive in the Americas have lost the position assigned to them by popular imagination in the cosmic arrangement. In Brazil, for example, the Yoruba god Obatala is known as Oxala. Soyinka used the example of the changes brought upon the essence of Obatala (Oxala) through his syncretic associations with the Christian God in the Americas to illustrate the relevance of the second keyword (aesthetics) in the title of the essay under discussion. A comparison of two versions of the Obatala passion play, one supposedly by a Nigerian playwright and the other by a Brazilian, helped Soyinka to advance his argument. In their associations with the Christian saints, the African gods in the Americas have inherited the Western mind's conception of deity as an Olympian archetype. This view of the gods is the direct heritage of the Platonic-Christian tradition which has encouraged the gradual erosion of Earth in the Western metaphysical universe. It runs counter to the very geocentric dispositions of the gods themselves which have brought them closer within the sphere of human fallibility in the African world view. In the play *The Imprisonment of Obatala*, the gods assert their *humanity*. They dine, wine, and chat with men and are prone to human foibles and weaknesses. In Zora Zeljan's play *The Story of Oxala*, on the other hand, the African gods emerge as transcendental deities, inhabiting a sphere separate from the humans. It is this sense of their remoteness, the differing attitude to the gods in the two versions of the Obatala tragedy (i.e., the contrast between Obatala's earthiness in the first play and Oxala's ethereal incorporeality in Zora Zeljan's version), that Soyinka seeks to convey with the term *aesthetics*. In the Brazilian play the gods' reality is defined by the "aesthetics of estrangement" (25). Soyinka holds that the gods are remote in the Brazilian play because in the Americas they have inherited the "attenuation of terrestrialism... brought about by the encounter of the gods with Christian saints" (24). And when this happens the moral imperatives of complementarity become meaningless:

> When ritual archetypes acquire new aesthetic characteristics, we may expect re-adjustments of the moral imperatives that brought them into existence in the first place, at the centre of man's effort to order the universe. (25)

But one wonders, however, whether the word *aesthetics* has been employed in its proper context in Soyinka's essay. Is it not, indeed, possible that Soyinka is merely attracted by the rhythmic resonance of the word *aesthetics* for its sake, which, in conjunction with the rest of the words in the title, reads like a line of verse? But equally implied in the term *aesthetics,* though not specifically illustrated in Soyinka's essay, is the staging logistics of the drama of the gods, the mode of presentation, details of space, music, poetry, and the producer's consciousness of the need to elicit from ritual archetypes "the emotive progression which leads to a communal ecstasy or catharsis" (5-6).

The third ritual essay, "Drama and the African World View," has two main thrusts, one expository and the other applied. The expository focus dwells upon the symbolic function of space in ritual theater. In the second part of the essay, Soyinka discusses two plays, J. P. Clark's *Song of a Goat* (1964) and Duro Ladipo's *Oba Koso* (1964), which appear to him to illustrate the way drama can reflect the African world view.

First, what are the main features of Soyinka's pet concept, African world view? These may be summarized as follows: the union of essences both divine and human in man and god, the replenishment and continuance of which guarantees unity of being in both man and god. Transferred to the world of nature, Soyinka sees this union as "animist interfusion of all matter and consciousness" (145). Cosmic balance is a function of the harmonious relationship between separate entities within the cosmic envelope, that is, the healthy interaction of the spiritual, the human, and the natural forces. This leads us naturally to the role of hubris as an agency of shock: it is nature's mechanistic device for its own regeneration. Without the challenge of the cosmic status quo through hubris, cosmic equilibrium runs the risk of being locked up in a condition of sterile harmony. Add to all this the movement of transition between the world of the ancestor, the living, and the unborn, and the reality of the fourth space acting as a channel for transition. This is linked to a cyclic conception of time whereby, in Soyinka's view, "life, present life, contains within it manifestations of the ancestral, the living, and the unborn" (144).

What emerges is a homogeneous world view in which the constituent elements are interrelated and inseparable from one another without the risk of disrupting the cosmic order. This view of the universe is not peculiar to the African mind. Elements of it can be observed in other cultures. There are, for instance, affinities between this world view insofar as its ultimate goal is a harmonious relationship between man and his environment and the ordered hierarchy of the Elizabethan world view.

Two plays are related to this world view: *Song of a Goat* and *Oba Koso*. We encountered *Oba Koso* in the essay on "ritual archetypes" where Sango attains apotheosis through self-sacrifice. The action itself is a heroic gesture in spite of the crime against nature that motivated it, and it turns out as an event that became beneficial to the human community. As a tyrant and a murderer, Sango was an abnormal growth on the body of nature. Nature can only be returned to a condition of harmony through a total excision of the abnormal outgrowth. Sango wins the reader's sympathy through his courage to dare the abyss. We have in the play a world reminiscent of the universe of *Song of a Goat* in which man's bonds with nature are visceral. Timi, one of the protagonists in the play, was encouraged by his consciousness of this union of man and nature to summon nature to his aid in his own rites of passage:

> I come this day to Ede town
> It is the gentle wind that says, blow towards me
> Spirits of swarming termites say, swarm towards me
> Two hundred rafters support the house
> Two hundred lizards support the wall
> Let all hands be raised to sustain me. (59)

The tragedy in *Song of a Goat* lies not in the crime of incest but in Zifa's sexual impotence and his sterile pride which threatens the continuity of the species. Therein inheres the worst breakdown in moral order. Soyinka explains:

> Where society lives in a close inter-relation with Nature, regulates its existence by natural phenomena within the observable processes of continuity – ebb and tide, waxing and waning of the moon, rain and drought, planting and harvest – the highest moral order is seen as that which guarantees a parallel continuity of the species. (52)

The theoretical focus of the third ritual essay deals with the metaphysical implications of the stage in ritual theater. These implications were enumerated early in the essay on "ritual archetypes." The stage, says

Soyinka, is a microcosmic copy of the chthonic realm, which requires the presence of "a challenger, a human representative to breach it periodically on behalf of the well-being of the community" (3). Soyinka made this statement with special reference to the drama of the gods, but he maintains that even in ordinary ritual drama or in the so-called realistic or literary drama, this view of the stage still holds. But it is the function of the stage in ritual theater, its metaphysical implications that exercise the greatest fascination for Soyinka. In its metaphysical context the stage is to be seen as a symbolic representation of earth and the cosmos, and the actor on the stage is a human challenger re-enacting man's existential predicaments. The stage is to be viewed as one arena in which man has attempted to come to terms with the spatial phenomenon of his being. Soyinka returns again and again to the cosmic definition of the stage. Two more representative citations might suffice:

> The concern of ritual theatre in this process of spatial definition....must....be seen as an integral part of man's constant efforts to master the immensity of the cosmos with his minuscule self. (40)

And again:

> Ritual theatre... establishes the spatial medium not merely as a physical area for simulated events but as a manageable contraction of the cosmic envelope within which man... fearfully exists. (41)

The insight revealed in these ritual essays distinguishes Soyinka as an accomplished critic of the ritual stage and must count as original contributions to dramatic theory and criticism.

Ideology or Social Vision?

Two matters concern us here, namely, the religious and secular dimensions of Soyinka's statements on works of social vision. Two of his essays are to be viewed as further clarifications of his position on the issue of ideological commitment in works of literature where ideological commitment connotes a sympathy for a Marxist view of art; and although Soyinka stretches the meaning of ideology to embrace the leading ideas behind such literary movements as expressionism, surrealism, and Negritude, the implication of the term *ideology* in the essays under consideration is Marxist oriented. This prejudice is understandable considering the frequency of Soyinka's own "passage" through the crucibles of Marxist literary anatomy at radical circles at the Universities of Ibadan and Ife, where he is found to be ideologically wanting. Soyinka has thus cause to restate and redefine his position in the context of the on-going debate on literature and ideology. He says yes to a social vision and no to a literary ideology because of the latter's tendency to limit and impose upon the free operations of the creative spirit. Works of literature, says Soyinka, are "essentially fluid operations of the creative mind upon social and natural phenomena" (61). In a literary ideology this fluidity yields to rigidity, and the creative imagination is compelled to follow the routes mapped out by ideological manifestoes. The choice for a social vision is determined, therefore, by Soyinka's regard for the integrity and autonomy of the creative artist, but autonomy does not preclude social relevance. The artist, as the popular saying goes, does not live in an ivory tower. His visionary imaginings have the good of society as their goal. A prime function of art in its social context, says Soyinka, is "the visionary reconstruction of the past for the purposes of a social direction" (106). This definition of literature's social role is a carry-over from Soyinka's earlier view on the role of a writer in a modern African state. In the essay on that subject published in 1967, Soyinka charges the African writer with a deplorable lack of "vision." The African writer is urged to abandon the "historic" vision inherent in Negritude so that he can the more easily center his gaze on the immediate realities of his society. Only through the acquisition of a realist vision, says Soyinka, can the writer resume the real essence of himself as "the record of the mores and experience of his society *and* as the voice of vision in his own time."[28] The writer's capacity to combine the gains of historic and realist visions into a constructive program for the future is what might amount to a social vision. The very conception of the writer's social program as an alternative that is attainable only in the future renders that image of society a visionary projection.

Soyinka is at pains indeed to define exactly what he means by "social vision." We have several tentative offerings:

(1) The reflection of experience is only one of the functions of literature.... And when that experience is social we move into areas of ideological projections, the social vision. (64)

(2) A creative concern which conceptualises or extends actuality beyond the purely narrative, making it reveal realities beyond the immediately attainable, a concern which upsets orthodox acceptances in an effort to free society of historical or other superstitions, these are qualities possessed by literature of a social vision. (66)

(3) A re-statement of the values of past or present in integrated perspectives of a future potential. (98)

The continuous search for definition is necessary because Soyinka insists on making a distinction between a social vision and a socialist (revolutionary) vision. If the distinction must be maintained, it follows that a socialist revolutionary fiction might belong to the category of social vision, whereas not all works of a social vision are transposable to the socialist revolutionary category. The problem is compounded by the introduction of a religious factor into Soyinka's conception of a social vision. The way out of the dilemma is to qualify again his definition of social vision in terms of its relationship to a socialist revolutionary fiction:

> Revolutionary writing is generally of this kind [the category of a social vision], though whether or not much of the writing which aspires to the label is always literature is another question. (66)

It is his suspicion that most revolutionary writings might not qualify as literature that compels Soyinka to prefer the expression social vision to the term socialist revolutionary vision. His preference for social vision enables him to bring a wide spectrum of fiction under the label.

The practical illustration of his thesis is easier for Soyinka than his theoretical definitions. Since he draws his examples from works of fiction, we can distinguish three categories: (1) social realist fiction; (2) socialist realist fiction; (3) social visionary fiction. Social realist fictions are generally novels of disillusionment, the kind of fiction that exemplifies the pressure on the African writer to assume a realist vision. Soyinka's first novel, *The Interpreters* (1965), belongs to this group. Others include Alex La Guma's *A Walk in the Night* (1964), Achebe's *A Man of the People* (1966), and Armah's *The Beautyful Ones Are Not Yet Born* (1969), to name only a few examples. The social realist fiction makes no pretensions to a social vision, although Armah's *The Beautyful Ones* moves from the social realist level to a social visionary plane at the tail-end of the novel when Armah envisions the symbolic, solitary flower positioned in the center of the elegiac inscription "The beautyful ones are not yet born." The birth of the "beautyful ones" is predicted in the image of the beautiful flower and fulfilled in Armah's fourth novel, *Two Thousand Seasons* (1973).

Under the second category we include Soyinka's own novel *Season of Anomy* (1973), Ousmane Sembene's *God's Bits of Wood* (1970), Armah's *Two Thousand Seasons* (1973), and Ngũgĩ's *Petals of Blood* (1977). Only two of these novels (*God's Bits of Wood* and *Two Thousand Seasons*) are discussed in Soyinka's essay. They qualify as works of social vision because they make projections on the nature of society. They have one thing in common: the image of society they envisage is one that is egalitarian.

Social visionary novels are those works that project an image of the ideal *status quo* that the author considers best for his society either now or in the future. This vision is similar to the hopes of the novels of the second category, but the novelist need not, in this case, embody his dreams in revolutionary terms. Soyinka is thinking here of the visions of ideal society entertained by a great many African novelists either from a religious salvationist or other (secular) ethos. Iconoclastic literature (which may not necessarily be socialist oriented) belongs to the category of social vision. The positive values held by the author may be inferred from the negative values he destroys. This is particularly true of Ouologuem's *Bound to Violence* (1971), which "upsets orthodox acceptances in an effort to free society of historical or other superstitions" (66). The superstition in this case is the Arab-Islamic colonization of Black Africa. Ouologuem, Soyinka believes, has deliberately countered Hamidou Kane's claim in *Ambiguous Adventure* (1972) that Islam is "one religion whose ethics, philosophy and form of worship reconciles races and encourages universal fraternalism" (77).

When we come to Camara Laye's novels, *The Dark Child* (1955) and *The Radiance of the King* (1956), Soyinka's thesis falters a little. We have a secular vision in these works which is not necessarily social. If we insist on Soyinka's other definition of social vision as "a re-statement of the values of past or present in integrated perspectives of a future potential," Laye's *Radiance of the King* does not embody a social vision. It restates the values of the past (the African world view) but offers no projections about the nature of society in the future. *The Radiance* is best understood in terms of its achievement as a work that vindicates the authenticity of the African world view just as that world view is best illustrated in drama by *Song of a Goat* and *Oba Koso*.

It is Achebe's rather ambivalent attitude to that world view in his third novel *Arrow of God* (1964) that creates some obstacle (in Soyinka's view) in our determination of the role of the gods in that novel. Incidents involving the supernatural or the mystical are not presented in a situation of sustained dignity in Achebe's novels. His attitude to the divine is cavalier, sometimes irreverent, and often determined by political rather than spiritual considerations. The imprisonment of Ezeulu, who is half-man half-spirit, was a good enough opportunity for the writer in the mythic mode to visit upon nature the cosmic implications of that hubristic breach of nature, but curiously, Achebe avoids any spiritual dimensions of the priest's experience of exile. In the earlier essay, "From a Common Back Cloth," Soyinka commends Achebe for according the mystical its due place in the order of things in his first novel *Things Fall Apart* (1958). We have in that novel a pattern of "understated mysteries... of psychical influences on daily routine, of a man's personal *chi*, of initiations, of guilt and purifications whose ethics are not those of a court of law but of the forces of Nature cycle, of the living and the dead."[29] In *Arrow of God* the story is different:

> Considerations of the authenticity of spiritual inspiration, or of manifestations which may be considered supernatural, or at the least, ominous coincidences, are given alternative (secular) explications in the casual reflections of members of his [Achebe's] Igbo community, coloured as always by individual problems or positions taken in sectional confrontations. In short, coloured by their *humanity*. (87)

These remarks underscore the difference between the temperament of the imagination of the two writers. It is a difference between the mythic imagination (Soyinka) and the historical imagination (Achebe).

Soyinka's reading of Achebe's novel from a mythic perspective is innovative, being so different from the general concerns of Achebe criticism. Most critics have tended to situate Achebe's novels merely in their historical and cultural context, but we have here a new approach which is refreshing.

Soyinka holds that religious factors may also determine a writer's conceptions about the nature of society. He is thinking here of two main religions: the Christian religion and the Islamic religion. The point here is that there are some novels in which the author's religious background has influenced the resolution of the plot. This resolution is often superimposed, thereby weakening the strength of the novels concerned. Such an interference from a religious ideology is comparable, in the secular sector, to a forced resolution which might have been determined by a socialist ideology. In William Conton's novel *The African* (1960) and in the play *The Rhythm of Violence* (1964) by Lewis Nkosi, the logical progression of the plot is distorted by a Christian salvationist ethic which pretends that a fraternal understanding between races could be brought about through the affirmation of Christian values. In Conton's novel the value asserted is forgiveness, and in Nkosi's play it is love. "These," says Soyinka, "are the ethical lines on which an envisioned regeneration of society will be based" (70), hence the author's social vision. Other writers ensnared, Soyinka thinks, by the illusions of the Christian vision are Alan Paton and Peter Abrahams: they were reprimanded in the earlier essay "From a Common Back Cloth" (1963). Nearly two decades later Soyinka had cause to return to them with his first judgments on these novels still unchanged.

The Islamic vision is represented by Hamidou Kane's novel *Ambiguous Adventure*. The summation of the Islamic viewpoint is contained in Soyinka's preliminary observations to his discussion of Hamidou Kane's novel, already quoted in part:

In colonial societies which constantly seek a world-view to challenge the inherent iniquities of any philosophy which can be associated with the colonial intrusion, we naturally encounter works which make a point of claiming that Islam... is one religion whose ethics, philosophy and form of worship reconciles races and encourages universal fraternalism. (77)

In Kane's hand the Islamic vision is shown to be less harmful to the creative imagination than William Conton's or Lewis Nkosi's handling of the Christian message of love and forgiveness in their own works. The Islamic vision is not consciously upgraded to the level of propaganda in Kane's novel, and because the question of propaganda is very remote from the author's mind, the novel achieves a more satisfying resolution of its conflicts through the author's evocation of his religious background than the mechanical imposition of Christian values on *The African* and *Rhythm of Violence*. Death is the logical outcome of Samba Diallo's apostasy. It is the doctrine of death, the standpoint of the grand master of the Word, the Teacher, which had the final word in the novel's logical and natural resolution of its conflicts, not the traditional Diallobe society, nor the West which was responsible for the weakening of Diallo's spiritual roots (85).

The closing paragraphs of the essay restate Soyinka's longstanding objections to Negritude. Three key issues are at stake here. The first (the Cartesian fallacy) is the naiveté of the founding fathers of the Negritude movement itself, a naiveté that manifested itself in their uncritical accept-ance of Eurocentric prejudices and racist ideologies. Descartes had said, "I think, therefore I am"; and that supreme Cartesian, Senghor, came up with a variant of the Cartesian proposition: "I feel, therefore I am." Soyinka wonders why an intellectual movement that is anti-European should borrow its self-characterizing definitions from a European system of thought. Negritude's "reference points took far too much colouring from European ideas even while its Messiahs pronounced themselves fanatically African" (127).

The second objection (the aesthetic fallacy) is Negritude's attitude to the principle of creativity; it adopted a defeatist self-justifying aesthetic stance which breeds a poetry of self-contemplation rather than a poetry of action. Soyinka regards the poetry of self-contemplation as a form of "narcissism." Soyinka recalls the points made in the earlier essay "And After the Narcissist?" in an important statement. One of the unfortunate by-products of Negritude was "a mounting narcissism which involved contemplation of the contrived self in the supposed tragic grandeur of the cultural dilemma" (130).

The third objection (the dialectical fallacy) was the fallacy of the dialectical self-resolution predicted by Sartre for Negritude. Negritude, says

Sartre, occupies a middle position in the ᵗhree-stage movement of an inexorable dialectical progression. The first movement (the thesis) is the assertion of white supremacy that gave birth to Negritude in the first instance; the second stage (the antithesis) is the countering of this supremacist ideology by Negritude, that is, the birth of Negritude; the third stage (the synthesis) will resolve itself in the ultimate cancellation of the racial concepts in both the thesis and the antithesis. This stage will witness the union of all the workers of the world (both white and black) in a proletarian struggle for the establishment of a raceless society. Soyinka commends Sartre and his dialectical ancestor, Descartes, for their logical thinking: they are people who think, white creatures in pith helmets in an African jungle who think, but their thinking should have opened their eyes to the one reality of Negritude: it was the property of a bourgeois intellectual elite, and as such it had no chance of integrating itself in the destiny of the working classes.

Although all these objections are interrelated, the most important of them all, because it concerns itself with the theme of creativity, is the second objection. And this brings us back to the subject of the essays in this section, the question of ideology and literature. Negritude tended to channel its creative energies through a particular mode of artistic expression – the contemplative narcissistic mode. This bending of the natural disposition of the creative mind to accommodate certain preconceived ideas is the bane of all literary ideologies. The principles of creativity cannot be legislated. "The practical effects," writes Soyinka, of literary ideology "on the creative process lead to predictability, imaginative constraint, and thematic excisions" (65).

All this does not mean that there is no fallacy in Soyinka's own argument. The definition of Negritude in terms of the Cartesian proposition runs into the same dilemma as the very act of writing African literature or Soyinka's literary criticism in a European language. We cannot accept the view which asserts that "the writer is far more preoccupied with visionary projection of society than with speculative projection on the nature of literature" (64). The writer in fact is concerned with both. Most great writers, Matthew Arnold, Yeats, and Eliot, have indeed speculated on the nature of literature and of its relation to society. Nor can we accept the reasoning that relegates the question of literary ideology to the province of the critic only. Ngũgĩ, Armah, and Sembene have steered their art along consciously formulated ideological convictions. "It is only in the socialist context," wrote Ngũgĩ in 1968 on the issue of an ideological program for African literature, "that a look at yesterday can be meaningful in illuminating today and tomorrow."[30] Nine years later Armah echoes this view: "In my people's world revolution would be the only art, revolutionaries the only creators. All else is part of Africa's destruction."[31]

The arguments of Soyinka's two essays on ideology and the social vision carry further the points he made in a lecture delivered at the University of Washington's faculty seminar in 1973. The lecture entitled "Drama and the Revolutionary Ideal" focused interest on the pitfalls of ideological commitment in drama. Soyinka's conclusion was that ideological interests were bound to weaken drama's integrity as an art form because drama is by its very nature a revolutionary medium. It is the only art form that is extremely vulnerable to ideological manipulation. To superimpose an ideology on an art form that is intrinsically revolutionary is to overburden the form. The insertion of an ideology into drama's structure could, however, be adroitly managed by a gifted dramatist through the medium of ritual, but in lesser hands the result is frequently a melodrama. Soyinka feels that the consciously worker-proletarian-motivated drama written by Arnold Wesker (*Roots*) or Edward Albee (*Who's Afraid of Virginia Woolf*) and the social visionary plays written by Lewis Nkosi (*The Rhythm of Violence*) and Alton Kumalo (*Themba*) suffer from contrived anguish and enforced resolution. He reaffirms the point I made earlier that literary ideology (usually the concern of the critic rather than of the writer) has the tendency to "dam up the creative paths natural to the writer's peculiar genius and lead him toward artificial concepts of proletarian art."[32] Since revolutionary tendencies are inbuilt within the dramatic mode itself, the less consciously ideological the dramatist appears to be the more effectively would the subversive intent of his message be disseminated:

> The creative ideal in revolutionary theatre is not a self-conscious pandering to any proletarian illusion on any level whatever, be it the spiritual level or the social-revolutionary level, because...the matrix of creativity, most especially in the dramatic mode, embraces at all times – both in individual and communal affectiveness – the regenerative potential of society.[33]

How do rituals function as vectors of social or revolutionary messages? Through the medium of audience participation. This, according to Soyinka, has been the secret of Ben Caldwell's achievement in *The Fanatic* and Imamu Baraka's success in his play *The Slave Ship*. In these plays the revolutionary message has been effectively disguised under the ritual idiom of audience participation.

Soyinka is firmly opposed to a conscious injection of ideological motives into works of imaginative literature. This attitude appears to be a self-defensive posture, one that is intended to justify the kind of literature Soyinka himself produces. But whether this attitude should lead to a denial of literary ideology in itself as well as of the achievement of writers with obvious ideological motivations is another matter. Also, Soyinka's essay suffers from a weak theoretical definition. He is unable to convincingly separate the term *literary ideology* from our understanding of what he calls social vision. However, Soyinka's evaluation of the works of the authors discussed in the essays is unquestionably insightful.

Controversies

Soyinka has come under attack as a writer from two radical schools of criticism. The most outspoken, though perhaps less publicized, is the Marxist school led by Biodun Jeyifo and Femi Osofisan among the Ibadan-Ife leftist critics. The other radical voice in Soyinka criticism is the school of neo-negritudist apologetics for authentic traditional African aesthetics led by Chinweizu and his group. The uncompromising posture struck by these two schools in their evaluation of Soyinka's work has drawn Soyinka into controversial polemics that are not strictly literary criticism but which, nevertheless, do contain some insights that further clarify Soyinka's conceptions on the nature of art.

First, the Marxist school of critics. This school of critics approaches a work of art from the materialist-historical perspective. Leon Trotsky has outlined some key issues in the materialist-historical theory of art.[34] These include such fundamental questions as the following:

(1) To what order of feelings does a given artistic work correspond in all its peculiarities?

(2) What are the social conditions of these thoughts and feelings?

(3) What place do they occupy in the historic development of a society and of a class?

(4) Under the influence of what historic impulse and conditions has the work been produced and in what ways have those conditions and contradictions been reflected in the work?

The Nigerian Marxist critics indict Soyinka for his supreme indifference to the responsibilities which the materialist theory confers upon art. It is the function of art, in the materialist-historical aesthetic, to reflect the historical processes which are at work in society at a given historical moment together with their internal contradictions and tensions (i.e., their dialectics). To the Nigerian Marxians every work of the imagination that dares an independent existence outside the framework of "historical materialism"[35] is prone to the charge of deliberate falsification of experience and reality. Other metaphors for falsification are such terms as *distortion, romanticizing, mythifying, mystifying,* and *prettifying.* Soyinka's natural predilection for a mythic exploration of experience exposed him obviously to the Marxist notions of falsification. Every utterance of the Nigerian Marxists echoes the view that Soyinka's perception of history is static, mythic, and therefore unrealistic. In a reading of Soyinka's tragedy, *Death and the King's Horseman* (1975), Biodun Jeyifo speaks of Soyinka's "mythopoeic" attitude to history, his constant penchant for transforming experience into metaphysical, trans-historical, mythic dimensions."[36] Femi Osofisan, in the essay "Drama and the New Exotic," ridicules the new exotic stage patronized by such playwrights as Soyinka and Ola Rotimi and peopled by animist gods and utterly indifferent to the logic of "historical contradictions in the dialectics of flux."[37] Omafume Onoge and G. G. Darah make the same point in their paper "The Retrospective Stage: Some Reflections on the Mythopoeic Tradition at Ibadan." They dismiss as "mythic" and "retrogressive" a dramatized historiography of the past where antagonistic contradictions do not exist.[38] "It is this undialectical approach," they affirm, "plus the pre-eminence of the supernatural in the artistic representations of the past that we have termed mythopoeic."[39] Applying the materialist theory to *Death and the King's Horseman,* Jeyifo finds the play to be guilty of mispresenting and misinterpreting the real identity of the indigenous society. The play, says Jeyifo, did not attempt to highlight the real objective differences between conflicting groups and classes in the indigenous society. What we have, instead, is a rationalization of "the rule of the dazzling FEW... over the deceived MANY."[40] In an earlier essay on Soyinka's *The Road,* Jeyifo concedes to Soyinka some awareness of the dialectical processes of history, but that awareness, he feels, is subverted by Soyinka's mythopoeic imagination that has led to a deliberate mystification or reification of a natural instrument of labor, the road, so that we have in that play a "hidden" class war rather than an open one:

> The reification of the road... is a mystification: the road (and the vehicles which ply it) is a product of man's labour, a specific item in the ensemble of the forces of production; it is not a manifest destiny unto itself.
>
> *The Road* is imbued with the heavy atmosphere of death, is obsessed by the deaths and "dangerous employment" on the road because it penetrates the "natural," normal aspects of a mode of production in which the relationship between the instruments and tools of labour and the labouring classes is distorted, mythified. [41]

Several years before the New Marxist radicals began to articulate their objections to Soyinka's works, the Kenyan novelist and critic, Ngũgĩ wa Thiong'o, had expressed some dissatisfaction with Soyinka's writings along the same lines as those of the Nigerian Marxists. We quote Ngũgĩ in full in illustration of a Marxist criticism that is sober, level-headed, pedestrian, and bereft of linguistic mystifications:

Although Soyinka exposes his society in breadth, the picture he draws is static, for he fails to see the present in the historical perspective of conflict and struggle. It is not enough for the African artist, standing aloof, to view society and highlight its weaknesses. He must try to go beyond this, to seek out the sources, the causes and the trends of a revolutionary struggle which has already destroyed the traditional power-map drawn up by the colonialist nations.[42]

Soyinka's reply to his Marxist critics is contained in the paper "Who's Afraid of Elesin Oba?" delivered to the Conference on Radical Perspectives on African Literature held at Ibadan, in 1977, and in the Inaugural Lecture he delivered at Ife in November 1980 entitled "The Critic and Society." The point of view proffered in these essays is identical, and a detailed analysis would only be undertaken at the risk of becoming repetitive. Soyinka reaffirms in these essays the points he had already made in the essay on ideology and social vision. He insists on the autonomy of the creative imagination. Its operations on social and natural phenomena cannot be legislated. Criticism must learn to evaluate works of imagination only in terms of the sociology of the works' own aesthetic universe. The criticism that seeks in every work of art a causal and historical and socio-economic network of society is reductionist and arbitrary; it imposes extra burdens on art. "Criticism – dealing with general principles and theories of creativity – has gone beyond its competence and dared to enlarge upon the legitimate purlieu of imaginative projection."[43]

On his addiction to myth and ritual, Soyinka believes, as would Jung, that both myth and ritual are relevant to the spiritual needs of modern man. It is only the Western-trained skeptics who would repudiate the element of mystery even in the present contemporary setting. Myth may be viewed as representing the spiritual dimension of the very historical processes which the Nigerian radicals accuse Soyinka of ignoring. The Nigerian critic, Stanley Macebuh, has noted that myth and history complement one another in Soyinka's works:

To the extent that myth and history are complementary, it may be suggested that Soyinka's persistent meditation on myth is an attempt to reveal the primal foundations of African culture, and therefore of history.[44]

Soyinka himself has affirmed his confidence in the mutual interdependence of myth and history.

My social temperament is not without its complementary objective study of the society we live in and the societies we do not live in but which do impinge on our immediate society.[45]

The message of the two essays is summed up in the epigrammatic statement: "When art ceases to imitate life, it does not thereby aspire to imitate ideology; while criticism which fails to emulate life ends up as an imitation of art."[46]

Soyinka is not the kind of writer who will give up easily in intellectual debates. His intellect appears to be easily stimulated by polemics. This is proven by the witty, pungent, and incisive replies he metes out to his critics. He tries to use the very logic of the Marxist critics to defeat their own arguments. Marxist criticism, says Soyinka, tends very often to reduce art to an economic commodity. It treats art even as bourgeois capitalists treat labor: "The work of art is the product of intellectual labour which, without any self-criticism, the critic appropriates to ends other than the ends for which the work is produced and marketed."[47] This capitalist attitude to art shows up in the language of the Marxist critic himself. In spite of his supposed sympathy for the proletariat, the critic's language is not proletarian. It is a "seminarist language replete with its infinite discursiveness submerging, distorting and finally appropriating the original commodity in its quotational garrulity."[48]

The next radical voice in Soyinka criticism is the school of critics led by Chinweizu. These critics examined, among other things, the attitudes and tendencies of modern Nigerian poetry between the 1960s and the early 1970s. The poets whose works were scrutinized are J. P. Clark, Christopher Okigbo, Michael Echeruo, Wole Soyinka, Romanus Egudu, and Okogbule Wonodi. These poets, in the opinion of the Chinweizu critics, are lacking in craft and are found guilty of the following faults: (1) old-fashioned, craggy, unmusical language; (2) obscure and inaccessible diction; (3) a plethora of imported imagery; and (4) a divorce from African oral poetic tradition. The poet most guilty of these charges may be Soyinka. Of Soyinka's *Idanre*, the Chinweizu critics delivered this verdict:

> The imagery is imprecise and opaque and lacking in evocative power. All we can decipher is the names of the various deities: Ogun, Sango, Ajantala, Esu, Orunmila, Orishanla [sic]. But in this narrative poem it is never clear who does what to whom and with what consequences. It is often difficult to tell who the many pronouns – *he, she, we, us* – refer to. We are shut off from the experience on both the intellectual and emotional levels. The language is a formidable barrier; and even after you have hacked your way through it, you still cannot understand what, if anything, is supposed to be going on.[49]

There is merit in these observations; for if, as Soyinka himself has claimed, works of literature are "fluid operations of the creative mind upon social and natural phenomena," his, indeed, have not always been so. He injects studied metaphysical strains into the free operation of the creative intuition upon social and natural phenomena. Critic Roderick Wilson had earlier complained of complexity and confusion in Soyinka's poetry.[50] The Chinweizu critics' endorsement of these charges lends them further weight. Soyinka replied to the Chinweizu critics in two essays: "Neo-Tarzanism: The Poetics of Pseudo-Tradition" (1975) and "Neo-Tarzanism: The Aesthetic Illusion" (1976). The argument of these two essays is similar, although their tones differ. Soyinka defends the disposition of his imagination as a creative artist in these essays. What he calls "selective eclecticism"[51] is the technical approach that rewards his imagination, enriching his sensibilities as a poet. As a creative artist, Soyinka is not limited to considerations of local color only (the flora and fauna of the African poetic landscape recommended by the Chinweizu critics) but transcends these to assimilate new experiences from other cultures and traditions. And so the "plethora of imported imagery" cannot but be persistent. Even his attitude to that local environment itself is more complex than an average mind comprehends:

> My African world is a little more intricate and embraces precision machinery, oil rigs, hydro-electricity, my typewriter, railway trains (not iron snakes), machine guns, bronze sculpture, etc., plus an ontological relationship with the universe including the above listed pumpkins and iron bells. This may result in a subtle *complication* in the "narration, reflection and resolution" of these phenomena but emphatically denies the deliberate *complicating* of them.[52]

But in spite of his eclectic sensibility it is still necessary to distinguish between the true poet and the imitative poet. The mind of the true poet assimilates disparate experiences only to transform them into a new mintage. The great poets of the world, both dead and living, form part of the cultural inheritance of every poet regardless of his background. What distinguishes the genuine poet from the imitative poet is his or her attitude to that cultural heritage. The mind of the true poet transforms what it borrows into a new whole, whereas it is the aspiration of the imitative poet to merely echo his or her master's voice:

> A distinct universal quality in all great poets does... exercise ghostly influences on other writers – however different in background – at moments when a similarity of the particularized experience is shared. For the genuine creative mind, this need not be a cause for self-flagellation. The resulting work is easily judged by its capacity to move one step further, or sidewise; a conceptual variant or sleight-of-thought, by the naturalness of the influence, the thoroughness of ingestion within a new organic mould, its felicitous re-emergence and by the original strength of the new organic entity.[53]

These essays help us to understand Soyinka's views about the nature of poetry. Poetry for him is that metrical composition that is "visceral and sensuous" and "engages the imagination."[54] Indeed the "principle of imaginative challenge... is one of the functions of poetry."[55] Also we have gained an insight from the essays into Soyinka's concept of image or symbol. What determines his choice of image is its peculiar potential to spark off "a dynamic relationship which consists of an internalized dialectic of phenomena and perception."[56]

Because the Chinweizu critics advocate a return to tradition, Soyinka labels them "Neo-Tarzanists" and calls them "advocates of a noble-savage school of poetics."[57] Tradition, he affirms in a different context, does not mean raffia skirts or menstrual loin cloth.[58]

Of the two essays Soyinka wrote in reply to the Neo-Tarzanists, "Neo-Tarzanism: The Aesthetic Illusion" is more sober, more weighty, less polemical, and more emotionally controlled than "Neo-Tarzanism: The Poetics of Pseudo-Tradition." The earlier paper might have been written on the spur of the moment. Soyinka appears to have been too emotionally involved with his subject for the essay to have been objective. His judgment in the later essay is more mature and more aesthetically distanced from its immediate target and, therefore, more effective as a literary polemic.

Conclusion

This study has not exhausted all that could be said in a full discussion of Soyinka's statements as a literary critic. It has only attempted to analyze the content of his major critical essays in order to understand what is being said in them and thereby to gain a fuller understanding of Soyinka's mind and art, for Soyinka's critical writings illuminate his own works. From his earliest criticism to his latest, Soyinka has urged upon the African writer the philosophy of self-acceptance: the acceptance of the true image of the African in works of the imagination. The philosophy of acceptance is the inspiration behind the Incidental Essays. Soyinka has quarreled with Senghor and others of the Negritude school for distorting Africa's true image in their writings. This denial of the authentic image is at the root of Soyinka's criticism of Negritude.

The Ritual Essays transport us into the world of Yoruba mythology, exploring the origin and nature of Yoruba tragedy and the role of hubris in the drama of the gods. Tragedy originates from Ogun's sacrifice of his being in the first archetypal space (the fourth stage). Taking their cue from Ogun's example, the other ritual archetypes – Sango and Obatala – have learned to face tragedy as reparation for a previous act of error. It is in the principle of challenge and restitution that (ritual) drama can be related to the African world view.

The insights derived from these essays illuminate Soyinka's own works; indeed, the essays are written with the kind of work he produces in mind, for he is a writer in the mythic mode as distinct from one whose imagination is historical. It is here (his mythic imagination) that Soyinka falls short of the expectations of Marxist critics. Indeed, his essays on ideology and social vision reflect the dilemma of the mythic imagination in a world of pragmatic ideology. This is the argument of his literary polemics whenever they do not concern themselves with the problems of poetics. The mythic imagination, he maintains, can hardly consort with ideology in the Marxist sense. But it can make projections for the good of the future. Such projections constitute what Soyinka means by "social vision."

In illustrating his theories with practical examples, Soyinka is an accomplished critic; in the formulation of these theories, however, he is not so clear and precise in his meaning. This is understandable, for Soyinka is primarily a creative writer, not a literary theorist.

NOTES

1. Clarence Hugh Holman et al., *A Handbook to Literature* (New York: Odyssey, 1960), p. 298.

2. Ibid., p. 299.

3. Bernth Lindfors, "The Early Writings of Wole Soyinka," *Journal of African Studies*, 2 (1975), p. 85. This article has been expanded in Lindfors's *Early Nigerian Literature* (New York: Africana, 1982), pp. 111-41.

4. Lindfors, p. 86, and Martin Banham, "The Beginnings of a Nigerian Literature in English," *Review of English Literature*, 3 (1962), p. 90.

5. Wole Soyinka, "From a Common Back Cloth," *The American Scholar*, 32 (1963), p. 393.

6. Ibid., p. 395.

7. Ibid., p. 389.

8. Ibid., p. 394-95.

9. Ibid., p. 391.

10. Ibid., p. 392.

11. Wole Soyinka, "And After the Narcissist?" *African Forum*, 1 (1961), p. 57.

12. Ibid., p. 62.

13. Cited from Erich Heller, *The Artist's Journey into the Interior and Other Essays* (New York: Random, 1965), p. 103.

14. Soyinka, "And After the Narcissist?" p. 53.

15. Ibid., p. 59.

16. Ibid., p. 60.

17. Wole Soyinka, *Myth, Literature, and the African World* (Cambridge: Cambridge UP, 1976), p. 150. Subsequent page references to essays in this book will be inserted in the text.

18. Soyinka, "And After the Narcissist?" p. 59.

19. Soyinka's essay first appeared in *The Morality of Art*, dedicated to G. Wilson Knight, ed. D. W. Jefferson (London: Routledge & Kegan Paul, 1968), pp. 119-34.

20. *University of Ife Newsletter*, 11 June 1980.

21. Friedrich Nietzsche, *The Birth of Tragedy*, trans. Francis Golffing (New York: Doubleday, 1956), p. 99.

22. Ibid., p. 97.

23. W. B. Yeats, *Essays and Introductions* (London: Macmillan, 1961), p. 288.

24. Nietzsche, p. 61.

25. Ibid.

26. Anthony Graham-White, *The Drama of Black Africa* (New York: Samuel French, 1974), p. 22.

27. Wole Soyinka, *Idanre and Other Poems* (London: Methuen, 1967), p. 62.

28. Wole Soyinka, "The Writer in a Modern African State," *The Writer in Modern Africa*, ed. Per Wästberg (New York: Africana, 1969), p. 21.

29. Soyinka, "From a Common Back Cloth," p. 393.

30. Ngũgĩ wa Thiong'o, "The Writer and His Past," *Homecoming* (London: Heinemann, 1978), p. 46.

31. Ayi Kwei Armah, *Why Are We So Blest?* (London: Heinemann, 1974), p. 231.

32. Wole Soyinka, "Drama and the Revolutionary Ideal," *In Person: Achebe, Awoonor, and Soyinka*, ed. Karen L. Morell (Seattle: African Studies Program, University of Washington, 1975), p. 87.

33. Ibid.

34. Leon Trotsky, "The Formalist School of Poetry and Marxism," *Marxists on Literature*, ed. David Craig (Harmondsworth: Penguin, 1977), p. 368.

35. For more information on "historical materialism," see Ernst Fischer, *Marx in His Own Words*, trans. Anna Bostock (London: Penguin, 1970), pp. 80-93.

36. Biodun Jeyifo, *The Truthful Lie: Essays in a Sociology of African Drama* (London and Port of Spain: New Beacon Books, 1985), p. 27.

37. Femi Osofisan, "Drama and the New Exotic: The Paradox of Form in Modern African Theatre," unpublished paper presented at a Department of Modern European Languages Seminar, University of Ife, 1978, p. 7.

38. Omafume Onoge and G. G. Darah, "The Retrospective Stage: Some Reflections on the Mythopoeic Tradition at Ibadan," *Chindaba*, 3, 1 (1977), p. 55.

39. Ibid., p. 53.

40. Jeyifo, "Tragedy, History, and Ideology," p. 35.

41. Biodun Jeyifo, "The 'Hidden' Class War in *The Road*," *The Truthful Lie*, pp. 11-22.

42. Ngũgĩ wa Thiong'o, "Wole Soyinka, T. M. Aluko, and the Satiric Voice," *Homecoming* (London: Heinemann, 1978), pp. 65-66.

43. Wole Soyinka, "Who's Afraid of Elesin Oba," paper presented at the Conference of Radical Perspectives on African Literature, Ibadan, 1977, p. 23.

44. Stanley Macebuh, "Poetics and the Mythic Imagination," *Critical Perspectives on Wole Soyinka*, ed. James Gibbs (Washington, D. C.: Three Continents, 1980), p. 201.

45. Soyinka, "Who's Afraid of Elesin Oba?" p. 10.

46. Ibid., p. 16.

47. Wole Soyinka, *The Critic and Society*, University of Ife Inaugural Lectures Series 49 (Ile-Ife: University of Ife, 1982), p. 9.

48. Ibid., p. 8.

49. Chinweizu *et al.* "Towards the Decolonization of African Literature," *Transition*, 48 (April - June 1975), p. 32.

50. Roderick Wilson, "Complexity and Confusion in Soyinka's Shorter Poems," *Critical Perspectives on Wole Soyinka*, pp. 158-69.

51. Wole Soyinka, "Neo-Tarzanism: The Poetics of Pseudo-Tradition," *Transition*, 48 (April - June 1975), p. 44.

52. Ibid., p. 38.

53. Wole Soyinka, "Neo-Tarzanism: The Aesthetic Illusion," unpublished manuscript, p. 15. The essay was later published as "Aesthetic Illusions: Prescriptions for the Suicide of Poetry," *Third Press Review*, 1.1 (1975), pp. 30-31, 65-68, but this statement was omitted.

54. Soyinka, "Neo-Tarzanism: The Poetics of Pseudo-Tradition," p. 40.

55. Ibid., p. 43.

56. Ibid., p. 31.

57. John Agetua, *Six Nigerian Writers* (Benin City: Bendel Newspapers Corporation, n.d.), p. 46.

58. Soyinka, "From a Common Back Cloth," p. 390.

SOYINKA
and the
CRITICS

The "Communalistic" African and the "Individualistic" Westerner: Some Comments on Misleading Generalizations in Western Criticism of Soyinka and Achebe

J. Z. Kronenfeld

Many African intellectuals – politicians, writers and other professionals – have been concerned with establishing the value of pre-colonial African life, in the face of hundreds of years of Western condescension towards and misunderstanding of "primitive" peoples. This essay concerns the use made of the terms of these African intellectuals in Western discussion of modern African literature, a use that sometimes leads the literary critic and the social scientist alike, away from, rather than into the actual nature of the works he is examining.

This attempt to establish a "positive" African identity, indeed to stress the unique values of African societies, has been intimately involved with the struggle for independence, and with nation-building. It has been characterized by the use of a series of contrasts between African and Western cultures, which are, by now, very familiar to the reader of modern African fiction and non-fiction, of Western discussion of African literature, and, finally, of African commentary, both on African literature itself and on Western criticism of it. Perhaps the most familiar of these contrasts is that between "communal" African society and "individualistic" Western society, which is often linked to the contrast between the "traditional" and the "modern," the "rural" and the "urban," and often closely associated with a distinction between a mystical attitude toward nature that does not separate the individual from the cosmos, and an empirical or rational attitude toward nature. The contrast between "communal" African society and "individualistic" Western society has become a touchstone for Western criticism of African literature; it has been put into service in the explanation of apparent differences between Western literature – in particular, the nineteenth- and twentieth-century novel – and African fiction, which, for example, less frequently involves conventions of extensive introspection.

The intellectual history of these familiar contrasts might plausibly begin with the distinction in nineteenth-century German social theory between

Gemeinschaft and Gesellschaft, originally found in Tönnies, but also present in Max Weber, and anticipated in Marx, who is certainly an influential figure in modern African thought. On the one hand, there are collectivist, cooperative, small-scale, homogeneous societies governed by divine sanctions, in which there are close personal bonds between individuals; on the other, individualistic, secular, heterogeneous societies in which it is the "cash-nexus" that controls relationships among individuals.[1] In many ways it is this kind of distinction that is passed on in Janheinz Jahn's influential works on "African" values and that appears in Léopold Senghor's writings. For the African intellectual and for the African politician, the positive connotations associated with the cooperativist side of the dichotomy are crucial: connotations of brotherhood, a non-materialistic outlook, of sharing, of a mystic closeness to nature, not an exploitation of it.

The question of the truth value of these distinctions between kinds of societies is a complicated one which belongs to the discipline of anthropology. However, one does need to keep in mind that these generalizations have been applied to the great range of African cultures, when it is not clear whether the "collectivist" description holds for anything but, say, hunting and gathering societies, and in what senses even there. Though I cannot go into detail here, I would like to suggest the possible usefulness of a distinction between the ideology of the "communal" society, with all its positive associations of sharing and absence of conflict, and the nature of "communal" society. For example, it is true that many African societies have communal "ownership" of land – that is, the "lineage," not the individual, "owns" the land.[2] "Ownership," as we think of it, involving rights of alienation on the part of the individual, is actually an inapplicable concept here. However, this does not mean that there is idyllic sharing of all valuables, that there is no differential access to valuables, that there are no disputes. We are very likely to associate such a situation with communal land tenure, because "ownership," as we think of it, is clearly an area in which disputes and tensions exist in our own society. However, individuals do matter in the African situation; they do have "use rights," which they inherit, and may sometimes procure in other ways. There may indeed be political squabbling about who gets what as well as differences among individuals as far as the ability to procure such rights goes, not to mention differences in wealth resulting from the nature of the land a person has rights to, among other factors. To put it bluntly, because people in different cultures do not dispute over exactly the same things, in exactly the same ways, does not mean that they have no disputes!

Similarly, the Western sense of the overall "religious" orientation of African, or non-Western, societies – a commonplace – may result from our particular perspective, from invalid comparisons, rather than from as great a difference in human behavior as is sometimes supposed to exist. What *we* call religious activities are relatively discrete, formalized and isolated from the rest of our activities, which we consider secular. However, an alien observer might consider that our religion is capitalism – involving such rituals as formal speeches about the virtues of the free enterprise system – which would then be seen to pervade all aspects of our lives. As alien observers looking at small-scale societies in which institutions overlap, we may see the same set of people involved in religious activities involving the supernatural, social activities involving arbitration of disputes, and economic activities – sometimes at the same time – and we may consequently think of these societies as pervaded by religion, and fail to make the necessary distinctions. We may then classify activities that are not primarily involved with the supernatural (e.g., visiting a herbalist, which is often pragmatic or empirical) as religious, because they have no exact counterparts in our society – given *our* classifications – even though they are in fact closer to medicine in our sense than not. Or, we may fail to see that activities in our own society which we exclude from the rubric religion (for example, psychoanalysis) have a great deal in common with activities in other societies that we think of as related to religion (for example, visiting a priest who may diagnose and suggest a remedy for a purely "social" illness such as tension among certain kinsmen, even if his supernatural sanctions *may* give him the power to make such a diagnosis).

The critic anxious to define African values as the basis for a discussion of African literature often makes use of the kinds of contrasts I have been discussing. However, he may fail to understand the facts upon which the contrasts need to be based in order to be valid, and thus may overstress the differences between cultures. He may fail to adequately distinguish between philosophical, political or celebrative aims and other kinds of aims that the artist may have, even when this distinction is necessary; he may fail to distinguish between the ideology of the nature of African society, and African society, when there is a distinction that should be made. That is, although these contrasts do not necessarily have a very clear content in his mind, the critic may impose them, with their valuations, on the works he is examining. While such terms are crucial background for the poetry of Senghor, for example, they are quite misleading when forced on most of the plays of the satirist, Wole Soyinka, Furthermore, the Western critic sometimes seems to be attributing the differences he observes in African literature as opposed to Western literature to an absolute difference of the African and Western psyches. Thus, the noted absence of introspection in some African novels (one need only mention the novels of Ayi Kwei Armah and Soyinka's novel, *The Interpreters,* as exceptions) is linked with the supposedly communal character of the African mind, rather than with the special political situation of the African writer which makes him more likely to deal with societal problems than with uniquely personal ones. The absence of "introspection," insofar as it exists, is more related to the absence of a developed literary tradition of introspection than to an eternal feature of the "African Mind." From the sociological point of view, perhaps there is a correlation of the less urgent need to establish uniquely African values, with such factors as the achievement of independence, or with the absence of a settled, landed colonial population in some parts of Africa, or with the degree of comfortable assimilation or acceptance of his own culture on the part of the African writer himself, which, in turn, would relate to the other factors. Certainly, once nations achieve their independence, their writers are more likely to become concerned with injustices *within* their own society. Even if a desire to create viable *art* might have to await conditions in which people can afford to care about art *per se,* there certainly are African writers who object to the overly polemical as incompatible with their growth as artists or the creation of art. Insofar as art involves fidelity to truth – as envisioned by the individual artist – even in order to be credible, we might expect some artists to take off from different assumptions than those involved in the familiar contrasts outlined here. Human conflict is the stuff of literature; sometimes those critics who find African literature "simple," do so because they assume the absence of conflicts, in accordance with their presumptions about African thinking about African society, when, in fact, those presumptions are not applicable.

The actual variety of opinion as to the nature of their own societies, of the influences of opinion and of personal experiences of Africans in differing circumstances and cultures should encourage a healthy reluctance on the part of Western critics to turn uncritically, and without some of the caveats outlined above, to individual sources for the "essence" of African culture on which to base a theory of the nature of African literature. If Senghor was influenced by Lucien Lévy-Bruhl concerning the "prelogical" mentality of primitives, modern African intellectuals show an awareness of the works of more recent anthropologists, such as E. E. Evans-Pritchard, who have gradually corrected the rather extreme views of Lévy-Bruhl by pointing to the logicality of "primitive" systems of belief within their own assumptions, to the attentions of people everywhere to pragmatic as well as supernatural concerns.[3] "Primitives" are aware of empirical causation just as we are; it is events that cannot be controlled empirically that require other means of control, just as in our own culture. Some African intellectuals find the presumed close association of drama and ritual (as in Francis Cornford's theory of Greek comedy) attractive, interesting, and in some cases exploitable for experiments in modern drama, since their own societies have ritual performances and animal sacrifice.[4] However, others suggest that the mimetic instinct is universal, that acting out is inherently pleasurable, and thus, that there is no intrinsic relation between religious feeling, and drama; rather, a "religious" occasion may simply provide the necessary formal circumstances for drama to take place uninterrupted, in small societies where everyone knows everyone else.[5] Such writers are in effect suggesting that the African is no more inherently and totally mystically oriented than anyone else.

Even though there is certainly a great deal of competent criticism of African literature, there still is something of a tendency to think uncritically in terms of these contrasting categorizations – especially "communalistic" vs. "individualistic" – without the necessary distinctions and caveats in mind. These categorizations encourage the misrepresentation of certain literary works, the underestimation of their human complexity and ambiguity, and the diminishing of their merit, when they are imposed on literature structured in different terms. I would like to examine the comments of two critics who serve as examples of these tendencies: first, a social scientist commenting on Wole Soyinka's *The Lion and the Jewel,* among other African works; second, a literary critic discussing Chinua Achebe's *Things Fall Apart.*

In his article, "Behavior and Cultural Value in West African Stories: Literary Sources for the Study of Culture Contact,"[6] Austin Shelton argues that Wole Soyinka's play, *The Lion and the Jewel* (one of four African works he considers), reasserts the value of traditional, communally-based society. Soyinka's comedy concerns the victory of a chief over a superficially Westernized schoolteacher in a rivalry for a village belle – whose head has been a bit swelled as a result of the appearance of her photograph in a glossy Lagos magazine. The play is assessed as follows, along with the other works Shelton considers: "The value most clearly approved ... is traditional communal responsibility, revealed partly in the condemnation of self-seeking individualism" (p. 41). Now the play does mock "modern" ways, but particularly insofar as they are espoused superficially, naïvely, or hypocritically by Lakunle, the village schoolteacher. In this sense, what is being exposed, as in comedies generally, is pretension. The categories of approved traditionalism involving positive qualities ("responsibility") and disapproved modernism involving negative qualities ("self-seeking") may derive from the literature that celebrates or seeks unique ethical values in African social institutions, but they are not the categories that structure this play. To come to the play with these preconceived notions in mind is to miss the *comedy.* The comic stance is a more objective one. As comedy, *The Lion and the Jewel* exposes self-seeking and inconsistency – beneath various guises – in *all* the characters. It shows how people use the "traditional" for "modern" purposes, and the "modern" for "traditional" purposes, in accordance with universal human motivations of pride, power, and sex, rather than out of loyalty to an abstraction such as "tradition," or even primarily out of religious or moral conviction. If "tradition," as exemplified by chief Baroka, wins (in the sense that Sidi the belle becomes his youngest wife), it is mainly because he is wilier than Lakunle, not because he has appealed to better values, which in themselves motivate behavior. Baroka and Lakunle may not be equally good choices as mates, for economic and other reasons, but the chief is equally subject to the penetrating comic glance that distinguishes the eloquent speech from the mundane motive.

As the play opens, Sidi, a young village girl, is being courted by Lakunle, the village school-teacher, who offers her a "Western" monogamous marriage. However, she will not marry him until he pays the bride-price; she will not have people say she "was no virgin / That [she] was forced to sell [her] shame."[7] We soon learn that Sidi has been photographed in various exotic poses for a magazine by a "Lagos man," who seems to have exploited the idea of "bush" beauty. After she has seen the photographs, her sense of her importance grows and indeed she does become more significant in the village. But, her inflated ego piques the village chief, even more than the pictures attract him to her charms. Although the chief's eldest wife brings Sidi her husband's offer of marriage, and explains the advantages of being the youngest wife in a polygamous household, Sidi does not jump at the chance. In fact, she is quite suspicious of the chief's motives. Baroka has manipulated events in the past to preserve the *status quo* and his own comfortable position; he bribed some roadworkers to encourage them to see the wisdom of not building a motor road through the village. Now he arranges a trap which both squelches Sidi's inflated ego and wins her as his youngest wife. He allows the rumor of his impotence to circulate through his gleefully unaware eldest wife, with the result that Sidi comes, uninvited, to his house, in order to enjoy this blow to his pride, to scoff. However, and partially because she is off her guard, believing she has the upper hand, he is able to seduce her by alternating a show of power and scorn with overwhelming eloquence and flattery, not to mention the aid of some available palm-wine. The flattery includes a promise to print stamps with her glorious image on them right there in the town on a machine obtained for the purpose. Whether or not Baroka really intends to use the stamp-machine is not clear. But it certainly would not be inconsistent with his character for him to turn the "modern" to his own uses by collecting a local stamp-tax. And it is part of the conception of human behavior in the play for him to use the same kind of flattery to win Sidi for himself as was involved in the photographs which made her think herself more important than him, rather than for him to appeal to her directly in terms of the value of traditional life and institutions. After Sidi has lost her virginity to him, although at first angered and humiliated, she decides to marry him. He has won in a show of strength and cleverness; it is best to make good one's losses.

This brief plot summary should make clear that the play does not really operate in terms of a simple antithesis between the modern and the traditional, and certainly not in terms of an antithesis between "self-seeking" modernism and "responsible" traditionalism, unless some explanation is forthcoming! Now, let us consider the comedy in more detail in order to see how its comedic aspects in fact undercut so simple a conception. Lakunle is in love with Western ways, and he attempts to make his "knowledgeableness" a selling point in his courtship of Sidi. Recent writings on West African popular culture suggests that Western styles of courtship, as observed in the cinema, for example,[8] are aspired to, imitated and enjoyed by some West Africans who, like Americans trying out "alternative life styles," get pleasure from being *au courant*. But Lakunle is presented by Soyinka with purely mundane motivations as well. It is suggested that he was unskillful at rural occupations (p. 36); it is not uncommon in rural situations for African children who show little aptitude for farming or fishing to be sent to school. His rejection of traditional customs has a strong economic cause; he simply cannot afford the bride-price (p. 36). Like the other characters in the play, he uses or abuses the "traditional" in accordance with his own needs and situation. Thus, he adopts a misinformed Western attitude toward bride-price ("To pay the price would be/ To buy a heifer off the market stall./ You'd be my chattel, my mere property." p. 8) partially because he is in a bad economic position. If that position encourages his fascination with Western values, the espousal of such values also compensates him – at least in his eyes – by boosting his low social status in the village. Yet, he is not above using a traditional argument when it suits his purposes. After Baroka has successfully seduced Sidi, Lakunle, at first reacting with shock, recovers himself (his love is "selfless – the love of spirit/ Not of flesh."); besides, she will agree:

> it is only fair
> That we forget the bride-price totally
> Since you no longer can be called a maid (p. 60).

Shelton's view of the play, as asserting the value of one way of life over another, would seem to require that the author or the characters – especially the "traditional" characters – be concerned with value judgements. However, the comedy clearly operates in terms of the characters adjusting ideology, or selecting convenient aspects of it, in accordance with their situations and their psychological needs, as Lakunle does here:

> 'Man takes the fallen woman by the hand'
> And ever after they live happily.

Moreover, I will admit,
It solves the problem of her bride-price too.
A man must live or fall by his true
Principles. That, I had sworn
Never to pay (p. 61).

Sidi's concern with bride-price makes her no more self-consciously an upholder of traditional values for their own sake than Lakunle's abuse of it makes him a sincere believer in "modern" ways. Neither traditional nor modern values and institutions are treated as abstractions, but in their relation to people's universal needs, which clearly can be met in a variety of ways. Sidi participates sufficiently in the village society to feel that marriage without bride-price would seriously undercut her self-esteem, making her a "laughing-stock," a "cheap bowl for the village spit" (p. 7). However, her self-esteem can be served equally well by modern means; once her ego has been flattered by the photographs, she becomes Westernized in her own way. She may reject the abandonment of brideprice, but she is quite willing to give up carrying firewood – which many West African women do – and to allow Lakunle to behave in a courtly, "Western" manner in this instance (p. 19). We might indeed call this an example of the selective adaptation of new customs! Although she rejects Lakunle's equation of the custom of bride-price with the concept of "property," she does seem to use his ideas in rejecting Baroka's offer of marriage. Indeed, "property" in a more generalized and universal sense *is* involved in Baroka's interest in her:

Why did Baroka not request my hand
Before the stranger
Brought his book of images?
....
Can you not see? Because he sees my worth
Increased and multiplied above his own;
Because he can already hear
The balled-makers and their songs
In praise of Sidi, the incomparable,
While the Lion is forgotten.
He seeks to have me as his property
Where I must fade beneath his jealous hold (p. 21).

In their different ways, both men want Sidi as extensions of their pride or self-images. Most ironically – not in accordance with a dialectic of pure tradition as opposed to impure modernism, but with the more universal and realistic terms in which the play operates – Sidi finally ends by taking from Baroka, the supposed traditionalist, what she refused from Lakunle, the supposed modernist: marriage *without* bride-price. Although the "fox" seduced her (like Volpone, by playing at impotence), she still would not be granted bride-price because of her loss of virginity, as has already been made clear (p. 7), and furthermore, she might not care to have her gullibility mocked at great length. She goes in the direction that salvages her pride. Like Lakunle, when it suits her situation and purposes, she makes light of "traditional" customs. As reported by Sadiku, Baroka's eldest wife, her comment is "leave all that nonsense to savages and brabararians" (sic, p. 62). In any case, the traditionalist in power – that is, Baroka – may always dispense with tradition, and more easily than someone like Lakunle. And, from Sidi's point of view, marriage to a chief upon whom she has some claim because he seduced her, even marriage without bride-price, is certainly a better choice than no marriage or marriage to a person poorer in status and wealth, or one who might use her "shame" as a bargaining point, to her disadvantage. In her present situation, she is indeed, to quote Shakespeare, "not for all markets."

Baroka's negative attitudes toward modernization stem as clearly from the threats it poses to his authority and status, as from his fondness for the old ways; they certainly do not stem from a moral preference unrelated to vested interests. His desire to "get" Sidi, apart from her evident attractions, is a desire to squelch an upstart, a "little fool" (p. 59), who would mock him and dare to think herself more important than him, and it is an aspect of the eternal war between men and women. Although his speech on the sameness of modern life (p. 52) is appropriate to the superficiality of modernization evident in Lakunle and is concordant with Soyinka's general dislike of the *unassimilated* facile imitation of other cultural styles,[9] Baroka's words are comically undercut in the dramatic situation. Baroka is, after all, trying to overwhelm Sidi with eloquence, and at the same time, enjoying her lack of comprehension of the joke he is about to play on her. His metaphors concerning change and tradition are so patently sexual, his posture so clearly a situation-related pose (the "body-weighed-down-by-burdens-of-state attitude," p. 54), that whatever concern for the traditional *qua* traditional he may have is qualified – to say the least – by his evident enjoyment of duping her. *He* is the old wine and *she* the new bottle:

Yesterday's wine alone is strong and blooded, child,
And though the Christians' holy book denies
The truth of this, old wine thrives best
Within a new bottle. The coarseness
Is mellowed down, and the rugged wine
Acquires a full and rounded body...
Is this not so – My child?
[*Quite overcome, Sidi nods*] (p. 54).

The Lion and the Jewel, as comedy, depends on seeing humans in terms of their universal motivations of pride, power and sex, which culture provides various means of satisfying, not in terms of their allegiance to old or new cultural values *per se.* Austin Shelton's brief comments on the characters seem to stem from preconceived notions about the concerns of modern African authors which are imposed on the play, rather than from the play itself. Shelton says that "Lakunle failed to obtain the 'jewel' because she had sense enough to succumb to the traditionalist Baroka..." (p. 411). However, we have seen that Sidi hardly has an unconstrained choice, that she does not make a self-conscious value judgment in favor of the traditional. *The Lion and the Jewel* is not a morality play in which Sidi is presented as freely assenting to "pure" traditional values, after having foolishly toyed with modernism, and having learned her moral lesson. Even were her choice unconstrained, Lakunle himself was not a very appealing example of a Westernized African, being too poor in goods and status. But there is nothing about Sidi's basic motivations, as they are presented by Soyinka, that would prevent her from responding more favorably to a government minister, albeit a virile one, who might offer her a monogamous marriage, should circumstances allow for such a possibility, just as there is nothing that prevents her from enjoying giving up carrying firewood, traditional as the practice may be for women. When Sidi does finally ceremoniously give up the magazine, she is capitalizing on the prestige and ego-satisfaction to be obtained from the choice she has been constrained to make. The same motives may be satisfied in the "traditional" and the "modern" situation.

Similarly, it does not seem appropriate to Lakunle's economic and psychological motives and his clear manipulation of "principle," to assess him simply in Shelton's terms, saying that he "possessed individualistic ideals,... and he extended these to Sidi, treating her accordingly" (p. 410), especially insofar as this description, taken in the context of Shelton's article, is meant to suggest a qualitative difference between the "self-seeking individualism" of Lakunle and the "communal responsibility" of Baroka. Again, there is nothing about Lakunle that would prevent his taking advantage of whatever combination of the "modern" and the "traditional" suited his purposes and situation. It is clear enough that he could enjoy the advantages of traditional polygamy, were he in the chief's situation, and that the fact that he cannot, encourages his attraction to the "modern."

> Ah, I sometimes wish I led his kind of life.
> Such luscious bosoms make his nightly pillow.
> I am sure he keeps a time-table just as
> I do at school....
> ... ...
> ...No! I do not envy him! (p. 26)

Alas, having several wives is expensive, and Lakunle cannot even afford one. Once again, the play seems to point out that people do not opt for the traditional or the modern as abstractions. The man who enjoys more privileges in the traditional situation than in the modern is certainly likely to be a "traditionalist." The traditional way is not inherently less likely to serve individual self-seeking than the modern. The plot alone makes clear that Lakunle did not fail to win Sidi because he did not "face the fact that what a young African woman really wants is to 'prove' her *raison d'être* through childbearing" (Shelton, p. 410). At the end of the play, Sidi does indeed look forward to "children, sired of the lion stock" (p. 64), but this comes after the fact, as it were, not before. The plot alone also makes clear that Baroka did not succeed by appealing to Sidi to consciously assent to her valued, traditional role, but rather, by coercion and by flattery. That flattery, which included the suggestion that there is a certain amount of prestige in carrying on the noble line, in assenting to the wisdom of the ancients, was particularly instrumental, since the only alternative was being thought "vain," with "a featherlight" head, and "always giddy/With a trivial thought" (p. 49). Bearing children is undoubtedly taken for granted as part of Sidi's idea of her future, but wanting to "prove" one's *raison d'être* requires more self-consciousness than she seems to possess, as well as a different sort of situation, in which the traditional as traditional *per se* is salient and chosen for ideological or political reasons alone.

Shelton's generalizations seem to be simply unrelated to the tenor of the play in that they suggest that it is primarily about the psychological and ethical value of the traditional way, which alone ultimately satisfies all the needs of the people, because of its inherent nature, and about which the author, if not the characters as well, think in abstract moral terms of "right" and "wrong." "Change to the white man's way is 'wrong' even if necessary, but return to the African way is 'right'...The individual... can regain 'wholeness' of self and proper orientation to behavior as well as obtain the deserved rewards only through his maintenance of traditions or a return to the traditionally sanctioned behavior" (Shelton, p. 410). The play does not assert the *moral* superiority of the old way of life, in fact making only a brief case for its esthetic superiority. Nor does it operate in terms of the possibility of a willed "return" to the "African" way, because it does not depend on the African way being qualitatively different, in the sense that it appeals to different motives, from the "modern" way. Rather, *The Lion and the Jewel* makes comedy out of human contingencies and inevitably mixed motives, in traditionalist and modernist alike. One wonders what the statement that Baroka "received full reward for his support of communal values" (Shelton, p. 411) can mean. Traditional ways, no more than modern, satisfy all the people all of the time. Indeed, Baroka's eldest wife, who had some good words to say about the advantages of being the chief's last wife, was not entrusted to win Sidi to the side of tradition, but played her role in accordance wih Baroka's knowledge that she would be delighted to make him a laughing-stock because of his "loss" of vigor! The war between men and women pits the "traditionalists" against each other, and, indeed, aligns the "modernist" and the "traditionalist" (for even Lakunle has sympathy for his rival when it is a matter of seeing manhood being mocked). Insofar as the debate between the traditional and the modern figures in the play at all, it seems to revolve around questions of status, and vested interests – both psychological and economic – which are frankly understood as such, more than questions of value. All of the characters are more or less constrained by their situations, and all of them seek to enhance or maintain their power and prestige by taking whatever chances offer. Individuals will conflict as each has his eye on the main chance, but not necessarily within the same fixed alliances, and the alliances are in any case not determined by an overriding loyalty to the traditional or the modern *per se.* Baroka, having more cards to play, succeeds in getting what he wants, but he is hardly acting in disinterested support of "communal" values, or out of any purer motives than anyone else. The play does suggest that traditional socialization is still operative, and that traditional institutions may still answer people's needs (not that they inevitably must), even that the older way of life is preferable to a superficial imitation of the new. But the traditional way of life has no monopoly on purity and nobility and does not inspire loyalty *on its own account;* the same kinds of human motivations and contingencies that result in its apparent preservation here, could as well result in significant modifications. *The Lion and the Jewel* does indeed tell us about culture contact and change, but in quite a different way than Shelton would have us think.

"Traditional" and "modern," especially as they are attached to positively-evaluated "communalism" and negatively-evaluated "individualism," may be rather meaningless and indeed misleading ready-made categories to use in the analysis of modern African literature. One suspects that such categories would also be troublesome for the social scientist. Soyinka's play seems very much related to the work of those anthropologists concerned with the selective adaptation to new institutions, and the incorporation of new ideas or practices into existent institutions, in situations involving rapid change, such as that of modernizing Africa. Soyinka's characters would easily fit into a world where a practitioner of folk medicine may live in an urban community and be saving money to send his son to college, or where bride-price becomes a matter of cash and is raised exorbitantly by parents of daughters. One danger of the categories is the assumption that change is an all-or-nothing experience. Another is that people act out of loyalty to abstractions, rather than in accordance with their needs, upon which many complex factors operate, including their socialization into their own systems. One might want to distinguish between situations in which people are likely to become self-conscious about "traditional" values conceived as such, or conservative for conservatism's sake, and situations in which they are not likely to act this way.

The tendency to use such concepts as "traditional" and "modern," "communalistic" and "individualistic" too carelessly and abstractly, without sufficient content in mind, and without regard for their fit with the literature being examined, is undoubtedly encouraged by the critic's awareness of what African intellectuals themselves have said, often for political purposes. Shelton does begin with the assumption that the African writer, like his society, is inherently communally-oriented, opposed to "any consideration of African literature as individualistic 'art for art's sake'." He asserts that the new African literature is reasserting a "traditional" African attitude toward art as "socially functional rather than merely aesthetically pleasing" (p. 406). In this he echoes the many statements made at African writers' conferences and by politicians such as Sekou Touré.[10] But politically motivated statements might overstress differences between cultures in this instance. A socialist or Marxist political leaning certainly encourages such an attitude toward art. The political need to establish a positive contrast between African values and Western values also would encourage such a position, especially when Western criticism has often been negative with regard to the lack of "individualization" in African literature. The African writer comes from a small intellectual class; he is rarely devoted to writing alone, but is often, as an educated person, a spokesman for his society, or pressed into the service of nationalism. His audience is both the local literate population and the rest of the world. The African literary movement in Western languages is of course very much tied up with self-explanation, identity-seeking and current conditions, hence the attraction of anthropology for so many authors. This is not unusual; in times of transition, writers often speak for their cultures. If these writers are more concerned with their societies and their nations than with unique experiences, this is a product of their circumstances, rather than an indication of their absolute nature as Africans, or of their inherent potentialities. Perhaps more literary reflection on uniquely personal experience needs to await a larger educated class and a more stable and diversified society, as well as a more stable political situation.

In any case, "socially functional," from the point of view of the political powers that be, can of course be quite different from "socially functional" from the point of view of the artist. Social purposes, in the sense of statements about one's society or its direction, often coexist with aesthetic purposes and interests. Indeed, "socially functional" could cover the gamut from the sheerest propagandistic didacticism to the subtlest satirical attack by the author, as minority of one, on majority values. It is also probably a bit rash to assume that traditional African art is only socially functional, whatever is meant by that term, simply because we have tended to ignore its aesthetic aspects.[11] The politician and intellectual, anxious that folk literature and art be credited with value in a world accustomed to written literature and signed sculpture, have stressed the values of "communal" and "anonymous" art. But individuals shape this anonymous art, even though their contributions do not get recorded as such, and the end result is constantly modified by performance in front of a general audience. More importantly, individuals have created modern African literature, and signed their own names to it. We cannot assume that they share precisely the same attitudes. We suspect that Shelton means that that African artist is "socially functional" in the sense that he voices "communally held" beliefs about the validity of ancient traditions and the corruption of the new civilization. But, even as a statement about what particular artists say they are doing, this is only adequate for some of the poets of négritude. Such a statement is particularly inadequate for those who reject excessively polemical or didactic straightjackets which they feel impede their development as *artists,* or which simply make for bad literature, which must delight, even in the service of teaching. Ezekiel Mphahlele has voiced such opinions; Wole Soyinka is notable for a consistent position of this sort.

For Soyinka, artistic concerns, which in large part involve a concern with truth, clearly are paramount. It is clear from his description of his position in "From a Common Back Cloth: A Reassessment of the African Literary Image,"[12] that he is concerned with art as the expression of the individual, not of the community in the sense that folklore and ritual are expressions of the community – that is, with the "validity of a creative imagination for the African, outside folklore and ritual" (p. 387). He finds that fiction is marred by sentimentality, inflation, "philosophical straightjacket[s]" (p. 389) of various kinds, including négritude, however politically useful it may be or have been. The African writer who accepts himself (p. 395) does not have to exoticize his past, does not have to share in or encourage the European critic's attitude, which he says too often becomes a condescending "Takes a simpleton to understand a child" (p. 387). When an author has been "selective to the point of wish-fulfillment" (p. 387), as he thinks Camara Laye has been in his nostalgic portrait of his African childhood (*The Dark Child*), such an attitude can be redeemed only by art: "Even if it grew precious, it carried an air of magic, of nostalgia, which worked through the transforming act of language" (p. 387). What Soyinka finds attractive in Mongo Beti, another African author, is instructive; simplification of human mixed motives is ultimately condescending.

In the literary effort to establish the African as, first before all else, a human being, Mongo Beti with this novel [*Mission to Kala*] has leaped to the fore as the archpriest of the African's humanity. Mongo Beti takes the back cloth as he finds it, asserting simply that tradition is upheld not by one-dimensional innocents, but by cunning old codgers on chieftaincy stools, polygamous elders, watching hawklike the approach of young blood around their harem, by the eternal trouble-making females who plunge innocents, unaware, into memorable odysseys. Hospitality is not, as we are constantly romantically informed that it is, nearly so spontaneous. There is a mercenary edge, and this, alas, is not always traceable to that alien corrupt civilization! (pp. 394-95)

This indeed sounds close enough to the situation in *The Lion and the Jewel* to reinforce the plausibility of the reading given. Soyinka rejects the simple formula that produces the kind of work that would fit Shelton's reading of *The Lion and the Jewel:* "A society, an intrusion, an all too predictable conflict" (p. 390).

Even if the writer in the emerging African national states understandably felt that he had to "postpone that unique reflection on experience and events which is what makes a writer – and constitute himself into a part of that machinery that will actually shape events," Soyinka suggests that the writer cannot be truly useful politically if, once again, he ignores the truth, becoming "blinded to the present by the resuscitated splendours of the past."[13] As he explains his attitudes about the political role of the writer in "The Writer in a Modern African State," Soyinka is undoubtedly thinking of the Nigerian Civil War, during which he was imprisoned for supporting the Biafran cause.

This was the beginning of the abdication of the African writer and the deception which he caused by fabricating a magnitude of unfelt abstractions.... The black tin-god... would degrade and dehumanise his victim as capably as Vorster or Governor Wallace.... The romancer and the intellectual mythmaker has successfully deleted this black portion of a common human equation.... The myth of irrational nobility, of a racial essence that must come to the rescue of the white depravity has run its full course.[14]

In accordance with these opinions, while some of Soyinka's plays do comment on materialism, they do not make "humanity" an inherent possession of Africans, nor do they associate the ethical life exclusively with traditional ways. As satirist, Soyinka shows the potential for exploitation in the older societies as well as the new – that is, he portrays *humans.* In *Kongi's Harvest,* both the traditional rulers and the new political leaders are clearly portrayed as subject to the same kinds of motivations. Furthermore, he may use the comparison of traditional and modern to touch on issues beyond it; in *The Swamp Dwellers*, neither the old religion (which is exploited by the cult priest) nor the new life in the cities can guarantee that there will be no risk, no loss in life.[15] Preconceptions about political or social attitudes and too hasty an attempt to generalize in terms of the "traditional" and the "modern," the "communalistic" and the "individualistic" can result in serious misreading of sophisticated literature, particularly when written by an author of Soyinka's cast of mind.

Chinua Achebe's novel, *Things Fall Apart*, although read most intelligently by such critics as Charles Larson and David Carroll,[16] has also been curiously misread on occasion. Once again, the reasons for the misreading lie in generalizations about "the African mind" or African society and too hasty an attempt to pin the nature of the novel on an "African" ethos. Perhaps because of his unfamiliarity with African societies, the Western critic is more likely to accept generalizations about "the African personality" without attempting to see them in context, whereas he undoubtedly would exercise more caution in the presence of generalizations about, say, the British or the American national character. It seems once again that an unexamined and unspecific notion of the "communal" nature of African society lends encouragement to this very tendency. Thus, for example, if told that Americans are ambitious, one knows the sense in which "making good" is an ideal, the many forms of "ambitiousness," and indeed, the senses in which it may conflict with other American values – more or less for different people and different situations – or, in fact, be rejected. One does not for a minute expect that all Americans will act as if they are molded of exactly the same materials. However, this complex sense of the variable responses to a cultural norm, of the discrepancy between *ideal* and reality, of the tensions that are inevitable because personality is variable, even if within culturally defined limits, seems to be abandoned when some critics confront African literature. Yet it is just this sort of awareness that is required for an open-eyed reading of Achebe's novel; anything less makes a naive polemic out of the fairly complex view of social change in the novel.

James Olney, in his recent critical work of considerable merit, *Tell Me, Africa*,[17] nevertheless serves as a significant example of these tendencies toward misreading. He begins with assumptions about the communal nature of African society based in part on what appears to be an imperfect understanding of clans and lineages. It is as if the mere existence of such kinship groupings is enough to guarantee a "community with one soul rather than a multitude of souls, held together by the will of the ancestors who speak group wisdom and timeless desires through the mouths of the present ruling elders" (p. 175), as Olney understands Achebe's portrait of Igbo society in the first part of the novel. Now, many peoples in the world have or have had extended families, lineages and ancestor worship – one might mention the Chinese – but no one has ever seen these mere facts as assuring no differences of interest within these groups, no conflict and no variation in personality, in short, a totally "homogeneous and coherent group character" (Olney, p. 175). Perhaps because of his lack of anthropological awareness – he does call the extended family "that uniquely African tie"! (p. 61) – Olney too readily attributes extraordinary significance to the mere existence of these forms of residence and affiliation, and ignores their contexts. Perhaps he grants these institutions more significance as indicators of African values of "community" than would automatically be granted them if he understood their specific roles in dictating residence patterns and inheritance, say, before leaping to their influence on an explicit or implicit African philosophy. In this, he follows uncritically, and here, irrelevantly, I think, those African writers who describe the "mystique" of lineage or ancestor worship. There is some point in this kind of background when the creative writer is himself speaking from such a position, as is the case, with qualifications, of Camara Laye. But Achebe, like Soyinka, takes a relatively objective stance. If Soyinka is objective as comic artist in *The Lion and the Jewel,* Achebe is objective as the anthropologist, or the documentarist might be in *Things Fall Apart.* He is concerned to "justify" pre-colonial African institutions in a rather anthropological way, by showing that they *worked* to keep society functioning, although not always perfectly. Such a view counters the view of primitive societies as *irrational,* common enough until recently. "I would be quite satisfied if my novels (especially the ones I set in the past) did no more than teach my readers that their past – with all its imperfections – was not one long night of savagery from which the first Europeans acting on God's behalf delivered them. Perhaps what I write is applied art as distinct from pure."[18] But, Achebe's is an *analysis* that allows for imperfections, not a nostalgic or sentimental eulogy of the past.

> Will [the writer] be strong enough to overcome the temptation to select only those facts that flatter him? If he succumbs he will have branded himself an untrustworthy witness. But it is not only his personal integrity as an artist which is involved. The credibility of the world he is attempting to create will be called into question and he will defeat his own purpose if be is suspected of glossing over inconvenient facts. We cannot pretend that our past was one long, technicolour idyll.[19]

Let us look at an example of Olney's reading of his sources, in order to illustrate how he has perhaps forced the available material into his categorizations "communal" as opposed to "individualistic," with the end result that he, too, imposes these categories on the literature he analyzes, and consequently distorts it. The Igbo are commonly described as "individualistic," as Olney says, yet he wishes to emphasize their "communal" character in order to support his reading of *Things Fall Apart*, and of modern African literature generally. This causes some difficulty which he resolves by referring to Victor Uchendu's description in the latter's ethnography of the Igbo, which Olney curiously classifies as autobiography. "Victor Uchendu, for example, though he argues that the Ibo 'lay a great emphasis on individual achievement and initiative,' is quick to acknowledge that this individuality, when considered in a Western perspective, is a partial and non-extreme thing: it is *Ibo* individuality, not personal, private individuality. 'Igbo individualism is not "rugged" individualism; it is individualism rooted in group solidarity.... There is a great emphasis on communal cooperation and achievement'." (Olney, p. 177). [20] At this point the distinction gets a bit muddy. American individualism is equally "American." Uchendu's comments must be put in the context of his ethnography, where he also says: "[The Igbo world is] a world that is delicately balanced between opposing forces, each motivated by self-interest; a world whose survival demands some form of cooperation among its members, *although that cooperation may be minimal and even hostile in character.* It is a world in which others can be manipulated for the sake of the individual's status advancement – the goal of Igbo life." (Uchendu, p. 20, my italics). On the basis of Uchendu's ethnography as a whole and of other works on the Igbo, it appears that Uchendu is trying to give a picture that takes account of two facets of Igbo life that appear contradictory: on the one hand, they *are* very much oriented toward achievement and the gaining of status, on an individual basis – and status is *achieved* by individuals and not ascribed; on the other, the Igbo are unusual in the number of self-help organizations they have. The individual is motivated to achieve by such institutions as title-taking, in which Igbos compete on an egalitarian basis, yet his achievement may also rebound to the credit of his group (town, family, age-group or whatever) and that group may facilitate his achievement as he in turn facilitates the achievement of other individuals within it. When put in these terms, the differences between our society and theirs *as regards self-seeking and cooperation* do not loom so large; "they" too appear to try to strike a balance. We too may in our individual achievements bring honor to our families or ethnic groups. We too have organizations – such as junior chambers of commerce – which encourage us to help ourselves by helping others. In fact, Uchendu presents Igbo society, not as a group with no conflicts of interest or unfavored people – he does of course mention the *osu* slaves, a group of outcasts, and mothers of twins who had to abandon them – but as a society that attempts to maintain a social and cosmological balance, a society that has to take different – even opposing – forces and claims into account.

But the Igbo believe that these social calamities and cosmic forces which disturb their world are controllable and should be "manipulated" by them for their own purpose. The maintenance of social and cosmological balance in the world becomes, therefore, a dominant and pervasive theme in Igbo life. They achieve this balance, for instance, through divination, sacrifice, appeal to the countervailing powers of their ancestors (who are their invisible father-figures) against the powers of the malignant, and non-ancestral spirits, and socially, through constant realignment in their social groupings....

Indeed, whatever threatens the life of the individual or his security as well as society is interpreted by the Igbo as a warning that things must be set right before they get out of hand....

The Igbo individual balances his conflicts in one agnatic group with his privileges in another. His...[mother's agnates...] stand with him against the perennial conflicts he faces among...[his own agnates]. Although he is exposed to physical danger among ... his [own agnates] his person is sacred to his [mother's agnatic] group....

Domination by a few powerful men or spirits is deeply resented. A relationship that is one-sided, either in its obligations or in its reward system, does not last long among them. Imbalance, either in the social or the spiritual world, is considered a trouble indicator. (Uchendu, pp. 13-15)

Indeed, *Things Fall Apart* does reflect the attempt to balance cooperation and achievement, to balance the idea that one is perfectly free to shape one's own life – which would encourage achievement – and the idea that one has a preordained fate – which may be used to put a damper on inordinate ambition. It also reflects the actual balance between one's mother's patrilineal kin, who act as protectors in times of trouble and one's own patrilineal kin, as well as the attempt to balance the "masculine" and the "feminine" virtues. One misses all of this, if one comes to the novel prepared to find simply a celebrative account of "traditional," totally homogeneous and "communal" African society.

Things Fall Apart has been interpreted in terms of Achebe's presumed or actual social aims as a defense of "traditional" Igbo life; it has also been interpreted as a tragedy similar to *Oedipus*[21] and, as such, is a book beyond social considerations, which, in fact presents its hero as calling the fates upon his head. Insofar as the book is a tragedy, a better model is the *Hippolytus* which concerns the inevitable tragedy of choosing or aligning oneself with one of two necessary and opposed forces, which are extremely difficult to balance, but must be balanced. David Carroll's view of *Things Fall Apart* as a book concerning "competing claims," in contrast to Olney's view, is totally reconcilable with Uchendu's description of Igbo society, which clearly supports and probably helped shape it.[22] Such a view in fact takes all Achebe's statements about the novel into account and, when extended as I intend to extend it here, makes it possible to reconcile the view of the novel as an analysis of a social system with the view of the novel as a tragic statement of human and societal limitations, the role of the writer as ethnographer and the role of the writer as artist.

Olney makes two assumptions that drastically simplify what he has already called "a vastly simple tale of cultural conflict resolved in tragedy" (p. 166). For one, he claims that Achebe portrays a society that falls apart simply because of external influence, but which experienced no conflict because of the "attitudes" and "appetites" of individual members until that time (p. 175). "Until it begins to disintegrate under the impact of a foreign civilization, the old Ibo community, manifest in the person of Okonkwo, is untroubled by internal dissension or individual conscience, by moral hesitation or disunity of purpose. Conflict in such a fiction as this will always be large and simple, external rather than internal, inter-tribal or inter-cultural or even international rather than inter-personal or intra-personal" (p. 181). Olney's second assumption is apparent in the above quotation; he claims that Okonkwo *exemplifies* Igbo society, that he is not individualized: "There is a virtual one-to-one relationship between Okonkwo as an individual and the Ibo as a people" (p. 170). From the point of view of common sense, it seems plausible that there may be less conflict of interest, one might say no competing world views, in smaller-scale societies in which most people do the same things or have similar experiences. Perhaps Olney has something like this in mind when he makes his broad statement about the necessary nature of conflict in the fictions he is considering. However, it is very clear in this particular fiction that there is *not* one cultural norm to which everyone fits, without difficulty, as if they are all cut from a master mold; and it is equally clear that insofar as there is a dominant norm, it is not one to which Achebe gives his wholehearted approval. The Igbo past, "like other people's past," as Achebe has said, "had its good as well as its bad sides."[23] Okonkwo is a representative figure, but he represents one pos-sible cultural type – albeit, perhaps, in a society with fewer possible norms that our own – rather than *the* Igbo type; everything in the novel reaffirms the idea that he overstressed manliness, when an ideal of balance was in fact available. And insofar as the norm he represents was a source of conflict in Igbo society, the destruction of that society comes as the result of the interaction of external *and internal* forces. As Achebe said: "This particular society... believed too much in manliness. Perhaps this is part of the reason it crashed in the end."[24]

David Carroll's penetrating analysis of *Things Fall Apart* makes it clear that Achebe analyzes Igbo society in terms of the polarity of the masculine and feminine virtues. Even if the masculine virtues of war and achievement define the dominant ethos of the society, it clearly also requires and gives a place to the feminine virtues of mercy and love. Just as Okonkwo did not *have to* suppress all feelings of tenderness, he did not have to internalize the shame he felt at his father's failure. Igbo society does not insist on heredity; both Uchendu (p. 12) and Achebe use essentially the same proverb to show that anyone can "get up": "As the elders said, if a child washed his hands he could eat with kings" (Achebe, p. 12). Carroll's analysis also makes clear that potential for change and actual changes, as well as conflicts between the individual and society, existed before contact with the white man. Rites had already begun to change on their own; cruel punishments for violation of the Week of Peace were modified because it began to be understood that they worked against their purpose. Individual characters show the existence of variations on cultural givens, and exemplify the senses in which cultural expectations were sources of conflict, or not all of a piece. Ezeulu urged Okonkwo not to personally participate in the killing of Ikemefuna because it would be a violation of an honorary kinship bond, and as such, a pollution of the Earth-Goddess. Obierika, a man of title (a masculine accomplishment), voiced the same opinion after the fact (although the men who refused to kill Ikemefuna were called effeminate) and questioned the exposure of twins, as well as banishment for an involuntary act.

To Carroll's analysis, I wish to add that the conflict in *Things Fall Apart* is not only a conflict between the individual and society, or human forces and divine, but a conflict within the divine realm as well that is, to some extent, a conflict *between* the Oracle and the Earth-Goddess, which is to some extent congruent with the conflict between the dominant ethos of masculinity and the necessary balancing virtues of feminity. Furthermore, a full appreciation of the novel must take into account the crucial difference between balance, which is possible, if difficult, and reconciliation, which is impossible.

The Earth-Goddess is described as follows: "Ani played a greater part in the life of the people than any other deity. She was the ultimate judge of morality and conduct. And what is more, she was in close communication with the departed fathers of the clan whose bodies had been committed to earth" (*Things Fall Apart*, p. 37). The local Oracle, her messenger, is in a sense subordinate to her. Victor Uchendu's comments on oracles (p. 100), which suggest that they had to be in close touch with public opinion in order to be popular, support the idea that Okonkwo was wrong in obeying the Oracle. However, Uchendu also indicates that oracles could sometimes give publicly necessary but difficult acts a spiritual sanction, thus taking the responsibility away from men. There seems to be an understandable reason for Okonkwo's assertion that "the Earth cannot punish me for obeying her messenger" (p. 64), even if he is judged as acting wrongly. The Oracle, who orders the killing of Ikemefuna, is to some extent associated with encouraging the masculine virtues of war and solidarity; it is to some extent responsible for the unity of the village by urging it to acts that enforce its integrity, even to somewhat cruel acts. No one questions the necessity of obeying the Oracle, although one does question the necessity of *Okonkwo's* obeying the Oracle. On the other hand, the Earth-Goddess, as both Achebe and Uchendu (p. 96) tell us, is merciful, slow to act, a source of morality – contrasting with the principle Okonkwo seems to represent: extreme quickness of action – and she opposes the slaying of Ikemefuna by Okonkwo. To some extent, then, although not perfectly, the roles of the Oracle and the Earth-Goddess overlap with the roles of the masculine and the feminine in the book. At the same time, as Carroll does indicate, there is conflict between these divine forces and individual humans: the Oracle is feared and causes suffering for Okonkwo when her priestess, Agbala, takes his daughter Ezinma, away; the Earth-Goddess who prescribes banishment for her pollution, even if accidental, allows the society to go on, since the offender is removed, but at a significant price to the individual.

As Carroll suggests, had Okonkwo agreed not to *personally* participate in the killing of Ikemefuna, he would have been able to strike a balance between "competing claims." But I wish to emphasize the tenuousness of such an equilibrium. Such an act only postpones the ultimate problem of reconciling conflicts in Igbo society, rather than merely balancing them. It would solve Okonkwo's immediate problem, but would it solve his son Nwoye's problem? The fact that his father did not participate in the killing of the friend he loved would not totally compensate him for the loss of the friend, whose *love* had inspired Nwoye to manly acts, thus temporarily reconciling the masculine and feminine polarities of Igbo society. For these reasons, the possibility of balancing claims is not the only context in which Okonkwo's behavior can be seen. That is, given the nature of Igbo society, Okonkwo does not represent a kind of behavior that can be modified in the direction of a community-accepted norm of moderate behavior, combining in one person, both the masculine and feminine virtues. Rather, from the tragic point of view, he participates in a society which is truly split. As in the *Hippolytus,* both of the opposing forces are necessary, and aligning totally with one at the expense of the other is dangerous, yet it is extremely difficult to take account of both, and impossible to reconcile them, since they conflict at the core.

Insofar as the masculine and feminine virtues tend to be associated with different people or sets of people, for example, discipline with one's father and "sympathy" with one's mother; one's "fatherland" with "good times" and one's "motherland" with "sorrow and bitterness" (p. 124), and insofar as the society encourages this sort of separation of functions and roles, balance is possible, however difficult. However, balance is not a solution for the *individual* who cannot exist comfortably in terms of the preferred role or norm assigned him in accordance with his situation and gender; he can find solace, but only at the price of loss of status. Reconciliation is what is required from the point of view of the individual – that is, the possibility of the acceptance of aspects of "masculine" and "feminine" behavior in the same person. Such a reconciliation is momentarily achieved in the friendship of Nwoye and Ikemefuna; it should be stressed again that it is the *love* of Nwoye for Ikemefuna (rather than his desire to achieve) that inspires Nwoye to *manly* acts. Persons such as Obierika are clearly asking the kinds of questions that might have changed the dominant norm of Igbo society. But, Igbo society as it is described in *Things Fall Apart* exists sufficiently in terms of the masculine virtues that it cannot *incorporate* the others without disintegration. As such, it is caught in a truly tragic dilemma. Insofar as individuals pay a personal price for community solidarity, the community is that much more open to threats from without, just as Nwoye's discomfort with Igbo practices such as the exposure of twins, make the religion of the invaders that much more attractive to him. On the other hand, without strictures on behavior that threatens the group, without punishment for certain crimes or without any encouragement of group solidarity in obedience to the local oracle, disintegration may take place from within.

Things Fall Apart, then, both describes a particular society and exemplifies a tragic dilemma of the type found in the *Hippolytus.* It describes a correctable situation, insofar as balancing claims was an available and meaningful alternative for an Igbo such as Okonkwo. But, insofar as *reconciliation* of such claims was what was needed from the point of view of the individual, although such reconciliation was incongruent with the very existence of the society, *Things Fall Apart* describes an insoluble tragic dilemma. This view accords with Achebe's comments on his book. The Igbo themselves are often given as a prime example of adaptation to modern circumstances. Yet the book itself and Achebe's comments make clear that he thinks of the Igbo society he portrayed as having experienced disintegration and downfall. He seems to think of the older Igbo society as fundamentally different from the new. "The weakness of this particular society is a lack of adaptation, not being able to bend. But I can't say that this represents the Ibo people today. I think in his time, the strong men were those who did not bend and I think this was a fault of the culture itself."[25]

In both the cases of critical misreading analyzed here, philosophical and political attitudes and categorizations seem to be imposed on particular literary works. It is possible that these categorizations, "communalistic," "individualistic," and so on, are also not very useful in generalizations about cultures, at least as they are used by the critics I have looked at. In any case, these critics do not seem to be sure enough about what they mean by these categorizations and hence allow them to encourage some simplistic readings. If the categorizations are useful, this must be shown in more precise definitions and more accurate readings of the works, achieved with their aid. As it stands, the roots of the misreadings discussed here seem to lie in a tendency to accept generalizations about other people that we would never accept about ourselves. It is with such generalizations in mind that James Olney comes to *Things Fall Apart* ready to find that the African author is inevitably synonymous with his culture, and the African individual, even in a novel, inevitably one with his group. He does not seem to feel the necessity to distinguish different groups and interests within a particular culture. It is hard to avoid drawing the conclusion that he assumes not only that African cultures are monolithic, but that they all can pretty much be summed up in the same way. And it is with such generalizations in mind that Austin Shelton argues for the relevance of abstract values appropriate to a political tract for a comedy that sees human behavior in all its contingent forms. Unfortunately, such critical assessments justify Soyinka's accusation that the Western critic is condescending: "Takes a simpleton to understand a child."

NOTES

1. This distinction is summarized in Marvin Harris, *The Rise of Anthropological Theory* (New York, 1970), p. 192.

2. See, for example, Paul Bohannan, *Africa and Africans* (New York, 1971), pp. 119-28.

3. E. N. Obiechina makes just such an argument in "Transition from Oral to Literary Tradition," *Présence Africaine*, 63 (1967), pp. 15ff.

4. J. P. Clark takes seriously the idea that tragedy stems from a ritual sacrifice in his play, *The Song of a Goat*; an actual goat is sacrificed in the course of the play.

5. Oyekan Owomoyela makes this argument in "Folklore and Yoruba Theatre," *Research in African Literatures*, 2 (1971), 121-33. The same argument may be found in the work of a British anthropologist, Robin Horton, in "The Kalabari Ekine Society: A Borderland of Religion and Art," *Africa*, 33 (1963), pp. 94-114.

6. In *Black Africa: Its People and their Cultures Today*, ed. John Middleton (London, 1970), pp. 406-12. Page references to Shelton's article will appear in parentheses in the text.

7. Wole Soyinka, *The Lion and the Jewel* (1963; rpt. London, 1966), p. 7. Further page references to *The Lion and the Jewel* are to this edition and will appear in parentheses in the text.

8. E. N. Obiechina, *An African Popular Literature: A Study of Onitsha Market Pamphlets* (Cambridge, 1973), Ch. IV.

9. See, for example, Soyinka's comment about those "contemporary interpreters of African themes [who] have not truly assimilated the new idioms. It is merely naive to transpose the castle to the hut...There are the new poets in Nigeria who regroup images of Ezra Pound around the oilbean and the nude spear." In "From a Common Back Cloth: A Reassessment of the African Literary Image," *The American Scholar*, 32 (1963), pp. 388-89.

10. Cf. Claude Wauthier, *The Literature and Thought of Modern Africa* (New York, 1967), pp. 173-74.

11. See, for example, Warren L. d'Azevedo, ed. *The Traditional Artist in African Societies* (Bloomington, Indiana, 1973).

12. *The American Scholar*, 32 (1963), pp. 387-96. Further page references to this article will appear in parentheses in the text.

13. "The Writer in an African State," *Transition*, No. 31 (1967), pp. 11, 12.

14. Ibid., pp. 12, 13.

15. See Gerald Moore, *Wole Soyinka* (New York, 1971), pp. 16-19.

16. See Charles Larson, *The Emergence of African Fiction* (Bloomington, Indiana, 1972), Ch. II, and David Carroll, *Chinua Achebe* (New York, 1970), Ch. II.

17. Princeton, New Jersey, 1973. Further page references to Olney's book will appear in parentheses in the text.

18. "The Novelist as Teacher," *New Statesman*, 29 January 1965, p. 62.

19. From "The Role of the Writer in a New Nation," *Nigeria Magazine*, 81 (1964), quoted in G. D. Killam, *The Novels of Chinua Achebe* (New York, 1969), p. 10.

20. Olney quotes from Victor Uchendu, *The Igbo of Southeast Nigeria* (New York, 1965), p. 103. Further page references to Uchendu's ethnography will appear in parentheses in the text.

21. Larson, *The Emergence of African Fiction*, p. 61.

22. Cf. Carroll, pp. 26, 28 and n. 7 (p. 49).

23. From "The Role of the Writer in a New Nation," quoted in Killam, *The Novels of Chinua Achebe*, p. 10.

24. "Conversation with Chinua Achebe," *Africa Report*, 9 (July 1964), p. 19.

25. Ibid.

"Larsony" with a Difference: An Examination of a Paragraph from *Toward the Decolonization of African Literature*

James Gibbs

One of the most influential books of African literary criticism, *Toward the Decolonization of African Literature* by Chinweizu, Onwuchekwa Jemie, and Ihechukwu Madubuike, has the stated aim "of probing the ways and means whereby Western imperialism has maintained its hegemony upon the literary arts of contemporary Africa."[1] In their analysis of British and American criticism of African literature, the authors employ with approval a term derived from the name of an American critic, Charles Larson: *larsony*. The term, coined by Ayi Kwei Armah, is defined as "that style which consists of the judicious distortion of African truths to fit Western prejudices, the art of using fiction as criticism of fiction."[2] In this paper I argue that the authors of *Decolonization* are themselves guilty of "using fiction as a criticism of fiction" in the sense that they present a tendentious, misleading, and emotive account of events as an adjunct to their literary criticism.

I intend to examine, in the context in which it appears, the passage in which they describe Wole Soyinka's return to Nigeria in 1960. The authors of *Decolonization* have not indicated the sources for several observations, and I have, on occasion, had to make assumptions about the points they make. I have, I think, tried to do this in a reasonable manner, but I do not suppose I will carry with me those who, to glance ahead, regard me as a laughing British imperialist. Nor do I suppose that my observations about Soyinka will in any way strengthen his case to those who are confident that he is, in the image of Chinweizu *et al.*, a cultural mercenary, a fellow traveller serving Western imperialist interests. He has made his own defense against some of the charges leveled against him, and his own work and life, in my opinion, refute many other charges most eloquently and effectively.[3]

In *Toward the Decolonization of African Literature*, as part of an argument concerning what the authors regard as "The Inculcation of Euro-modernism in Nigerian Poetry: The Scandalous Leeds-Ibadan Connection," we read:

> Then Wole Soyinka with his brand-new reputation, is parachuted in (1960) from Leeds and the Royal Court Theatre, and lands amidst much fanfare blown by such colonialist propaganda organs as *Encounter* magazine, and goes into action to flush out and swat the remnants of the native resistance to Anglo-Saxon pseudo-universalism. This Marshall Ky of African culture (remember Vietnam?) rehearses in the pages of *The Horn* an early draft of his tigritude counter-insurgency slogan bomb. The local opposition melts before the gun of his "duikeritude." British imperialist triumph over a nascent Nigerian cultural nationalism is complete! Ridicule by voices like Aig-Imoukhuede's merely cry "Amen," and bring laughter to the teeth of the triumphant Britishers and their fellow travellers![4]

I suggest that this statement is ill-informed and misleading: the tone of the argument confuses, and the paradigm of the process of factors affecting changes in cultural attitudes is naive and simplistic.

Soyinka returned to Nigeria, as the passage indicates, in 1960, but I take exception to the description of his reputation as "brand-new." It suggests that Soyinka was known only for what he had achieved during his five-year stay in England. This was not the case: his achievements abroad, such as his fame as a broadcaster on the BBC's *Calling Nigeria* program, had been added to reputations he had earned at school, in Lagos and while an undergraduate at Ibadan. During the late 1940s he had become known beyond the gates of Government College, Ibadan, where he was at school, by winning prizes for his poetry and for his recitations at arts festivals. While working in Lagos in 1950 and 1951, he had written stories and plays which were broadcast by the Nigerian Broadcasting Service. He had continued to write for radio during his two years as an undergraduate at University College, Ibadan (1952 and 1954), and had taken an active part in campus life. His poem "Thunder into Storm" was published in *The University Voice*; he edited the newspaper, *The Eagle*, put out by a student political party; he co-founded a fraternity, the Pyrates, which still flourishes; and his performances of leading roles in student productions of plays by James Bridie and George Bernard Shaw earned him considerable acclaim.[5]

I have spent some time on this issue because the tactic of suggesting that Soyinka's reputation has been essentially earned in Europe and America – that he is "a prophet" more honored abroad than at home – is one which is frequently employed by his critics, among whom Chinweizu *et al.* must be counted. Soyinka has long moved easily through international gatherings; he has been praised by British and American – and Cuban and Zimbabwean – critics. He is committed to human rights and the welfare of writers in many parts of the world, but his prime commitments are to his continent and his country. He is deeply involved in Nigerian academic, theatrical, and political life; he devotes considerable energy to trying to make the roads in Nigeria safer, and he particularly enjoys hunting; he is a Nigerian who is committed to Nigeria, and he is by no means without honor in his own country.[6] To allow "brand-new reputation" to pass unchallenged would be to connive at the establishment of a misleading impression.

By saying that Soyinka was "parachuted in" to Nigeria, Chinweizu et al. are insinuating the image of Soyinka as a mercenary, a tool of interventionist forces. There is no evidence that he was, or is, an agent of imperialist interests, but, in view of the attack on his integrity, his means of support and his means of returning to Nigeria must be scrutinized.

While in England Soyinka had been supported at first by a scholarship awarded by the colonial government and later by an income derived from his first wife's wages, supply teaching, broadcasting, writing, and work for the Royal Court Theatre. He returned on a research studentship financed by the Rockefeller Foundation to a position which was, in some respects, a privileged one. He had no teaching responsibilities; he had the use of a Land Rover (with a petrol allowance), a tape-recorder, and a camera. The only obligation placed on him seems to have been that he would write a book on Nigerian drama. He was, however, a member of the Junior Common Room and was housed in a student hall of residence. Soon after his return he expressed his dissatisfaction with this accommodation and, after a spell off-campus, persuaded those responsible to rehouse him in a chalet that he occupied rent free. After negotiation he was gazetted as a "research fellow." He traveled tens of thousands of miles in the Land Rover at the foundation's expense and returned the vehicle at the end of his two-year "fellowship" with bald tires, a flat battery, and without a door. He did not write the expected book, and he did not return the tape-recorder. In certain circumstances this conduct might be regarded as, at least, discourteous; in the present context, it may be used to draw attention to Soyinka's independence. He took the Rockefeller Foundation, literally, for a ride.[7]

This may all seem disingenuous. There may be those who will argue that Soyinka was inevitably compromised as soon as he accepted a colonial scholarship or Rockefeller grant and had become, in the decolonizers' idiom, a mercenary. Such people may cite the observation that "he who pays the piper calls the tune" in support of their case. I do not regard this as a valid line of argument, and I invite anyone tempted to support it to note that Chinweizu himself held a Rockefeller Research Fellowship at Massachusetts Institute of Technology during 1976.[8] If he preserved his integrity while being maintained by the foundation, why should not Soyinka have done so as well?

I do not take exception to the decolonizers' expression that Soyinka returned "from Leeds and the Royal Court Theatre" – those two locations represent his major points of contact with English life. I think, however, that it is pertinent to remark that both places represent traditions of radical opposition to the British establishment and to British imperialism. At Leeds, Arnold Kettle had, by 1950, contributed a distinct Marxist element to the teaching in the School of English. At the Royal Court Theatre there was considerable support for the Campaign for Nuclear Disarmament (CND) and tremendous anger at the way in which the British government was conducting affairs in Kenya. Many members of the community which was centered on the Royal Court took part in CND marches, and an anti-colonial, agit-prop production entitled *Eleven Men Dead at Hola Camp* was mounted. The theater encouraged committed socialists, including Arnold Wesker, and provided a London venue for the plays they wrote.[9]

The authors of *Toward the Decolonization of African Literature* write that Soyinka arrived "amidst much fanfare" blown by *Encounter*. They do not indicate what form the fanfare took and without sources and authorities to refer to the reader is left to work out what is meant. This is a difficult process and one which almost inevitably gives Chinweizu and his co-authors an obvious line of reply: Gibbs assumes *this,* but we meant *that*. However, without cited authorities, an assumption must be made, and my assumption is that the fanfare was blown in the pages of *Encounter*. During 1960, the year in question, several articles on Africa were published in the magazine, none of which mentioned Soyinka. The only reference I have found to him in the 1960 issues was in a report of the playwriting prize awarded in connection with Nigerian Independence.[10] Near the back of the December number, after the letters to the editor and under the headline "African Playwrights," extracts of a letter from Ulli Beier were quoted. They consist of a very brief résumé of the theme of *A Dance of the Forests*, a few lines on Soyinka, and some comments on the runner-up, Nkem Nwankwo, and his entry. Of Soyinka we read "[he] is known in London where he presented 'An Evening at the Royal Court Theatre' in 1959, including readings from his poetry, scenes from his plays and songs for the guitar." This is at most a chord on the piano; it is certainly not a fanfare. Incidentally it draws attention to work by Soyinka which Chinweizu *et al.* should have taken into account and which must have caused them, if they were open-minded, to reassess their judgments. The Royal Court program included songs "in a blues idiom," a poem in memory of a victim of racial violence in London, and an anti-racist drama.

The playwriting competition sponsored by *Encounter* which Soyinka won brought him the modest prize of one hundred pounds and gave him a certain amount of prestige in Nigeria. The judges included Chinua Achebe, one of those to whom *Decolonization* is dedicated, and it would be very hard to argue that the competition was arranged so as to give Soyinka publicity. He has shown himself to be the major Nigerian playwright of his generation, and there is every indication that he deserved the prize. Since a similar competition was held in Sierra Leone, it would seem highly unlikely that the whole event was engineered to give Soyinka's reputation a boost.

The critics describe *Encounter* as a "colonialist propaganda [organ]." This is not an appropriate description, although the integrity of the journal was called into question when it was discovered that it had, in ignorance, been partly funded by the Central Intelligence Agency (CIA).[11] In my opinion, no opprobrium should be attached to a writer merely because he has been praised or awarded a prize by a journal which, unknowingly, received funds from the CIA. Apart from *Encounter* the CIA provided covert support for *African Forum, Black Orpheus*, and *Transition,* journals which published the work of several Africans and people of African descent of whom Chinweizu *et al.* approve, to whom, indeed, *Decolonization* is dedicated. These include Langston Hughes, C. L. R. James, Kwame Nkrumah, and Léopold Sédar Senghor. In 1975 an essay by Chinweizu *et al.* entitled "Towards the Decolonization of African Literature" was published in *Transition*, at that time edited by Soyinka. I may have labored the issue, but the point must be made that CIA money was used to subsidize the distribution of work by authors whom the decolonizers regard as "giant voices of the Black World" – and even of their own work! This association does not provide grounds for suspicion of the integrity and loyalty of authors, be they Soyinka, Chinweizu, Jemie, or Madubuike. Soyinka's reputation should not be called in question on the grounds that he was mentioned in *Encounter* and won a competition sponsored by that magazine.

The impression Chinweizu and his co-authors create in the subsequent lines from the paragraph under consideration is that Soyinka went into action soon after his return "to flush out and swat the remnants of the native resistance to Anglo-Saxon pseudo-universalism." In this summary the military, interventionist imagery established by "parachuted in" is taken up: "flush out and swat" recalls the "search and destroy" missions of American troops in Vietnam, a neo-colonial war which surfaces in the prose a little later. In fact, Soyinka was certainly very busy on his return, but his activities had little or nothing to do with promoting "Anglo-Saxon pseudo-universalism." For instance, he acted in Bertolt Brecht's *Good Woman of Setzuan*, wrote a play for radio, sang Afro-American songs at concerts, and published poems – including one in pidgin and one in protest against French nuclear bomb tests in the Sahara.[12] These poems, once again, are not mentioned in *Toward the Decolonization of African Literature* and, also once again, call in question the value of the judgments made about Soyinka's verse in that book. Soyinka's article on African literature was first announced as forthcoming in volume 3, number 4, of *The Horn*, but following apologies for the delay, it did not appear until several issues and many months later.[13] This is "go[ing] into action" at a dead march; it suggests that Soyinka's priorities were quite different from those imputed by the decolonizers.

Does Soyinka stand, as his critics suggest, for opposition to "native" resistance to "Anglo-Saxon pseudo-universalism"? Or, put another way, does he promote "Anglo-Saxon pseudo-universalism"? The answer is no, as a reading of "The Future of West African Writing" and such creative work as "Death in the Dawn" and *The Lion and the Jewel* confirms. The ideas Soyinka explores, the conventions he manipulates, and the vision he embodies in his work are profoundly informed by African – specifically Yoruba – experiences and values.[14]

Chinweizu *et al.* describe Soyinka as "This Marshall Ky of African Culture." But this comparison is so far-fetched, so inappropriate, so clearly the result of emotional imbalance as to be ridiculous. Objective observers – and those who have been swayed by what I have already argued – will regard it as part of a smear campaign, designed to condemn by association. It does not, particularly when we "remember Vietnam," stand up to scrutiny.

The kind of emotional and hectic innuendo characteristic of the passage under examination continues in the comments on Soyinka's article in *The Horn*. To be brief, Soyinka wrote "The Future of West African Writing," in which he argued for self-acceptance and against the "authentic," "'unspoilt' stuff" demanded by foreigners and foreign-influenced tastes – among such tastes he included "Negritude," which he described as an "inherently invalid doctrine." In the course of the paper, he wrote, "The duiker will not paint 'duiker' on his beautiful back to proclaim his 'duikeritude'; you'll know him by his elegant leap."

Those curious about *The Horn* have often gone to an article by W. H. Stevenson entitled *"The Horn*: What It Was and What It Did," which was published in 1975.[15] After pointing out that it was "a slight, typewritten, amateur, student publication," and that he had not been able to assemble a complete run of issues, Stevenson analyzed the contents and the impact of the publication. In commenting on "Negritude," he made the point that, though written about with enthusiasm in the first editorial and occasionally present in subsequent issues, Negritude was an idea that took only shallow root in Nigeria. He observed that after Soyinka's article the word was, he thought, "never again used in *The Horn*, except once," and "poetry dependent on the concept almost [disappeared]." The "once" is in a satiric poem by Frank Aig-Imoukhuede.[16]

The authors of *Decolonization* drew on Stevenson; indeed, they quote extensively from his article. The significant addition is that they see the fate of Negritude in the student publication in terms of a "diversionary coup." They describe "the derailment of African cultural nationalism and the substitution in its place of 'universalism' " as a characteristic British ploy to keep control. This interpretation begs many questions; for instance, if *The Horn* was an instrument of British imperialism dedicated to destroying Negritude, why was J. P. Clark given a chance to sound "a positive and welcoming note on Negritude and on black cultural consciousness" in the first issue? Why were sixteen out of twenty-seven of the issues that are known to have been produced edited by men with some sympathy for Negritude, Clark and Abiola Irele? And why were Irele's Negritude-influenced verses published in volume 6, number 1?

In the passage under consideration the authors maintain, in the military imagery with which they have conducted much of their argument, that, "local opposition [melted] before the gun of his duikeritude." Then, presumably following Stevenson, they summon Aig-Imoukhuede's voice as evidence. It is not clear what "local" means in this context. In Stevenson's article the setback to Negritude is confined to the pages of *The Horn* and for him "local" would mean, perhaps, the Department of English at University College, Ibadan, or, perhaps, the college as a whole – a very small, though very influential, community.

In *Decolonization* the paragraph falls between comments on the ideas prevalent at University College, Ibadan, and remarks about the fate of Negritude in what are described as Britain's "African 'commonwealth' possessions." The authors of *Decolonization* maintain that, due to Soyinka's attack on Negritude at the Kampala Writers' Conference, "the spread of Negritude into the British colonies and neo-colonies [was] contained, and whatever variants of active African nationalist consciousness its example might have triggered off [were] diffused."[17] This seems to represent confusion about the process by which ideas spread: sarcastic remarks in student literary magazines and poets' comments at writers' conferences do not create public opinion, though they may, if succinct and witty like Soyinka's, articulate it and become part of the common currency of debate. For a fuller awareness of the growth, development, and fortunes of cultural nationalism in Nigeria, which is the point at issue here in relation to "duikeritude," the authors should have ranged more widely than they did and should have taken into consideration studies such as those by M. J. C. Echeruo on Victorian Lagos and by Ebun Clark on Hubert Ogunde.[18] It remains for Chinweizu *et al.* to provide evidence for their provocative claims about the influence of Soyinka's comments on African nationalism. Even those who like to think that the pen is mightier than the sword – and the voice of the poet louder than the roar of the cannon – may find it hard to accept that a few words could have affected so many in such distant and different places.

Chinweizu, Jemie, and Madubuike use the term *larsony* but, I suggest, their own discourse employs "larsony," that is, fiction as a criticism of fiction. They use dubious arguments, present facts in heavily emotive terms, slander by association, neglect to examine relevant material, and extend findings quite unjustifiably. This is "larsony" with a difference, "since the prejudices which produce the distortion are not, of course," Western.

NOTES

1. Chinweizu, Onwuchekwa Jemie, and Ihechukwu Madubuike, *Toward the Decolonization of African Literature*, vol. 1 (Enugu: Fourth Dimension, 1980).

2. Ayi Kwei Armah, "Larsony, or Fiction as Criticism of Fiction," *Positive Review* (Ife), 1 (1978): 14. My use of the term *larsony* should not be taken to imply that I accept Armah's analysis.

3. For instance, Wole Soyinka, "Neo-Tarzanism: The Poetics of Pseudo-Tradition," *Transition* (Accra,) 48 (1975): 38-44.

4. Chinweizu *et al.*, 203-04.

5. For details of published work from this period, see *Critical Perspectives on Wole Soyinka*, ed. James Gibbs (Washington: Three Continents, 1980), and Bernth Lindfors, *Early Nigerian Literature* (New York: Africana, 1982). See also Wole Soyinka, "Gbohun-Gbohun," *The Listener* (London), 2 Nov. 1970, 581-83. For information about Soyinka's youthful activities, I am grateful to Modupe Oduyoye, Mary Welch, and Harold Preston.

6. See my Introduction to *Critical Perspectives on Wole Soyinka* and my articles: "The Masks Hatched Out," *Theatre Research International* (Oxford), 7 (1982): 180-206, and "Tear the Painted Masks," *Research in African Literatures*, 14 (1983): 3-44.

7. Correspondence regarding Soyinka's "studentship/ fellowship" is on file in the University of Ibadan Library.

8. Chinweizu *et al.*, xi.

9. See, for instance, Arnold Kettle's *Introduction to the English Novel*, vols 1 and 2 (London: Hutchinson, 1951, 1953), and Richard Findlater, ed., *At the Royal Court* (Ambergate: Amber Lane, 1981).

10. "African Playwrights," *Encounter*, 15 (1960): 87.

11. For background see Ellen Ray, W. Schaap, K. van Meter, and L. Wolf, eds., *The C.I.A. in Africa* (London: Zed Press, 1980), and various issues of *Transition,* including 45.9 (1974): 66.

12. For instance, "Poisoners of the World Unite" and "Proverb: Okonjo the Hunter," *The Horn*, 3.3 (1960): 4-7, 9.

13. Wole Soyinka, "The Future of West African Writing," *The Horn*, 4.1 (1960): 10-16.

14. I have argued this in my study aids to *The Lion and the Jewel* (London and Beirut: Longman & York, 1982) and to *Kongi's Harvest* (London: Collings, 1973). See also my monograph on Soyinka for Macmillan.

15. W. H. Stevenson, "*The Horn*: What It Was and What It Did," *Research in African Literatures*, 6 (1975): 5-31.

16. Frank Aig-Imoukhuede, "The Poor Black Muse," *The Horn*, 4.2 (1960): page unknown.

17. Chinweizu *et al.* 204.

18. M. J. C. Echeruo, *Victorian Lagos* (London: Macmillan, 1977), and Ebun Clark, *Hubert Ogunde: The Making of Nigerian Theatre* (London: Oxford UP, 1979).

Gibbs's Gibberish

Chinweizu, Onwuchekwa Jemie, Ihechukwu Madubuike

First of all, we wish to thank Bernth Lindfors for his courtesy in sending us James Gibbs's article so that our reply could be published simultaneously.

We must confess that our first reaction was to ignore the piece on the grounds which we have stated so often, namely, that the responsibility for the critical evaluation of African writing and the establishment of reputations for African authors belong to Africans themselves, for they are the primary audience. However, efforts by Westerners to impose their views on Africans have been quite persistent, and for reasons of history and colonialism, what the James Gibbses of this world publish in Western journals on African literature still has considerable influence on African thinking. Thus, it would not be safe to ignore them until Afrocentric criticism has reevaluated all our writers and powerful African forums have emerged for presenting the African assessment of African writing.

In order to stop the reputations Westerners insist on fabricating for African writers from filtering in and polluting African judgment, our present situation makes it necessary for us to respond to Western interlopers like James Gibbs. Like members of a household which is faced with a guest who insists on imposing his views and preferences upon it, it is our job to throw him out.

Gibbs's central charge is that we committed "larsony" by presenting Soyinka's role in the anti-Negritude campaign of the 1960s as interventionist on behalf of Europe's pseudo-universalism. But really, Gibbs cannot claim we committed "larsony," that is, fiction as criticism of fiction, unless he successfully challenges W. H. Stevenson's account of the career of Negritude in *The Horn* or our account of the impact at the Kampala Writers Conference and thereafter of Soyinka's "tigritude" attack on Negritude.

Gibbs does not in his article challenge these accounts, and we believe he cannot do so without blatantly distorting the historical facts. His charge of "larsony" against us is, therefore, simply false, and an attempt to confuse everybody by brandishing distractions.

Gibbs's real gripe seems to be against our dramatizing the imperialist campaign against Negritude in the imagery of military interventionism. Specifically, he is against our portraying Soyinka's role in the imagery of a

Marshall Ky performing a cowboy sheriff act, going on a search and destroy mission, parachuting down, flushing out and swatting the nationalist opposition, etc. What's bugging Gibbs? Not the underlying facts as already presented by Stevenson and us – he did not challenge the facts; rather it is the imagery used in a dramatic summary of the facts. However, in keeping with what imagery must do to be apt, our extended metaphor was faithful to the facts and, like all effective metaphor, simply helped to make clearer the nature of Soyinka's role.

That Gibbs happens not to like what emerges from the clarification is his problem, a matter of his own tastes, sensibilities, and loyalties. Of course, most people are not pleased with cartoons which sharpen and thus make memorable the correct points being made about their heroes. So we sympathize with Gibbs for his very human sensitivities, but we must also point out that his sensitivities do not turn into fiction the correct points made by such a cartoon.

Having made the essential point, we might have stopped here. But since his misdirected arguments are enlightening about other things, let us grant Gibbs an honorary *locus standi* in an African discussion of African literary reputations and spare time for a few main remarks.

Gibbs objects to our characterization of Soyinka's reputation upon his return to Nigeria in 1960 as "brand-new." But then, Soyinka's reputation upon his return was the one he had just made in England from his work at the Royal Court Theatre, culminating in his presentation of an evening of songs, poems, and excerpts from his plays in late 1959. That was an unprecedented achievement for any African and formed the basis of the reputation with which he landed in Nigeria, a reputation which therefore was "brand-new" at the time.

Here, incidentally, is Gibbs himself on Soyinka's reputation at the time:

> Soyinka returned to Nigeria after five years in England with a fine sense of timing: he arrived in Lagos on the first of January 1960. His reputation as a poet and playwright had preceded him to Ibadan and he soon became well known in the Western Region as a writer and broadcaster, an actor, and a singer. (*Research in African Literatures*, 14 [1983]: 14)

In other words, Gibbs in 1983 agrees with us that Soyinka's reputation when he arrived in Nigeria in 1960 was the one he had just made in England. But Gibbs in 1985 thinks otherwise. Has he discovered any new facts? Or is this just another case of somnambulist criticism such as we wrote about in *Decolonization?*

Gibbs tries to confuse the issue by pointing to Soyinka's youthful student writings, his juvenilia produced before he left to study in England, as evidence of a pre-existing Nigerian reputation. In this, Gibbs misses the essential point. What gave weight to Soyinka's pronouncements against Negritude? Soyinka's juvenilia or his newly blossoming national and international reputation? Since when did the circumscribed reputations in schools and local communities give national and international clout to anybody's pronouncements?

Like countless others, Soyinka did not acquire literary prominence, in Nigeria or Africa, by winning school prizes, publishing in college or university magazines, and having occasional stories read on the national radio.

He came to national prominence only after his return from Leeds and the Royal Court Theatre and precisely through his having presented something there (1959). He consolidated that reputation chiefly with his play *A Dance of the Forests*, which was staged as part of the Independence Celebrations in 1960 and which won the *Encounter* magazine prize for that year; with the staging of plays by the 1960 Masks, the drama troupe which he founded; with the popularity of his poem "Telephone Conversation"; and with the publication of a book of his plays by Mbari in 1963. This was how Soyinka came to stand out from the many other Nigerians who had published college and undergraduate poems, or had had their stories read on radio, or had won arts festival prizes, etc. And it was this new and growing reputation which at the time gave clout to his literary pronouncements, including his clever "tigritude" quip at Kampala in 1962.

Soyinka's youthful student writings did not go into the making of his reputation; they were brought to public attention much later when hardworking academic moles such as James Gibbs dug them up. That Gibbs has to resort to those juvenilia shows that he really has no case.

We were rather amused by some of the irrelevancies which Gibbs thought pertinent to the case he was making. It may well be, as Gibbs seems to imply, that Soyinka's subsequent (1970s) road safety campaign, his enjoyment of hunting (date unspecified), his commitment to human rights throughout the world, the ease with which he reportedly moves through international gatherings, etc., etc., are evidence against the notion that "Soyinka's reputation has been essentially earned in Europe and America – that he is "a 'prophet' more honored abroad than at home." But we fail to see how it shows that the reputation with which he arrived in Nigeria in 1960 was not "brand-new," or that his anti-Negritude remarks of the early 1960s did not aid the imperialist cultural campaign against Negritude and African nationalist consciousness.

Second, we wonder why Gibbs thought it necessary to argue that Soyinka was not a mercenary. To our knowledge, no one has accused him of that. The issue is not whether Soyinka studied on foreign scholarships or fellowships. Many prominent Nigerians of that period did, including those of unquestionable nationalist persuasion. One can take foundation or CIA money and not do what they want, or do what they want without ever taking their money. Our view of Soyinka's role in the anti-Negritude campaign is not derived from the sources of his funding, but from the attitudes, views, and values he propagated and from the vital part his pronouncements played in the imperialist campaign to put down Negritude.

Gibbs appears to be contesting our claim that there was such an interventionist cultural campaign by doubting whether the pro-Negritude editorial would at all have appeared in *The Horn* if there was such a campaign. Gibbs seems to think that if British interventionist forces had indeed been at work, the Negritude tendency would not have surfaced at all. Which shows that he has not really considered how interventionist forces work and why.

The fact that you are interventionist does not mean you are all-foreseeing and omnipotent and thus able to prevent things you do not like from ever emerging at all. But it does mean that when you see things moving in a direction you do not like, you intervene to constrain them to go the way you prefer. Which was precisely what the powers that were in the English Department at Ibadan, particularly John Ramsaran, did on *The Horn*, with considerable help from Soyinka and his "duikeritude" attack, as we reported in *Decolonization.*

Gibbs further writes as if what took place in the English Department at Ibadan and on the pages of *The Horn*, and later at the Kampala Writers Conference, should be played down as inconsequential, and he accuses us of "confusion about the process by which ideas spread." In actual fact, it is Gibbs who is confused about how the pseudo-universalist idea was spread and the Negritude idea sidetracked in that particular campaign. Wars, whether of ideas or of troops, are not won by every battle but by the decisive engagements. And in the campaign against Negritude, what took place in *The Horn* and later at the Kampala Writers Conference proved to be decisive engagements where the forces of Eurocentric pseudo-universalism checked the threatening momentum of Negritude and of African nationalist consciousness in English-language African literature. And on both occasions, Soyinka used his powers of ridicule to undermine the African nationalist side.

It would appear that Gibbs has a special talent for missing the point. He shouts "larsony" where there is none; in the matter of Soyinka's reputation, he focuses on irrelevant juvenilia; to the demonstration that Soyinka served the imperialist interest in the campaign against Negritude, he irrelevantly counters that Soyinka was not a mercenary; he misses the point about interventionism and finds it convenient not to see the importance of *The Horn* and the Kampala Writers Conference in the battle of ideas which took place around Negritude.

We should, therefore, like to enter a last note of warning to Gibbs and his kind not to waste everybody's time by spinning confusions, trumping up irrelevancies, and filling the air with false accusations. When next Gibbs is tempted to make his confusionist interventions, we suggest that he takes pains to discover what is central or even germane to the case. Had he done so, we believe he would not have wasted everybody's time with this gibberish. And may Ogun save Soyinka from such inept defenders.[1]

NOTE

1.   For the continuation of this exchange see Gibbs' rejoinder to this article in *Research in African Literatures*, 17, 2 (Summer 1986), pp. 317-22, and Soyinka's comments in *Art, Dialogue and Outrage* (Ibadan: New Horn, 1988), pp. 265-78.

Beating the White Man at His Own Game: Nigerian Reactions to the 1986 Nobel Prize in Literature

Bernth Lindfors

When Wole Soyinka won the Nobel Prize for Literature in October 1986, there was national jubilation in Nigeria. For weeks following the announcement, his achievement dominated the headlines, editorials, political cartoons, advertisements and letters to the editor in all Nigerian newspapers and news magazines. Congratulations poured in from every corner of the country and from countless countrymen abroad. When Soyinka, who happened to be in Paris at the time the news broke, returned home the next day, he was greeted in Lagos with a hero's welcome and official national honors, being awarded the prestigious CFR (Commander of the Federal Republic) by Nigeria's President. It was the national pride evident in this spontaneous public celebration that was most gratifying to the honoree himself: "I was very moved," he said, "by the fact that, from President Ibrahim Babangida down to the ordinary people in the street, it was taken as a national honour ... To have it shared, really shared – I've never been through an experience like that ... . To me, that is the great thing about the prize, that it was really a national thing" (Duodu 28). Nigeria exuberantly congratulated herself on having produced a son worthy of the highest international recognition.

But there were also a few loud grumbles beneath the noisy acclamation, some of them directed pointedly at Soyinka, some at the Nobel Prize, some at both. Like any famous personality, Soyinka does not lack detractors, several of whom have crusaded tirelessly over the years to deflate his soaring reputation. The Nobel Prize gave these enemies another opportunity to snipe at their favorite target, now borne aloft on what they saw as a transient bubble of over-inflated public adulation. Yet in launching their slings and arrows against Soyinka's outrageous good fortune once more, the best marksmen among these critics were not acting frivolously, for they sincerely believed that writers like Soyinka do more harm than good to a literary civilization. They were objecting not to his notoriety as a public figure but to his obscurity as a poet and playwright – that is, not to his way with the world but to his way with words. By questioning the very tools with which he worked and the value of

341

what he fashioned with them, they were reopening an important debate on the relevancy of high art to everyday life in modern Africa.

This debate had started in earnest more than a decade earlier, when three Nigerian critics – Chinweizu, Onwuchekwa Jemie and Ihechukwu Madubuike – had co-authored essays on Nigerian poetry and literary criticism that were originally published in *Okike* and *Transition* under the title "Towards the Decolonization of African Literature" and later were expanded into a book with more or less the same title. Their basic argument, presented in an engagingly irreverent idiom typical of what came to be known as *Bolekaja* ("Come down, let's fight"[1]) criticism, was that

> contemporary African culture is under foreign domination. Therefore, on the one hand, our culture has to destroy all encrustations of colonial mentality, and on the other hand, has to map out new foundations for an African modernity ... If African literature is not to become a transplanted fossil of European literature, it needs to burst out of the strait-jacket of anglo-modernist poetry and of the "well-made novel" and it needs to find more ways of incorporating forms, treatments and devices taken from the African oral tradition (239-40).

Soyinka was not the only Nigerian author to be branded "anglo-modernist," but he was among the principal poets singled out for abuse, particularly for his "obscurantism, ... his fidelity to the Hopkinsian butchery of English syntax and semantics, and ... his deliberate choice of Shakespearean and other archaisms as models for his poetic diction" (156). In short, by writing "Euro-assimilationist" literature, Soyinka was betraying a nationalist and pan-African struggle to affirm the integrity of indigenous cultural expression. He was a sell-out to the West, a brainwashed colonial cringing obediently before alien literary gods.

Soyinka, stung by this sharp needling, was quick to respond with his own verbal pyrotechnics. Dismissing his antagonists as a "troika" of "unsure critics and superficial traditionalists," he ridiculed their conception of poetry as simplistic, primitivistic, ignorant and stiff-necked. Such would-be critics, he maintained, "do not know what they are talking about"; they are merely "neo-Tarzanists" promulgating a "poetics of pseudo-tradition" which has no authentic African foundation (38-44).

The war of insults between Soyinka and the *Bolekaja* critics had begun, and it flared up spectacularly again in October 1985, when Soyinka was rumored to be on the shortlist for Nobel Prize consideration. In fact, only a few hours before that year's winner in literature was announced, a Nigerian newspaper reported that the contest had been narrowed down to only two candidates: Soyinka and an unnamed Czech writer (Odemwingie 1). When the award then suddenly went to Claude Simon, a little-known, avant-garde

French novelist, there were howls of disappointment heard throughout Nigeria. The Swedish Academy was vilified by the press as narrowminded, incurably Eurocentric in outlook, even latently racist. Else, why were Africa's most accomplished writers being consistently ignored?

It was at this point that Chinweizu, a regular columnist for *The Guardian*, one of Nigeria's leading dailies, inserted his *Bolekaja* barbs into the discussion. In a brief piece entitled "That Nobel Prize Brouhaha," he said that "somebody asked what I thought of the prize not having gone to Soyinka. Well, I was actually disappointed. In my view, the Nobel Prize and Soyinka's works deserve one another. It would be an excellent case of the undesirable honouring the unreadable."

Chinweizu went on to spell out why he considered this prize undesirable for Africans:

> namely, its role as a bewitching instrument for Euro-imperialist intellectual hegemony, and the conceit that a gaggle of Swedes, all by themselves, should pronounce on intellectual excellence for the diverse cultures of the whole wide world. Likewise, I am not one of those who stand in uncomprehending awe before Soyinka's literary works ... Maybe, if [these] works were even harder to make sense of, and even more pandering to Graeco-Roman mythology, they might have edged out the hard-to-decipher species – the French *nouveau-roman* – which got the Swedish Academy's nod. As for all the heartaching in some circles, I don't see why any self-respecting African who understands the cultural role of the Nobel Prize, would lust for a moment for the damn thing (5).

Soyinka did not respond to this provocation – at least not immediately. However, his supporters rapidly took up cudgels in his behalf. Titi Adepitan, reacting to "Chinweizu and his hang-ups," suggested that "we examine the merit in the pronouncements of a critic whose position is underlined more by an unrelieved animus for the object of his strictures than any concern for a balanced appraisal ... Though he may not know it, I suspect Chinweizu is suffering from some incurable mutation of that disease Harold Bloom has diagnosed as the anxiety of influence. He should learn to control it or seek solace in silence" (8).

This put-down prompted an essay in defense of Chinweizu by Naiwu Osahon, an energetic pop writer best known for his prolific production of children's books and soft-core pornography – both good money-spinners. Osahon prefaced his remarks by commenting on what he construed to be Soyinka's disappointment, especially financial disappointment, at not having won the Nobel Prize:

> Soyinka himself would only say, when cornered recently over the prize, that he had no comment to make. For someone who normally is very articulate on most

issues, his no comment position could either be interpreted to mean that he was unhappy for not winning the prize or that the prize was not worth his or our bother. However, if the loss was so painful as to silence Soyinka, then one can only conclude that Chinweizu, Jemie and Madubuike were very perceptive in their assessment of Wole Soyinka as a not-so-steadfast an 'African' writer. Of course a quarter of a million dollars or so prize can be a great temptation even across racial and patriotic lines (9).

This was too much for Soyinka to swallow in silence, so he published a rejoinder in *The Guardian* a few days later, entitling it "Ethics and Aesthetics of Chichidodo." His immediate purpose was to repudiate Osahon for "imputing to Wole Soyinka emotions which at no time in his existence, he has never yet experienced" [sic], but his real aim was to get back at Chinweizu, whom he referred to as "a human incarnation of the bird *Chichidodo*," a creature in Ayi Kwei Armah's novel *The Beautyful Ones Are Not Yet Born* which "screams out loud its hatred of excrement but loves to feed on the worms that breed in it." Soyinka then proceeded to dump a large tangle of scatalogical nightcrawlers on Chinweizu and his "'Brouhaha' group," whose heads, he said, "are stuck in a latrine bucket ... Their sickness is too far gone for ministration. A centre of pus substitutes for grey matter in their head and they have never made friends with the word 'integrity' " (9).

Such earthy mudslinging sparked a controversy among readers of *The Guardian*. In a letter to the editor, Epaphras Edward offered lefthanded thanks to the "unreadable professor" for demonstrating in his essay that "he is an obscurantist *par excellence*" but very respectfully warned him of the consequences of soiling his reputation for highmindedness by engaging in gutter brawls with the *Bolekaja* critics: "Dancing with the Chichidodo to the gallery is not a healthy development for him and the rest of us ... When the eagle flies very low, children will think it is a vulture and will start stoning it" (8).

Indeed, the stones soon started flying, but not before a few air raid shelters were hastily erected. Kunle Oresulu argued that "a writer does not become unreadable, irrelevant and undesirable solely because the majority of his readers cannot understand him at first reading. The problem seems to be that most Nigerian readers are lazy and cannot be bothered to read a novel twice even if it is simple and interesting, much less when such novel is a little difficult to understand ... Why should some ill-informed, ill-motivated (and sometime) envious pseudo-writers want to crucify Soyinka for his supposedly obscurantist writing style?" (8).

Olu Hamz had an answer to that: "A writer should know that it is absolutely essential that the meaning of all what he or she is writing should be clearly understood by his readers. It is no use having the most original and exciting ideas if you are unable to pass them on to anyone ... A writer should be involved in making use of his medium to educate those who need education ... The public is not interested in big grammar" (8).

But Oladeji Popoola was more tolerant of poetic license and literary diversity: "There are writers and there are writers. I have no doubt in my mind that Soyinka is readable and has been effortlessly readable since the past one decade. In any case, two equally intelligent people can interpret a simple and straightforward play or novel differently ... Let us have the so-called readable writers. Let them write a billion novels. The Nigerian literary sky can accommodate any type of bird without their flagging each other down" (8).

U. Icheku, agreeing that Osahon and Chinweizu had overstated Soyinka's alleged obscurity, offered to help them and others out: "I have read, enjoyed and understood all Soyinka's works that I have read, including poems, essays and a novel. And willingly, I will give free lectures to those who find his compositions a bit above their comprehension" (8).

At this point Chinweizu re-entered the fray with a six-part series of weekly columns containing his "Reflections on Nigeria's Literary Culture," followed by a two-part series on "Pan-Africanism and the Nobel Prize." In these essays he emphasized that the writer's primary responsibility was to contribute to nation-building and that he couldn't fulfill this important social rôle if he alienated himself from ordinary people by writing pretentious works that they couldn't decode. Chinweizu was most contemptuous of writers like Soyinka who spouted "shamanist mystifications":

The jokers in the literary community are that small coterie who fancy themselves as seers, shamans, or pathfinders on some mystic "Fourth Stage", and who go about claiming that their heads are buzzing with prophetic and priestly "visions" ... those who refuse to write what even their friends would be eager to read, those drunk on private visions which they find great difficulty in communicating to bystanders – they make it difficult for the public to either accept writing as valuable work or see the career of a writer as anything but a lunatic pact with needless poverty (23 February, 5) ...

But why do shamanists ... insist on mystifying the role of the writer, even when for their pains they are often punished with poor sales and alienation? I submit that to the extent that these mystifications succeed, they yield great psychological gains to their propagators. It should be noted that the point of this kind of mystification is to make out the writer as a special kind of cultural hero. If he is a pathfinder, then he should command our special reverence, and we ought to grant him a special status. This type of mystification provides him with a cult-following whose hero worship ministers to his megalomania by assuring him that he indeed is a literary Napoleon or demigod.

In imitation of what religious shamans enjoy, the literary shaman expects to gain enormous authority from the propaganda that he communicates with the spirits and has privileged access to the transcendental world. He expects to be feared for these powers; he expects never to be contradicted, and that unfavourable opinion will never be expressed about him or his work, not even behind his back.

The aura of holy madness which surrounds a shaman aggrandizes whatever legitimate reputation such a writer might acquire from his writing. This overblown reputation, if properly manipulated, can be made to yield him enormous material rewards from awed patrons of culture. For if the man is special, we ought to honour him with gifts and tribute (9 March: 5).

Such writers, though prime candidates for the Nobel Prize, have a perniciously harmful effect on the young, who seek to emulate their success as enigmatic obfuscators: "For those who find Soyinka turgid and obscurantist, his imitators are even less attractive ... To experience all this is to know at first hand just how much havoc the idolatry of these pioneer shamanists has inflicted on Nigerian literature. All that misdirected effort; all that wasted work!" (16 March: 5).

And the Nobel Prize, Chinweizu argues, just aggravates this deplorable situation by further disorienting writers and destroying their ability to contribute productively to the cultural integration of their own society:

African writers, following the prescriptions of their western mentors, may mimic some fashionable styles from western literature. If their works are consequently incomprehensible to African readers, that does not matter to them so long as scouts for western prize-givers are delighted. The result is a euro-assimilationist literature which is bewitched by western claims of cultural superiority, and which grovels for acceptance into the tributary streams of western literature. Yet other African writers might contrive to make their euro-assimilationist works appear authentic products of the African tradition by craftily giving them enough Africanesque patina and inlays to satisfy the western tourist taste for exotica. Such works become sophisticated literary versions of airport art. It is thus that the eurocentric disorientations induced by the Nobel Prize divert some African writers ... from devoting their full energies to developing African ... literature (20 April: 5).

A month later, in May 1986, Chinweizu boldly penetrated enemy territory to deliver, albeit *in absentia*, the same message at a conference of African writers in Stockholm attended by Soyinka himself. Chinweizu's paper, circulated to participants but not read aloud as part of the proceedings, concluded as follows:

Africa does not need the cultural disorientation and subservience which western prizes promote. By its origins and operations, even the most globally prestigious of these prizes, the Nobel Prize, is a local European prize, and should go back to being just that. If it wishes to become the international prize it gives the impression of being, it should stop lending itself to hegemonic uses. Its terms of reference, its selection procedures, and its award committees should then all be internationalized ... It is, of course, most unlikely that the West would agree to a genuine internationalization of the Nobel Prize. That would end their control of it, and end their ability to use it for hegemonic purposes ... It is up to the rest of the world, in a bid to stimulate a long-overdue New International Cultural Order, to publicly withdraw allegiance from the Nobel Prize, and so reduce it to its proper minitude as a local European prize ("Literature and Nation Building in Africa" 19-20).

I have quoted Chinweizu's opinions on this subject at length for he offers the most coherent articulation of a pan-Africanist argument that seeks to make literature subservient to a concrete political and cultural goal – in this case, the complete intellectual liberation of Africa. The title of his latest book, which brings together many of his journalistic pieces on this theme, sums up his ultimate objective: *Decolonizing the African Mind*. The Nobel Prize, by continuing European domination of African cultural expression, by rewarding extravagantly those writers whose works bear the greatest formal resemblance to those produced in the West, by giving young African authors the misleading impression that the best writing is the sort that resists ready interpretation, perpetuates the intellectual enslavement of Africa to its former colonial rulers. True nation-building cannot rest on such treacherous foreign foundations, undermined as they are by racist assumptions of inherent European superiority. Africa needs to set its own priorities for literary development and therefore needs to award its own prizes for literary excellence. It cannot continue to allow a "gaggle of Swedes" to define what is best in African literature.

Nonetheless, when Soyinka won the Nobel Prize, Nigeria sang his praises loudly and rejoiced mightily. Most Nigerians took great pride in his achievement, seeing it as confirmation by the outside world of what they already suspected: that their nation in a relatively short period of time had produced an important literature. Tributes to Soyinka and outpourings of national self-congratulation glutted the press. People recognized that this was an historic moment and reveled in the glory and gaiety of it. A festive holiday mood prevailed.

It is worth looking at what was said about Soyinka during this period of national euphoria, for the adulation itself affords interesting evidence of some of the contradictory critical principles underlying Nigerian aesthetic preferences. But instead of relying on middlebrow journalistic accolades for this kind of data, let us take our samples from two extremes in the educated community: 1) the highbrow assessments of university professors and literary critics who wrote thoughtful essays for the press on the significance of the prize, and 2) the lowbrow evaluations of ordinary university students who reacted more viscerally to the excitement generated by news of the award.

Some of the top academics in Nigeria published brief articles in *The Guardian* and other media in the weeks following the historic announcement. First to appear was "Reflections on the 1986 Nobel Prize" by 'Molara Ogundipe-Leslie, a feminist critic teaching at Ogun State University. Taking the bull by both its horns, she argued that Soyinka's excellence resides in precisely those areas where many of his detractors find him deficient: his transcendent universality and his daring experiments with language. "It is this universality of the final meaning of his themes," she said, "which irks critics who feel that his work should be situated more historically and materially in his own social context," yet she found his depiction "of the plight of man on earth as both creator and destroyer ... a profound existential theme that has particular universal significance and relevance in these times." Morover, as far as his handling of language was concerned, "Soyinka's mastery of English is at that high level where expertise breaks the semantic barrier to poetic efflorescence and linguistic newness. At that level of control, one becomes one of the makers of the language. The artist dares to break the rules to create new ones." Ogundipe-Leslie, in tackling these issues head-on, was challenging two of Chinweizu's cardinal charges against Soyinka: mystic shamanism and unreadability. She went further and applauded the Nobel laureate as a writer of "world stature" who "makes the whole world his audience"(9).

Isidore Okpewho, a professor of English at the University of Ibadan who specializes in oral literature but writes novels as well, saw Soyinka's achievement in a different light:

> On the aesthetic side of things, I think that Soyinka has demonstrated – much more than any African writer has done to date – the essential *mythic* foundations of the creative activity. By this I mean that he has, throughout his work, revealed quite convincingly the stress between a loyalty to life as it starkly and (in the peculiar case of Africa's socio-political conditions) painfully presents itself to us and the urge to construct a scale of reality towards which we ought constantly to strive. In this regard, he has plumbed the mythology of his people (the Yoruba) and identified a figure who for him captures the essence of this stress: the god Ogun, patron of metal and of the arts and occupations derived therefrom ... It is therefore fair to say that, more than any writer on this continent, Soyinka has subjected his indigenous traditions to true creative alchemy and derived a symbolic essence which has served him well in an examination of the large issues of human existence.

This sounds a bit like the old "universality" argument again, but it is grounded more solidly in an appreciation of the indigenous "mythic essence" of Soyinka's work, and Okpewho concludes by reclaiming the laureate as an African through and through: "Although he writes mostly in a European language, and although he speaks to a larger human universe, Soyinka is perhaps the most truly African writer today because he articulates the African condition through the medium of aesthetic essences derived from the timeless cultural history of his people" (11). So much for Chinweizu's contrary contention that Soyinka is a totally colonized euro-assimilationist!

Next to put in a word on Soyinka's behalf was his old friend Abiola Irele, a professor of Modern Languages at the University of Ibadan and one of Nigeria's most distinguished literary critics and scholars. To Irele, Soyinka, though certainly universal and indisputably African, is above all a writer who responds in his work to specifically Nigerian stimuli. He may be large enough to belong to the whole world and Negritudinous enough to appeal to the rest of Africa, but his greatest relevance is to the society that produced his sensibility. But let's let Irele speak for himself, as he does quite eloquently in this essay:

> If the African experience on which his work is centred assumes a particular value for him as a measure of the universal problems of the human condition, it is not only because this is the experience closest to him, one in which his immediate responses are called up but also because our recent emergence into the realities of the modern world poses anew certain fundamental issues of collective life and moral conduct to which writers and thinkers at other times and in other climes have turned their hearts and minds; issues related to how best society can be organized in order to provide fulfillment for the individual. This is a problem with which we are confronted in this continent, and especially in this country, in the most dramatic way ... Soyinka's work finds its place at the very heart of this specific complex of historical and social factors, enacts the drama of ambiguity and the conflict of moral choices which confront the awakened consciousness in the contemporary African situation. It proceeds from the sustained activity of his mind and sensibility upon this situation, in an effort of imaginative reflection directed towards a comprehension of its inner workings. More than this, it is a means of experiencing deeply and pervasively within the artistic mind the implications as well as the promises of our situation
> .... .
>
> The significance of Soyinka for us resides then, first and foremost, in the act of revelation that his quest implies, and his sharing with us of those insights into the murky mire of our collective soul, however disagreeable and even terrible these insights may be ... Wole Soyinka is significant because in his work, he has been responding to his situation, in his time and place, in a way that I can only call vital: full-blooded, deep and serious. This situation is also ours, and he is doing the responding for us so as to awaken in us the very essence of our

humanity, that is to say, the free exercise of our faculties as moral agents, and of the sense of responsibility that this entails (17).

Soyinka, Irele wants his countrymen to remember, is and always has been, at heart, one of them.

The parade of cap-and-gown appraisals ended with yet another high-flown interpretation of Soyinka's significance hoisted into the wind by Biodun Jeyifo, a Marxist critic teaching at the University of Ife who formerly had been one of Soyinka's most energetic "leftocrat"[2] hecklers. Maybe the Nobel Prize disarmed this radical critic or made him feel in a more charitable critical mood, for in a long essay, published in *The Guardian* in several instalments, he made the rather lofty claim that "Soyinka is the greatest mythopoeist in contemporary African literature and as such the scale of values and referents within which his works are conceived embrace the cosmic framework of man's terrestrial existence." In short, Soyinka is not just universal, African or Nigerian, as the earlier commentators had claimed, but is a cosmic mythopoeist, an extraterrestrial wonder-worker. What's more, "Soyinka's mythopoeisis has a personal, idiosyncratic dimension as well as a matrixed, cultural source" (6 December: 13). In other words, the way he works his wonders is peculiarly individualistic yet is rooted in an exclusively Yoruba ethnic ethos, the spiritual embodiment of which is the god Ogun, whom Soyinka, as an artist, is said to resemble:

Soyinka's own artistic and cultural activities have sought to realize the variety of ideas encompassed by this "essence." His prolific and sustained creativity, the diversity and range of his literary output, the ferocity of his opposition to tyranny and injustice, his penchant for mysticism and the esoteric arts, the robustness, vitality and lyrical power of much of his writings, all these collectively approximate convincingly to the array of significations which Soyinka has assigned to the Ogun "essence" (20 December: 13).

Jeyifo thus continues but simultaneously reverses the direction of the remarks made by the critics who preceded him. Ogundipe-Leslie had Soyinka as a universalist, Okpewho saw him as an African, Irele identified him as a Nigerian, and Jeyifo now claimed him as primordially a Yoruba and on top of that an incorrigible individualist, but in the process of squeezing him into these smaller and smallest categories, Jeyifo also transformed him into a superglobal essence and a god. It's as if Soyinka gradually had been sucked by these critics into an ever blacker and blacker black hole only to emerge on the other side larger than life and lighter than the brightest incandescence. Who said that Proteus is dead? Or, to indigenize the analogy, who said that Eshu is not still alive and kicking? There is shape-shifting confusion enough here to boggle the mind of any reader, even those veterans whose minds may have been boggle-hardened by repeated readings of Soyinka's more elliptical works. Evidently Nigerian literary critics are not in perfect accord in their assessment of the source and character of his creative genius. He remains many different things to many different interpreters, a deep mystery imperfectly plumbed.

But if we turn from the academic eggheads to those embryonic young minds whose literary impressions are still in a gelatinous process of formation – from the hardboiled critics to the parboiled, that is – we find symptoms of the same scrambled confusion. I base this generalization on a fascinating collection of brief statements made by students at the University of Lagos who inspected an exhibition of Soyinka's works mounted as a "Tribute to the 1986 Nobel Prize Winner" by their University Library between 17-28 November 1986. The librarians had included on a table in front of the exhibition a notebook where spectators could record their reactions.[3] More than three hundred people took the time and trouble to do so, usually signing off by identifying themselves by name and departmental affiliation. The preponderance of their remarks, as befits a tribute, were enthusiastic ejaculations of praise for Soyinka and what he had accomplished. "You remain a living legend and a star in a galaxy of peacocks," wrote an English student. "Wole Soyinka, to my mind, is the reincarnated William Shakespeare," exclaimed another from Business Administration. A less confident Engineering student confessed, "Soyinka's works I find hard to understand, 'cause of it's high grammatical content. Nevertheless, I consider him to be the greatest of his time." A representative from Civil Engineering, equally impressed but perhaps also equally befuddled, put forward the view that "Wole Soyinka writes for advanced minds of generations yet to come. He has come much too early for this age." Someone else agreed that "He is just too much for a man. I can't understand his works. Nevertheless, I say more grease to his elbow" – a sentiment voiced so frequently that were such wishes to come true, Soyinka would be blessed with well-lubricated elbows for the rest of his life.

The vast majority of University of Lagos students were quite tolerant of Soyinka's obscurity and more than willing to salute him without understanding much of what he had written. A few, however, had some harsh words to say. An English student wrote, "You are an 'alienated native,' apology to Chinua Achebe. There is neo-colonialism in your language." Another, who sounded as if he had been reading Chinweizu's columns carefully, said, "I am happy for you for this big award but the only thing is that the award is not given to you by Africans. It's high time we Africans too have our own award which we call world award, why should the whites dictate everything for us, does god made us to be slaves to the white man?"

There were in addition a number of comments more difficult to interpret as positive or negative assessments of Soyinka. One student noted that *"The Man Died* is a banned book. Why is it displayed?" And someone from the Department of Psychology, perhaps a believer in positive reinforcement, said, "Bravo! Try better next time." A third, who identified himself merely as a squatter, remarked that "$200,000 is a lot of money. Hope it flows to others." Some Nigerian students obviously were beginning to look beyond the award to its possible beneficial consequences for the nation at large.

And that may ultimately be the biggest question of all to ask about such an award: who in Nigeria will benefit from it? Many citizens took vicarious pleasure in Soyinka's winning of a major intellectual sweepstakes, but after sharing with him that brief glow of international recognition, will any of them be any better off than they were before? Will Soyinka's accomplishments as a writer enrich them in any way? That may be the question that finally determines whether Soyinka becomes a *fixed* "star in a galaxy of peacocks."

Some, like Chinweizu, already entertain serious doubts about the value of what Soyinka has done. Others may go on acclaiming him even while openly acknowledging they cannot comprehend his works. The real test may come many years from now, when Soyinka is a remote ancestral figure rather than a dynamic, forceful presence influencing contemporary events. Will the works outlive the man? Some past Nobel Prize winners have already been forgotten because their writings spoke only to their contemporaries, not to future generations. Is Soyinka's voice strong and clear enough to echo through the ages?

One of the sanest reactions to the 1986 Nobel Prize in literature came not from an academic critic or a student or a journalist but from a fellow Nigerian writer who himself has been nominated many times for the same honor. In his presidential address at a conference of the Association of Nigerian Authors held in Lagos in late November of 1986, Chinua Achebe said:

> This is the year of Wole Soyinka's Nobel Prize. We rejoice with him on his magnificent achievement. A lot has already been said or written about it and no doubt more will be said. For me what matters is that after the oriki and the celebrations we should say to ourselves: *One of us has proved that we can beat the white man at his own game. That is wonderful for us and for the white man. But now we must turn away and play our own game* (2-3).

Achebe didn't specify what that game was or how writers should play it, but by situating it a good distance from Stockholm, he may have succeeded in putting the Nobel Prize into proper perspective for creators and consumers of African literature.

NOTES

1. Chinweizu, Jemie and Madubuike define *Bolekaja* in these words, explaining that it is "a term applied in Western Nigeria to passenger lorries ('mammy wagons') from the outrageous behavior of their touts" (xii).

2. This term was coined by Soyinka in his inaugural lecture at the University of Ife on 30 October 1980: "The Critic and Society: Barthes, Leftocracy and other Mythologies."

3. All quotations are taken *verbatim* from this notebook, which very likely has been preserved at the University of Lagos Library.

WORKS CITED

Achebe, Chinua. "Presidential Address." Unpublished speech delivered at the sixth annual convention of the Association of Nigerian Authors, Lagos, 27 November 1986.

Adepitan, Titi. "Chinweizu and His Hang-ups." *The Guardian*, 24 November 1985: 8.

Chinweizu. "That Nobel Prize Brouhaha." *The Guardian*, 3 November 1985: 5.

---------. "Reflections on Nigeria's Literary Culture." *The Guardian*, 16 February 1986: 5; 23 February 1986: 5; 2 March 1986: 5; 9 March 1986: 5; 16 March 1986: 5; 23 March 1986: 5.

---------. "Pan-Africanism and the Nobel Prize." *The Guardian*, 13 April 1986: 5; 20 April 1986: 5.

---------. "Literature and Nation Building in Africa." Unpublished paper circulated at the Second African Writers' Conference in Stockholm, 11-17 April 1986.

---------. *Decolonizing the African Mind*. Lagos: Pero Press, 1987.

Chinweizu, Onwucheckwa Jemie, and Ihechukwu Madubuike. *Toward the Decolonization of African Literature*. Washington, DC: Howard UP, 1983.

Duodu, Cameron. "Africa's First Nobelist." *South*, December 1986: 27-29.

Edward, Epaphras. "Ethics and Aesthetics of Chichidodo." *The Guardian*, 19 December 1985: 8.

Hamz, Olu. "Writers Who Don't Communicate." *The Guardian*, 31 December 1985: 8.

Icheku, U. "I Find Soyinka Readable." *The Guardian*, 1 February 1986: 8.

Irele, Abiola. "The Significance of Wole Soyinka." *The Guardian*, 1 November 1986: 17.

Jeyifo, Biodun. "What is the Will of Ogun? Reflections on Soyinka's Nobel Prize and the African Literary Tradition." *The Guardian*, 6 December 1986: 13; 13 December 1986: 13; 20 December 1986: 13.

Odemwingie, Tommy. "Soyinka may be named Nobel Prize Winner." *The Guardian*, 17 October 1985: 1-2.

Ogundipe-Leslie, 'Molara. "Reflections on the 1986 Nobel Prize." *The Guardian*, 27 October 1986: 9.

Okpewho, Isidore. "The Mystic Essence." *The African Guardian*, 30 October 1986: 11.

Oresulu, Kunle. "Soyinka and His Critics." *The Guardian*, 30 December 1985: 8.

Osahon, Naiwu. "Titi vs. Chinweizu." *The Guardian*, 1 December 1985: 9.

Popoola, Oladeji. "Leave Soyinka Alone." *The Guardian*, 13 January 1986: 8.

Soyinka, Wole. "Neo-Tarzanism: The Poetics of Pseudo-Tradition." *Transition*, 48 (1975): 38-44.

----------. *The Critic and Society: Barthes, Leftocracy and Other Mythologies*. Inaugural Lectures Series, 49. Ile-Ife: University of Ife Press, 1982. Reprinted in *Black Literature and Literary Theory*. Ed. Henry Louis Gates, Jr. New York and London: Methuen, 1984. 27-57.

----------. "Ethics and Aesthetics of Chichidodo." *The Guardian*, 7 December 1985: 9.

INDEX

Index